So Down to Prayers

So Down to Prayers

Studies in English Nonconformity
1780 – 1920

Clyde Binfield

Department of History
University of Sheffield

J. M. Dent & Sons Ltd
London
Rowman and Littlefield
Totowa N.J.

All rights reserved
Made in Great Britain
at Biddles Ltd, Guildford, Surrey
and bound at the Aldine Press, Letchworth, Herts
for
J.M. Dent & Sons Ltd
Aldine House, Albemarle Street, London
First published 1977

First published in the United States 1977
by ROWMAN AND LITTLEFIELD, Totowa, New Jersey

This book is set in IBM Journal 10 on 11 point

Dent edition
Hardback ISBN 0 460 10366 0

Rowman and Littlefield edition
Hardback ISBN 0 87471 959 3

British Library Cataloguing in Publication Data
Binfield, Clyde
    So down to prayers: studies in English
    Nonconformity, 1780-1920
    Bibl. — Index
ISBN 0-460-10366-0
    1. Title
    301.45'28   BX5203.2
    1. Title
    Dissenters, Religious — England

274672

Contents

This book is dedicated to all who have worshipped with the churches gathered at Zion, Russell Street and High Street Dover;
Emmanuel Cambridge;
Broompark and Trinity Sheffield;
And especially to my great-grandmother, Sarah Parton (1846-1901)
To my grandparents, Florence Sara Goodfellow (1877-1968)
and Arthur Thomas Goodfellow (1879-1965)
And to my parents, Margaret Florence Binfield (1913-76)
and Edward John Binfield (1911-76)
Whose lives expressed all that was progressive in the Free Churchmanship of their generation,
Whose influence has continued among those who knew them,
Whose memory remains with their descendants.

J. C. G. B.

Preface

> . . . while the great current of political intrigue and courtly pomp flows on glittering and lauded with noisy publicity, there is also a deep, though quiet undercurrent of unpublished labour, and unlauded piety and virtue, which is far nobler and more beautiful, and which is indeed the stream.
>
> (C. Armitage, *Some Account of the Family of the Armitages from 1662 to the Present Time*, 1850, pp. 97-8.)

> In one village, with a population of 2,400, there was the parish church, a Congregational chapel, a Wesleyan chapel, a Wesleyan Reformed chapel, a Friends' meeting house, a Brethren's room, and just one mile off there was a Supralapsarian place. Just seven churches in that village — as many as there were in the whole of Asia Minor years ago — [much laughter] — and they must have the seven influences of the Holy Ghost before they could amalgamate.[1]

It cannot be done, of course. A history of Nonconformity which aimed to be other than an urbane rehearsal of events and names would need the seven influences of the Holy Ghost to be credible, let alone readable. This is not such a history. It is an account neither of events nor denominations. It will not greatly assist those who need to unravel past controversies or follow the developments of doctrine. It is not so much selective as exclusive. Yet it attempts to do justice to a section of English life without parallel for influence or variety, still taken too easily for granted by all save the professionally curious and no more conformable than ever it was to the prevailing standards of acceptable living.

This book seeks to evoke atmosphere. It does so, after an introductory section, by a series of studies which trace the enlargement of horizons as Dissenters became Nonconformists and Nonconformists became Free Churchmen, and their numbers increased thirtyfold. Each study is complete in itself, but each leads into the next. Their concerns include literature, architecture and education, politics and churchmanship, war and foreign mission, but since Nonconformity had to do with man's salvation, these studies are about men and women. Issues emerge distilled through the vagaries of personality.

Not the least remarkable aspect of Nonconformity, remarkable that is for a movement whose existence depends on what mortal people *feel* rather than what they take for granted, is its continuity, and therefore its separateness. In the 1960s the Congregationalists of Wrentham, in Suffolk, still recorded their baptisms in a book in which the first names came from the 1640s, people to whom the Pilgrim Fathers were, literally, Pilgrim Uncles or Cousins. When the churches finally unite, the Church of England which emerges, not merely reformed but recreated, will in no sense be a home to which any of its members have *returned*.

If Nonconformity's separateness and continuity need to be recognized, so does its pervasiveness. Tacket Street Congregational Church, Ipswich, was of seventeenth-century origins. It had revived with the nineteenth century, its membership expressing all the self-consciousness of Victorian England: multiple drapers; maltsters and millers; large farmers; solicitors; engineers and shipowners; printers. They filled prosperous farms around, or the villas in new avenues, or the opulent houses overlooking the river. In 1869 nearly a quarter of the church's 259 members lived in such areas, many of them prominent in municipal affairs and recognized as local leaders of the Liberal interest. They were also deacons. They supervised branch chapels and superintended the Sunday School. One of them founded a separate church in an artisan district. All of them overlapped into other churches and other denominations. They were representative; there was nothing exceptional about Tacket Street.[2]

They were part of a way of life. This was not just religious, nor even the religious stretched into the political or the intellectual, for it could be light and delightful, like family life and the trust and laughter of friends. The Taylors, 'of Ongar', were engravers, writers, thinkers, preachers, scientists. One married a Chairman of the Congregational Union; another, in Anglican guise, designed architecturally naughty churches in the north-west. If one of them was over-polished, as thoughtful Nonconformists were apt to be, another wrote 'Twinkle, Twinkle, Little Star', and recalled fondly the Christmas dances, blameless card-games, and dashing silk pelisses and feathers of the pious plain Dissenters of her youth.[3]

This book is about such people, Nonconformity's opinion-formers at least in the sense that they provided its public face in an age when influence, education and worth still depended on property and when so many Nonconformists clustered uncomfortably at property's cutting edge.

It is chiefly about mainstream Evangelical Nonconformity, Methodists, Baptists and, especially, Congregationalists. Quakers, Unitarians, and others, walk on as soldiers in the stage army of the wider

Nonconformity but they have been celebrated elsewhere.[4] Congrega-tionalists have appeared less attractive to the historian, and consequently less accessible to the general reader, and yet they may plausibly be regarded as the most representative of Nonconformity's opinion-formers.

There remain two further points: this book is about *English* Nonconformity, and it is biased.

Although the great pulpiteers were as often as not Welshmen, Scotsmen or Irishmen, and there were few congregations without their Celtic infusion, English Nonconformity differed fundamentally from its Celtic counterparts. Scotland was another nation. Its Established Church, moreover, was firmly within the Reformed tradition, and although those who dissented from it included Episcopalians (the most Nonconformist of all) most did not differ in churchmanship from the Kirk. Ireland was dominated by the fact that most Irishmen were Roman Catholics, and most Protestant Dissenters were Presbyterians, and that there ceased to be an established church in Ireland after 1869. In Wales the significant facts were that Protestant Nonconformists formed the majority of Welsh Christians; that what was most vital about them was expressed in the Welsh language, and therefore a different culture; and that the Welsh middle classes were relatively few and relatively new — the social composition of Welsh Nonconformity differed significantly from that of England. English Nonconformity, however, was long established and well established. It was closer to the economic realities of the world's foremost industrial nation, and it was harnessed to the natural governing party of that nation. And yet it was inferior, the victim of continuous discrimina-tion. It needs separate treatment.

The book is biased. Its title, *So Down to Prayers*, derives from the comment which my great-grandfather, who was a deacon and grocer and knew what he was talking about, made about his fellow grocers: they would adulterate their sugar stocks with sand, and then go down to prayers with their families and assistants.[5] My great-grandfather, it seems, was not that sort of deacon. He gave winter provisions to the poor, his wife smoked in private, played cards (but never for money) and wrote pleasantly slangy letters to her eldest son who had run off to join the army in India. His daughter kept him to the mark where radical politics were concerned. Theirs were positive, sensible lives, more truly the product of Nonconformity than sanded sugar.

It still seems to me that what they stood for was right, and that those who failed to share their views could not be quite so right. Such confessions are sometimes necessary, even for historians who do so like to be objective. In this instance confession is doubly necessary since had I been a Baptist, or a Methodist, let alone an Anglican, this would have been a different book, assuredly for reasons as respectable as those which justify its present form.

Clyde Binfield

Acknowledgments

Inevitably a book of this kind has resulted from the encouragement, courtesy, and hospitality of innumerable people. My acknowledgments, cannot be other than inadequate.

First I must express my gratitude to many who made available their time, advice and private papers: the Very Revd G. W. O. Addleshaw, W. J. Alexander, J. H. G. Archer, W. B. Armitage, G. A. H. Bousfield, Miss A. L. Bulley, Dr. R. Carwardine, the Revd K. W. Clements, T. Copeman, the Revd R. W. Courtney, the late B. Cozens-Hardy, the executors of the 4th Lord Cozens-Hardy, M. Darby, the Revd J. R. Englefield, H. Fairhurst, Professor J. Ferguson, P. Ferriday, Dr D. Fletcher, Miss I. M. Fletcher, C. O. Foster, A. Goodyear, Mrs A. C. Gunter, A. M. Haworth, Sir G. Haworth Bt, the Revd E. S. Herbert, Miss M. Hirst, the Revd Canon R. Holtby, R. C-H. Horne, Mrs V. Horton, J. L. Hulme, the Revd W. E. Hurley, the Revd A. Jestice, C. B. Jewson, the late Dr G. Kitson Clark, A. D. Lee, Mr and Mrs H. Marshall, Miss F. R. McLaren, the late Revd Dr N. Micklem, the Revd T. C. Micklem, J. E. Mitchell, K. Moore, E. W. Moxey, Dr and Mrs G. Newton, the Revd Dr C. Northcott, the Revd Dr G. F. Nuttall, the late W. J. Onions, Miss P. A. Pemberton, Lord Pilkington, Miss B. C. Preston, C. Price M.P., J. S. Rebecca, the Revd D. Rowland, the Revd W. E. C. Sewell, Miss M. C. Shuttleworth, A. A. Smith, H. Stead, the Revd C. E. Surman, Dr E. Sykes, Professor J. N. Tarn, B. L. Thompson, G. B. Tobey, the Rt Revd O. S. Tomkins, Professor W. R. Ward, the Revd J. P. Watkins, R. Watkinson, R. J. Watson, the Revd Dr J. S. Whale, the late Mrs M. Willans, J. Willans, the trustees of Dr Williams's Library, the Revd and Mrs H. A. Wilson.

I owe a special debt to the courtesy and tolerance of the librarians and staff of the Cambridge University Library, Dr Williams's Library, Essex Record Office, East Suffolk Record Office, the Fine Art Society Ltd, Kirklees Libraries and Museums Services, Knutsford Branch Library, Manchester Public Library Archives Department, Mansfield College Oxford, New College London, Norfolk and Norwich Library, the Print Room of Victoria and Albert Museum, Rochdale Libraries and Arts

Services, Rotherham Central Reference Library, the Royal Institute of British Architects, Sheffield City Library, Sheffield University Library, the Whitworth Art Gallery, the William Morris Gallery Walthamstow.

Such a study as this results from a criminal exercise of academic larceny. I must express my debt to those from whose typescripts and dissertations I have gained immeasurably: Miss R. Allwood, Dr D. Bebbington, Miss J. Beck, Dr A. D. Gilbert, Dr J. Lea, J. R. Lowerson, Dr G. I. T. Machin, the late Revd Dr R. Mansfield, Dr H. R. Martin, Dr H. McLeod, Dr J. E. B. Munson, Dr J. S. Newton, R. J. Owen, Dr R. W. Ram, Dr G. M. Weston, Dr J. Wigley, Dr D. G. Wright.

I am grateful to the administrators of the University of Sheffield's Research Fund, whose consistent generosity has made much of this work easier than it might have been.

There remain certain private debts — to successive generations of Sheffield 'Liberal friends' whose scepticism, bafflement, and unexpected interest, have provided a salutary discipline; to my wife and aunt, whose typing has provided a clear accompaniment to the tangled thickets of my handwriting; and to A. N. Cass, whose criticisms have preserved me from grosser errors than this book yet retains, and who introduced me to *Grey Pastures*.

Book I

Introduction

Chapter 1

For Here was Good

'*Chapel begins* at eleven and *leaves* before one. We *attend* Bethel. The *Interest* at Mincing Lane is very low. But there are several other *causes* in the town. They want *supplies*. They say they can't *sit under* so heavy a preacher. They have the *ordinance* every Sabbath. But not many *sit down*. Few are *coming forward*. At the prayer meetings there are often none to *engage*. But better things are hoped for after the anniversary, when the Church is to take tea in the chapel, and they expect assistance from the friends at Grub Lane, and Bread Street, and Ebenezer, and Mount Zion, and Square, and Adullam.'

(Newman Hall's parody of chapel jargon, *Congregational Year Book*, 1867, p. 71.)

'On any showing, the Free Churches are important, if secondary, institutions in the life of England, at least comparable in social significance to, say, the public schools or the Liberal party.'[1] This sentence has unexpected charm, for the Free Churches, like the public schools and the Liberal party, produced some of the most radical responses to the tensions of nineteenth-century living. Unlike the public schools and the Liberal party, they possessed the benefit of effortless inferiority, to which, however, should be added that most powerful of all superiorities, spiritual superiority. No wonder that studies of nineteenth-century England should be incomplete without some reference to Nonconformity, baffled, frequently irritable, often respectful, seldom affectionate.

By any stretch of the imagination the period from the 1780s to the 1920s is fascinating for the student of Nonconformity, not least because the Nonconformity of the later twentieth century has closer parallels with that of the earlier eighteenth century than with the intervening generations. The Nonconformity of our grandparents' youth, which only the very elderly can now recall, belongs to a different order of life, which makes it hard to appreciate the extent to which we remain bound to it; for nothing is wasted in history.

At the beginning of the period Nonconformity experienced rapid growth, more than commensurate with the increase in population, and kept to the mark by the petty apartheid endured by all who refused to conform to 'national' standards. Towards the end of the period Nonconformity was the nearest it could ever get to establishing its vision of an alternative society. In between there was an adventurous history whose theme was the riddance of grievances built into Nonconformist life by the circumstances of the Toleration Act of 1689, but whose variations ranged from promoting religious issues of principle, to sharing in secular issues of equal principle, to internal squabbling. All these issues overboiled from the 1830s. All had a political dimension, partly because their champions had never quite been excluded from the political classes, but chiefly because they involved the nature and ordering of society.

Between the failure of Lord Sidmouth's shabby attempt to regularize the status of Dissenting preachers in 1811 and the passage of Carvell Williams's Burials Act of 1900, which largely settled the question of Nonconformist burials in parish churchyards, most grievances were smoothed away until only their flavour remained. Unitarians were brought within the scope of the Toleration Act in 1813, and all Dissenters of standing were brought formally into the political classes by the repeal of the Test and Corporation Acts in 1828. There remained the question of marriage, since only Quaker marriages were recognized, of death, because of the burial issue, and indeed, of birth, since the burial of unbaptized children complicated what was already a fraught issue. For the propertied there were the burdens of church rate and of tithe, especially for countrymen and Quakers. For the clever there were university tests: undergraduates at Oxford had to subscribe to the thirty-nine articles on matriculation, and at Cambridge at graduation. Tithes were commuted in 1836, although Quaker opposition to a rent charge was withdrawn only in 1873; church rate went in 1868; Nonconformist marriages were legalized in 1836, and freed of the stigma of notification of the Poor Law Guardians in 1856, though it was only in 1898 that Nonconformist ministers could act as registrars; and the older universities opened successive doors to Nonconformists in 1854, 1856 and 1871.[2]

All this kept Dissenters in political training and alerted them to issues whose fundamental importance was not to be denied, like national education and disestablishment of the Church of England. Neither problem was solved but both brought Nonconformists into the heart of Liberal politics and thence to the compromises of Westminster politics.

From there it was a natural step to secular issues of which Free Trade was the most successful, and temperance the most easily assimilated to Gospel values. John Bright, the legendary Free Trader, was a Quaker, and Wilfrid Lawson, the fox-hunting squire who brought prohibition within the range of Liberal party policy, had a Congregational upbringing and kinsmen. Matthew Arnold could make fun of Nonconformity's fixation with marriage to a deceased wife's sister, but there was nothing funny about its concern with the Contagious Diseases Acts, to understand which demanded clear views on morals, the proper place of women and, therefore, of all personal relationships. The Victorian Nonconformist Conscience was a vital factor in producing the liberal, 'permissive' society of the following century.

Undergirding this was the question of communication, natural to people who made an art of the sermon. Nonconformity produced notable editors from Josiah Conder of the *Eclectic Review* to Henry Allon of the *British Quarterly*, from Edward Baines of the *Leeds Mercury* to Edward Miall of the *Nonconformist*, from numerous editors of the *Daily News* to Robertson Nicoll of the *British Weekly*. It produced publishers — Hodder, Stoughton, assorted Unwins — and paper manufacturers, of whom the many Spicers may stand for many more. For people of the Word, words transcended deeds; they penetrated politics.

Nonconformity's history, however, was punctuated by civil wars. This was its unacceptable face and no denomination was free of it. There was perpetual sniping between Unitarians and the rest, exemplified in the evangelical uproar which greeted the Dissenters' Chapels Act of 1844, a reasonable attempt to confirm Unitarian congregations in their possession of premises first provided by Trinitarian ancestors. Of course this could be seen as a betrayal of the evangelical past, but the current touchiness really reflected the perennial insecurity of evangelicals when faced with the suavity and the fine manners of rational Christianity. At the other end of the spectrum the Quakers lost members to Baptists, Congregationalists, Plymouth Brethren and Low Church Anglicans, in the disruption which followed the publication in 1835 of a book by an influential evangelical Quaker which most Quakers construed as an attack on their traditions of worship, conduct and doctrine: Isaac Crewdson's *Beacon to the Society of Friends*.[3]

In between Methodist history was littered with schism from the 1790s to the 1850s. The Kilhamite secession of 1797, called after Alexander Kilham, an ardent spirit who battled — not always logically — for the rights of the Methodist laity, resulted in the Methodist New Connexion. The Protestant Methodists, who issued from the Leeds Organ Case of 1827, had agitated against the rights of the trustees of Brunswick Chapel, Leeds, to install an organ: their local protests began a storm which ultimately brought into question the methods and authority of Conference itself. The 'Warrenite' agitation of 1834-6, when Samuel Warren unavailingly attacked the way in which it was proposed to establish a Wesleyan theological institution, led to the Wesleyan Methodist Association. Most numerous of all were the Wesleyan Reformers who emerged from the 'Fly-Sheet' disruptions of 1846-9, provoked by the way in which Wesleyanism's 'London clique' dealt with a series of 'anonymous' pamphlets attacking their dignity and integrity.[4] Each of these were necessary stages in the emergence of Wesleyan Methodism as a denomination, if not a church. Each produced a distinctively Methodist organization, none very large, several rather noisy, each defined by the personalities and issues – some doctrinal, some social, all concerned with questions of freedom and authority – which had first caused them.

It was not so very different with the Baptists. From the first quarter of the century Baptists endured the agonies of the open-closed debate: should the privilege of communion be extended to other Christians than those baptized as believers? The complexities of this dispute make it impossible to see Baptists as a homogeneous body with an influence proportionate to their numbers. At the end of the century, in 1887, Charles Haddon Spurgeon propelled Baptists into the Down-grade controversy, the most notorious of a series of general scares about the way evangelical doctrines were going. There were others about conditional immortality or 'the larger hope' and Baptists were especially worried by Samuel Cox's *Salvator Mundi* (1877).[5] Such worries were the stock-in-trade of nineteenth-century Christians beset by higher criticism, higher education, higher incomes and higher expectations.

Congregationalists experienced no schism and little scandal, but they suffered more than has been realized from the nagging patterns of petty disruption, caused by a variety of irritants but usually explicable in doctrinal terms. Thus T. T. Lynch's foolishly pretty hymns (their nature reflected in the title of his collected verse: *Hymns for Heart and Voice: the Rivulet*) shocked his denomination with their pantheism in the *Rivulet* controversy of 1856, Samuel Davidson's ill-advised biblical scholarship (his revision of the second volume of Hartwell Horne's: *Introduction to the Critical Study and Knowledge of the Holy Scriptures*, was a gift to the heresy hunters) scandalized Manchester cottonmen in 1857, and elderly pulpit princes were stampeded into criticism by the woolly young warmhearts of 1877, with their Leicester Conference and their yearning to include all men of goodwill within the bonds of communion.[6]

·Such notorieties were merely the iceberg's tip. Congregationalists may have been free from schism, but perhaps their ineradicable 'middle classness' owed something to the nature of their discontents.

The context of these adventures was numerical growth, rapid to 1840, decreasingly so thereafter, turning into decline with the close of

Edwardian England. But it was growth for mainstream Nonconformity — Methodists, Baptists, Congregationalists — not for Quakers and Unitarians; these declined, whatever their profound effect on contemporary society.

The decisive factor in this was Methodism and its reaction with the Old Dissent, those Baptists, Independents, Presbyterians and Quakers who were children of the Reformation centuries, blooded by the English Revolution, schooled by the Restoration Settlement and its aftermath. The reaction was complex, involving a parting of the ways for the Old Dissent. Most Baptists and Independents (increasingly describing themselves as Congregationalists), and many Presbyterians (indistinguishable from Congregationalists in practice though not in theory) renewed their evangelicalism, acting increasingly with Methodists, marching from eighteenth-century Dissent into nineteenth-century Nonconformity (*Dissent* is querulous; *refusal to conform* is manly). Many Baptists and Independents, however, and most Presbyterians followed their intellects into Unitarianism. These, with the Quakers, those cats of Protestant Dissent walking perennially by themselves, drew apart from the mainstream.

Their isolation was never complete, partly because of heterodoxy's social and intellectual charms and also because the parting occurred over many decades and was filtered through a multitude of personalities. Indeed, it is arguable as to whether Congregationalists or Unitarians were more truly the inheritors of Presbyterianism.[7]

In the nineteenth century Evangelical Nonconformity was complicated by two more strands. The first concerned the growth of evangelical Presbyterian congregations, chiefly in towns, usually for expatriate Scotsmen, though sometimes linked in north-eastern England with indigenous Presbyterian communities. In the 1840s they were fuelled by the impact of the Disruption in the Church of Scotland, that dramatic time when Scottish evangelicals stood out (and eventually came out) for their national church's spiritual independence in the face of an encroaching state. The Scottish seceders were Dissenters from necessity, not conviction, and something of their unwillingness flavoured the English congregations, most of which sided with them. In 1876 the various pieces of this new English Presbyterianism united to form the Presbyterian Church of England; thereafter a chaste courtship developed with the Congregationalists. It resulted in 1972 in the United Reformed Church, the first formal union since the Reformation of British churches from different confessions. The second strand concerned the persistent growth of sects from the Plymouth Brethren of the 1820s to the Salvation Army fifty years later, taking in groups as diverse as the Catholic

Apostolicals and the Peculiar People, the former a rivetting combination for rich, intense people of the Catholic and the charismatic, of liturgy and speaking in tongues, the latter a revivalist sect for poor Essex people, inspired by an exWesleyan shoemaker. Fissiparous, inward-looking, numerically insignificant, they represent tendencies towards religious primitivism as important in their way as the rediscovery of catholic, churchly virtues elsewhere. They attracted wealth as well as poverty, thereby escaping the political stresses affecting middle-class Nonconformists, for life eternal promised more than those temptations of daily life which lured most articulate Christians. If Strict Baptists and much in Primitive Methodism and among the Bible Christians are added to these, they represent a ceaselessly attractive Dissenting alternative whose significance was that it made inevitable the failure of the Nonconformist Conscience; for here were numbers without activity.

Nonconformist numbers will never accurately be gauged. Perhaps in the middle of the eighteenth century the Old Dissent in England could claim 50,000 *members*: perhaps in the first decade of the twentieth century English Evangelical Free Churchmanship could claim 1,500,000 *members* of whom nearly 850,000 belonged to the Methodist Churches. There is no accurate means of assessing adherents.

Numbers mean people. The connexion between the nature of people and their numbers is caught by Alan D. Gilbert in his analysis of religious practice in an industrial society.[8] He draws four conclusions of interest for the present study, concerning the national pattern of Nonconformist strength, the peak years of its growth, the extent of its recruitment, and the nature of those recruited.

The motifs to the national pattern are that Methodism tended to be strongest where Anglicanism was weakest, but that Old Dissent was strong where the State Church was also strong, while from the 1780s to 1840, Nonconformity of all kinds grew and the State Church was everywhere at a profound disadvantage.

Where it concerns the years of peak growth for Nonconformity, the first motif is that the peaks in the years of greatest growth were less high and more isolated as the century progressed, until at their highest they were still lower than the general average of the first years of growth.[9] The second is that these peak years were not always times of overt religious revival: they also coincided with epidemics of disease or with the kind of political excitement which brought great issues into play.[10] The cumulative excitements of cholera, Moody and Sankey, and Mr Gladstone, profoundly influenced many Victorians minds. When it was said of George White, the Baptist backbencher from Norwich, that he viewed 'all political problems as through the windows of a Baptist Meeting

House',[11] the judgment was neither sentimental nor commonplace, and the extraordinary rhapsodies which greeted Gladstone's return to power in 1880 need also to be seen in such a light. 'We would gladly anticipate and dwell on some of those great measures out of which the golden future is to be made; but we may safely leave them in the custody of England's greatest statesman. . . .'[12]

The golden future was one of numerical decline, whatever the compensating spiritual joys, but in the nineteenth century the matter was best seen as a question of changing recruitment rather than positive declension. Not the least useful of Dr Gilbert's conclusions is that while the churches inevitably suffered as young converts became old members and then died, the real problem was their failure to replenish their stock from outside.[13] Early in the nineteenth century they had been outstandingly successful in doing this, in conscious interaction with secular society. At the end of the century they successfully held what was already theirs, but the recruits had gone, and the churches conducted their dialogue with society from the wings, projecting their voices more to their own children than to the children of the world.

But who had been the recruits? In the light of retrospect Nonconformity appears to have been shockingly middle class. Dr Gilbert contends that in its heroic years all but 8.6 per cent of its strength came from that 67 per cent of society which fitted between the professional classes and the unskilled: the artisans, the good poor who might become the better rich in an expanding society.[14] The implications of this are important, if unsurprising.

The first is that all the denominations were strongly artisan stretching, as the century progressed and society developed, into the lower middle classes. This needs to be remembered when such communities as the Independent Meeting at Witham, or East Parade Leeds, or Kensington Chapel, are considered.[15] The second is that while no denomination lacked its very rich or even its very poor, the determining factor lay in the proportions of very poor or very rich in its pews: hence the significance of East Parade Leeds, or the Witham and Kensington Chapels, or Bowdon Downs, Altrincham.[16] The third is that in a society whose politics was based on property, the public voice of any denomination was bound to be a propertied voice. Hence the apparent middle classness of Nonconformity, and the extent to which Congregationalism appeared as Nonconformity's golden mean.

There remains the most important question of all: why was Nonconformist growth so massive between the 1780s and 1830s? This was the generation burdened by the French Revolution which W. R. Ward describes as 'the most important generation in the modern history . . . of most of the Christian world'.[17] His reason for so striking a judgment is that within these years in most parts of Western Christendom the terms which conditioned the working of religious establishments were decisively altered.

There was some piquancy in the British situation for here authority was already weak. The Toleration Act of 1689 had built Dissent in to the establishment. It had done so grudgingly but irrevocably. Toleration of Dissent became a useful check in the balanced system of the Whig supremacy. It made room for apathy; it also injected a strain of voluntaryism into the workings of the Established Church itself: the eighteenth century was distinguished by a small army of benevolent agencies, manned by Anglican voluntaries.

The careful mechanism of the eighteenth-century constitution — as mythical a beast as the Nonconformist Conscience of the following century — worked remarkably well in a rural society. But from the middle of the century English society was unbalanced. The cumulative effect of the Industrial Revolution and the rapid impact of the French Revolution revealed the weaknesses of the English established order. Men's minds as well as their lives were at issue, and there seemed to be more of them within the boundaries of the political nation than might once have been dreamed. Dissent, that licensed critic within the gates, could only gain from society's confusion, provided that it was prepared to pay the price of its own transformation.

It was transformed but, as W. R. Ward has explained, the distinctive note of the transformation was an outpouring of undenominational evangelical religion, of 'Catholic Christianity' to use a phrase which was sometimes in vogue, which was the most natural religious response to a society in which the established disciplines had been shaken. Nineteenth-century evangelical Nonconformity never quite lost the flavour of this transformation. At its most exotic it is characterized by Amelia Alderson Opie, artist's widow and novelist, a Unitarian turned Quakeress who once nearly turned Methodist. At its most stately it is characterized by Thomas Wilson of Highbury, the London silk merchant who retired early to devote his energies to the nurture of evangelical pastors, their flocks and their pastures, or by those London ministers, the Claytons, father and sons. These were men known by 'their gentlemanly demeanour, and their large intercourse with ministers and people of other denominations', Congregationalists taking pride in 'uniting intense Evangelical sentiments to what might be called liberal views of Church polity'.[18]

Stately or exotic, they nonetheless represent those most vulnerable to the new outpouring, numberless men and women at the edges of the articulate classes with most to gain (and therefore to lose) in an age when accepted values were abrogated. The new evangelicalism was inevitably coloured with Dissent even where it kept closest to Anglicanism. In many places it was caught and braced by formal Dissent. In all places it provided a manner of living and a reason for it which owed little to established modes and made sense in a senseless society. This was the power of such communities as Salem, Leeds, or its grander successor at East Parade, islands of social control in the uncharted seas of the new industrial society.[19]

Or, more precisely, the new *industrializing* society. East Parade and Salem were tiny islands but the chapels in towns which were still little more than industrial villages — Morley, Heckmondwike, Cleckheaton, the earlier stages of Ashton-under-Lyne, Huddersfield or Halifax — were another matter. Their world was overturning, not overturned; it was semi-urban, and therefore semi-rural; its workers were often outworkers, its capitalists often 'yeomen'. This world produced the distinctive figures of nineteenth-century Nonconformity, Baines of Leeds, Titus Salt the alpaca prince, Crossleys the Halifax carpeteers, the innumerable Manchester Armitages, and, at one remove, Samuel Morley the shirt and stocking philanthropist.

It was a northern and midland world, of vast and once deserted parishes whose incumbents found themselves confronted by new communities in inaccessible corners, proof not merely of a new society and alien values, but also of the inadequacy of existing disciplines in coping with them.

But it was not only a northern world. In eastern England the aggressive face of Nonconformity was also an industrializing face, its features those of the Colmans of Norwich and the Courtaulds of Essex, the Prentices with their gun cotton factory at Stowmarket, or the Gurteens, whose French Renaissance factory dominated Haverhill, in concert with their spiky chapel, Old Independent. These families saw themselves as focal points of political Liberalism and religious freedom, and where they connected with older Dissenting communities they were as often as not connecting with communities formed in the earlier industrial world of Norfolk or Essex textiles. However rustic the values which had intervened, old Dissent no less than renewed Dissent testified to an established world at risk, and justified those who were taking the risks. This was the function of the new breed of minister, related by marriage as well as faith to the new industrialists, and of the new breed of communicator, the newspapermen of provincial England, their cousin-hoods ablaze with preachers and entrepreneurs.

This is the context of Chapel, a model of self-control expressed collectively, offering a life of obedience, discipline, duty and noseyness to individuals. In a world where you had only your feet to stand on, there could be no better recipe for stepping heavenwards.

The implications of this were announced by Thomas Binney in his notorious address to the Congregational Union in 1848: 'Revolutions are convulsing the world: and they are doing so partly through the medium of ideas consecrated by us . . . and, it must be confessed, that if our ideas be right, or, whether right or wrong, if they should predominate, our mission is, and would seem to be, revolutionary.'[20] This classic expression of Nonconformity in a dissolving society was voiced after the heroic age had ended, to people who were decreasingly able to respond. Thomas Binney celebrated the movers and moulders of the modern world. The Christianity which he represented had been that world's spiritual midwife: but formation needs more than midwifery.

The undenominational religious outpouring of the later eighteenth century caught the aspirations of the mobile classes of a new society. Its natural tendency was towards Dissent, since its values could not be established values as traditionally interpreted. Its inevitable conclusion, therefore, was a renewed denominationalism, at once deplorable and necessary. It turned Dissent into Nonconformity; *movements* became *churches*; Nonconformists turned at last into Free *Church*men. The inferior establishment implied by the Toleration Act of 1689 reasserted itself, marked now by swollen numbers and a new self-consciousness. The process may be symbolized by the changed standing of the twin inheritors of the congregational principle, the Baptists with their Baptist Union of 1813, and the Congregationalists, who launched their national Union in 1831. These bodies were never more than expressions of evangelical convenience, but by the second half of the century they were the established voices of established denominations.

The reasons for this development fit into two categories, of which the first, the growth of 'churchiness', has been analysed by W. R. Ward and A. D. Gilbert. When towns became cities the island nature of even the most successful chapels was exposed, and their 'churchy' image grew in self-defence. These responses to religious outpouring now erected flood barriers. And very properly so, since the 'churchy' image was also a response to the developing needs of those who had been swept in before the flood barriers were set up. Many of them had ceased to be on the edges of society. They had moulded their towns and moved with them, and their churches expressed their care of them in ways better suited to their new circumstances. But they were not replaced. As their towns turned into cities, so artisans became the labouring poor, decreasingly accessible to the self-conscious chapels of a society which had finally become class-conscious. At the same time the movers of urban England became less confident of their ability to mould it, hence the mounting concern with the quality of life, the defiant assurance of civic buildings, and the studied civilization of the English suburb.

All these aspects are reflected in chapel life, whether in the gravelled drives and gothic tracery of late Victorian Bowdon;[21] or in those successive generations of Congregationalists who had turned to moulding Huddersfield in the 1820s and found it running away with them in the 1880s;[22] or in Salem, Leeds, growing with its city, moving to the central opulence of East Parade in the 1840s, but ending with the new century in a suburb, as Trinity, 'churchly' as its name, seating fewer people than ever East Parade had done, a sign that the masses were beyond reach, and that the faithful, nurtured in the church family were few enough.[23]

Yet it needs stressing that if one aspect of Chapel development might be seen as 'churchiness', a defensive thing, a second might be seen as 'churchmanship', which is a much more positive thing. For the 'churchiness' of many chapels reflected a need for symbols seldom met in times of evangelical outpouring; and symbol can be a mark of strength. It is certainly a mark of thought, and since much of the new denominationalism met up with earlier traditions of scholarship, culture and churchmanship, forged, refined and strengthened by the experience of the Reformation centuries, there was bound to be stress on such matters. Churchmanship may never be discounted, neither may its intermingling with culture.

The heroic age ended with strife. The rivalry between Church and chapel entered a new phase from the 1830s, and in the 1840s internal strife beset Christians from English Wesleyans to Scottish Presbyterians. Perhaps these unlovely bickerings reflected tensions general in Western society which the churches could no longer comprehend because their brittle new denominationalism (which aggravated the bickerings) had itself been a response to earlier tension.[24] They certainly accompanied a heightened awareness of enemies within the gates and beyond, the twin R's of Romanism and Rationalism chief among them.

Rationalism was a dreadful bogey because it infested factories and city streets, captivating those whom Nonconformity ought to have reached, 'the humblest mechanic is heard denying the immortality of the soul, the inspiration of the scriptures'.[25] Rationalism's twin, Romanism, was regarded as dangerous as atheism, if only because of the numbers of Irishmen filling the industrial cities and because it offered more scope for flavoursome denunciation than the drab philosophizings of rationalistic mechanics. It also touched a particularly painful Nonconformist nerve, because Rome's most signal success appeared to lie with the Church of England.

13

> Now, once again, in many a town and village of this Protestant land a bastard Popery raises its bedizened and shameful front, and seeks to lure back by Ritualistic pomp, by priestly 'nods, and becks, and wreathed smiles', to the half-deserted sanctuaries the people who had fled from the cold and lifeless ministration of un-sanctified though State-appointed teachers.[26]

Whether in the guise of the bastard Popery of the 1870s or the more restrained rediscovery of Catholic truths thirty years earlier, it is clear that an important element of Nonconformist defensiveness lay in the revival of Anglican vigour at the very moment when Nonconformity was losing its numerical impulse. The element of competition was inescapable, and it was on the State Church's terms. It was a determining factor for Victorian Nonconformity most strikingly expressed by the unique but memorable religious census of 1851.

> If, by a happy miracle, on Sunday, March the 30th, 1851, an universal feeling of devotion had impressed our population, and impelled towards the public sanctuaries all whom no impediment, of physical inability or needful occupation, hindered; if the morning or the evening invitation or the service-bell had called, no less from the crowded courts of populous towns and the cottages of scattered villages than from the city mansions and the rural halls, a perfect complement of worshippers; for what proportion of the 17,927,609 inhabitants of England would accommodation in religious buildings have been necessary?[27]

The answer to this question, suitably analysed by Horace Mann, and published in 1853, exercised all serious people for the rest of the century.[28] He assumed that, all allowances made, the 'public sanctuaries' should seat 58 per cent of the population; which meant 10,427,609 sittings. In fact there were only 8,753,279 accessible sittings, and the urban areas, where population outpaced sittings, made the distribution more unequal still, and likely to continue so; for if since 1821 the overall provision of new sittings had outpaced the growth of population, the increase was not where it was most needed. This was disquieting enough, but Mann then observed that if 12,549,326 people could have attended a service on the relevant Sunday, in fact only 7,261,032 had done so, and at any one service the likelihood was that little over half the seats would be taken.[29]

Such figures were of general Christian concern, but arranged denominationally they were peculiarly interesting to Nonconformists. For every 100 sittings provided by the 'National Church', Nonconformity could find ninety-three, and the ratio was echoed in attendance. This must seize every Nonconformist imagination, obscuring such unpalatable facts as the pronounced decline since 1841 in the percentage increase of accommodation in all the major Nonconforming bodies, or the equal failure of

Nonconformists in filling their pews, not least in the towns which housed their wealthiest chapels.

The census revealed plainly the massive advance of Nonconformity in the past half century, displaying a numerical equality with the Church 'of England', which must now lead to social and political equality. This would be the refrain at stonelayings throughout the land. It also revealed to every pulpit, pew and annual assembly Nonconformist inadequacy in salvaging the nation's spiritual life, 'Is it true that more than five millions of England's population are habitually absent from public worship? . . . What can I do to remedy so fearful and gigantic an evil?'[30]

A further goad to competitive Nonconformity, uncertain whether to be more aggressive or defensive, came in 1862 with the bicentenary of 'Black Bartholomew's Day', 1662, when those valiant clergymen ejected from the State Church of Restoration England for refusing to assent to its Prayer Book, first endowed Nonconformity with traditions and a purpose.

It fell to the Congregationalists, as Old Dissent's most numerous heirs to lead a satisfying confusion of self-sacrifice and self-congratulation. Joshua Wilson, the son of Thomas of Highbury, an antiquarian who supplemented the family tradition of generosity to evangelical causes with a denominationalism more in tune with the age, entered zestfully into the fray. He prepared a paper for the Birmingham Autumnals of 1861.[31] 'Our watchword should now be "London and the large towns"', and he trusted that none of the hundred hoped-for commemorative churches would be in towns of under 3,000. He aimed for the middle classes, Congregationalism's 'special vocation', yet he spoke too for 'that most interesting class — the working men and their families'. He wanted a memorial in Bunhill Fields, the Dissenters' Valhalla, and a Memorial Hall to house the agencies of the Congregational Union. He wanted to propagate the old principles by lectures and histories, and popular tracts to 'let the people of England know on what an antichristian and sectarian foundation the Ecclesiastical Establishment in this country was reconstructed in 1662'. In short, census lessons confirmed the spirit of the age, class consciousness, denominationalism, symbolism and all. His proposals were 'rapturously adopted'.

The results were mixed. There was a lot of noise. A Nonconformist historical society was not formed, though ephemeral publications sold well. It was ten years before the Memorial Hall was built. Moreover, by 'originating the Bicentenary Conference and promoting the objects of the Bicentenary Fund, we are accused of aggressive action on the Church of England, and of promoting strife and alienation among Christian brethren'.[32] That too was the spirit of the age, and it found its expression

15

in the commemoration of two hundred years of past history.

There was a more permanent commemoration, because the next decade was a great church-building age. Its churches were 'churchy' and competitive, but they were full responses to the needs of the communities which used them. This was home extension 1860 style, costly, tiring and inhibiting, despite the ingenuity of chapel architects and their building committees.

Congregationalists especially were conscious of the architectural expression of their strength and faith. In 1860 their Autumnal Assembly deemed 'the Chapel-building movement of the present day one of the important signs of the times.'[33] Ten years earlier they were urged to remember 'that the men for whom we build have taste, and not religion', and to hope that gratification of the one might lead to the other.[34] Henry Allon, of Union Chapel Islington, spoke pointedly in his stock stonelaying address: 'Whatever name the edifice might bear; whether the conventional but unmeaning and Popish designation *chapel*, the homely and furtive designation *meeting house*, or the more seemly and significant designation *church* − that which pertains to the Lord. . . .'[35] These fine new churches were not just symbols: they were facts. 'The burst of spiritual life in connection with the Free Churches during the past sixty years has been the springtime of Christianity in England; we now wait for the summer fragrance and superabundance.'[36] It was, at best, an English summer.

The census enumerated people, the bicentenary commemorated people, and the new chapels symbolized the spiritual and material dimensions of people. Septimus March had an enjoyable time at the Congregationalists' Ipswich Autumnals in 1873:

Chapel must be Gothic and cruciform, regardless of comfort and acoustic properties; a chancel is indispensable; the pulpit must be put on one side, to give a good view of the coloured window and the table draped like an altar; the prayer, if still extemporaneous, must be mainly composed of memoriter repetitions from the Church of England liturgy; and choral must supplant congregational singing.

He prefaced this happy parody with a sharp survey of the snares of fashion, leaving his Free Church hearers to draw their State Church moral:

She who is most particular about going into mourning in Lent, will blossom out in most extravagant ballroom attire in Easter, he who thinks of his fish on fast days will think more of his flesh on feast days, the opera will be deemed the most fitting sequence to the 'miserere', the stage will be viewed as the holiday side of the chancel, and dancing as the proper physical balance for genuflection. So it has been and will be − sackcloth and ashes alternating with carnival and sugar plums.[37]

So of course it already was, for why talk like this unless to a prosperous audience in a provincial town whose 'Decorated' Congregational Church was already the cynosure of all Nonconformist eyes? And what Septimus March described was achieved by Arthur Reed Ropes, Congregationalist, Fellow of King's and collaborator in musical comedies from 'Our Miss Gibbs' to 'Lilac Time', with the 'Merry Widow's' English libretto thrown in, patron saint of the Nonconformist chancel's holiday side.[38]

There was a price for such delights. They came to laymen of refined sensitivity shrinking from their fathers' evangelical brashness. The evangelical father was 'more vehement and passionate in his feelings and devotions, more given to self-discipline and godly behaviour'. His son was 'more self-restrained; he neither rises to the same ecstasies of devotion, nor sinks to the same depths of despondency'.[39] Such a man was far from the classes with which his father's church had grappled, and the evangelical imperative was weakened accordingly, for prayer meeting and mission hall needed men of coarser fibre, like ministers.

Where it concerned denominational affairs, however, lay leadership remained at a premium, the lines of acceptable lay activity clearly demarcated in all the denominations, with predictable results. 'No squire ever entered the family pew of the parish church with a more conscious feeling that he was exercising his hereditary right than my father entered any Congregational Church which he chose to attend.'[40] What his son wrote of Sir Albert Spicer could have been written of many more.

They were outsize men, and no hard and fast rules should be drawn from Christians conditioned to 'think in individuals', but the sociological implications of these trends in the more eligible pews have been explored by Dr Gilbert, who has drawn parallel conclusions from trends in the pulpit.[41]

There was a general hardening of ministerial status. Ministers needed maintenance, which meant that their growing status had implications for future evangelism. Much of their ministry lay in serving existing needs rather than uncovering new ones. The implications of this for the conscientious were captured by the strategic siting of many chapels on the social frontiers of urban life.

The Wesleyan ministry had originated to meet the need for peripatetic evangelism. Congregationalists, and to a lesser extent Baptists, retained the traditions of a settled pastorate and in many churches an intense partnership developed between minister and people, in which personality outweighed status. Such partnerships existed between Alexander Mackennal and Bowdon Downs, R. F. Horton and Lyndhurst Road Hampstead, or Arnold Thomas and Highbury, Bristol. They were the glory of a congregational system, possible neither in the Methodist

17

connexional system, nor in Anglicanism with its parson's freehold. They were partnerships in which minister and people grew — and aged — together.

Congregationalists were nonetheless worried by their ministry. On the one hand it was felt that 'the less desirable element in the effects of Methodism is nowhere more conspicuous than in the Nonconformist ministry of this country'.[42] On the other hand, and a generation later, R. W. Dale, Birmingham's intellectual heavyweight, plaintively asked whether the Divine Call must 'never come to anyone who is over four and twenty, and is too old to enter college?'[43]

For more ministers could not always mean better ministers and much of the growing professionalism may be attributed to the fears of vulnerable men acting in self-defence. As Joseph Parker of the City Temple put it: 'The Minister is a superior kind of woman, too full of Greek and catechism to know much about the ways of the world. . . . He is revered so profoundly as to be profoundly ignored upon all practical questions. He is the victim of an idolatry so sentimentally complete as to amount to practical annihilation.'[44]

But was he a governess or a maid of all work? That depended on his stipend. Olympian ministers, chiefly Congregationalists, might expect between £700 and £1,000 in the second half of the nineteenth century, but the generality were not nearly so grand. In 1867 a Manchester Congregationalist claimed that the highest ministerial income was less than a responsible clerk's, and advocated a minumum stipend of £150 for a village pastor with £250 for his small town and £300 for his larger town counterparts.[45]

This problem was never solved, and stipends had failed to keep pace with costs well before 1914. Hence ministerial *esprit-de-corps*, for if their abilities outran their means and therefore their standing in the world, in Conference or Assembly, with cousin ministers and son-in-law laymen, they formed a powerful and singularly motivated denominational group.

How did it end? At one level it culminated in the golden age of Nonconformist mayors and M.Ps. There were even Nonconformist peers. Yet W. R. Ward has portrayed the churches as pushed permanently to the borders of the nation's life.[46] There was not again to be a large outpouring of popular, free evangelicalism, and the nineteenth century's transdenominational movements provided no substitute.

This predicament was most painfully felt by the Primitive Methodists, Methodism's most consciously popular branch yet not its largest. When, in 1848, they entered Witham, 'with a good intention we have no doubt', they caused the resignation of two members of the local Congregational

Church: 'We humbly believe, God has sent this people into this town to do a work that no other denomination of Christians are so well calculated to do because they are not quite so plain — not quite so willing to be counted singular — and not quite so willing to stoop so low, as to go out into the highways and hedges and compel the Poor and needy, and outcasts of society to come into the fold of Christ'.[47]

Nearly thirty years later the Primitives clung to their national mission, rejecting overtures for union with more churchly bodies:

In the animal and vegetable kingdom varieties of species may be produced, but when species are blended the race is ended. Under such circumstances, unity is destructive. . . . And so, we think, that Primitive Methodism, being a distinct denomination, having sprung from a distinct and independent root, must have a separate existence if it is to assume the purpose for which God has brought it into being.[48]

Even so, they spoke as a *denomination*; and unity came.

If evangelical primitivism belonged to the age of Nonconformity's lost innocence, there remained the 'Nonconformist Conscience' or, as W. R. Ward puts it, the Nonconformist 'platform'.[49] Joseph Parker ruefully surveyed it in 1876: 'We have to disestablish the Church, modernize the Universities, rectify the policy of School Boards, clear the way to burial-grounds, subsidize magazines, sell hymn-books, play the hose upon Convocation, and generally give everybody to understand that if we have not yet assailed or defended them, it is not for want of will, but merely for want of time.'[50]

The manning of this platform appeared to be Nonconformity's mission as it moved into Free Churchmanship. It was the task of men consciously eschewing 'churchy' activities for immersion in a world which they believed to be God's; Edward Miall was their *beau idéal*.[51] They shared his obedience to an alternative vision of what society might be: 'Our country is the Palestine of the modern world. . . . This land of wonders reigns over a colossal empire equal in size to the continent of Europe. On the fiat of our statesmen the destiny of millions on millions depends. And never shall its glory depart while Bible Christianity faithfully does its work through English Churches.'[52]

This Congregational vision of the 1860s was placed in a cultural context by a poetic Baptist: 'We have left the old Puritan error. We no longer despise the beautiful and artistic, but claim them as divine things, and enlist them in the divine service. We no longer consider retirement from the world a sign of holiness, but believe that all man's life and work can be dedicated to heaven.'[53] It was a secularizing work; necessarily so, because it involved a search for power, which meant politics, which meant compromises, which meant that there could never be any clear victory, though there would be many unclear ones, battles in a war whose most hopeful conclusion must be a negotiated peace.

In 1841 the five eastern counties, heartlands of rural Puritanism, returned one M.P. with close Dissenting affiliations, and these were Unitarian. In 1885 nine were returned, all of them Liberals, six with strong Congregational connexions, the seventh a Baptist with a wife from a Congregational family, the eighth a Primitive Methodist and the ninth a Unitarian.[54] But it was a pyrrhic victory, for the war's course had already turned. The political world was on the verge of realignment, and Nonconformity's accumulating political experience was helping to plane away any denominational angularities as it discovered the values of united action and turned towards an ecumenism which was based on proper understandings of churchmanship.

Political and ecclesiastical realignments were not to run in harness. The 'churchly' apparatus, for all its insights, proved to be inadequate when faced with the tensions of late Victorian society. Despite its coarseness of detail, Matthew Arnold's *Culture and Anarchy* had perceived this as early as 1869. The Nonconformity which had filled the spiritual vacuum of an industrializing society had already solidified into a middle-class establishment which Arnold believed to be outdated. It seemed inconceivable that it should fill the voids of a fully industrial society.

Nonconformists, however, would not go away. While the Liberal intelligentsia turned to panaceas for replacing decaying systems, Nonconformists looked to their Central Halls and missionary Forward Movements. They too had the world view and the social concern, and if in the years before the Great War they turned too easily towards the facile optimism of the Brotherhood Movement, or even of R. J. Campbell, with his 'new theology' grey and fascinating in the City Temple's great white pulpit,[55] /they were mistaken only inasmuch as the lessons which they then learned were not those which they had been trained to expect.

Chapter 2

The Evolution of Irreconcilables

... a Methodist, or melancholy Calvinist of some sort.

(Harriet Martineau, *Autobiography: with Memorials by
Maria Weston Chapman*, 3 vols, 3rd edn 1877, vol. I, p. 11.)

The Methodists were the pacemakers of revival and were caught most
firmly in the toils of their own initiative, the Baptists experienced the
most spectacular transformation, and the Congregationalists became *les
hommes moyens sensuels* of the new Nonconformity.

Methodism was the key factor in revival's first outworking, religion's
popular response to the tensions of the eighteenth century. By adding a
vast dimension of freshly evangelical souls to the drying remainder of
historic Dissent, bruising and breaching its exclusiveness, it helped to
forge Nonconformity and then led the way into Free Churchmanship.

Methodism's most distinctive facets — Wesleyanism, which was the
most numerous; Primitive Methodism, which was the most popular; and
the Bible Christians, who were the most rural — were seldom in
competition with each other. Their origins were spontaneous and initially
at least they often attracted different sorts of people. Its most confusing
facets — the Methodist New Connexion; or the Protestant Methodists and
Wesleyan Methodist Association and Wesleyan Reformers who combined
to form the United Methodist Free Churches in 1857; or the scattered
individual circuits and societies which remained aloof from any of these —
were dissidents from Wesleyanism, attracting similar people from similar
places. Thus Sheffield and Leeds, or Ashton-under-Lyne and Rochdale, or
Norfolk, were stong in Methodism of most sorts, but Ashton was a New
Connexion stronghold at Wesleyanism's expense, and the Free Methodists
sapped Wesleyanism in Rochdale or Norfolk.

But whatever its facets, Methodism was strongest where the Established Church was weak, meeting needs which that church was ill-
equipped to meet, its connexional organization outpacing both the
'gardens walled around' of historic Dissent and the traditional parish
disciplines of Anglicanism, responding to their inadequacy, supple-
menting their weakness and eventually competing with them.

21

Inevitably all the elements making for 'churchyness' were at work in Methodism, accentuated by the disruptions which distinguished Wesleyanism after Wesley. The organization which had emerged to let revival take root and conversion multiply was equally helpful for generations whose Christian 'mateyness' was softening into connexional inwardness. The refining sensibilities of Methodists whose disciplined lives were bearing material fruit in the new industrial England needed to be tended, whether by theological institutions for their ministers, or proprietary schools for their children.

They also needed to be wary of a reviving Anglicanism. The strength of Anglicanism's parochial system, once the necessary legal and spiritual adjustments had been made, was that it could tap almost unlimited resources. No other Christian body could command such a combination of tradition, status, money, personality and spirituality. Therefore, partly in self-defence, and partly in response to the needs of its own members and preachers, a denominational sense developed in all Methodism's branches.

All non-Anglican evangelical Englishmen believed in a 'felt' religion, stressing personal experience but expressed in community. More of them were Methodists than anything else and Methodism's experiential, revivalistic element poured into the old evangelical bodies, jerking memory into life.

The impulse was Methodist, but it was not *essentially* Methodist, neither was it all revival and no reason. Indeed, the closeness of Methodist organization added a fresh dimension of reason to the existing disciplines of evangelical living. The Methodist belonged to God, and was therefore worlds away. He was also God's instrument, and therefore here, now, and active. His life was subject to methodical control, the more so in a world beyond control. His appearance was a discipline: if he was a Primitive Methodist preacher he had to wear his hair 'in its natural form' until 1847, and 'in a plain form' thereafter.[1] His singing too was a discipline, a loud, long, outpouring effective only in concert, fusing words, emotions and souls, a conviction of destiny.

There was, in short, a movement in the Methodist discipline, not so much *from* as *through* this world to the next, demanding head as well as heart. Depending on place, time and personality, and on the chemistry which can turn chronic tension into sudden explosion, Methodists were as open to the pressures and politics of normal English life as any other nonconforming Christians: which probably meant reform. 'If Christian brethren of some other denominations solicit us as Ministers to join them in their organized opposition to the continued union of the Church of England with the State, our reply to them is this — that our spiritual charge is too absorbing, and at the best too imperfectly fulfilled to allow of our entering on such a course', stated the Wesleyan *Minutes of Conference* in 1848;[2] but the Congregationalists noted nearly thirty years later that 'the armed neutrality so long maintained by our Wesleyan friends is yielding to decisive action'.[3]

If the Wesleyans' armed neutrality crumbled rapidly after this, other Methodists had long shared political enthusiasms with established Nonconformity. As the Wesleyan Methodist Association *Minutes* of 1850 put it: 'this Assembly renews its expression of approval of the object sought by the Anti-State Church Association'.[4] All this made the emergence of an enlarged Evangelical Nonconformity, sharing that strange platform which came to be called the Nonconformist Conscience, not quite so strange after all.

In one particular respect, this platform Nonconformity was powerfully attuned to its age. Its strength lay in community, but its inspiration was entirely personal. It excelled at mounting crusades to allow individuals to be their best selves. Men and women were to be neither selfish, nor self-indulgent, but self-conscious, and Methodist societies, like Baptist or Congregational Churches, were collections of such people. They were sustained by national organizations prepared to fight for the nation to become a nation of redeemed individuals, but this growing collectivity was always to service the individual.

This was also the ethos of English Liberalism. One of the mercies of nineteenth-century English life was that, in a country which had escaped violent revolution and so never entirely repudiated traditional values, the natural party of government should be a party of movement, whose most consistent supporters were Nonconformists by conviction, which meant by salvation. Liberal England, like Nonconformist England, believed in Englishmen as individuals, though it was never frightened of acting collectively if that were best for individual Englishmen.

But what if such beliefs were proved to be inadequate? England's established constitution and Established Church were interpreted for long periods of the nineteenth century by a party whose most distinctive supporters had suffered from that constitution and whose instinctive churchmanship was not merely autonomous, but localized. The tensions and complexities of this were fascinating enough, but they were sharpened in the context of a society whose upending was continuous, piling complexity upon complexity.

It became decreasingly obvious that personal religion was the best way of defeating vice, or even that the old personal vices like drink and gambling were still the chief social evils. The discipline which had held Nonconformity together and kept it apart from the world while yet harnessing it to the most hopeful forces in that world, seemed less relevant. The simple virtues of self-reliance, always a frail barrier against chronic disease or depression, even when cocooned by Chapel, were subject to rigorous scrutiny.

It was at this stage that Nonconformity provided its own solvents, the disciplines which had enlivened its self-conscious young to engage the world and so be engaged by it: for self-consciousness is a pre-condition of civilization. The world was there to be used. Perhaps in the end it was Chapel that was used. The tension between individual and community now became crucial, not least in Methodism, which had given most to Nonconformity.[5]

And not least to the Baptists. In an important article W. R. Ward has described the period between 1780 and 1830 as encompassing a striking shift in the Baptist frame of mind.[6] It was the Baptist reflection of the readjustment which the new society demanded of all evangelical Christians, and Professor Ward expresses it by tracing a new view of history, which emerged from the mid-eighteenth century, in which it might appear not merely that offers of Grace were being freely made, and that history bore this out, but that they were being made to Christians far beyond the bounds of Calvinistic churchmanship.

The implications were profound for Calvinistic churchmen, as most of the older Dissenters were. There had to be a revaluation of mission, a reassessment of organization, and a review of doctrine. The problem to be faced by Christians reared in gathered churches, subject to the gentle fluctuations of biological, family growth was that of large and rapid recruitment from the outside world. The new recruits had experienced salvation, so doctrine needed to be phrased accordingly. The gathered church which received them was transformed into an evangelical instrument, associating with other such instruments for the practical purposes of further evangelism. A new empiricism was grafted on to the older churchmanship. 'It was expressly declared and determined that the Band of Union in this church was and should be *Christian Love and Virtue* only and not any sentimental covenant and that Members should be admitted merely on the Apostolical declaration or confession that Jesus is the Christ.' Thus the Cambridge Baptists in 1790, the essence of pragmatism, but expressing tensions peculiar to Baptists.[7]

The extent of the Baptists' predicament and of their opportunity may be suggested by the Suffolk Baptist churches. In that strongly Baptist county only three Baptist churches listed in Victorian handbooks existed in the first half of the eighteenth century, and none was of seventeenth-century origin. Nonetheless, the rapid advance experienced by Suffolk

Baptists in the early nineteenth century owed most to the missionary vitality of a church which had flourished since the seventeenth century, across the border in Essex: Eld Lane, Colchester.

The tensions inherent in Baptist advance were fourfold. The first was that the associations of Baptist churches which had arisen to communicate revival should naturally harden into denominational structures; the beloved 'Association Tent', that perfect expression of Christians meeting in concert to promote home mission, became the annual symbol of organized togetherness. The second lay in the balance to be achieved between missionary pragmatism and Baptist churchmanship. The covenant relationship between people and God could not entirely be wished away, even in Cambridge. The walls around the holy garden could not be completely slighted. In short, there was a place for the church as symbol. This led to a third tension which lay in the ministry itself, because the church's minister, for all his call to evangelism and the meeting of new needs for new Christians, could never cease to be a pastor of a settled flock. And, fourthly, there was baptism. It was this which set Baptists apart from other Christians, building radicalism into them and then tempering it with an equally inbuilt conservatism.

The radicalism was twofold. On the one hand there was the explosive effect on socially downtrodden Calvinists, trained to see prayer as the Spirit's work, but now discovering that prayer was also the church's work, even that 'God is . . . at the command of the prayer of faith; and in this respect is, as it were, under the power of his people'.[8] No wonder Joseph Kinghorn of Norwich rejoiced 'at the destruction of that most infamous place the Bastile'.[9] Then there was the effect of baptism itself. For Baptists the rite was not sacramental but confessional. It was for believers; and since it demanded the total immersion of believing adults and not just a gentle sprinkling, it was a radical act. The old life was drowned by it, and the new life was totally new and not just a continuation on more hopeful lines made memorable by a striking interruption.

Here the difficulties began. If believer's baptism were a prerequisite to the privileges of membership, sitting at the Lord's table chief among them, then what was the status of other Christians among whom God had clearly worked? What of Congregationalists who shared everything with Baptists save believer's baptism? Hence the prolonged agonies of deciding whether or not to open church membership — and therefore the Lord's table — to infant-baptized or unbaptized Christians. For if membership were open where was the 'Baptistness'? If it were closed what then was the price of maintaining the divisive symbolism of Baptist Churchmanship? Might it not be quietism, a stemming of the free outpouring of revival?

These problems never ceased to exercise Baptists. There seems to have been little difference between the larger and more obviously busy Baptist churches and the general run of Congregational churches, and on leading issues the Baptist Union and prominent Baptists made similar noises to the Congregational Union and prominent Congregationalists. But it is not entirely clear that such Baptists were in fact the mainstream Baptists, even if they contributed largely to the mainstream of evangelical Nonconformity, and the appearance later in the century of 'Spurgeonism', reviving small causes, weaning stricter Baptists to the cause of wider evangelism, but with its conservatism crystallized in the 'Down-Grade' controversy, further complicated matters.[10] Spurgeon towered among Nonconformists, but 'Spurgeonism' reflected a growing pessimism about the way things were going, which had the effect of drawing Baptists away from Congregationalists. This was a ragged process, but it suggested that mainstream Baptists were after all to be found in the residuum of quiet Baptists, village Baptists, strict Baptists.

There remain the Congregationalists. As the most numerous evangelical heirs of the Old Dissent, the largest united Nonconformist body after the Wesleyans, and the most consistently active, they assume particular significance as representative Free Churchmen.

If it is true, following A. N. Whitehead, that Protestantism is chiefly concerned with what a man does with his solitariness, it is certainly true that Congregationalists best expressed the tensions hidden in this concern. Even their name was ambivalent. They were at once *Independents* and *Congregationalists*, the latter never entirely superceding the former. Their position was most aptly expressed by Henry Allon at the Congregational Union's Manchester Jubilee meetings of 1881. His paean of individualism turned into a call for brotherhood:

> The future will be with the Church that most fully and practically recognizes the prerogatives and responsibilities of the individual life. For thus only can the highest conditions of belief, the truest sympathies of brotherhood and the most vital bonds of union be constituted. Our own Churches stand on these lines of progress. Their distinctive principle is that of individualism.[11]

This really was the spirit of the age, the religious parallel of the journey taken by intellectuals and politicians away from that convenient old myth, *laissez-faire* individualism, towards a truly liberal collectivism of men freely banded to help each other. These were the prerogatives *and responsibilities* of the individual life.

The journey was also a fight. The establishment was consciously breached for the first time since Cromwell's time, and those who were most consciously breaching it were the descendants of Cromwell's

Ironsides, educated, solid citizens on the underside of society. It was, therefore, a fight for social recognition. But it was fundamentally a religious fight, concerning values which were at odds with established values, endowing those who fought for them with an integrity which might even survive a drawn battle.[12]

Above all the journey was an evolution, as men who were apparently individualists of deepest dye in fact expressed their own sort of social control firmly cast in the successful *communal* image of countless chapels.

Some like Edward Miall extended this.[13] From the dissidence of his Dissent he craved union with the lower orders, expressing in the 1840s all the guilty yearnings of Toynbeean intellectuals of the 1880s. It seemed clear to him that if middle-class Nonconformists could unite with the progressive forces undermining established society, then the contest with the Established Church would be won. A tempered version of Miall's radicalism became Congregational orthodoxy. Of course Congregationalists would rather be gentlefolk than artisans, but they were never allowed to forget that the future was probably an artisan one, hence perhaps the appeal of the *Christian* gentleman, who might even be an artisan.

But what would this do to Congregationalism? 'The Church of the future. . .', Baldwin Brown told Congregationalists in 1881, 'will have to launch out into the deep, by recognizing all human activity, which tends to development and progress, as belonging to its realm.'[14] The extent and urgency of that launching into the deep became so clear in the 1880s that it could no longer be taken for granted that the church of the future would be recognizably Congregational. It was not enough, it seemed, for the Church to be a church. The context of this evolution was such that there could be no clear end to it.

In the half century after 1780 society was unbalanced and malfunctioning, and Nonconformity provided the most striking religious answer. In the half century after 1880 society was still malfunctioning, nowhere more irrefutably revealed than in the London Congregational Union's pamplet of 1883, *The Bitter Cry of Outcast London*. The Congregationalists' sense of malfunction, schooled by decades of Miallism, was alerted on several fronts.

For slum London's was not the only bitter cry. There was the cry of the lower middle classes, rapidly growing, fighting hardship with respect, producing Congregationalism's ministers and teachers. There was also the women's cry, the most obvious evidence in church of a malfunctioning society. 'I am poor, I have no money: but worse, I dwell under the accursed thraldom of womanhood. Could I but burst these bonds asunder, and be free, if only for once! Yea, I am confident that they will one day be broken: perhaps even in my time I may see them loosened.'[15] This was not a frustrated spinster's cry, but that of a highly educated girl, who remained firmly within deonominational boundaries, without ever relaxing her first sense, of 'showing what a woman can do'.

But if Congregationalists were alert to the cries, they could only respond on unfavourable terms, for society had become more complex, and their own resources had become constricted. They no longer lived on income. Only capital remained.

There was one other reason why there could be no clear end to the Congregational evolution. It concerned union. The very existence of Nonconformity was evidence of a divided society. Nonconformists were divisiveness incarnate and there is nothing more divisive than the snobbery of middle-class self-consciousness. Yet they craved union and extolled harmony and the truest middle-class values are all of harmony.

Perhaps the moral is that the divided best appreciate harmony, and that Congregationalists, poised at the edge of every class, products of a 'felt' Christianity but heirs to a rigorous intellectual tradition, were more vulnerable than most. Christians have not solved the conflict between intellect and experience, Hebrew and Hellene, action and thought, any more than that between individual and community, or church and society, and there is no reason why they should. But middle-class Christians, with just enough money and leisure and education are in the midst of these tensions.

The chapters which follow describe some of the ways in which Nonconformists, chiefly represented by Congregationalists, tried to resolve the irresolvable. They were faced with working out the consequences of the historic view which had emerged for most of them in the course of the eighteenth-century revival. God was at work with His people.

Yet who was God, or Jesus, or the Spirit? The trouble with history is that it poses questions, plays with answers, and promotes scepticism. Nineteenth-century Christians, sensing progress, agonized and fretted over such matters, fumbling towards fresh understandings of Christ's fulfilment.[16]

A few came to terms with that hardest of propositions for the Nonconformist: that it is possible to live with the irreconcilable. Such an acceptance, however, demanded a certainty which was no longer part of the age. No commanding thinker or statesman emerged to help Nonconformists on their way, and they had to make do with impressions of Browning or Gladstone, amidst their bouts of doubt and self-criticism. As one reared, unwillingly, at Lyndhurst Road, Hampstead, put it, 'I grew up in an atmosphere of belief in progress curiously mingled with apprehension . . . with a myth in my mind of the world having resolved itself from past history, correctly, like a sum. Yet there was also, paradoxically, a feeling that the best times were over'.[17]

Book II

From Dissent to Nonconformity

Chapter 3

'Old-Fashioned Dissenting Narrowness': Crabb Robinson and the Pattissons

The gradual emergence from narrow intellectual conditions in a Puritan pedigree is always interesting.

(John Addington Symonds, quoted in C. Mackenzie,
My Life and Times: Octave One 1883-1891, 1963, p. 19.)

'Witham Hundred is one of the pleasantest and most fertile divisions of Essex.'[1] The little place which gave its name to the hundred, well-sited on the coaching road from London to Colchester, close to Chelmsford, and easily reached from other small Essex towns — Maldon, Coggeshall, Braintree — was a perfect example of the stage at which village became town and country life was refined into urban society. In 1841 its population was 3,158, a thousand more than in 1801 and three hundred less than in 1861. It had two parish churches, one of them just built, British Schools as well as National Schools, both of them new, a good Congregational Chapel, recently built, and some smaller chapels. There were several gentleman's houses in the neighbourhood, modish places like Hatfield Priory where the Wrights lived. Some of the Witham families, like the Pattissons of Witham House, had risen from the local shopocracy. Others, like the Du Canes or the Luards of Witham Lodge, noted for their clergymen and sailors and other public servants, had been Huguenots. The Shaens of Crix were closely connected with London lawyers and merchants. The Strutts of Terling had left corn-milling for a peerage and family ties with an Irish duke. The Vicar of Witham for thirty years in mid-century was a Bramston and therefore in the heart of county society, and Witham's curates had included Van Mildert, the last Prince-Bishop of Durham. There was also a solid class of farmers, brush manufacturers, millers and tradesmen — the Dixons of Wickham Mills and Blue Mills, the Thomasins, Butlers, Fosters — and there was the workhouse, moved in the last two years from Chipping Hill.

Early in 1837 two brothers, one of them married with a child, the other still seventeen, both of them silk weavers out of work, were admitted to Chipping Hill, ordered to strip, and dressed in the leather uniform of breeches, coat, low shoes, ribbed stockings and 'hairy cap with peak'. They were set to making flocks, and were there for a fortnight before being moved on.

The degradation of it all was clear enough but it was lightened at the suggestion of two seasoned inmates: 'as soon as they saw us they gave us a hint to put our names in as Dissenters, although he was a grave-digger at Coggeshall Church and we had been brought up to the Established Church: yet we turned Dissenters because the Church was close to the door of the Union. The Chapel was in Witham Street, a long way off; this gave us a good walk every Sunday.'

The younger brother, John Castle, remained a chapel man for the rest of his life, a modest example of the model artisan, precariously making good by way of a mixture of chapel, self-help and the co-operative movement, one of Edward Baines's statistics and Edward Miall's heroes.[2]

The decision to go to chapel rather than church was prudent as well as healthy. The minister was Richard Robinson, amidst his longest pastorate.[3] The membership was not large, but it was solid — shop-keepers, maltsters, millers, schoolmasters, farmers, the exciseman, the master of the workhouse in 1849 — and it was maintained. Robinson received 215 members between 1825 and 1847. There were also the subscribers and together the members and subscribers formed a substantial body, revealing a social variety more characteristic of nineteenth-century Congregationalism than has sometimes been realized, and also revealing a social strength which was the distinctive mark of Congregationalism in the small towns of Essex. Many of the names decorate lists beyond Essex Congregationalism, like the Harveys and the Shaens. Matthew Barnard Harvey provided the almshouses which were connected with the chapel and his son Daniel Whittle Harvey shot into a radical notoriety of which Essex Dissenters were affectionately tolerant. The Shaens of Crix were a wealthy, well-connected and high-living family of Unitarians but they submitted to, and attended, the Congregational cause at Witham.[4]

This picture is enlarged by old men's recollections of their youth. John Robinson, the minister's second surviving son, who owed his drift to Unitarianism as much to the good offices of the Shaens as to any other factor, later claimed — with the exaggeration proper to an editor of the *Daily News* — that his father baptized, married, preached to, and buried nine-tenths of the people.[5] He may have done, though he certainly failed to convert them. John Robinson's contemporary, R. Walker Dixon, had a similar recollection, telescoping his memories of chapel life so that they encompassed his grandparents' prime in the early 1800s as well as his own youth in the 1830s.

Dixon was a boy when John Castle met Dissent at Witham Chapel. Like

Castle he stood for a type of Congregationalism. For several generations Dixons had milled at Wickham Bishops, prospering sufficiently by the 1820s to send their sons away to school. Dixons had been deacons at Witham since 1823, and in the 1830s they were prime movers of the British Schools. They were socially inferior, of course, to the Shaens, but they were firmly entrenched in Essex farming and milling and by the middle of the century — Walker Dixon joined the church in 1849 — they were related to Nonconformist families already prominent in rural commerce and radicalism, most notably the ferocious Browns and Goodmans of Huntingdon. Henry Allon of Union Chapel, Islington, Congregationalism's finest ecclesiastic, was Walker Dixon's brother-in-law.[6]

Dixon wrote his 'Reminiscences of the Old Dissent at Witham'[7] just before the Great War, an octogenarian from the generation of militant Dissent. He used the memories of childhood acquaintances extending almost to the chapel's foundation in 1715. The chief value of his account lies, however, in its re-creation of a Dissent which was neither militant nor heroic, its solid features only slightly touched by evangelical fire, but bearing all the marks of accumulated goodness; an alternative society which would have been surprised to see itself as such. He provides moreover an indispensable background to people and attitudes not immediately associated with Dissent but nonetheless part and parcel of it for several generations.

At the heart of Dixon's reminiscences was Richard Robinson's best-loved predecessor, Samuel Newton, minister from 1786 to 1822. Newton, his meeting-house, and his people reflected each other to perfection, examples of an apparently insensible movement of generation in stirring times, innocent of Methodism or the new industrialism, orthodox as of right and almost by default.

There was nothing isolated about Witham Dissent. Newton's father ministered in Norwich at the important Old Meeting from 1757 to 1810, and Newton himself preached in large London chapels. Newton was tall and heavy, small-featured and pock-marked, with 'a decided chin and massive lower jaw',[8] a dry sense of humour and a rich first wife. He took in pupils with an eye for the ministry — W. J. Fox, the Radical politician and Unitarian was the best known.

All this was incidental to his genius for fashioning a church. His chapel was a meeting-house for mind as well as personality. He was sufficiently learned, and his sermons were strong. 'His manner of preaching was very quiet; for three fourths of the time he would stand with his hands behind him. His printed discourses often appear coldly argumentative.'[9] This was of a piece with the man who built up the Christian life of his people from

35

the cradle to the grave. When children baptized by him reached the age of fourteen he wrote to them on serious topics, the mark of an older evangelical orthodoxy: 'His hearers were often strongly wrought upon. I have heard that once a woman went into a fit of hysterics while listening to a specially moving address — a result which Mr Newton afterwards deprecated by a characterization more forcible than polite.'[10] Sometimes, out in the country, he would lift his hat, and pray 'to the Great Creator of all'.[11]

Mr Newton's chapel, built in 1715 and enlarged for him in 1795, had galleries on three sides, supported by round wooden pillars. The singers' pew was in the gallery opposite the pulpit, with a raised table for the musical instruments — flute, bassoon, bass viol, clarionette. In the centre of the chapel was the Table Pew, for the ordinance: at other times it provided free sittings for the poor. 'Straight high-backed old square and oblong pews of various sizes were scattered about the sides of the building under the galleries and opposite the pulpit.'[12] Ventilation came from four holes in the ceiling. Light came from candles fixed to the pillars, but these were seldom used since services were held in the morning and afternoon, with worshippers from a distance eating between times in the vestry.

The services were more congregational than might appear. The sermon was long and so were the prayers, and the minister expounded as well as read the scriptures, but for the 'long prayer', the congregation 'stood, turning their backs to the minister, frequently kneeling on the seats', and this atmosphere of individual conversation with God was intensified in song. Dr Watts's hymns caught up each member of the congregation and disciplined them. They were sung sitting, their lines given out two at a time by the chapel clerk, to help those who could not read: 'well-known hymns sung to well-known tunes, led by the choir and assisted by various instruments of music. Fugal tunes were in vogue; sometimes an intricate tune with runs in the different parts would tax the power of "the singers" and excite the admiration of the people. . . .'[13]

The congregation was as disparate yet as united as the singing. The Dixons drove from Wickham in a sort of procession — a yellow-hooded chaise, then a yellow gig, and then a springless covered cart for children and servants.

Three sedan chairs used regularly to be brought up to the door of the meeting-house, one of which was occupied by Mrs Newton, the minister's wife. From Hatfield came an old family coach, swinging on high springs, with coachman and footman in cocked hats and powdered wigs; this was occupied by an old lady and her daughters, her son following on horseback. Three old labouring men used to hobble in, the last relics of the time when they wore the cocked hats of the period.[14]

So to the working men in their smocks and breeches, and the women in summer cotton gowns or winter kerseymere ones, scarlet cloaked and coal-scuttle bonneted and iron pattened, and the charity school children. Walker Dixon put few names to them. The old fashioned gentlefolk from Hatfield were surely the Shaens of Crix; and there were the Pattissons.

In 1856 John Robinson revisited Witham, to find it much the same as at any other time, from the drapers to the chief lawyer 'driven by in a four-wheeled chair by a fashionably dressed lady whom I found to be the little child I had patronized in her babyhood'.[15] This was J. Howell Blood, of Blood and Douglas, Deputy County Treasurer, magistrates' clerk and union clerk,[16] or it was his cousin, J. Howell Pattisson of Witham House, on the eve of the spectacular bankruptcy which swept him from the county.

Pattissons had been the mainstays of Samuel Newton's ministry; indeed they had been connected with the Witham Meeting since early days. They were a many-branched Essex family of farmers and rural tradesmen — in Witham they were 'eminent shopkeepers' and became 'eminent attorneys' — who prospered in three small towns, Maldon, Coggeshall and Witham. There they were chapelgoers, trustees, deacons, givers to good causes. The Pattissons of Maldon and Coggeshall dissented into the second half of the nineteenth century, the Witham Pattissons only into the 1820s.

'The Pattissons, eminent shopkeepers here, have of late adorned this place with good brick houses, more than any other persons'.[17] This adornment began in the 1730s, and it eventually included their own Witham House, 'a large brick Building with tasteful pleasure grounds behind it'.[18] A mixture of providential mortality and commerce would seem to have caused this prosperity, enabling these shopkeepers to assume the vital role of rural capitalist which brewers assumed elsewhere. Their small families allowed for a consolidation of property spiced by inheritance from childless kinsmen.

The first Witham beneficiary of this appears to have been Jacob Pattisson (1733-1805), whose two sons by his first wife, reflecting their father's enhanced prosperity, effected the family's removal from the commercial to the professional classes. The elder, another Jacob, went to Edinburgh University where he died in his early twenties, in 1783, 'being at the same time President of the Royal Medical, Speculative, and Philosophical Societies'.[19] The younger, William Henry Ebenezer (1775-1848), was apprenticed to a country attorney. His legal friendships ensured a modest immortality for his family.

The chief of William Pattisson's friends was Henry Crabb Robinson. Robinson too came from a prosperous, Dissenting, provincial background, Presbyterian rather than Independent, whose connexions added the chapel families of Bury St Edmunds, Royston, Melbourn and the villages south of Cambridge to the natural circle of Pattisson acquaintance; Robinson too was apprenticed to a country attorney, at Colchester in 1790. Eventually he became a barrister on the Norfolk Circuit and practised between 1813 and 1828 when he retired with a modest income assured for the rest of his life. He died in 1867.[20]

But Robinson's life was cast on a wider stage than the Norfolk Circuit and the small towns of eastern England. From 1796 he lived in London, latterly in Russell Square. He was immensely clubbable, an early member of the Athenaeum and noted for his Sunday breakfasts. He was a common-sense Romantic, an amateur of drama, poetry and philosophy, a traveller, a bachelor, a journalist, and one of the earliest and most influential of English Germanophiles. His views, once youth's revolutionary passions had faded, were Whiggish. He was a man of exalted friendships — Goethe, Coleridge, Wordsworth, Charles Lamb. Above all he was an observer, his observation fired into action in his diaries and his correspondence. Like many bachelors he was a warm and family man, his Wedd, Fordham, Nash and Pattisson friends and kinsmen in the eastern counties serving as his family. He entered into their quarrels and lawsuits, he showed them London, he corresponded with four generations of them, often on political matters but most happily when sharing the accumulated treasures of literary discovery. He corresponded as a friend and equal with William Pattisson, his stepmother, his wife, his sons and daughter-in-law and his grandsons. His Unitarianism tested and broadened their orthodoxy, although eventually some of them found it hard to bear. With literature he was on safer ground, and Wordsworth's latest sonnet and Scott's latest novel were anxiously read, debated and enjoyed at Witham, where Samuel Newton himself once observed that even Byron could not be *all* bad.[21]

It is from Crabb Robinson's correspondence that the elder Jacob Pattisson survives at all — 'I know . . . but few characters that are read with so much difficulty . . . he appears to the world too cautiously niggard, he is in fact very benevolent and to be benevolent, there must be discretion, and attention to the Income to make Expenditure the larger'[22] — and it is from the same correspondence that the most attractive of the Pattissons takes shape.

Elizabeth Pattisson was Jacob's cousin as well as his second wife. Childless she concentrated her affections upon her stepson, William, and later upon his two sons; and William's friend Robinson kept her in the current of the thought and letters of the world beyond Witham. Towards the end of his life Robinson remembered her fondly as 'a most excellent and amiable woman deformed in figure, with a face scarred by *Variola* there was an expression of benignity in her countenance so sweet as to render [it] all but handsome'.[23] She lives in his correspondence as a person of vigorous, loosely disciplined intelligence, fortunate to be a woman of property in a generation where politeness had yet to vanish in gentility. There was an earthy good sense, even an assumption of equality about her which her daughter-in-law and her grand-daughter-in-law lacked. These later Pattisson wives equalled her in intelligence and strength of character and surpassed her in education but they were ladies at the mercy of the etiquette necessary to an enlarged and urban society. Theirs were the generations which created the 'woman problem'.

She was the sort whom pious biography dismisses too easily as the spirited mother whose example and prayers set her sons on right paths. Her letters provide a rare backing for the stereotype, uncovering a housewife's breathless chatter, the tastes of a reading woman of leisure, and the concern for eternity of the thinking church member. 'She was one of the best specimens of the Independents of the last generation',[24] and one of the reasons for the continuity of orthodox Dissent.

'Pray see that the Ivy Leaf Geranium has the branch tyed up lest it should be broke off as they are rather tender I told Betty to set in the Green house but I think it may stand abroad a week longer if it has a dish which I think it had not when I left home I have not found any thing of the dimness (I had had before I left home) since I came hither', she wrote to her husband from near Southend, in July 1789. 'We are to drink Tea with Mrs Crisp this afternoon. William desires his Duty and also that I will tell you he liked the Water very well. Pray remember I like to receive Letters better than to write them.'[25] Twelve years later, and still out of breath, she was writing to her daughter-in-law concerned that she had forgotten to send some fresh fish by coach, telling of visits, of her husband buying pigs and herself wandering about the garden 'to gather evergreens to have as fine Bough Pots as Mrs Strutt'.[26]

To Crabb Robinson she wrote about novels. In November 1794 she asked about the Colchester Circulating Library, though she preferred to pay for her novels by the volume rather than by the day. She was particularly interested in Charlotte Smith's *The Old Manor House*, hurriedly assuring her young friend 'that she does not (by her earnestness to see Mrs S — s Novels) desire to be supposed to give her full *assent* and *consent* to all Mrs S — s sentiments but can read her publications, as others Study fine pictures, without *approving all* though she *admires much*'.[27] A month later, satisfied as to the Colchester system, she sent a list of books — *Mysteries of Udolpho, Anna St Ives, Woman as She Should be* — and expressed her delight about *Man as He is*, 'yet I hope all men are not quite so much, or so easily misled as Sir George Paradyne, however Mr Holcroft has not committed the mistake of drawing, Man as he aught to be, and so putting many people out of humour with themselves. The Authoress of The Romance of the Forest, has the power of terrifying in a high degree, and her poetry is pleasing.'[28]

Sixteen years later Elizabeth Pattisson had herself turned authoress, explaining it away to her friend Robinson with engaging diffidence when she sent him one of her works:

As there is no dedication or preface or anything to give the Authoress an opportunity to speak for herself, I shall just say I did not write such a meer baby's book for boys of six or seven years old; it was written five years ago, when William [her elder grandchild] used to want me to tell him stories, and my recollection not serving me, I try'd a little invention; and afterwards finding other children amused by hearing it read, and their mothers pleased, 'by the persuasion of friends', I had it printed.

Her pride was shadowed by grandmotherly regret. 'The time is now come for them to want little amusement from me for William leaves us this day se'ennight for school, a necessary, but painful circumstance in a boys life, as it is the first loosening of the tie to home, parents, and friends. I hope his mother will bear it with tolerable fortitude.'[29]

The intrusion of school into this small and affectionate family circle is a reminder of its Dissent, for young Master Pattisson's new school, Mr Carver's at Melbourn, catered for rich Dissenters, and his grandmother, with her liking for the novels of Mrs Radcliffe, Mrs Smith, Mrs Inchbald and Thomas Holcroft, was an Evangelical Dissenter. Robinson's Unitarianism pained her, and he told her plainly that Samuel Newton's orthodoxy deterred him from Christianity. She rallied him bravely.

For myself I can hardly suppose I am a Calvinist — you shall judge — I cannot tell you the five points, and think if I could I could not understand them. There then I take the liberty to stop. If I meet with anything *above* my comprehension that is a *subject of revelation*, I can acknowledge it as a Truth, for I cannot think a thought, or look at an object, that, properly attended to, does not fill me with wonder, but when a human being claims my full assent and consent to his unintelligible explainations, I think myself fully justified in stopping where scripture stops . . . as to the Athanasian Creed, if I were at Church when that was read, I should be disposed to close my prayer book, and sit down.[30]

Robinson first met William Henry Pattisson, Elizabeth's stepson, at the home of mutual friends and kinsmen, the Isaacs. Mr Francis, the inferior attorney to whom Robinson had been articled, had no room for Pattisson who went to Meadows Taylor of Diss instead, which was an altogether more professional opening.[31] The Taylors were Unitarians, kinsmen to the Norwich Taylors who with the Martineaus and Aldersons added such intellectual flair to the famous Octagon Chapel close to the older Newton's Old Meeting. Such society was not new to Pattisson since he had been educated at Rochemont Barbauld's school at Palgrave, near Diss, and the Barbaulds ran the Taylors close in literary — and heterodox — distinction.[32] Pattisson entered into the swim of things in Norwich, where the revolutionary tide was at its highest.

Pattisson was a fourteen year old holidaying with his stepmother near Southend when the Bastille fell. He was in Norwich when the Gallic radicalism of middle-class young men, many of them Dissenters, ran most headily in a town with one of provincial England's most consistently sophisticated political traditions. Norwich was no longer the nation's second town, but it was still a sizeable manufacturing city, rare for so large a place in possessing a truly representative corporation.[33] The combination of such a town and such society with the literary education for which Barbauld's school had been noted, and the sharp intelligence of professional youth on the edge of twenty proved irresistible. In the 1790s William Pattisson in Diss, Crabb Robinson in Colchester, and a third friend, also a solicitor's clerk but a Churchman this time, Thomas Amyot, in Norwich, corresponded enthusiastically. Some of their letters were high-flown treatises, drafts of essays for fugitive periodicals, their pomposities mercilessly deflated by the candour of friendship. Amyot, the Churchman, was a natural conservative, but his friends affected Jacobinical views and the journals for which they wrote — Benjamin Flower's *Cambridge Intelligencer* or *The Cabinet*, published in Norwich by ardent young radicals very much in the Octagon mould[34] — were wide open to legal proceedings. The notorious treason trials in London of Thomas Hardy, the Piccadilly shoemaker, who founded the London Corresponding Society, and John Thelwall, Coleridge's friend, with ten other seasoned reformers, turned the spice of excitement into the reality of persecution and when both Pattisson and Robinson moved there in 1796 to continue their legal training, a metropolitan dimension was added to the triangular correspondence.

Politics invigorates these letters, but their chief interest lies in the emergence of taste, and therefore of attitudes. This trio, Independent, Unitarian and Churchman, none of them pacemakers, show how it was that reasonable Georgians became fine romantics, and since two of them were Dissenters, we are reminded of an aspect of middle-class culture which is easily overlooked, although it contributed as much, for example, to the world of Edward Miall as any prayer meeting.

The note was best struck by Robinson in a letter to Pattisson written from Colchester, a neat combination of Augustan reason, Victorian chivalry and the heady opportunities of political economy: 'I will like a Knight Errant of the Days of Chivalry maintain that the fair beautiful and peerless System of Godwin is superior to all other systems. And I will defend with my Sword and Buckler its incomparable Worth. . . .'[35] Robinson was bowled over by the 'new and splendid Edifice', William Godwin's *Political Justice*[36] and in April and May 1795 he tried out a long 'Essay on the Profession of a Barrister' on his friend Pattisson. It was a dogged attempt to convince himself of the propriety of the law as a profession, but its political implications were unavoidable, and the two friends' mutual criticisms highlight the intellectual development of intelligent young Dissenters.

Robinson thought well of his essay, though admitting that it owed much to Godwin 'and is an abridgement of his Morality'. He intended, business-man's son that he was, to prove that law was a natural profession for moralists:

> The necessity of procuring subsistence would furnish him with motives for Industry, and his incessant search after Truth and Love of virtue, will prevent the accumulation of wealth. The moralist will perhaps be averse from entering into a large field of Commerce or Business. He will prefer some Employment of the mind and Body which does not require a perpetual Attention to the minutiae of Profit and Loss. He will select that Profession which has the fewest Temptations to vice, and . . . the most intimate Connection with morality.[37]

He will select the Law.

So he talked of law, and truth, and understanding. He refused to see Original Sin in mankind and he seized on the kernel of the matter for 1795: 'At the present time it must be allowed that the most efficacious means of improving the State of Society are by Correcting (if not destroying) the Institutions of existing Governments. This can be effected only by those who are Lawyers as well as moralists'. He ended by trouncing poor Pattisson's criticisms of his earlier draft: 'You have written 5 or 6 lines as consummate nonsense as can be conceived. You have ascribed it to Montesquiou . . . your extract was taken from some puerile Essay in a trumpery magazine signed Montesquiou and you having a mind to express obliquely your opinion of me compare me to him by calling us "Doctors". I am very much obliged to you.'[38]

Neither Robinson nor Pattisson was fitted for the destruction of institutions. In October 1796 Amyot wrote to Pattisson a very sensible, Anglican, letter broken only by exasperation that Tom Paine's 'vulgar Abuse, his ignorant Assertions and his blasphemous Bawdry are almost enough to make pious Believers . . . run mad'.[39] Two years later Pattisson remained sufficiently radical to write unforgivingly of Edmund

Burke, whose inconsistency he could not excuse: 'I admire his abilities but I have very little short of a detestation of the Man.'[40] With the new century, however, the ardours finally cooled. Revolutionary France, as Burke had been the first to prophesy, hardened into military dictatorship, and prudent Essex people were alarmed at the prospect of invasion. Pattisson did his duty:

> Every thing is military and the common salutation is now to what Corps do you belong, for myself I have enrolled as a Guide whose office is to be the carriage of Dispatches and the direction of the Troops to any particular spot — Every Body is arming, and when the Porcupine has his quills ready to throw, not even Bonaparte shall dare to touch him — We are all ministerial men, and tho' I should never like the work of Death, yet without . . . the prevention of the Test Act I might at this time have been Captain of a Volunteer Corps, of which I have been repeatedly solicited to take the command — There is no longer a difference of Political Opinions, but we are united hand and heart to drive back Invaders.[41]

He was still a Dissenter, at the mercy of the Test Act should it ever be invoked, and at election time, if a contest offered, he still drove to vote for the opposition, his own views as sensibly whiggish as might be, though when the uproar of the Great Reform Bill in the 1830s once more threatened 'revolution under the promise of reform', he shuddered and placed his faith in 'sober common English sense'.[42]

When Pattisson wrote full of the invasion scare of 1803 Robinson was in Germany pursuing the studies which are his chief intellectual claims to fame. This prompted Pattisson to some unmerited philistinism: 'that you have gained much by the study of German Metaphysics we sincerely rejoice and yet we are almost ignorant what German Metaphysics are. . . .'[43] His literary tastes, always on the ponderous side, were nonetheless accomplished and their provincialism was more in his mind than his bookcases. Moreover he had acquired a London wife.

The friends' letters invariably commented on the literature of the day, its tendencies pulling them in all directions. Elizabeth Pattisson was not alone in relishing novels, although her stepson tried to maintain a nice discrimination. In 1796 Amyot, pretending to forget William's scruples — 'Pattisson, the Classic, the Theologician, the Lawyer turns his nose up at novels' — had permitted himself a comparison between the novels of Fanny Burney and those of Mrs Radcliffe: 'in the Ball Rooms and Breakfast Parlours of the former I am pleased with the Taste and Elegance which is displayed and am so glad to find myself in good Company that I care not to leave it; in the Castles and Forests of the latter I am hurried and harassed by noises and apparitions and my mind is impelled by the curiosity of Terror to unravel the mysteries that perplex me.'[44] Thus perhaps was Jane Austen's readership prepared, although for reasons which she would not have countenanced.

The letters flowed on. In December 1798 Pattisson favoured Robinson with an imitation of Ossian ('the world is then an unweeded Garden') and chatted about books. Richard Graves's 'Collumella the Distressed Anchorite' ('you will easily procure it at a circulating Library – it is an old Book'), alas, was 'a prospective view of the William Pattisson of 20 years hence', but an authoress 'many years wife to two Consuls at Petersburgh', gave the 'best description of Russian manners of any Book I ever saw'; he even learned much from the 'Arabian Night Entertainments'. Then, gloomily: 'All your conjectures respecting any petit l'amour are Groundless my connexions . . . are at present trifling and the thread may be now easily dissolved, and you may be assured that I shall not try to make this thread a Cabal Rope.'[45]

Ten months later this thread, or some other one, had most certainly become a cable rope. On 9 October 1799, amidst the pressures of Quarter Sessions at Chelmsford, Pattisson wrote a letter whose gist was nowhere in doubt. It was long, tangled and pompous. It took refuge in high-sounding asides about the chicaneries of English justice. It was patronizing – 'To me is much more agreable one native charm than all the gloss of art, or the pageantry of grandeur. I seek not the pleasures of Life but its comforts' – but it began and ended as what it was, a first love letter: 'My dear girl I now know what it is to love . . . God bless you my dearest Girl. à Dieu.'[46]

Nearly three weeks later and certain now of his conquest, Pattisson broke the news of his dearest girl to Robinson,

I have formed an attachment for a Girl, whose manners are generally admired, whose amiability is esteemed, and whose abilities are those of ingenious activity, and vivacious animation – methinks I hear you ask where, how, who, and when, the place was Witham, the manner was the consequence of frequent interview and the insensible growth of respect into esteem and affection, and who, is a Miss Hannah Thornthwaite of Islington.

His feelings were not to be contained: 'Oh my dear Henry I have a heart teeming with love towards you and desirous of assuring you of its sincerity by the most unreserved avowals . . . you must not now be jealous of my superior regard for another . . . I who was deemed cold and phlegmatic am converted into Life and Spirit.'[47]

Hannah Thornthwaite charmed Henry, who inscribed William's letter 'Son Amour: A good letter – Substantially good Pattisson was seriously a good man – And Mrs P. his Wife beautiful and graceful'. She charmed William's father who feared a misalliance for Miss Thornthwaite had no fortune. Her father was a London tailor, and they lived at Islington in

Colebrooke Row. Her Dissenting ancestry was impeccable, and though a cousin became a Unitarian minister in Halifax, Hannah's own views were firmly orthodox. She had been away to school, and a tearful passionate letter survives from a school-friend begging her not to allow marriage to disrupt old ties.[48] She was altogether more conventional than her mother-in-law, and she was never quite at ease with Henry's easy intellect and bachelor ways. Yet she was keenly intelligent, and Robinson enjoyed her company, delighting to form her tastes and adding the Thornthwaites to his miscellaneous London acquaintance. William's marriage fulfilled all expectations since those first 'sweet interchanges of the sympathies of feeling' at Islington and his friendship with Henry remained unimpaired.

William and Hannah Pattisson so confirmed the orthodoxy of each other's taste that Robinson could do little more than dent their certainties and wait for fashion to have its way with them: 'You may if you please think Locke a great metaphysician and Pope a great Poet, you may laugh in your ignorance at Kant and refuse to understand and feel that Wordsworth has deep moral feeling and high poetic conceptions of man . . . and for all these heresies against good taste and sound philosophy I shall never be a whit displeased. . . .'[49]

That was in 1809, a bantering episode in his long, devoted bombardment of his friends with Coleridge, Southey and Wordsworth. 'Poor Coleridge! the name awakens a number of interesting reflections. How insufficient is mere genius for moral purposes', he carefully wrote to the Pattissons on Boxing Day, 1810, describing a Sunday dinner party, and fearing that Coleridge would leave no memorial 'unless he is to be considered, as perhaps the Greek philosophers were, a public instructor, a desultory educator of adults'[50]

Four years later, spending Christmas at Witham, Robinson read Coleridge's *Christabel* aloud after tea to the Pattissons, 'the first of my hearers who have not relished it'.[51] Criticism for the Pattissons was largely a matter of moral feeling. In September 1815, again at Witham, Robinson tried Southey on them. 'We began *Don Roderick*, Southey's last heroic poem, the religious character of which I thought, must, at all events, render it acceptable to the ladies.'[52] He had judged the ladies too easily. 'The greatest fault of the poem' he decided nine days later, 'is that it is too uniformly religious. Even Mrs William Pattisson was not satisfied with the religion. Probably she thought it not quite sincere in the author; and I do think, after all, that Southey belongs rather to the *Philo-Christians than the Christians*. It is, I suspect, the poetic capabilities of Christianity which have charmed him'.[53]

The Pattissons' response to Wordsworth taxed all of Robinson's tolerance. In October 1812 he read extracts from *Peter Bell* aloud to Mrs

Pattisson, and was vexed that she only half enjoyed them.[54] Then came *The Excursion* in 1814. Robinson looked through it in August, devoured it in November and was entranced by it. In December he forced it upon the Pattissons. Robinson found it 'unquestionably the noblest ethic poem I am acquainted with', and he was relieved that 'the alternating beauties of picturesque description and moral sentiment seemed not unfelt by Mrs Pattisson'.[55] Nonetheless Mrs Pattisson had her criticisms to make. She found the work doctrinally inadequate, its pantheism mixed with 'hyper-orthodox assertions as to the influence of baptism, which Wordsworth seems to represent as actually washing away the stains of original sin'. To this she added a further objection. She found in Wordsworth

a want of sensibility, or rather passion, and she even maintained that one of the reasons why I admired him so much is that I never was in love. We disputed on this head, and it was at last agreed between us that Wordsworth has no power because he has no inclination to describe the *passion* of an unsuccessful lover, but that he is eminently happy in his description of connubial felicity. Mrs Pattisson allowed him to possess sensibility, but a sensibility extended over a great number of objects even inanimate, and not concentrated on the nearest and best objects of affection.[56]

It was a drawn battle. Robinson scored heavily by producing the *Eclectic Review*'s account of the poem which was as enthusiastic as an evangelical journal could be, while still criticizing with equal propriety any portrayal of 'the study of nature as a sanctifying process'. Robinson later discovered that the *Eclectic's* reviewer was the Sheffield hymn-writer, James Montgomery, a poet entirely to the Pattissons' taste, and he wrote charmingly to tell the Pattissons so. 'My last Witham visit was in no respect uncomfortable and the want of an entire sympathy in regard to the Poet and the Poem only served to stimulate a salutary exercise of reasoning and — forbearance.'[57]

The Pattissons were a much tended outpost of their friend's intimacy with literary England, sharing his information where they could not always share his taste, living vicariously with poems and romances, passing them on to the local book club or the gamely apprehensive Mr Newton, and sometimes sampling them first hand, their doubts conflicting with their curiosity, and planed away by the insistent Robinson.

Thus in May 1812 Robinson treated Hannah Pattisson to a cold London luncheon and then a digressive sort of lecture from Coleridge at Willis's Rooms, who 'spoke of religion, the spirit of chivalry, the Gothic reverence for the female sex, and a classification of poetry into ancient and romantic. Mrs Pattisson was, however, sufficiently delighted by the sight of eminent persons. She also found out Wordsworth when talking to

Coleridge . . . Wordsworth came and chatted with us a few moments'.[58]

In June 1815, he noted a victory of curiosity over consistency, but found it better not to reproach Hannah with it:

> We then drove to David's pictures of Buonaparte which I refused to see, and to Lefèvre's picture of the same man, which Mrs Pattisson took her boys to see also. I was half displeased with her for such a rage for seeing an object she could have no moral interest in, and I almost reproached her with a vulgar curiosity to look at the copy of a being she ought to entertain an abhorrence of. I was afterwards pleased to find that in my repugnance to pay homage to the shadow of a villain I was supported by Wordsworth.[59]

London lectures and literary lions bound together by Robinson's letters and readings aloud, were no more to be resisted than were novels. Hannah Pattisson enjoyed them as much as her mother-in-law, and with greater reason. In February 1819 Robinson urged two quite different novels upon her, praising their artistry and truth in a perfectly pitched criticism. One was *Pride and Prejudice* — 'The women especially are drawn after the life and Mrs Bennet is a very jewel — equal to any of Ostade or Gerard Dou's portraits, and these you know are not prized for the beauty of the originals. Mr Collins too, the sneaking and servile parson, is quite a masterpiece' — the other, 'a still better book', was *The Heart of Midlothian* and he extolled old douce David 'as a sort of Christian hero', avowing disarmingly that he 'should have the lowest opinion of the understanding of a Unitarian who did not enjoy the fine characteristic speech in which *Socinian Vermin* are spoken of with a contempt and horror quite boundless'.[60]

Barely twenty-five years separated Elizabeth Pattisson's reading of *Udolpho* and Hannah Pattisson's introduction to *The Heart of Midlothian*, but with Walter Scott and Jane Austen, Coleridge, Southey, Wordsworth and latterly Keats, filtered through the Witham Book Club and sometimes censored by Samuel Newton, the foundations for Victorian literary culture had been laid, and given the moral discrimination which the Pattissons brought to the task, goaded by their Unitarian friend, the foundations were particularly strong for well-placed Nonconformists.

Foundations were laid in another respect. William Pattisson was, to all intents, an only child, and he had only two children, William, born in 1801, and Jacob Howell, born in 1803. For these generations, therefore, the Witham Pattissons were a small family, their cohesion accentuated by their chapel loyalties. It was also accentuated by unrestrained mutual affection. The Pattisson household had none of the coldness which John Stuart Mill, recalling his own pinched childhood, attributed to the English middle classes, or which came as a matter of course to many aristocratic households, with the 7th Earl of Shaftesbury as the most notable victim.

If anything there was too much sun in the childhood of the Masters Pattisson. 'I quite long to introduce them to their father's best loved friend', wrote their mother to Robinson shortly after Jacob's birth in 1803.[61] Five years later, when Robinson was in Spain, Hannah wrote about the boys. In William she discerned

a singular acuteness of remark, indications of a delicate discrimination, in character and feeling, with much good sense, yet he is wholly free from any marks of precosity and has rather a desirable than a wonderful mind — He is a child whose dispositions require unremitting attention, high spirited and ambitious, yet ever alive to the observation of affection or self-evident truth. He is slow in comprehending a new subject, but he will not be satisfied till he fully understands it, while Jacob catches a thought or lesson just as quickly as he forgets the one and the other, says a great many witty things without flippancy, has unbounded vivacity with the most perfectly disinterested soul I ever knew — You would love the simplicity and generosity of Jay's character, a character which you will think a Mother has painted — Would that you were here to *tell* me I am very partial. . . .[62]

In 1810 William went away to school; the choice was determined less by the Pattissons' wealth than by their Dissent. It was happier than might have been expected in the circumstances.

William Carver ministered at Melbourn Congregational Church, on the Cambridge-Hertfordshire borders, between 1791 and 1825. Melbourn was smaller than Witham, but its chapel attracted a similar auditory of farmers, lesser squires and professional men. Crabb Robinson was on as close terms with the Nashes, Wedds and Fordhams of the surrounding villages, as he was with the Pattissons of Witham, and his uncle, Habakkuk Crabb, a gentle Arian, had ministered in Royston sixteen years before.[63] These families contained all the shades of Dissent, but the Carvers were orthodox. Mrs Carver was the daughter of a London minister and connected to those stately persons, the Claytons of Poultry, the Weigh House and Walworth. Her connexions, together with local Dissent's respectability and Melbourn's accessibility made it sensible and profitable for the Carvers to keep a school. It lacked the breadth of Barbauld's, but its pupils remembered it affectionately, and the biographer of one of them, Samuel Morley, called it 'the best of its kind in the country. Mr Carver prided himself upon being able to turn out gentlemen as well as scholars, and spared no pains to train the boys in good and useful habits'.[64]

Carver's was as sheltered as any boys' boarding school could be. It harboured neither the brutality of contemporary public schools, nor the inefficiency and corruption of some ancient grammar schools; it encouraged the exercise of parental care. In 1816 Hannah Pattisson wrote to her younger son, interspersing Witham news — about the curate, the health of Grandmama Pattisson, a local attorney and poor Lucy who 'died happily trusting in God' — with motherly exhortation and careful advice about the boy's future. Jacob wished to become a solicitor; Hannah had ambitions for the Bar.

I hope that you often *review* your choice of being an attorney. Have you considered the pleasure of argument, the gratification of public speaking, your aptitude in making happy allusions, your unusual self command when haranguing and the extended fortune and importance attached to a barrister? in the latter, I include the power of benefitting the oppressed. I grant there is another side to the picture, or as I had better have said, let us contemplate the reverse.

For you know Jay, as speech is a gift distinguishing us from the brutes, so we aught to value and cultivate its perfection. *Absence* from fond parents, residence in London greater responsibility, and infinitely increased temptations, are inseparable from the choice of a counsel's profession. Yet as you told me many years since 'Joseph of Arimathea was a counsellor and a good man'.[65]

Jay did become an attorney, however, and it was his brother William who became a barrister subject to London influences. This occasioned an anguished letter to Robinson, between whom and William there was a special bond. Hannah poured out her concern — 'I have written as the thoughts have occurred and you will believe I shall not retain a copy' — lest Robinson's religious views should mislead her son. She told of her pain at the latitudinarianism of some of her London relatives and the lightness of their speech.

Another topic remains. . . . You once stated before *me*, as the acme of your deceased friend H's character his *perfect purity* adding that at 36 you believed it a unique circumstance. The world is, and may be very bad, I hasten on to say, that as you have always been held up to W[illia]m and J[acob] as a pattern of *high moral* excellence I feel such an expression from you would deeply impress Wm as involving otherwise good characters and his present horror of one transgression, which the sad fall of a youth has led him unequivocally to develope, might be *lessened*: — though I trust it would not act as a *consoling* thought in vice — If my dear friend, you feel offended with one iota of this letter, forgive the friend for the sake of the mother: writing it has cost me many tears and no little repugnance have I overcome.[66]

The sheltered atmosphere of these Essex gentlefolk constitutes their claim to immortality. In 1811 the boys were painted for 160 guineas by Thomas Lawrence.[67] The portrait took a long time painting, but engraved after the artist's death as 'Rural Amusements' it became known as a delightfully, innocently civilized picture, accessible to all of gentle taste, midway in the Lawrence canon between 'Pinkie', of 1795, and the

luscious 'Master Lambton' of 1825. 'Rural Amusements' was charming. It
lacked all sense of fun and was as rustic as a *cottage orné*. It portrayed Jay,
in green velvet, half-kneeling on a grassy knoll, clasping the neck of a
whimsical donkey, while behind him William, in red velvet, held the
animal's bridle, his right arm at once stroking the donkey and protecting
Jay. The boys were curly haired, red lipped and cheeked, and their eyes
sparkled with health and honesty and intelligence.

Thomas Lawrence was a natural choice for fashionable people: the
Pattisson connexion is less obvious. Crabb Robinson was the intermediary. Robinson had been sketchily educated at the school run by an
uncle, who was a Dissenting minister in Devizes. Lawrence, who was six
years older than Robinson and the grandson both of a Dissenting minister
and a country clergyman, was also the sixteenth child of the landlord of
the Black Bear at Devizes. His career was astonishingly rapid.[68] By 1789
he was settled in London and had connexions at Court. By 1811 his
position as a portrait painter was unsurpassed, he had moved to Russell
Square, and he was expensive. He charged from 2-400 guineas for a
full-length portrait: 'Master Lambton' was to cost Lord Durham 600
guineas.

Lawrence concentrated on portraits. His most celebrated subject
picture, 'Satan Summoning his Legions', illustrating a scene from *Paradise
Lost*, and exhibited at the Royal Academy in 1797, was likened by a critic
to 'a mad sugar-baker dancing naked in a conflagration of his own
treacle'.[69] In a portrait treacle became flattery and acceptable. There was
a drawing-room quality about his work, sophisticated, always pleasing,
never profound. He excelled with mothers and children — when the
Pattisson picture was broached Robinson sensibly took Hannah Pattisson
and her elder boy with him — but his practice comprehended the great
world, from Mrs Inchbald to Napoleon's conquerors and some of their
ladies.

The Pattisson commission, therefore, was out of the normal run,
perhaps at a reduced price for friends of his acquaintance Robinson. Some
of the commercial families whom he painted had Dissenting connexions
but very few had active links, with the exotic exception of 'Pinkie',
Elizabeth Barrett Browning's aunt.[70]

This might explain the slow progress of the Pattisson portrait.
Lawrence had little business sense, was pursued by debts, and immensely
busy. Between 1810 and 1812 about seventy-five portraits and seventeen
drawings were started, completed, exhibited or in progress, his sitters
ranging from the Duke of Devonshire to the Persian ambassador, from
Castlereagh to George Canning.[71] Quite simply Lawrence lost interest. In
1812 he sent the portrait to the Pattissons unfinished, and it was only

their persistence and Robinson's good offices that secured its completion in 1817, when it was hung at the Royal Academy.

The Pattissons were proud of their picture collection, William's portrait by Archer Shee, family portraits by Charles Hayter, landscapes which included some Turners, all part and parcel of their Dissenting life. William Pattisson was not merely a chapel subscriber: he was a church member, and he became a deacon in 1817. His minister, Samuel Newton, was one of the enjoyable hazards of Crabb Robinson's visits. In 1809 Newton was 'in a constant alarm lest I should pervert the minds of his flock. I recollect on this visit a very angry dispute on poetry — he declaring with vehemence that Collins's odes were blasphemous on account of the application to allegorical or mythological beings of the language used of the true God, and that it would have been a blessing to man and saved the souls of many sinners from perdition if Shakespeare had never lived. . . .'[72] In 1813 Robinson and Newton again disputed, this time about Southey's *Curse of Kehama* 'which he arraigned as profane, not having read it'.[73]

Pattisson, like Newton, was missionary minded. In 1806 he entertained John Campbell, the African traveller, and Mr Frey, a converted Jew, who were on missionary deputation. Campbell had Islington in common with Hannah Pattisson, whom he found 'very amiable'.[74] In 1814 another minister who had visited them on deputation wrote for advice about the case of 'the *dear, beloved,* and *interesting* but *deserted TOUSSAINT LOUVERTURE* — the supposed or pretended son of the late but immortal African chief of that name'. It was a lost cause, but Pattisson followed it up, with the endorsement: 'whilst in this world we must not be weary of well doing.'[75]

Throughout Newton's ministry Pattisson's well-doing was certainly unwearied. In July 1819 he read the first annual report of the Essex Auxiliary of the London Missionary Society, which Newton had largely founded: the reading followed a four-hour service, on leaving which the auditory silently expressed 'their gratification by very liberal contributions'.[76]

On 6 June 1822, however, Newton died suddenly, of dysentery, at Bath. Pattisson took charge of the funeral arrangements, writing to Newton's friends of this latest call 'by the great Disposer of all events . . . from time to Eternity'.[77] It was a fitting funeral, the shops and houses of Witham shuttered, and chaises, gigs, horsemen, two mourning coaches and seven gentlemen's carriages in attendance.[78] There was now the problem of finding a new minister.

The problem was not satisfactorily solved. The chapel's male subscribers demanded equal voting rights with the church members, and fifteen of them withdrew their support when Pattisson took the advice of local ministers and refused their request. In November the church had to decide whether it was scriptural for women to vote on church matters ('it was unanimously determined not in all church matters'), especially in the choice of a minister. That was defeated by twelve votes to nine, although particular attention was paid to the individual views of 'those sisters who were single women or whose husbands were not members'.

These precautions failed to preserve harmony. William Wright, Newton's successor, was acceptable to all the women save two, but only to two-thirds of the men. Eventually there was a secession and although it was healed in 1825 by the departure of Wright and his replacement by Richard Robinson, the secession's minister, it was at the cost of Pattisson's support.

Despite the drift of members to the new meeting, deacons and people of substance among them (Deacon Dixon of Wickham Bishops suspected Wright of preaching other men's sermons), Pattisson had remained with the old cause. Now he felt that his consistency was at stake and in April 1825, before Robinson was formally invited to minister to the reunited church, he resigned his office: 'I feel set at liberty from those ties, which through evil and good report I have held sacred and unbroken.' A year later, in August 1826, when charges were made against his morals, he withdrew with Hannah from communion.[79]

Old ways died hard, though the disenchantment was complete. In 1828 the Pattissons with Robinson and his brother Thomas attended the great London dinner in celebration of the repeal of the Test Act, and William and his younger son still acted legally for the Witham Dissenters and helped them in establishing the British School in the late 1830s.[80] In August 1849 the chapel Sunday School used Jacob's pleasure grounds for their treat, 250 scholars feasting on cold meat, hot potatoes, cold plum pudding and tea.[81] By then the surviving Pattissons were out of all sympathy with Dissenting aspirations, which they felt to be of a piece with the unquiet radicalism of the new age. 'Nothing can redeem the Country, but a good ministry of Conservative Reformers', William Pattisson wrote to Robinson in September 1837, '. . . I think, with you, the Political Dissenters have much damaged the ministry, by their violence and assertion of the Voluntary Principle, to the annihilation of the Establishment — Our lives have been lives of agitation, from the French Revolution to the present discussions'.[82]

The Pattisson tablets in Witham parish church give no inkling of their Dissenting lives. Indeed, by the late 1820s their affinities were all with established society. Hannah died in 1828, and her husband twenty years after, a justice of the peace now, President of the local Bible Society, and giver of land for All Saints Church and the National Schools.[83]

Of his sons, William went to Cambridge, where he was Dissenter enough not to take his degree. He became a barrister, more sanguine in his views than his father or brother, with the prospect of a political career ahead of him.[84] He married well, although the fashionable ways of his wife's family, the Thomases, who were London bankers, were distasteful to the Pattissons and Robinson. The young William Pattissons were drowned in September 1832 while on honeymoon in the Pyrenees, their tragedy commemorated in Witham parish church by a white Carara marble bas-relief by C. Augustus Rivers, from a sketch by Thomas Uwins, depicting Hannah Pattisson receiving her eldest son and his bride in the sky from the Pyrenean lake. Jacob also went to Cambridge. He settled in Witham, as a solicitor. In 1836 he married Charlotte Luard of Witham Lodge, and lived a life of increasing Toryism until overtaken by bankruptcy in 1859. His art collection was sold at Christie's in 1860, the 'Masters Pattisson' among them, for 200 guineas.[85] He died at Tonbridge in 1874.

Crabb Robinson continued to refresh the Pattissons with his rational Nonconformity. As he wrote to Jacob in January 1860:

I wish your Son may be able to breakfast with me occasionally on a Sunday Morning — Mrs Pattisson need not fear his being withdrawn from Church, for I dismiss my party at a few minutes before 11. Several of my Church friends would not stay a moment beyond Church time — This was Spender's case a grandson of Betsy Isaac. — And shall I say — a Convert or an apostate (convertible terms) from Independency to Episcopacy?[86]

With this he spanned the generations of kinship and churchmanship and poetry too. Betsy Isaac was kinswoman to both Robinson and Pattisson. Her Spender great-grandson, Harold Spender the journalist, returned to Independency, though of a Hampstead type. For some years he attended the ministry of R. F. Horton of Lyndhurst Road, the spiritual distillation of literary and artistic culture, living, as his son Stephen has recalled, unconsciously echoing William Pattisson in the 1830s, 'in a style of austere comfort against a background of calamity'.[87]

Chapter 4

'Self-harnessed to the Car of Progress'. Baines of Leeds and East Parade: A Church and a Dynasty

There was a remarkable correspondence between the spirit of Mr Baines and the spirit of the age. It was the spirit of improvement. . . . Self-harnessed to the car of progress, it was his happiness and honour to do what in him lay towards the great movement.

(E. Baines, *The Life of Edward Baines*, 1851, pp. 5-6, 8.)

No one can edit the *Leeds Mercury* for thirty years with impunity.

(John Morley on T. Wemyss Reid, quoted in A. Birrell, *Things Past Redress*, 1937, p. 262.)

I *Baines, Leeds and the* Mercury

'We don't now live in the days of Barons, thank God — we live in the days of Leeds, of Bradford, of Halifax, and of Huddersfield.'[1] So Henry Brougham, advocate, reformer and audacious carpet-bagger, assured Leeds in July 1830 in the course of that celebrated Yorkshire county contest which seemed to prove (by electing him) that the days of Leeds had already dawned amidst the shadows of the unreformed House of Commons. To many, however, it was merely a new rank of baronage that had emerged, the 'Bainesocracy', to use the name recently coined by Leeds Tories to describe the sort of men who had made possible Brougham's nomination for the nation's most prestigious county seat.[2] One man, Edward Baines of the *Leeds Mercury*, the 'Great Liar of the North',[3] stood for them all.

Eighteen years later, in July and the first days of August 1848, Baines lay dying in his house in King Street, Leeds. The deathbed, which was prolonged and edifying, was improved by a pamphlet: *A Father's Dying Addresses.*[4]

The last illness began on Monday, 10 July 1848. On the 14th, Bastille Day, it was insufficiently advanced to prevent his attending a meeting of

54

Directors of the Leeds and Thirsk Railway, but from the 21st he kept to his bed and his children began ominously to arrive, Margaret from Norwich, Anna from Lancaster, Thomas across from Liverpool, Talbot from the House of Commons. By the 22nd Baines knew that he was dying, and his son-in-law Wade 'spoke to our dear Father of the sustaining power of faith. "Ah", he replied, "my faith is very languid." '

There followed in the next ten days a strange mingling of the uplifting and the complacent: a large and prosperous family awaiting the great leveller, convinced of the efficacy of their evangelical faith and conscious that their earthly tasks — the running of an important provincial newspaper foremost among them — were efficiently done. Towards noon of the 24th Baines spoke about the family business, likening it to the British Constitution in its gradual perfection. 'I see nothing to regret or to wish altered. . . . We are in the desirable position of being removed from temptation. Our position is independent.' That evening he turned to religious topics, and wished that his feelings were more intense.

On Sunday 30th, at eleven in the morning, there came a change for the worse. Most of the family had gone to Belgrave Chapel to hear Raffles of Liverpool preach a memorial sermon for Winter Hamilton, a Congregational minister, eminent and stately, whom Baines had much admired. They were summoned back from this unrelieved gloom to King Street where, revived by brandy and water, comforted by his sons and with his wife holding his hand, the dying man reflected that Winter Hamilton was now 'spending his Sabbath among scenes of a very different kind from this', and felt uneasy that he should be so calm at the approach of 'the common destiny'. He talked about this to his wife, Charlotte, whose soul's most earnest desire, so she told him, 'has ever been that God would hear my prayers for *your* salvation'.

Thus he prepared to talk to his children, who came in one by one from the library. Matthew Talbot, the eldest, after a youthful period at the *Mercury*, had been set apart for politics and the law. He was a Trinity man who had been President of the Cambridge Union in 1818 and Member of Parliament for Hull since 1847. Already his political career was bright with promise. He would sit for Hull until 1852, and then for Leeds until 1859. From 1849 to 1855, excepting the Disraelite interlude of 1852-3, he would be President of the Poor Law Board and in December 1855 he would enter Palmerston's Cabinet as Chancellor of the Duchy of Lancaster. He was a Churchman, but his continued sympathies and family ties with England's most articulate Nonconformists gave him rare significance. 'Your example has tended to elevate the character of the rest of the family', to which Talbot replied: 'May I have grace to follow your example'.

Then followed Edward, who inherited the newspaper with his father's genius: 'In the whole course of my life I never saw stronger evidence than in you of high integrity of religious character, of love and dutiful obedience to parents, or of a resolution to render most useful a public station', and the older Edward spoke of the younger's engagement in a great work: 'you are giving education to the ignorant, and that of the soundest kind and in the best way.'

So to Frederick, recently widowed, who joined with his brother in the management of the *Mercury*, but lacked his flair: 'If I have had any pet, it has been you. . . .' As to his daughters, Baines rejoiced that Charlotte's husband was 'a public officer of the church, whose duty it is to make known the truth of the Gospel', and he urged Anna's husband to exercise special care in the selection of a new minister for East Parade Chapel, which was the Baines church, and pastorless like Belgrave. He sympathized with his charitable, childless, daughter Jane and with his high-spirited daughter Caroline, 'placed in a certain degree among strangers' down in Sheffield, where her husband was a solicitor. He trusted that the 'approving eye of God' was upon her. The youngest daughter, Margaret, was only four years married: her husband, Charles Reed, was a printer in London, with a knighthood and a political career ahead of him. Baines was especially gratified by this son-in-law, for Reed was devoted to the cause of Sunday Schools, and he referred to Reed's endeavours 'amidst all his avocations, to improve the rising generation . . . a task which to some persons might be irksome seems to him a source of pleasure and delight'.

Thus it continued, through the children — there was an affectionate message for his son Thomas, who was editor of the *Liverpool Times* —, and to the children-in-law, to the grandchildren, and even to two boys, sons of town missionaries whom Baines maintained. Politics and commerce, religion and philanthropy, the House of Commons, the *Mercury*, the *Liverpool Times*, Sheffield, London and East Parade, Leeds were swept together into the eye of eternity. It was a farewell in the grand manner, and it took one and a half hours.

On the morning of 3 August it became apparent that Baines could not last the day. 'Frederick had just raised him in bed, when a sudden ghastliness came over the face.' There followed 'a beautiful placidity, succeeded by a glorious smile'. He blessed his family, taking the hands of his eldest sons, while Watts's verse was repeated:

> A guilty, weak, and helpless worm,
> On Thy kind arms I fall;
> Be Thou my strength and righteousness,
> My Jesus and my all!

'How beautiful', he said, as he listened.

He died at a quarter to midnight. At his widow's suggestion the mourners moved into the library to praise God in prayer, the widow, her children and grandchildren, a sister and a nephew, the servants and four widowed or maiden ladies who were friends of the family.

A representative Victorian scene; but of what was it typical? No account of nineteenth-century Nonconformity would be complete without the Baines family, yet their combination of family connexion and political and religious views was not precisely echoed outside Congregationalism, and even within their denomination their views were by no means universally held. There can be no description of Leeds between 1800 and 1890 without some account of Edward Baines, father and son, yet neither of them properly belonged to that important group of mercantile and professional families of the upper middle class which distinguished Leeds from other Yorkshire towns: they were not even very wealthy men. Yet to the intelligent outsider Leeds and Baines were as synonymous as Baines and respectable Nonconformity.

Leeds ceded little to any northern city in terrible romance. It was, no doubt, a poem.[5] Samuel Smiles's *Self-help* was conceived there.[6] In the nineteenth century its population grew from 50,000 to 400,000. In 1831, when the 'Bainesocracy' had become tangible, its 123,000 inhabitants made it Britain's sixth city, slightly smaller than Birmingham. In the preceding decade its population had increased by nearly 50 per cent. But although Leeds was obviously a new city in the physical sense, it possessed an established urban tradition, mercantile rather than industrial, woven into the life of the surrounding county.

The elder Baines arrived from Preston in 1795, a young man with enough expertise as a printer and stationer to make his way as a master craftsman in a town of master craftsmen. Leeds society, however, was not dominated by master craftsmen but by merchants, wealthy capitalists numerically and financially at their height in the 1790s, connected by origin as well as by marriage and sympathy with the landed interest, investing their capital in property or government stock rather than in industry: part, therefore, of pre-industrial Britain.[7]

It was here that the tensions began. Yorkshire was a stronghold of the agricultural interest, but Yorkshire's West Riding was also a stronghold of the new industrial society. By the third quarter of the eighteenth century it exported nearly half of the nation's woollen goods. This was the reflexion not merely of new factories and therefore of the energies of a new class of manufacturers, but also of the energies of a new type of merchant. Leeds continued to prosper as a local marketing centre and as a centre of the finishing trades for locally manufactured woollen cloth, but it suffered increasingly from the competition of Bradford with its worsted industry, or Halifax, Huddersfield and Dewsbury whose woollen merchants were more closely associated with local manufacturers than the gentlefolk of Leeds, and whose lighter cloths were more attractive than Leeds broadcloth. The European wars which closed the century meant that new overseas markets had to be developed. On all counts the conservative Leeds merchants were at a disadvantage. Yet if the future lay with bolder spirits, the old mercantile influence remained strong and the 'Bainesocracy' never quite succeeded in breaching its defences.

Leeds, therefore, saw the emergence of a new class of merchant and of manufacturers on a new scale. It also witnessed a host of new trades and industries: it ceased to be wholly dependent on textiles. To the tensions within the textile industry were added the tensions natural to these other industries. Taken together they projected a further dimension: that of size. To the gentlemen merchants and master craftsmen of a provincial town were added not merely brash new men of substance but factory operatives by the thousand. By the 1820s Leeds, as much as Liverpool or Manchester, let alone London, was faced with the practical problem of moulding what had become Europe's first properly urban society. Could a civilization be produced from it, and if it could, who was to set the pace in this?[8] For England's rulers, like Leeds's gentlemen merchants, were men who continued to believe regardless of party or expertise that rural values were the fundamental values.

This was the problem which confronted the Baineses as self-confessed moulders of opinion, and their associates, new men, self-consciously producing the new Leeds. It was a problem of capturing existing structures, and then of forming their own order, frequently in conscious reaction to the 'order' of the older Leeds. For such men, 'self-harnessed to the car of progress', meeting the stern challenge of the age, the first stage must lie in self-order: in self-control.[9]

Self-control is not static, and it need not be selfish for it admits of a triple responsibility, to God and fellowmen, as well as self. This responsibility determines movement and amidst the chaos of industrialism such movement is best defined within the family circle, or perhaps the family church. The adaptation to wider disciplines, and the attempt to reconcile these with the continued integrity of the family, or the family church, or their particular sections of the middle classes, was a large part of the story of the new men of the industrial cities. It was at once a political and an educational process. Here at least the Baineses were typical, and inasmuch as they were professional educators, they were representative.

The Baineses were acutely conscious of the communities to which they belonged, and of which they were the mainstay: their cousinhood, for example, which within three generations infiltrated most corners of the public life of orthodox Dissent, to form a new Puritan inheritance; or their comfortably disciplined chapel communities first at Salem, then at East Parade, finally at Headingley Hill. These were without doubt gardens walled around from the wildness of contemporary Leeds.

Leeds was as horrifying as any industrial city.[10] Most of its people belonged to the various shadings of the working class, densely packed in districts which had become national bywords. The town was ill drained and unsewered; the houses lacked water and sanitation, and because they were often back-to-back and clothes lines needed to be hung somewhere, their streets were unpassable as well as unpaved. Their inhabitants were the first to succumb to epidemics and were always vulnerable to the commercial depression endemic in an industrial society.[11] The cumulative impact of disease and depression made self-help a mockery and improvement a delusion.

Yet it is not clear that the enormity of the problem was, or should have been, as self-evident to contemporaries as it appears in the light of retrospect. Disease and unrelieved poverty were not new but their novel concentration in a Leeds or a Manchester at least made them obviously intolerable to society, without making the suffering any more unbearable than it had ever been. There were further grounds for hope, for if those who prospered in the new Leeds remained vulnerable to financial disaster and their suburbs were still smoky and unhealthy, they were nonetheless tributes to a condition which had been mastered, however precariously. The battles which preceded the erection of the villas and the chapels, of the magnificent town hall, of the waterworks and the sewers, were landmarks in this seemingly irresistible conquest.

It was the victory of self-control. But the organizers of this victory were men whose communities could be sanctuaries as well as outposts, and the attitudes of mind developed by their communities to ensure survival could prevent them from using victory when it came.

This was largely a Nonconformist problem, for Leeds was a chapel town. It was especially a Baines problem. In 1843 the younger Edward Baines characteristically defended the apparently horrible state of Leeds by arguing that its ne'er-do-wells were mostly 'the children of idle and profligate parents who are attracted to a large town by the various resources which it offers to enable them to escape regular labour. They do not belong to the working population of the district': they did not belong to the *community* of Leeds.[12] Could such views be enlarged?

Leeds was a Methodist town. 'The real fact is', claimed Vicar Hook in

1837, 'that the established religion in Leeds is Methodism, and it is Methodism that all the most pious among the Churchmen unconsciously talk'.[13] Leeds Methodism had already produced the Leeds Organ Case of 1827 which was followed by an inevitable secession, and in the 1840s much of the 'Fly Sheet' agitation centred upon Leeds, but Methodism continued to flourish there. In 1851 nearly 42 per cent of Leeds churchgoers were Methodists compared with only 32 per cent who were Anglicans. In 1888 Wesleyans stood second, Primitives third and Free Methodists fourth (tying with the Congregationalists) in the number of their chapels, while the Wesleyans came second in their sittings to the Congregationalists' third: Anglicans came first with both churches and sittings. This preponderance was reflected in the restricted sphere of the town council four years later when nineteen out of twenty-seven Liberal councillors whose religious links have been traced, were Methodists, fifteen of them from the smaller Methodist bodies.[14]

In the light of this the prominence of other Nonconformists becomes noteworthy. As always, the Unitarians formed a class apart, and their Mill Hill Chapel was pre-eminent for the first half of the century at least in its civic and intellectual influence. The Congregationalists and Baptists stood together by 1851 with the Congregationalists slightly stronger in numbers, and much stronger in influence.[15] Three of their five central chapels in that year — East Parade, Belgrave and Queen Street — were of national repute in their denomination, their memberships reflecting more uniformly than those of most other chapels the men who were out to master the new Leeds, and thereby the new England.

Chapel was a basic stage in the process of control. In so Methodist a town as Leeds, Congregational Chapel could not fail to have political implications. The Baines family expressed this at all levels. From 1834 to 1841, and from 1852 to 1874, a Baines was one of the Leeds M.Ps: from 1847 to 1852 a Baines sat for Hull and from 1868 to 1874, and 1885 to 1892, Baines sons-in-law sat for Hackney and Halifax respectively.[16] Indeed, something of this Liberal tradition survived the century, for if a great-grandson of the elder Edward Baines failed to be elected for Leeds North in 1895, another great-grandson was a Liverpool M.P. between 1910 and 1918.[17]

At the municipal level the Baines influence was less direct, but no less pervasive.[18] With Hull and York, Leeds was the only important Yorkshire town in the early nineteenth century to have a corporation. Its charter of 1626 ensured the dominance of the gentlemanly wool merchants and until the Municipal Corporation Act of 1835 the Leeds corporation was their Anglican, Tory, preserve. Their political influence, however, no less than their economic power, had been subjected to the severest scrutiny. It had been affected by local Whig parliamentary triumphs in 1806 and 1807 and between 1818 and 1822 the corporation lost control of the Vestry, the Improvement Commission and the Workhouse Board. By 1835 some of the newer Leeds merchants were already to be found in the corporation itself.

Superficially there was little difference between the reformers and their opponents. Both sides included merchants and professional men. But socially there was a distinction since the reformers included the newer men and manufacturers. Above all there was a religious distinction: the reformers included Dissenters and Edward Baines senior was their epitome. In 1818 he became a trustee of the Workhouse, and by 1820 he was elected chairman of the Workhouse Board: it was his influence which secured the publication of the Board's accounts. From 1819 he agitated for the publication of the Churchwardens' accounts, which he secured in 1822: in 1833, for the first time, a majority of Dissenting Churchwardens were elected. In 1825 Dissenters, urged by Baines, initiated a new Leeds Improvement Act: by 1829 over half of the Improvement Commissioners were Dissenters. These were signal victories for open government and efficient agitation by way of reasoned debate.

The implications of this became clear with the municipal reform of 1835.[19] Apparently a wealthy Anglican oligarchy had been replaced by a wealthy Dissenting oligarchy, differing from their predecessors chiefly in the insecurity of their traditions and the unpredictability of their crotchets. The reality was more complicated.

Before 1835 there had been thirty-eight members of the unreformed corporation; the new council had sixty-four members, of whom forty-eight were councillors, over half of them Dissenters. George Goodman, the first mayor, was a Baptist. They were men of means and leisure, subject to property qualifications which were much modified but not completely abolished in 1869 and 1882, to the facts that council meetings were unpaid and in business hours, and to the demands of an electorate which before 1868 was over twice the size of the parliamentary electorate, and large by the standards of comparable cities: about 10 per cent of the population in 1840, 13 per cent twenty years later. There was a further subjection: councillors represented wards, and their electoral success reflected the efficiency of their ward committees. In short, opinion and efficient agitation by way of reasoned debate became institutionalized. The new oligarchy was, like Edward Baines, 'self-harnessed to the car of progress'.

Leeds became a county borough in 1889 and a city, by Royal Charter, in 1893. Latterly the car of progress had a bumpy ride, though driven until 1890 by Liberals of various standing. In 1842 the Improvement

Commission, in which the younger Edward Baines played an increasing part, was manoeuvred out of existence and a remarkable Improvement Act gave the corporation powers (should they care to use them) over drainage, sanitation, paving, housing, lighting and all manner of other amenities: it has been hailed as a pioneering measure in the history of public health in England.[20] This promise was not maintained. In the 1840s it was blighted by fears of Chartism and depression, and by the emergence of radicals whose watchword was economy, always suspecting Whiggish extravagance. It was also blighted by the education issue.

In the 1850s, the decade of the new town hall, drains and waterworks, the battle continued: smaller men, shopocrats, emerged to fight professional men. Improvement meant rates; it also meant increased power in the hands of officialdom. Where, then, lay the truly efficient humanity and the real economy? The issues were nowhere simple, when the hardest battles were between shades of Liberal. In the 1870s the tensions were increased by the emergence of temperance as an electoral issue and by the re-emergence of education.

Throughout these years the municipal system in Leeds ticked over. 1878 saw the completion of Leeds's first deliberate slum clearance, but no action followed the Artisans' and Workmens' Dwellings Act of 1876 and this typified the whole spectrum of local reform. It was only in the 1890s that the promise of the 1842 Improvement Act was redeemed. Only then might the local conflicts between efficiency and economy, expenditure and common-sense humanity, intertwined with wider conflicts about intervention or education, all of them mingling principle with self-interest, seem to be on the verge of resolution. And it was then that the Liberal domination was not merely threatened, but broken.

The Baineses were not active in the council, although Edward the elder declined to serve as an alderman in 1846, but they were active in every facet of the political organization which the reformed system necessitated, and they had been instrumental in voicing the principles and initiating the debates which determined that system's form in Leeds. They also contributed more than any other family to the complexity of such matters, and their contribution had a national impact because of the one level of politics in which they were truly master craftsmen: the press. It was through the *Leeds Mercury* that the Baineses and their dependants became known as a dynasty of ruthless, calculating, high-minded, doctrinaire, coldly Christian grandees.

It has been claimed that newspapers heralded change in Britain's politics in the 1820s rather as transistor radios heralded change in African politics in the 1950s. They not merely met a growing demand for information — and thereby increased it — but they were able to meet it because the processes of paper-making and newspaper printing were among those transformed in the course of the Industrial Revolution.[21] The *Leeds Mercury* was the foremost provincial beneficiary of these trends.

Its first issue appeared on 7 March 1801. There had been an earlier *Leeds Mercury*, but this had ceased in 1755 and when revived twelve years later as a conservative and thoroughly provincial journal with a more successful rival in the *Leeds Intelligencer* it fared only moderately well. In 1794 it was purchased as a business speculation by Binns and Brown, the printers and stationers to whom young Baines was apprenticed in 1795. It continued to do badly.[22]

This was the situation in 1801 when a group of notables enabled Baines to buy the *Mercury* and the goodwill of the printing business which accompanied it, for £1,552. The notables included R. S. Milnes and James Milnes, who belonged to the local Whig squirearchy, and Marshall, the textile manufacturer. Marshall was an industrialist on the new scale, the Milneses were Unitarians, all were reformers and therefore new men. Edward Baines joined them as a public figure: from the first he was independent.[23]

Baines's 'constant tendency towards judicious improvement ... enterprising without rashness, and cautious without timidity'[24] vindicated the intentions of his backers. Within its limits – under a dozen men produced it in the mid-1820s, and in the mid-1840s its price of 6*d*. restricted it to a prosperous readership – the *Mercury* was a portent. In thirty years Baines had so built up revenue from advertisements that the annual profit was £3,000. He was to the fore in his use of new machinery. By 1807 two editions were produced each weekend, one for country areas, and one, with fresher London news, for Leeds itself. Repeatedly in the 1820s the size and appearance of the newspaper were improved. From its earliest years it pioneered with its reporting of elections and assizes and Parliament: by 1825 it maintained a London correspondent. There was a conscious purpose in this, for opinion was not merely to be reflected, it was to be moulded, and from the start, handled with increasing confidence, the vehicle for this moulding was to be editorial comment, a dangerous as well as a novel experiment for the provincial press at the time of the Napoleonic wars.[25]

There could be no doubt as to the success of this: in 1801, 700 copies circulated and each issue stood at 21,000 words; in the 1840s, 10,000 copies circulated and each issue stood at 180,000 words.[26] The *Mercury* had become the leading provincial newspaper, and its proprietors were becoming a dynasty. In 1827 the younger Edward Baines formally became a partner, and there were dynastic alliances with other provincial journals. In 1829 Robert Leader, whose wife and Mrs Edward Baines senior were cousins, purchased the *Sheffield Independent* and the Leaders thereafter were to Sheffield a slight reflexion of what the Baineses were to Leeds. From 1829 Edward's third son, Thomas, was editor of the *Liverpool Times*, his daughters marrying impartially into Liverpool politics. In 1834 the *Bradford Observer* first appeared, whose editor and eventual proprietor, William Byles, founded a family of Liberals and Congregationalists as active in public works as the Leaders and the Baineses. The Byleses were not related to the Baineses, and their Liberalism differed, but the links were there. In 1867 the first minister of the new Headingley Hill Congregational Church in Leeds, which several Baineses promoted, was Alfred Holden Byles, son and brother of successive proprietors of the *Bradford Observer*. By this time the *Mercury* had become a daily paper, managed by four Baines partners. The genius of its founder was diffused: his creation had become an institution.

The *Mercury* had its moments of press history. In its columns in August 1802 Richard Edgeworth advocated the general use of railways, always a Baines enthusiasm.[27] It achieved its finest coup in 1817 with the exposure of Oliver the Spy, a government *agent provocateur* active in the West Riding; in 1819 the younger Baines was at the Peterloo massacre.[28] Between 1830 and 1832 it thundered away for Reform and it was a correspondence in the *Mercury* in October 1830 which helped to provoke the Ten Hours agitation.[29] By the 1830s it had become not merely the unchallenged organ of Yorkshire Liberalism, but also a platform for views dear to all intelligent opinionated men.[30]

Perhaps it traded unduly on this. As the 1830s moved into the 1840s and religious controversies enflamed educational and social issues, so the *Mercury* moved from its broad appeal. It became thoroughly crotchety as well as thoroughly respectable. Yet at no time could its influence be discounted. In the 1860s it consistently championed the Northern cause in the American Civil War.[31] In 1880 it was rare among the provincial press in predicting the Liberal triumphs,[32] and in 1885 it helped to determine the sequence of events which led to the split over Home Rule.

Since 1870 the editor of the *Mercury* had been T. Wemyss Reid, the first man to hold that position outside the Baines family. He was, however, the son, brother and uncle of Congregational ministers, replacing T. B. Baines, one of the younger Edward's sons, who had cut his active ties with the *Mercury* on leaving Congregationalism for the Plymouth Brethren.[33] He became, therefore, a man of note in provincial Liberalism. It was Reid in late 1885 who told the M.P. for Leeds West, Herbert Gladstone, the Grand Old Man's not very grand son, of Liberal moves to shelve the Irish question by keeping Lord Salisbury's Conservative administration in power. Reid begged for guidance. It was this which led Herbert Gladstone to state his father's views on Home Rule in the so-called 'Hawarden Kite', published in the *Leeds Mercury* on 16 December 1885, and in the London newspapers the next morning.[34] The uproar which followed was doubtless more noise than substance, but it was the last time that the *Mercury* was of visible Liberal note. Its clumsy attempts in 1886 to play its part in healing Liberal dissensions were unwelcome to the Gladstonian leadership; and in 1887 Wemyss Reid left Leeds for London.

Thereafter the *Mercury* became what perhaps it already was, merely the leading Liberal newspaper of an important city, nothing more. Occasionally it showed unexpected flashes, as when it espoused Lord Rosebery's Liberal Imperialism, but its financial decline was unimpeded and in 1901 the Baineses sold out to the Harmsworths. It survived until 1939 when it merged with the *Yorkshire Post*. It had long ceased to be even nominally Liberal, and the newspaper which had once barred gambling news latterly traded on the fame of its racing tipster, 'The Duke'.[35]

II *Baines the Elder*

What distinguished the *Leeds Mercury*, the *Liverpool Times*, the *Bradford Observer* or the *Sheffield Independent* was less their Liberalism, or even their success, than the Nonconformity of their editors and proprietors. The Baineses, Byleses and Leaders did not so much represent Nonconformity as *know* about it, which was rare among public men.

Yet for all that he expressed Nonconformity the elder Baines was properly Nonconformist only by slow conviction. Baines's way of life, therefore, should be seen as natural for any prudent man. It so happened that Baines's wife, children and closest friends were all committed Nonconformists. Only when he united his commitment with theirs, by joining Salem Congregational Church on 3 January 1840 might it be urged that he truly expressed the distinctiveness of Dissent.[1]

'It is believed', recalled his filial biographer of the time just before the *Mercury*'s launching

that the conduct of Mr Baines . . . was a perfect model for young tradesmen; and that his humble but happy household was also a model for young husbands and wives. . . . He always drank water. He never smoked, justly thinking it a waste of time and money, and that to gratify a taste that does not exist naturally, but has to be formed. He took no snuff. Neither tavern nor theatre saw his face. The circle of his visiting acquaintance was small and select. Yet he was not an earth-worm. He took an active part in the Benevolent or Stranger's Friend Society, and was a man of public spirit. The pure joys of domestic life, the pleasures of industry, and the satisfaction of doing good, combined to make him as happy as he was useful.[2]

The pleasures of industry and the satisfactions of well doing retained their charms when he was thirty-six years older, and a Member of Parliament: 'When I tell you that I presided at the Baptist Irish Society at seven o'clock this morning, that I was at the Sheffield Gas Committee at mid-day, and that I have to attend on Mr Buxton's motion in the House of Commons this evening, as well as to take the chair at the Irish Evangelical Society at six o'clock, you will conclude that I have not much time for correspondence.'[3] Even his leisure was highly serious. In the summer of 1822, he attended a fancy-dress entertainment during the Preston Guild Merchant, 'in the plain and grave attire of Dr Franklin, to whom he bore so considerable a resemblance in character and history. The personation was excellent'.[4]

To his son the English Franklin was in all things moderate, in height, appearance and dress. His hair was brown, his complexion fair. He spoke well, but plainly. He was a good committee man. As a young man he lived on half his income and kept a single servant. In later life he kept no carriage. His literary taste was as it should be: Fox's speeches, Addison, Hume, Goldsmith, the 'homeliness of Crabbe', the 'plain and nervous' Cobbett; 'he luxuriated, though sparingly in Shakspeare'.[5]

He was, nonetheless, a public man. He was even one of the landed interest, since from 1821 he leased 1,100 unpromising acres of Chat Moss. He did his best to improve them, farming with as much enthusiasm as science. Baines of Barton Grange is a less expected figure than Baines of King Street, Leeds, or even than Baines the courtier, who fell and loosened two teeth, hurrying to the coronation of Queen Victoria.[6] Yet they were all of a piece, as the Liberals of Leeds realized in November 1841 when they presented Baines with a silver service. Its centre-piece was a massive candelabrum on a triangular base, of which each face was a tablet. One was a landscape in bas-relief, 'with emblems of agriculture in the foreground, and a railroad in the distance'. A second represented a printing press and emblems of commerce and manufacture. The base's corners were occupied by figures, 'very beautifully executed in frosted silver', of Truth and Liberty and Justice, while palm trees grew from it, six branches springing from their foliage to hold lights.[7]

This was also of a piece with his upbringing. Baines liked to describe how he had crossed from Lancashire to Yorkshire, on foot, with most of what he owned on his back. He was no more self-made, however, than many successful men. The Baineses had been tenants of the Dukes of Devonshire near Ripon. They were Anglicans, the sort of farmers who produced country clergymen and country surgeons. Edward Baines's father, Richard, moved to Preston for a flightier career as exciseman, grocer, cotton spinner, coalmerchant and land agent. In the course of this he rubbed against the pretensions of Preston's closed corporation, a foretaste of his son's experiences in Leeds.[8]

There was a pattern book inevitability about Edward's youth: the education of Hawkshead and Preston Free Grammar Schools, as brutal and rebellious as such places then were, followed by apprenticeship to Thomas Walker, a local stationer. But these were the years of the French Revolution, and Walker was known as a Dissenter and believed to be radical. In 1793 he launched the *Preston Review*, with Baines to help him. It failed, suspected of all manner of Jacobinism and in 1795 Baines tramped to Leeds, to join Binns and Brown of the *Mercury*.

No doubt his views were eminently moderate and his conduct frank but his associates were often Dissenters — Congregationalists, Unitarians, members of the Methodist New Connexion — and his leisure was spent with discussion groups, hardly a blameless pursuit for young men in the 1790s.[9] At the same time John Pye Smith, the future principal of Homerton College, and a cousin of Mrs Edward Baines, was associated with James Montgomery and the Sheffield *Iris*, and consequently suspected of unnecessary radicalism. If their experience of the 1790s forced moderation to the point of caution into these men, they were nonetheless discovering the consistent discipline of reason. Among true Whigs this fostered that spirit of gentle insubordination which was their chief distinction. Translated to the sphere of rising tradesmen the spirit was less polite, though no less moderate, and the insubordination no less persistent.

The Glorious Revolution tinged Edward Baines's memory almost as much as that of Lord John Russell. His first involvement with parliamentary elections came in 1807 when he supported the Whig Fitzwilliam interest in the Yorkshire county contest, and he retained this loyalty: 'I always had considered the Whigs the mainstay of the country', he stated in 1835.[10] He converted his *History of the Wars of the French Revolution* into a *History of the Reign of George III*, 'a clear, candid, and honest narrative of events of transcendant importance', and when his wife saw George IV's entry into Dublin in August 1821, he wrote to her with powerful restraint: 'it was perhaps your charity towards him which suggested that his real appearance was what it ought to have been.'[11]

In the long, dead, years of the French Wars powerful restraint was the only course for a public man in his position. He was accused of Jacobinism, Napoleonism and Americanism. 'Suffice it to say', his son concluded, 'that Mr Baines took the views of Fox, Grey, and Whitbread'.[12] The views of Fox, Grey and Whitbread, echoed by the Baineses and those like them, became the commonplaces of later Liberalism. They were the foundation of that famous catchphrase: Peace,

Retrenchment and Reform. 'War is the harvest of Ministers — it is a period of extensive patronage', Baines claimed in words which any Victorian Liberal could have used; and in 1815 he saw no reason why Bonaparte's return from Elba should precipitate further war.[13]

Such views were sometimes wrong-headed, necessarily shocking, frequently imprecise and invariably moderate. The repressive atmosphere of the years before 1815 dictated this strange combination of qualities. For Baines was a Reformer. His Preston upbringing, his position in Leeds, and his association with the lordly Fitzwilliams determined this: his temperamental and religious affinities with Dissent meant that his support for Reform could never be mere Whiggery. His starting point was admiration for that eighteenth-century constitutional balance which had been lost. His intentions were the eminently conservative ones of seeking to redress the balance, but in the circumstances of the time and however circumspect his methods or practical his proposals, the implications of a return from imbalance were profound.

Logical conservatism can be disconcertingly reformist. Before 1815 he could not advocate specific reform, for that would invite prosecution for sedition; after 1815 he remained over-careful to dissociate himself from agitation. He feared that agitation could promote reaction which might end in despotism, but his insistence upon open, reasoned activity led him to brave meetings which verged upon agitation. In January 1817 he spoke on Parliamentary Reform for an hour in a snowstorm in the Cloth Hall Yard: 'we shall always be ready to meet our countrymen in public and in the light of day'. In June 1819, two months before Peterloo, he spoke to working men on Hunslet Moor, as bold in attacking their demands for universal suffrage and annual parliaments as in calling for triennial parliaments and a taxpayer's franchise. His speech as the workers' candid friend turned into a sermon: 'many of you are, I am sure, in such a situation as to stand in need of all the consolations which religion can afford. Religion will be useful to you in this world, and will prepare you for another.'[14]

This was Salem Chapel reform. Ten years earlier Salem's minister, Edward Parsons, preached on the 'True Patriot'. 'The mixed form of government under which it is our distinguishing happiness to live, is the noblest monument of political wisdom and justice ever exhibited in the world. By the union of the monarchy, the aristocracy, and the democracy, we are equally protected against the tyranny of an individual, and that worst and heaviest of all scourges, the tyranny of a depraved multitude.'[15]

Salem's congregation expressed the mean between an individual's tyranny and that of a depraved multitude. It was at once exclusive and excluded demonstrating an imbalance in society which was the practical outworking of the imbalance in the constitution. Salem was also an unmistakably successful expression of social order amidst chaos. Such a demonstration of excluded but propertied discipline surrounded by disorder was bound to have a political face. Its features were those of Edward Baines.

Baines the editor was a public figure long before 1815. From 1815 he became a public figure in his own right, an assiduous speaker as well as organizer. From 1830 he was a man of national repute, whose influence had secured Brougham's candidature for Yorkshire, thereby ensuring the Bainesocracy's most famous victory. In the autumn of 1831 Lord John Russell consulted him about the likely effects in so important a place as Leeds of a £10 franchise as against one of £15. Baines responded diligently with the statistics which were becoming his family's hallmark; the effects even of the £10 limit would be encouragingly moderate.[16] Indeed, throughout the excitement of the First Reform Bill, Baines's shrewd, careful, steady politicking did much to engineer the support of hesitant men. From 1834 to 1841 he sat in Parliament for Leeds. In one sense this merely extended his local importance. His predecessor, T. B. Macaulay, had resigned on becoming a Member of the Council in India. Famous men like Brougham, now Lord Chancellor, or Macaulay, were all very well, but they could be very inconvenient, and at least Leeds need not fear that Baines 'would take his seat on the woolsack, or take a trip to India'.[17]

Nonetheless he was a portent. He represented too many new things — the power of the Press, orthodox Dissent, the northern business and industrial classes. His constituency reflected this: Leeds's reformed corporation produced only Nonconformist mayors in its first decade.[18] Clearly he could never be other than a backbencher, but he worked unusually hard for one in his sixties, and he was courted by all wings of government. He was fortunate to enter Parliament at a time when the Whig grip was slack and the Philosophic Radicals, that intellectual corps of coldly resolute spirits, were convinced that their hour was come: indeed from 1837, one of them, Sir William Molesworth, was Baines's running-mate at Leeds. Baines's attraction lay in what he stood for in the country, and at Westminster he represented the undistributed middle of M.Ps.

The Philosophic Radicals believed that he could so easily be one of them, but they could not get him to commit himself. The logic of his approach was close to theirs — he too advocated the ballot, could countenance further extension of the suffrage, criticized Whig colonial attitudes — but he disliked their methods, and there remained his

Nonconformity. There were specific religious grievances to be redressed. Tories would not do this; Whigs might — and they were a more credible alternative at Westminster than the Philosophic Radicals, whose hopes faded rapidly after 1837 into the world of dreams and then of memories.[19]

At Westminster even the most Baines-like backbencher must succumb to the lure of the higher politics if he seeks the illusion of getting things done. Whatever might be the case in Leeds, when in London the olympians must win if it came to a choice between routs at Mrs Daniel Gaskell's or dinners with olympian grandees:

> The dinners are very sumptuous, but the conversation is of a very miscellaneous kind, partly political, partly statistical, but principally such as you find at the dinner tables of private gentlemen. There is no excess in drinking. The company generally sit down about half-past seven, and separate after tea to be home about eleven. The most perfect freedom, and I may say equality, prevails. There is no affectation of rank or dignity, and the conversation is as free and easy as you would find at the table of a Leeds merchant or a Leeds printer.[20]

Such revelations were an education rather than a capitulation. They did not unduly affect the views which undergirded his politics, whatever the Westminster realities to which he must adapt.

His views were predictable. He opposed the Corn Laws, and his first public speech was an attack on them, in 1815, the year of their first operation. He also opposed duties on raw materials used for manufacture. Indeed the prohibition on the export of British wool 'was his only heresy as a Free Trader', and he recanted even that in 1824.[21]

His views on factory reform were equally predictable. He opposed the Ten Hour Movement, and criticized Bradford's Parson Bull with especial bitterness. He had no time for that 'reverend bruiser'.[22] The *Mercury* was on its mettle since publishing Richard Oastler's sensational letter on 'Yorkshire Slavery' of 16 October 1830. The sheer blindness in Baines's attitude cost lives as well as votes: there was 'not a set of children in this kingdom better fed, better clothed, better lodged, and more healthy than the children in the factories', he told his fellow M.Ps in 1836.[23] There was a 'heartless doggedness' about Baines,[24] but what is at once terrible and terribly reasonable about his attitude is that it was benevolent. He could accept an eleven hour limit, with shorter hours for the youngest children (he 'objected to all interference with the labour of adults — only sanctioning interference with the labour of children because they were not free agents'[25]). Yet how could he support more, when he suspected that the Ten Hour Movement was a Tory ruse, and when his statistics persuaded him that if hours were cut, foreign competition would lower working men's wages when they already suffered from the loss in family income caused by restrictions on the working hours of their able-bodied children?

He was as generous as any man of conscience with his philanthropies, especially towards Irish immigrants, but order must begin somewhere. 'His benevolence did not . . . prevent him from firmly reproving the errors of the working classes', and when, in 1842, a body of strikers called at Barton Grange to seek help in their distress, he freely assured them of his pity and disapproval. He could not condone actions suggesting interference between employers and working men: they must return to work, seeking as good a price for their labour as they might get. It was their duty.[26]

Such duty and order were Salem-tinted. So was an issue which might lead such men towards the interference which their reason forbade — temperance. In 1830 Baines was a founder of the Leeds Temperance Society, one of the earliest in England. Four years later he sat on the Parliamentary Committee appointed to inquire into drunkenness. The committee's report had no immediate issue at Westminster, but it was profoundly influential in temperance circles, not least with its twin assertions that 'the *right* to exercise legislative interference for the correction of any evil which affects the public weal, cannot be questioned, without dissolving society into its primitive elements' and that 'the *power* to apply correction by legislative means, cannot be doubted, without supposing the sober, the intelligent, the just and the moral portion of the community unable to control the excesses of the ignorant and disorderly'.[27] Here was the opportunity to extend Salem attitudes into wider spheres than church fellowship, or the Leeds corporation. As with the Leeds Improvement Act the opportunity was taken fitfully.

If Salem's religion became Baines's religion, it was his wife's doing. Charlotte Baines was a Congregationalist. She married against her father's wishes, and it was forty-two years before Edward joined the church of which she had been a member since their first meeting. It was intensely painful to her that her husband should unite all the virtues and yet not be a truly serious person. His life was passed among Dissenters: he printed and published their works, and the *Mercury* was their secular Bible, much as the *Manchester Guardian* later became. He lived and worshipped with them and fought for them, but the final commitment eluded him. At first he worshipped impartially with the Unitarians of Mill Hill Chapel and Salem's Congregationalists, and he retained this impartiality in his friendships with powerful Leeds Unitarians, and his support for the Unitarian inspired Dissenters' Chapels Bill of 1844.[28]

Salem, however, became his spiritual lodging-house[29] and eventually the pressure of his wife's prayers and her minister's tactful suggestions had their effect. Baines's seriousness deepened in the 1830s. There were fewer Sunday lapses, and the deaths of friends and kinsmen were intimations of a world from which as yet he was excluded. He became convinced of inward change towards the end of 1839, and on Christmas Eve Pye Smith of Homerton wrote in delight at cousin Charlotte's joy on such 'evidence of vital religion in the highest object of creature affections'.[30] So his spiritual lodging became his spiritual home. It was a suggestive time, because Salem's people were about to leave their downtown chapel for the pillared grandeur of East Parade, close to Park Square, King Street, and the houses of Leeds professional men: the foundation stone was already laid.

It is important to grasp the temporal significance of the step as well as its claim upon eternity. In the eyes of the world Baines was already synonymous with Dissent. He had battled against Church Rate since 1819 and in the 1820s he had argued for Catholic Emancipation and Test Act Repeal. In Parliament he spoke for Dissent as well as the north and he brought Dissenting grievances to the attention of M.Ps on innumerable occasions. Where tithes, church rates or university tests were at issue, he could usually be depended upon; but he had less sympathy with the mounting agitation for disestablishment, and no sympathy with the militant Dissenters of the *Nonconformist* who made the running in the 1840s. His embarrassment was cruelly exposed as early as May 1834 when he chaired a meeting of 400 Dissenters at the London Tavern: only three voted against a motion on disestablishment.[31]

Baines's political inclinations tied him to government at the very time that his religious inclinations found anchorage. Edward Baines might represent only himself and his religion might be too tepid for his wife, but he remained a portent and he had sons to continue his gentlemanly fight. Salem had become East Parade, and the Baines family a dynasty. It was a change of generation, but church and dynasty were now intertwined.

III *The Moulder Moulded: East Parade and the Younger Baines*

The Baineses and Leeds Nonconformity coincided. Charlotte Baines became a member of Salem, Hunslet Lane, in 1797, seven years after its formation; her grand-daughter, Mrs Eustace Conder, was the last of her descendants to continue in membership, surviving the First World War on the 'distance list' of Trinity Church, Woodhouse Lane, into which time transformed the original Salem. Between 1820, when Charlotte's eldest daughter joined Salem, and 1890, when Charlotte's great-grandson

Arthur Conder joined East Parade, seven of her children and seven children-in-law, twenty grandchildren and seven grandchildren-in-law, two great-grandchildren and four step-great-grandchildren, followed her. Her son Frederick married a sister of Henry Robert Reynolds, minister of East Parade from 1848 to 1860, and her grand-daughter, Annie Catherine, married Reynolds's successor, Eustace Rogers Conder.

The Baineses were not the only extended family to worship at Salem and East Parade. The membership lists included political and municipal allies of the Baineses — the Thomas Plints, father and son, the George Rawsons, father and son, the Claphams and the Leutys — they included professional men like Thomas Scattergood, the Park Square physician, wool merchants like the Portways, textile manufacturers like the Nusseys, Willanses, and Morleys, who were a branch of Samuel Morley's family, ex-Quakers like the Jowitts, whose kinship with the Crewdsons of the 'Beacon' controversy might explain their transition, and distinguished birds of passage like Wemyss Reid of the *Mercury* or Russell Reynolds, the fashionable physician. These families became prominent in Leeds and some were the core of Nonconformist cousinhoods, widespreading beyond Yorkshire and often beyond Congregationalism. They were socially and politically formidable, the more so for their 'inferiority'. Four of Salem's members became Liberal M.Ps; the rest were the organizers of victory.[1]

There is a further point. The church, in its guises of Salem, East Parade, and Trinity, was large. In August 1833 its membership would seem to have been 266. By 1846 this had increased to 484 and in 1863 it was 570. In the next forty years, despite the formation of new causes and the pressures inevitable to a central church in a city embraced by suburbs its membership kept generally above 450. Even in 1903, faced with an over-grand building in an over-churched area, and learning new methods after three decades of Dr Conder, the membership was still 300, and it rose thereafter.[2]

The significance of this is that even in so stately a church as East Parade most members came neither from the wealthier families, nor their households, and certainly not from their work-people, but from artisans and the lower middle classes. East Parade was not socially homogeneous in the sense that many chapels, especially among the smaller Methodist bodies were; it was socially varied. It was, at least until the 1870s, living proof of the common sense of voluntaryism and the feasibility of the statistics with which the Baineses so conscientiously misled their denomination. East Parade stood on the lines of progress.

Edward Baines, father and son, sat under four ministers befriending all and kinsmen of two. Edward Parsons, minister until 1833, attracted the elder Baines to Salem and received four of his children into membership. John Ely, minister from 1833 to 1847, migrated with his people to East Parade in 1841, the year of Dr Hook's rebuilding of the parish church, leaving Salem's building to house a new fellowship of Congregationalists.

East Parade expressed a ceremonial Congregationalism, in a chapel seating nearly 2,000 and costing nearly £15,000, of which over £1,000 came from the opening services.[3] Of the £6,000 which had already been raised Edward Baines and his sons gave £500, five Willanses gave £1,150, and three Wades gave £500. There were 375 subscribers, their aims imprinted on the brass foundation tablet: '. . . the publication of that Great Mystery of Godliness, the Incarnation, Vicarious Obedience, Atoning Death, and Mediatorial Exaltation of the Only All-sufficient Divine Saviour, the Lord Jesus Christ. . . . In recognition of the sole authority of the Scriptures, the inalienable rights of conscience, and the obligation of brotherly love towards the whole Catholic Church. . . .'[4]

Perhaps such aims were best achieved in the 1850s under Ely's gentlemanly successor, Henry Robert Reynolds, friend of Matthew Arnold, kinsman of Thorold Rogers, acquaintance of Mr Gladstone and future President of Cheshunt College. East Parade was a demanding charge for so retiring a scholar. It had been one of the elder Edward Baines's dying wishes that Reynolds should assume the pastorate and ten years later Reynolds surveyed his church, disciplined ('we have been compelled to exclude four persons from our fellowship, on account of acts of gross inconsistency'), but sociable (Reynolds was 'At Home' on Wednesday afternoons), and above all inquiring. Miss Rawson's Sunday afternoon class for Young Women in Service, and Mr Rawson's class 'for the Sons of Members of the Congregation', witnessed to that; so did the Day and Sunday Schools at East Parade and its two branches. The younger Edward Baines superintended the mother church's Sunday School.

In 1858 the three Sunday Schools housed 999 children and 125 teachers while the church had 496 members. In the previous decade 405 people had joined East Parade, of whom 108 had since moved.[5] This picture of a fluid yet disciplined community is sharpened in the census note which Baines's brother-in-law, John Wade, made in March 1851. Wade estimated that the chapel's average attendance in the year before Census Sunday had been 800 in the morning, with a further 180 school-children, and 900 in the evening. On Census Sunday there were 748 in the morning — with 198 schoolchildren — and 587 in the evening, when there was a thunderstorm.[6] The attendance, therefore, was nearly twice the membership, but even on the best Sunday only half the sittings were filled, and only 162 were free: suggestive statistics for the Baineses' church in the decade when it most nearly closed the gap between reality and opportunity.

Eustace Rogers Conder of Poole ministered from the spring of 1861 to that of 1892. Under him East Parade passed from its summer to its Indian summer. Conder was among the most acute of what had become the old school of ministers by the 1880s. For his first ten years a steady stream of Baineses joined East Parade; then removal to Headingley Hill, with its spired suburban eligibilitys took its toll; so did the Church of England.

The struggle to keep pace is reflected in the *Church Books* of the 1860s and 1870s.[7] The membership dropped from 570 in December 1862 to 483 twelve years later. The church's income, which had been £2,125.11s.11d. in 1858, was £2,093.16s.6d. in 1874, although contributions to the London Missionary Society tended to increase: £538.8s.4d. was raised in 1874. These were valiant figures, their import suggested by Conder's annual letters to his people, bearing equally upon the quality of the church's worship and the nation's life.

Conder inculcated the worshipful spirit. Indeed his poem, 'Ye fair green hills of Galilee', survives as a children's hymn. In the 1864 *Church Book* he urged his congregation to join in the Lord's Prayer, and added, 'An audible "Amen", at the close of every prayer is suitable, reasonable, and scriptural. The occasional "Amen" often heard among our Methodist brethren — when low breathed, not shouted — is to my ear and heart very encouraging and inspiring.' Eight *Church Books* later he urged that spoken prayers should be 'arrows shot at a mark, and hitting it', and he pleaded for promptness at morning worship. If only latecomers 'knew the inexpressible pain, disturbance and discouragement . . . *from which sometimes the minister's mind does not really recover throughout the whole service*'. Prayer and promptness were part and parcel of living together, enfolded in the bonds of Christian courtesy: 'fittingly to lead the worship of the Church in free prayer, more imperatively requires than does even preaching, a composed mind, a heavenward spirit, and a sense of spiritual sympathy with the assembled worshippers'. Such an exposition is a suggestive reflexion of Nonconformist 'anarchy' and 'individualism'.

From the discipline of worship flowed that of mission. In November 1865, thirty-four East Paraders were transferred to the new church formed at Beeston Hill: 'we must *colonize*, and work from new centres. . . .' A year later a similar number, two Baineses among them, were transferred to Headingley Hill. In the 1870s a fresh concern appeared. Conder yearned to end pew rentals, that it might be 'universally understood that the house of God is free to all comers'. A monthly evening service was to be held for those 'to whom the term "working classes" is commonly applied', and there was to be an 'Invitation

Committee', 'having for its chief object to superintend and stimulate the invitation of street passengers and loungers . . . to our services'. By 1875 he discerned — though as yet without reference to Moody and Sankey, and with critical reference to the Convention movement — signs of revival and 'the penetrating thrill of the still small voice'.

Eustace Conder became the younger Edward Baines's son-in-law in 1871. His ministry saw the peak as well as the decline of the Bainesocracy and inevitably East Parade's *Church Books* dwelt on the great events. Conder's retrospect for 1866 was an exercise in gloom, depicting military violence in Europe, terrorist violence in Ireland, industrial violence, ferocious weather, agricultural disaster, commercial disorder and political disruption. The world was diseased and Britain in decline. 'Probably more Englishmen have met with violent deaths in the past year than in any preceding year when our country was not engaged in war.'

His retrospect for 1867 was more hopeful, but still thoroughly Bainesish. There had been a great reform: 'we must recognize the loud call which it utters to the Christian Church in England . . . no country, however wealthy or however free, can be even safe, much less truly prosperous, large masses of whose citizens are devoid of education and estranged from godliness.'

The 1870s were clearly a watershed, a crisis in the true sense, for Liberals and Nonconformists, and particularly for the Baineses and East Parade. Conder prefaced the *Church Book* for 1873 with fears of luxury and 'fraudulent speculation'. He perceived the end 'of old party ties and boundaries', and at a moment when young Baineses were slipping away to the parish church, he declared that disestablishment 'has become a question, not only of national religion, but of national morality'. The plain fact of the matter was that 'the Established Church is being worked as the engine of an organized conspiracy to reconvert England to Popery'.

Conder was not a scaremonger. He was as solid as East Parade appeared to be, the younger Edward Baines's pastor as well as his son-in-law, whose church was much more than the place where Baines chanced to worship when in Leeds: it was a community celebrating the best aspirations of the new society, a model of voluntary discipline, as soundly based as might be. 'In sacred Truth I am a thorough Conservative, because I believe Truth to be unchangeable', Baines wrote in 1886, 'But . . . our little company, in clinging to essential Truth, do not reject improvement. We sail with delight down the majestic stream, and find ourselves continually advancing nearer to the illimitable ocean.'[8]

There were rapids and whirlpools to be navigated, and sometimes the little company could have done with lesser pilots than Edward Baines, but he was not the only one with his Master's ticket, and any assessment of his career which is based chiefly on his public image and ignores the dimensions afforded by East Parade, will miss the extent to which his life was a victory of duty over temperament. East Parade is the key to him. Thus when a scholar has remarked that 'Baines and his fellows sought to create men in the image they knew to be safe . . .', East Parade may be seen as the context; and when he continues that Baines's 'was the excitement of the nineteenth century. The "spirit of the age" moved him and held him fast',[9] the judgment applies equally to East Parade, and to the denomination of which East Parade was a part and Baines a member.

Similarly the portrait presented by another scholar, of Baines as a man of archetypal Whiggish views moulded by a career of extra-parliamentary agitation[10] — infected, therefore with immoderation — makes best sense when viewed from East Parade. It was East Parade which fuelled his voluntaryism, which bound together his temperament and his profession, which transformed this exemplar of law and middle-class order into the herald of an alternative society. It was East Parade which first guaranteed his respectability and then ensured that he should never be safe: and it was Matthew Arnold who first captured this and then distorted it in *Culture and Anarchy*.

Arnold's own church had ensured that Nonconformists should never reflect adequately the high views of life which had made them Nonconformists in the first place, so it was easy for him to claim that the 'great works by which . . . the human spirit has manifested its approaches to totality and to a full harmonious perfection . . . come, not from Nonconformists, but from men who either belong to Establishments or have been trained in them. . . .'[11]

A Nonconformity which expressed itself in clattering teacups, carping resolutions and iron-columned Gothic was neither perfect nor perfectible, and Arnold caught it to perfection and the Baines-like men who led it. Yet this was not the whole truth about Nonconformity, whether Baines-led or Baines-moulding, neither was it a helpful guide to perfection. *Culture and Anarchy* was a study in impertinence — most clearly so when most on target.

The younger Edward Baines was second-generation in town, business and Congregationalism. He carried moderation to the point of philistinism. In his twenties he visited the proper places of Western Europe like any cultivated man of means, but he used his tour as much to develop his ideas on cemeteries, manufactures and industrial relations as on the pleasures of art. For this was the true Romanticism of the nineteenth century and his father was delighted in it: 'You seem to have done that at which I wish you always to aim, namely, to have lived in a handsome, comfortable way at a moderate expense. By economy alone can a man of moderate income ever be respectable.'[12] Baines's comfortable economy was duly rewarded: he left £165,818 gross when he died.[13]

The same busy moderation which accompanied him through Europe had already convinced him of the impropriety of the theatre: the spoken word was for open debate, not pretence, and it was generally best written anyway. When C. E. Mudie formed his circulating library in 1864, he told Henry Allon of his need for shareholders 'with *quite open minds* (and open hands) as regards literature' and added that 'one of the very few dissenters I shd like to have is Edwd Baines and this on account of the high position that gentleman occupies in the "World of Letters", as well as in active public life'.[14]

Doubtless Mudie's Library was the limit for common-sense philistines, but Mudie's testimony is important for his library circulated much sweetness and some light in a thoroughly efficient way. Baines was a remarkably flexible doctrinaire.

It all came back in the end, however, to the limits set by East Parade, or, rather, forced on East Parade by the Establishment. In 1868 Baines told Henry Allon of his deeply satisfying election at Leeds: 'Never was a purer or a quieter election: not a cab, not a pot of beer, to be seen: all was fought with the weapons of reason and the Constitution.'[15] So of course it was: except that the weapons of reason and the Constitution wielded by East Paraders or any other Nonconformists were used on ground selected by their opponents. The outcome was seldom in doubt. The interest depended on the quality of the fight, a piquant reflexion of the Victorian attitude to games.

This is the context for an understanding of the younger Baines's views on social and economic matters, on education, and on politics, although in his scheme of things these separate issues were inextricably fused.

There was a cool predictability about his social and economic views, there was less an armchair than a deskchair quality about them. They issued from the relentless consideration of meticulously prepared statistics, refined in the atmosphere of Headingley Lodge and St Anne's Hill, sooty-leaved islands in the ocean of proletarian Leeds. Yet it is unfair to deduce that they permitted no concept of a separate working-class culture. As Sunday School superintendent at East Parade, Baines saw such a culture at close quarters, working from a church which was as socially varied as might be reasonably expected in a Victorian city. It was this which gave Baines so firm a base for his views and which infused them with the breadth of a careful conscience. It was this too which ensured his self-deception.

East Parade was a model society, tied to no class, but drawing from all and refining them. This meant that it could not accurately reflect any class: to that extent it was unreal. It could be an inspiration, but it was not a mirror. Nonconformist churches gave men a rare perspective of social variety, so significant that it was easy to forget the artificiality of it, for they would have glimpsed it nowhere else. When Edward Baines opposed the Chartists' Six Points with six of his own — Education, Religion, Virtue, Industry, Sobriety, Frugality[16] he was advocating what East Parade had already achieved, but outside East Parade they sounded too much like the clichés of the threatened bourgeoisie: yet clichés are the proof of common sense. He effectively controlled the *Mercury* from 1822, which meant that from his earliest twenties he articulated his family's views, perfecting a unique blend of fact and fancy. His duty was to moralize Leeds. His first task, therefore, was to secure social cohesion, or at least social balance. The chasms between the classes could not be abolished, but they could be bridged, and the materials for the bridge could be found in the economic factors which had brought Leeds into being: and East Parade, Belgrave and Queen Street, and every other chapel proved that it could be done.

The great fact of modern Leeds was the factory system. It had for some time been the great fact of South Lancashire, and Baines had applauded it as an aid to men as well as masters in his classic *History of the Cotton Manufacture in Great Britain* of 1835. Indeed, he had applauded it nine years earlier in his first characteristically effective pamphlet addressed to the 'Unemployed Workmen of Yorkshire and Lancashire'. He was not blind to the evils of the system, but he was terrified by the likely effects of improper interference with anything so dynamic, and improper interference generally meant the intervention of a government infected by the values of the landed interest. This motivated his opposition to the Ten Hours Movement, whose implications, he was sure, threatened despotism to England as well as ruin to industry. The answer to the humanitarian yearnings of Oastler and Ashley lay surely in the humanitarian efficiency of masters and men, for whom there was already a formidable network of local benevolence. 'The best and kindest lesson which can be taught the poor is that their comfort depends on their own good conduct', he wrote in 1833.[17] 'The mill-owners to a very great extent offer labour and wages, but *they compel no man to accept them*', he announced in 1841.[18] Such utterances appear less blinkered when seen in the context of the twin dynamisms of industry and voluntary benevolence. Baines's statistics told him all about the former. First-hand experience was teaching him about the latter.

If the factory system could be moralized, there was no problem about Free Trade. Love of gain stirred men to their uttermost. It stoked the fires of invention and adventure. Its acquisition created leisure and fostered the gentler pursuits of mind and soul. At this point moral values must infect it. Free trade was the prerequisite for such perfection. When voiced by Richard Cobden there was limitless excitement in such views, but there was about Edward Baines a golden mediocrity — in the Jacobean sense of 'golden mean' — which prevented him from ever taking flight. Free Trade was a great issue and he was immersed in its West Riding affairs.[19] Yet Cobden felt that Leeds was a weak link in the Free Trade chain, and blamed Baines for it, misinterpreting Baines's caution and misunderstanding the complexity of Leeds politics.[20] It was not possible to be single-minded in Leeds, as Baines was discovering on the educational front. Trade and industry must be accompanied by improvement, voluntary but efficient, and it was inconceivable to think otherwise. This was the moral pre-condition for unfettered commerce. If ever the general welfare was harmed by individual freedom, then appropriate curbs must be placed on the individual. Baines's career should be seen as a painstaking discovery of the proper limits of these spheres, rather than as a last defense of individual freedom.

The spirit of improvement entered his innermost being. In the 1820s this meant canals. In the 1840s it meant railways, municipal expenditure on parks and the lighting and draining of streets: a sort of communal voluntaryism. What was done municipally at least since 1835, could be controlled, and a reservoir of local expertise was in the making. By the 1860s improvement meant public health with the *Mercury* championing sanitary reform, this time with Edward Baines being fuelled by his youngest brother Frederick, who now managed the newspaper.[21]

Throughout these years the cause of improvement was undergirded by issues at once vital for the well-being of the individual, and of national significance and complexity: temperance and education. Baines was a notable temperance reformer — his *Fifteen Years Experience of Total Abstinence* of 1852, reissued in 1857 as *Twenty Years . . .*, had a circulation of 284,000[22] — but his predictable gradualism was painful to prohibitionists, and eventually he suffered politically from their bitterness.[23]

His chief notoriety, however, concerned education. It was here that gradualism, when voiced by a Nonconformist, assumed the features of fanaticism, and reason seemed to become its opposite.

IV *Education and the Limits of Freedom*

In 1833 there was the first state grant towards English education: its £20,000 was about one twentieth of the Prussian annual grant.[1] In 1870 there was the first comprehensive English Education Act. The intervening years saw an educational battle royal encompassing every shade of prejudice and controversy. The Act which inaugurated the war was the most harmless imaginable, barely denting the barrage of voluntary goodwill which had sustained elementary education since the formation of the two chief school societies, the British and the National, earlier in the century.[2] The Act of 1870, which was more comprehensive in intention than in practice, was the prelude to compulsory schooling, then to free schooling and ultimately to secondary and technical schooling.

The clue to the war was less that of the state's proper place in education than that of religion's, and since the separation of religion from education was a painful concept for most nineteenth-century Englishmen of the thinking sort, the problem was complex beyond belief. It was largely an English problem; Scottish education was more efficiently managed than English, and from 1831 the Irish evolved a remarkably successful compromise. When tried in Liverpool it lasted for only five years.[3]

It was also a problem born of the success of the pioneer school societies. A reservoir of public interest was collected, akin to that sustaining foreign missions, and concerned about syllabus, about the training of teachers and the placing of schools.

It was here that the question of state aid became important: but state aid could only supplement what the societies already provided and naturally they provided best where their supporters were most prosperous, and the most uniformly prosperous were Anglicans. Educational provision, therefore, was uneven and all attempts to remedy this were doomed to sectarian bedevilment. An issue so close to conscience and social prosperity was bound to evoke at its most fatally reasoned the Nonconformist sense of exclusion and long discrimination.

Edward Baines the younger was a Nonconformist whose business depended upon education, for journalists were professional educators. He was in his prime between 1833 and 1870.

His concern extended from his youth. In 1818 he advocated a cultural and debating society for the Leeds middle classes, and by 1821 he was on the council of the Leeds Literary and Philosophical Society. There shortly followed an enthusiasm for Mechanics' Institutes which became lifelong. He became a director of the Leeds Institute, and the cause's advocate throughout the West Riding.[4]

There was little doubt as to the success of the Leeds Mechanics' Institute, but it did not attract mechanics and common sense suggested that the reason lay partly in their leisure, partly in their schooling and chiefly in the inadequacy of both. Here his concern met another early, unwavering passion — Sunday Schools. It was in the massive Sunday

Schools of the industrial cities, attached to their chapels rather as the white dominions were to the mother country, that benevolent youth first glimpsed the magnitude of the gulf between the good poor and the rest, and began to work out the consequences. Edward Baines had taught in Sunday Schools since his schooldays.

The stage was set. In 1833, while William Cobbett dismissed that first government grant as a doctrinaire French sort of plan, to 'force education',[5] Baines, as a matter of experience and common sense, welcomed it, hoping that there would result 'a proper application of the voluntary principle to a system of national education, aided by . . . an enlightened and paternal government'.[6] The vanity of his hopes was apparent within six years; their impossibility, within ten.

The parting of the ways came in 1839, when Lord John Russell, victim of the logic that grants from the state meant accountability to the state and therefore a closer supervision, concerned too for teacher training, and perhaps impressed by the success of the 'Irish System', made certain proposals. These uncovered a hornets' nest, but the chief of them survived as the Committee of Council on Education, a board of five Privy Councillors whose prime concern was the consideration and supervision of grants.

The cost was incalculable. Lord John's sensible suggestions came towards the close of a discredited administration at a time when the State Church was unusually sensitive about its role as national conscience and educator. They infringed this role and the violent Anglican opposition which they aroused showed how far any subsequent scheme would need to defer to Anglican scruples. As a corollary, the Nonconformists, who tended to approve the scheme, had been shown the limits beyond which lay discrimination: Edward Baines, who admitted its merits, found it inequitable.[7] Voluntaryism in education had always seemed desirable. Now, just when it might suitably be called into question, it became inescapable.

It was additionally unfortunate that Leeds provided Baines with a statistical foundation for his deepening convictions. He convinced himself that working-class children needed only five years schooling, between the ages of five and ten. His experience testified to the efficiency of Sabbath School instruction. In Leeds in 1839 a twelfth of the population attended day schools, and 13.9 per cent went to Sunday Schools. On this basis he urged that adequate day provision existed for all who needed it: there was a sound foundation for further development, within the competence of those who were already responsible.[8] He was equipped, therefore, to grapple with the proposals of 1843 and 1847, which converted suspicion into belief and from which he emerged to lead the voluntary cause.

The logic of voluntaryism was entirely natural, even admirable: education divorced from religious values was a nonsense, and since the state was incompetent to deal with religion it followed that its incompetence extended to education. When the bloody-mindedness and self-centredness which obscured the debate is penetrated, and when the size and novelty of the problems surrounding the education of a newly industrial nation are recognized, the debate is revealed as one about freedom. It was the voluntaryists, whose attitude is easily dismissed as short-sighted, and whose fight was doomed from the start, who defined that debate. They knew about freedom, but their vision of it restricted their horizons, and closed their imaginations. It warped their power of logic. There was nonetheless a nobility about voluntaryism, where many have seen pettiness.

The tragedy of the 1840s was that governmental insensitivity born of ignorance, combined with the impact of that fraught spiritual rebirth known as Tractarianism, and channelled into the partisan simplicities dictated by good propaganda and organization, forced men concerned with this most delicate of issues into crudeness beyond the bounds of philistinism.

Most English Christians agreed that education and religion should not be separated, and an increasing number maintained a prejudice against state control of education, which the facts of modern life might confound. As elsewhere in the 1830s and 1840s, the debate would centre on the stage at which necessary state aid turned into improper state control, and how one saw this depended on how one saw the State Church. This was the point of explosion.

It came in 1843. Its force converted Nonconformists suspicious of state control into opponents of state aid. It postponed all hopes of truly national education until 1870, and it affected the form even of that unsatisfactory measure. It turned the younger Baines into the spokesman for Nonconformity, at least in the eyes of its opponents.

The explosion was detonated by the educational clauses clumsily tacked on to a much needed Factory Bill. If passed, the measure would have resulted in a national system of elementary education at once perpetuating and extending the religious discrimination which came so effortlessly to the English ruling classes. The Bill was the responsibility of Sir James Graham, an outstanding Home Secretary in an age of accomplished administrators, who should have known better: his brother-in-law, Wilfrid Lawson, fostered Congregational causes from his Cumbrian estates.

The measure hit Nonconformists doubly below the belt, interfering at a stroke with industry and education, threatening despotism. Baines greeted it as an outrage on liberty, but he brought an ominously unWhiggish tone to bear on his criticisms: the Bill declared war 'against all the Dissenters of the Kingdom'.[9] He issued pamphlets, perfecting his techniques of emotion disguised as statistical analysis. He was in the closest liaison with the Bill's London opponents, addressing an open letter to Andrew Reed of Wycliffe Chapel, Stepney, chairman of the London committee formed against the measure, whose son Charles was engaged to Margaret Baines, and was the committee's secretary: 'Believe me, our opponents are importunate. Half the objects of life are carried by importunity. Our senators must be troubled on the subject. Send up short and emphatic memorials; ask for no modification, but simply demand that the Bill, so far as it is educational, be withdrawn.'[10] Such importunity worked. Petitions and public anger voiced by all Nonconforming denominations, had their effect. The Bill was withdrawn.

Nonconformist vehemence surprised the Government. Wesleyan Methodist anger was especially notable, because Wesleyans had sided with the State Church in opposing the 1839 proposals. It would be many years, if at all, before Wesleyan attitudes could be generally equated with those of other evangelical Nonconformists, but for individual Wesleyans the uproar of 1843 marked a shift of some importance. As it was the nuisance value of Protestant Nonconformity had been demonstrated; it now became a permanent factor in the calculations of the political classes. The potential of the press had been exploited, and so had the techniques of organization. The public pressure and efficiency which contributed to the victory of 1843, was on a par with the public pressure and efficiency which in the same decade motivated the Anti-Corn Law League, the great missionary societies and a host of useful philanthropies from Ragged Schools to the Y.M.C.A. A new generation of politically oriented do-gooders was blooded. As Andrew Reed, whose son Charles was one of that generation, put it in the Exeter Hall: 'We ask, in short, that we shall be free: in labour, free; in trade, free; in action, free; in thought, free; in speech, free; in religion, free — perfectly free. We ask freedom for others, freedom for ourselves, freedom for all, without distinction, that breathe in British air, and rest on British soil.'[11]

So unanimous a stress on freedom, undergirded by the apparatus of sound organization, was bound to be misleading. It appeared to give Nonconformity a homogeneity when the fact of the matter was that Nonconformist homogeneity was a negative thing. The defence of freedom can be organized, and occasionally, if the issues are clearly defined, an extension of freedom may be planned, but the expression of freedom is not a matter for organization. Yet the stand of 1843 committed the Bill's opponents to proving that freedom in education could be organized: that schools could be provided. The logic of this was particularly rigorous for Congregationalists, who seldom had day schools attached to their chapels, since they relied on the British Society's Schools; and British Schools received government grants. Congregationalists must be urged to build their own, truly voluntary schools.

The Congregational Union came to grips with the problem at Leeds in the autumn of 1843. Edward Baines was much in evidence, and to all outward appearances the denomination swung behind him. A fund provided for school buildings and a Committee of General Education was formed. In 1845 this was strengthened by a Board of Education, which was to be the denomination's recognized body for such matters, into whose constitution voluntaryism was writ large. Two Normal Schools were established in London. By 1853 Baines could compare the 453 schools housing 50,000 scholars which he claimed that the Board had established in the previous decade, with the 514 schools for 80,000 scholars which it had taken the British Society fifty years to found.[12]

Yet the denomination was not united. Influential Congregationalists still tolerated state aid, while some were attracted to secular daily education. Indeed, James Kay-Shuttleworth, Secretary to the Committee of Council on Education, a pace-maker in the first great age of civil servants, and a man determined 'to assert the claims of the civil power to the control of the education of the country',[13] had been reared amidst Congregational influences. To those who saw the magnitude of the problem were added the larger number who experienced it at first hand when they discovered that their schools could not be run efficiently without the help of grants, or at least of the grant-aided British Society. The voluntary principle in education spurred Congregationalists to great things, but it was never vindicated by results, neither was it fully incorporated into Congregationalism. This was spelled out when the Board of Education ceased its official connexion with the Union in 1857, but it had been so since the explosion of 1843, and the Union's autumnal resolution:

That *without pronouncing a decided opinion on the propriety of Government interference in the education of the people,* this Meeting entertains the gravest doubts whether any compulsory interference can take place without establishing principles and precedents dangerous to civil and religious liberty, inconsistent with the rights of industry, and superseding the duties of parents and of churches; while all the plans of national education by the agency of Government, suggested of late years, have been very objectionable either to the friends of the Established Church, or to the Dissenting bodies. This Meeting, therefore, concludes, without despondency or regret, that both the general and the religious education of the people of England must be chiefly provided and conducted by the voluntary efforts of the various denominations of Christians.[14]

This was voluntaryism born of necessity rather than principle: a classic plea for the emergence of such circumstances as might alter hard cases.

For Edward Baines, however, who emerged from the 1840s unusually case-hardened, necessity was entirely transmuted into principle. In 1846 he attacked the Vicar of Leeds's sensible schemes and in 1847 he turned the vials of his wrath upon further proposals from Lord John Russell. The Committee of Council requested an enlarged grant to improve the selection and training of teachers, by a system of apprenticeships, examinations and certificates. The scheme was imaginative. It promised to give elementary teachers greater status. Indeed, it encouraged social mobility since it was especially attractive to pupil teachers from the labouring classes.

Edward Baines found it objectionable. The despotism which he feared under the Tories in 1843 was now compounded by the Whigs. He foresaw less a new race of respectable teachers than a servile host of bureaucrats, 88,000 of them, all in receipt of state pay, susceptible to state influence, and costing £1,742,500 a year. He proved as much in a further spate of pamphleteering, adding a series of open letters to Russell and Lord Lansdowne, President of the Committee of Council, to his series of 1843 to Lord Wharncliffe and Sir James Graham.[15] His was the traditional Whig suspicion of improper Government influence, transformed by Dissenting exclusion and updated by statistics with a dash of quite genuine Liberalism. Prussian standards were all very well, but they must not entail Prussian methods, and in another of his open letters he reminded William Ewart that the arm of government had a handcuff at the end of it.[16] Even the introduction of the proposals was tainted with skullduggery, for the Committee of Council had no legislative power, it was strictly irresponsible and its proposals were brought forward as a money vote rather than as a bill for debate. It was deplorable that the nation's educational establishment should be reconstructed in so unstraightforward a manner.[17]

These objections brought the elder Baines to his last public meeting, when on 17 March 1847, he faced Vicar Hook, and assorted Whigs, Tories and Chartists in the Leeds Cloth Hall Yard, and by quoting Lord Lansdowne against himself and noting that state education had not contributed to the freedom of Continental countries, brought the meeting round to his way of thinking, with Bainesian sleight of hand and mind.[18]

The voluntaryists lost the battle of 1847. Russell was able to accommodate the qualms of Catholics and Scotsmen, and the Wesleyans retreated from their militancy of 1843. The Nonconformist power which threatened in 1843, was, after all, only of nuisance value.

Baines's energy hid the fact that voluntaryists could now do no more than service what was already theirs. In Yorkshire the political repercussions were such that Liberalism was split, and Baines was at scarcely concealed odds with Richard Cobden, who sat for the West Riding between 1847 and 1857 in decreasing sympathy with his voluntaryist constituents.

Yet Cobden's annoyance was not entirely justified. Baines's importance lay neither in his statistics, nor in the reasoning which flowed from them, but in the emotion firing that reason. Nonconformity demanded a leap of faith not reason. Its prerequisite was freedom, to permit a delicate balance of self-reliance and mutual responsibility. Baines cloaked this emotional base with politics, giving it form and influence. He gave a confidence born of passion, not pamphlets, to men who were entering the political classes. At least he taught them to distinguish between selfishness and self-interest. At most he converted their defensiveness into concern. This was an educational task and it took natural shape on the issue of popular education, their education. Circumstances forced Baines into a position which retarded truly popular education. This does not invalidate the principles on which he based his stand, and it is not clear that they could have been so powerfully voiced at that time in any other way.

For some years to come it was possible to believe in the ultimate victory of educational voluntaryism. Statistics, such as those to be gleaned from the 1851 census, appeared to confirm this, and there was always a place for scaremongering: 'In plain fact, the philosophy of national education is that of communism ... it is based on an entire distrust of individual energy and a hatred of free competition: and it rushes with Robert Owen and Louis Blanc into a forced co-operative society of the entire nation.'[19]

Whether it took the form of creeping communism or creeping despotism, there could be no doubt as to centralization's advance and the steadily mounting education votes, steadily by-passing Parliament and free debate, proved this. These dangers of the 1840s were as real in the 1850s, confirming the earnest conviction that the best education was self-chosen, and paid for. Free education was an improper freedom, because it blunted appreciation and a sense of value; compulsory education was impossible without state intervention of the most despotic kind. Various attempts, supported by influential Nonconformists, to provide alternatives or compromises, were thus easily condemned. The Lancashire Public Schools Association of 1847, with its emphasis on secular, free, compulsory education, was attacked with characteristic logic: 'It is quite as possible to violate the conscience by excluding religion or forbidding a religious duty, as it is by compelling a man to perform a religious rite which he believes unsanctioned by Scripture.'[20] The Manchester and Salford Committee on Education was hardly less objectionable, since it sought impartially to support secular and religiously based education from local rates, thus allowing denominational bodies to use publicly raised funds.

These suspicions surged yet again in March 1856 when Lord John Russell produced twelve resolutions of which five consolidated the previous Minutes of Council and the remainder struck frighteningly new ground: compulsory local taxation for education, compulsory education at the employer's expense for all children employed below the age of fifteen. Such compulsion was the merest tip of the iceberg; Baines rose to the bait and wrote to *The Times*. His arguments were the same mixture as before; and in the event Russell's resolutions were withdrawn.[21] They helped, however, to crystallize the views of the man who has damned Baines for posterity: Matthew Arnold.

Arnold had been an Inspector of Schools since April 1851, with a particular concern for British Schools.[22] He saw Nonconformist education at its best, unsectarian and impartial, and admired it accordingly. At its best, it offered the best answer for public education. More frequently he saw it at its worst, the victim of its own principles, debarred from expansion because it refused grant aid, lagging behind in equipment until forced to apply for aid for which it was no longer competent to qualify.

Arnold's views, distilled into *Culture and Anarchy* in 1869, formed rapidly in the 1850s. He was confirmed in his dislike of the Bainesite rhetoric of freedom and independence, and in his beliefs that England's future lay in free, compulsory, state education for the poor, with an efficient system of secondary education fusing the aspirations of all classes. He was in no doubt as to the power of the Bainesite classes: the vital thing was to enlarge their horizons. There must be a cultural transformation. His vision, however, was insufficiently acute for him to appreciate the responsibility of his class and culture for the Bainesites' philistinism. This precluded him from seeing the extent of Nonconformist culture. It was easy for Arnold to urge a national system, since the state was simply Englishmen in their corporate character, but in the 1850s and for most of the 1860s there was little reason for Nonconformists to see the state in this guise; indeed it had been hard enough to see Leeds or Manchester so. It was not their imagination which was at fault so much as Matthew Arnold's.

Culture and Anarchy came too late, since in the 1860s circumstances altered even Edward Baines's case. In the early 1860s voluntaryism enjoyed an Indian Summer. At the Congregationalists' Birmingham

Autumnals in 1861, Dr Vaughan of Manchester, Baines's weightiest Congregational critic, declared his conversion to the cause, leaving it to R. W. Dale of Carr's Lane to maintain the Congregational advocacy of a national system.[23] In the same year, following the Newcastle Commission's report into elementary education, the Committee of Council proposed the system which eventually emerged as 'payment by results', a notorious piece of rationalization, condemned by Matthew Arnold, Kay-Shuttleworth and the leaders of the teaching profession, but acclaimed by the voluntaryists. It was as if Robert Lowe, the scheme's father, had capitulated to Baines. Both sections misunderstood him. Certainly he aimed to simplify the system of grants into one grant dependent on pupils' performance in the three Rs, and this had its charms despite the criticisms of contemporaries and the general condemnation of posterity.[24] It provided a sort of educational utilitarianism, taking education from the hands of educationists, and therefore from bureaucrats, and reducing its cost at the same time. In this way it appeared to assuage two of the voluntaryists' deepest suspicions.

Thereafter Baines changed course. By 1864 his voluntaryism was wavering and he asserted — 'nothing was better known' — that the prime intention of the system whose working he had steadily attacked since 1846 was to 'stimulate voluntary contributions': he was almost back to his stance of 1839.[25]

In 1864 he was appointed, still the arch voluntaryist, to the Taunton Commission into Secondary Education. This was the third Commission in the 1860s to reveal the gross inadequacies of English education,[26] and Baines's careful attendance at its meetings convinced him not merely of this but also of the value of an inspectorate and the practicability of government control.[27]

The Taunton Commission provided him with the reasoned experience into which he needed to fit other pressing factors. He had been an M.P. since 1859, and now saw government from a new angle. It was not merely that he was on terms with men of affairs, but that the parliamentary pressure for Reform, which issued with such verve in the Act of 1867, enabled his sort for the first time to see the state as Englishmen in a corporate character, Nonconformists among them. Internationally the Prussian victories of 1866 and the Federal victory of 1865 (which Baines's *Mercury* had steadily championed) appeared to bear on the educational efficiency of Prussia and the United States, and it seemed from the Taunton Commission that educational efficiency need not have Prussian overtones. Nearer home the investigations of the Manchester and Birmingham Education Aid Societies, formed in 1864 and 1867, suggested the need for free education: the Bainesite insistence on the ability of parents to pay for education, and the moral value of such payment, was severely shaken.[28]

Such was the context of Baines's conversion. The Taunton Report was signed in December 1867 and became public in January 1868: but Baines had already proclaimed his conviction that voluntaryism was not enough at the Congregationalists' Manchester Autumnals of October 1867.[29]

Educational voluntaryism was dead and Baines, perhaps because he contrived to maintain a remarkable consistency in his views, ceased to lead the most distinctive strand of Nonconformist opinion. He accepted the necessity for state intervention, but he was careful to define the limits of that necessity. The aim must be a judicious supplementation of the existing system. In this way that individual responsibility which lay at the root of voluntaryism would be preserved. Thus Baines's voluntaryism turned into denominationalism and he found himself at one with those Anglicans who had so impressed him on the Taunton Commission. While Nonconformity's pace-setters turned, in their agitation for the now inevitable Education Bill, to the National Education League, formed from Birmingham in February 1869 to press for free, compulsory and secular education, Baines turned to the National Education Union with its Anglican, Conservative, flavouring and its prejudice against free, compulsory schooling. He stood now with Earls, like Shaftesbury and Harrowby.

It was natural, therefore, that he should give general support to Forster's Bill of 1870, which sought to supplement the existing system, and therefore to incorporate denominationalism permanently into the state system, and which allowed for the formation of locally elected School Boards to remedy deficiencies, but left the thorny question of compulsion and religious instruction to the discretion of those Boards. It was doubtless an inevitable compromise and it aroused inevitable criticism, not least because a Liberal government had ensured that Anglican pre-eminence was built in to the new system. Baines's acceptance of this savoured of betrayal, rather than fidelity to what remained of the voluntary principle.

Yet there was some injustice in the isolation which Baines suffered after his stand. Twenty-five years of steady agitation had taught Nonconformists about education. However much they now differed from Baines, he had prepared them: they were ready to cope with School Boards. Moreover, if Forster's Bill left too much to chance, and therefore to Anglicans, especially in the rural areas, it was a different matter in the towns, where the system of cumulative voting entailed in electing the Boards offered golden opportunities to carefully organized pressure groups: the *Mercury*'s headline summary was accurate as well as sensational: 'A truce to strife! Let us all try to get the best school boards and the best schools we can!'[30]

There was an ultimate irony about Baines and education, at one with his indispensable wrongheadedness, and proof of the salutary harm which a good and intelligent man can do.

It was sometimes said that Congregational resistance to state inter-ference in education ended by confirming the sectarian system.[31] As late as 1881 the Anglican National Schools alone educated over half of all elementary schoolchildren. Yet already the Board Schools were over-taking them, as Anglican standards fell, caught in the downward spiral which had so retarded the Congregational schools back in the 1850s. The educational dominance of the Church of England had after all been destroyed;[32] and the Baines family, voluntaryists still at heart, remained committed to a dwindling cause. The last Baines to be nationally concerned in elementary education was Edward's nephew, Talbot Baines. He was Secretary of the National Society from 1905 to 1918.[33]

V *East Parade and Beyond: The Conclusion of Bainesocracy*

Edward Baines was M.P. for Leeds from 1859 to 1874. Like most Nonconformists he came too late to the Commons to adapt easily to the agility and finesse of the parliamentary game. He was, nonetheless, a backbencher of unusual importance, a rainbow of Liberalism, uniting crotchets and conscience with the *gravitas* appropriate to the backbone of Victorian England's ruling party. He was essentially a man of 1832, always saving his Nonconformity, but he entered Parliament in the year of the meeting at Willis's Rooms which brought into coalition the chief components of what became the Gladstonian Liberal Party. His own contribution lay in the furtherance of franchise reform.

There was a strong element of East Parade in his advocacy of this: it was the lower middle classes whom he sought, the ballast of chapeldom, all pride, poverty and pianos, and the stuff of self-reliance. He concerned himself with their enfranchisement, at least to the municipal level, from 1848, but he opposed household suffrage rather as he opposed free and compulsory education: it would diminish self-reliance.[1] There was a Gladstonian ambiguity about his views. He told Huddersfield in September 1859 'that everyone who could fairly be considered as qualified to exercise the franchise should have the franchise'.[2] There was an equally judicious ambiguity about his actions. He could be all things to too many men. In 1860 he supported Russell's abortive Reform Bill, and found it too moderate. In October he secured Palmerston's presence at the Leeds Mechanics' Institute, in December he heard John Bright address the Leeds Working Men's Parliamentary Reform Association: the first time that Bright had spoken under the direct auspices of the lower orders.[3] Baines's own proposals stopped short of the lower orders.

In 1861, 1864 and 1865 he introduced measures to extend the borough franchise. They were vain hopes, their presentation engulfed in statistics, but they were portents. In 1861, presciently fearing Disraelite opportunism, he opted for the £6 franchise. His measure was backed by little external pressure, and it was studiously ignored by the Government, only Gladstone lending tacit support. Gladstone's attitude was doubtless as grandly selfish as most of that great man's political activity,[4] but it was consistent and when compared with the lukewarm attitude of Russell or Palmerston, it becomes easy to see how he built up an admiring support in unlikely parts of the back benches.

This was shown in 1864 with Baines's second attempt at the borough franchise. This time there was wider enthusiasm, at least in Leeds. It was still a forlorn hope, but it was introduced with an eye to the next election, and perhaps to Palmerston's extreme age. Gladstone's enthusiasm for it ensured the Bill's notoriety, Palmerston's displeasure and his own transformation as the People's William. It hardly mattered that Gladstone's celebrated phrase about the Pale of the Constitution, generally taken to herald his public conversion to the cause of wide franchise reform, was as ambiguous as Baines's earlier words at Huddersfield, or that Baines proclaimed the moderation of his proposals: 'Two thirds of the population ... would still remain without the franchise. . . . The upper and middle class would still constitute two-thirds of the voters in the boroughs.'[5]

His Bill of 1865 was also more important for its manner than its matter. The debate on it provoked open Tory opposition and the intervention of that group of right-wing Liberals soon to be christened the 'Adullamites', whose antics later brought down the Liberals, let in the Tories, and so ensured wilder reforms than they or Baines ever dreamed.[6]

Even in Leeds Baines's Bill was a nine days' wonder, complicated in the General Election of July 1865, by the appearance of Earl Russell's heir, Lord Amberley, as Baines's running mate. Baines was uneasy about Amberley whose charm and brilliance paled beside his fitfulness and inexperience ('I am inclined to regard Mr Baines's Bill with great favour, and it is very probable that I might vote for it. . . .')[7]. The Bainesocracy's accumulation of electoral wisdom was inadequate for the occasion, and Amberley joined the Quaker suffragist Joseph Sturge, the Congregational capitalist Remington Mills and the evangelical Sir Culling Eardley as one of Edward Baines's forlorner parliamentary hopes.

The passage of the Second Reform Act bemused and engulfed Baines as much as it did any upholder of self-reliance and responsibility, and he clung to Gladstone's storm-tossed leadership. He still distrusted household suffrage, and failed to see how the vote could be a natural right. He was embarrassed by the Reform League and appalled by the Leeds Manhood Suffrage Association.[8] Yet the Reform's immediate effect was to present him with his final triumph: he topped the poll at the 1868 General Election, handsomely ahead of his running mate, Alderman Carter of the Manhood Suffrage Association. Leeds Nonconformity — Barran, Marshall, Leuty, Clapham, Conder, Conyers, Lupton — turned out for Baines and Carter, and so did the Irishmen of the East Ward.[9]

Thereafter his comfortless moderation, intensified by his senatorial responsibility, isolated him. Now that the Leeds electorate was over 37,000 he was further removed than ever from the realities of Leeds politics. His newfound educational moderation was compounded by his refusal to support Home Rule for Ireland or the teetotal prohibitionists' Permissive Bill, and he criticized Trade Unions.[10] In each case he opposed the compulsion which such measures involved, however much he sympathized with their underlying principles. At the 1874 General Election he was placed fourth. His masterly compromises had aroused the opposition of a succession of major interests, although it would appear that he was chiefly defeated by the intervention of a temperance candidate.[11] So much for thirty-seven years of total abstinence.

His parliamentary defeat brought the Bainesocracy from autumn to early winter. In January 1874 Baines was presented with his portrait by the people of Leeds. In February he was defeated at the polls and in 1876 he was passed over as Alderman Carter's replacement in favour of John Barran, the Baptist clothing manufacturer, South Parade Chapel to Baines's East Parade, twenty years younger and more radical than Baines, a first generation man, but with over twenty years experience on the Council behind him, rich and Gladstonian, though with the Chamberlain stamp about him.[12]

Yet the Bainesocracy was not replaced by a Barranage, and the moderation which was its chief legacy to Leeds Liberalism maintained a powerful refining influence into the 1880s, the more remarkable in the light of interests affronted or manipulated by the Baineses since the 1820s. They had been objects of the deepest suspicion to working men since the 1830s; true Whigs mistrusted their crotchety voluntaryism and Radicals despised their truckling to true Whigs. They maintained their distance from the minutiae of municipal affairs, and from 1859 this distance increased when Westminster matters took the younger Edward away from the *Mercury*.

Seen thus the defeat of 1874 might be attributed to the sins and omissions of sixty years and the sinner's inability to adapt to the organizational demands of an enlarged politics. Yet when organization emerged, it was Baines-tinted, recalling Cobden's old despairing cry: 'By hereditary prestige, rather than by any native qualities for leading such a constituency, he occupies a position from which he cannot be deposed.'[13]

The Leeds Liberal Association which emerged after 1876 had a turbulent pre-history. It began in the late 1860s from a union of the old, Baines-fostered, Whig, Registration Association and the Leeds Reform League. It split in the early 1870s and was then re-formed. Leeds Liberalism, like that of any Victorian city, was an unnatural coalition of class (shopkeepers, working men, manufacturers), protest (Nonconformists against clerical assumption, all manner of men against rates, radicals against privilege) and government: Leeds was a Liberal city and therefore municipal expenditure was Liberal expenditure, and the protesters were also the governors. Such chaos must be organized; a matter of cliques and coteries had become a question of wards.

In the ten years after the Association's formation, ward organization was perfected and the care exercised in parliamentary and municipal elections was carried over to school board elections.[14] That this was done without the capitulation to wild Radicals which Baines feared, owed much to Wemyss Reid of the *Mercury*. Reid accepted the new order and influenced it. Baines, and others of the old guard followed him.

Reid was the Bainesocracy's last leader, working harmoniously with the Unitarian Kitsons and the Baptist Barrans who had replaced the Baineses in prominence, though not yet in prestige. In the 1880s Leeds became a great Gladstonian city, with Herbert Gladstone as one of its M.Ps, and in 1886 it swung almost united behind Gladstone on Home Rule. For a while it looked as if it might take Birmingham's place as the hub of the National Liberal Federation.

This did not happen. Reid left the *Mercury* in 1887. London became the centre of Liberal organization, and the efficiency of Leeds Liberalism was severely tested by the redistribution of seats which followed the Reform Act of 1884. Leeds was turned from one three-member constituency into five single-member constituencies, of which two were safely Conservative. In 1895 Leeds returned two Tory M.Ps, Herbert Gladstone barely scraped in at Leeds West, and a Labour candidate stood, albeit ingloriously, for Leeds South: and the Town Council became Tory for the first time.

Edward Baines was knighted, at Windsor, on 16 December 1880. Two weeks previously there had been a public presentation to him at the Leeds Albert Hall, its proceeds going to that most provincial but least philistine of causes, the Yorkshire College.[15] He died in March 1890 supposedly Europe's oldest working journalist, and certainly East Parade's oldest member.[16]

He outlived the Bainesocracy and he almost outlived Baines control of the *Mercury*. His was a strange legacy. His family had risen in the wake of the old Leeds oligarchy whom they replaced politically but never quite socially. They were in their turn replaced in what was largely the outworking of their own principles. In 1842 the Leeds Council contained twenty-four large-scale men of business; in 1892, there were six.[17] If it was Leeds's misfortune that the big men, Barran apart, lacked the verve of leadership, it was doubly unfortunate that the little men replaced them neither in standing nor imagination, because the little men were the products of those mechanics' institutes, Y.M.C.As, Sunday Schools and mutual-improvement societies which the Baineses had done more to foster than a whole brigade of Matthew Arnolds.

East Parade did not long outlive Sir Edward. Eustace Rogers Conder continued his ministry until 1892. He resigned in the spring and was dead by midsummer, and was buried at Poole, the setting of his first pastorate. From 1874 East Parade was living on borrowed time, and the first proposals were made that it should move, now that the rich men's houses had made way for shops and offices. From the 1880s the search began for a new site, accompanied by painful adjustments to new men and their rhetoric. East Parade's circumstances were permanently reduced, although it was to be several decades before this showed through its fine appearances.

In December 1875 there were 510 members; ten years later there were 519. This apparent steadiness hid a rapidly increasing mobility: Conder reflected that in twenty-five years at East Parade he had received 958 into membership and lost 957. In his last six years it proved impossible to maintain the balance. Reviewing 1887, he noted that 'no fewer than thirty members have withdrawn to other Christian bodies or resigned their membership', and a melancholy record had been set: for the first time no Congregationalist had transferred membership to East Parade. By January 1891 the membership was 459. This was an inflated figure for if the members at the branch church were excluded, the active membership was nearer 320, and the highest communion attendance was merely 162. It was an ageing membership and the *Church Book*'s obituaries steadily lengthened, but age had little bearing on attendance. The best attenders were the oldest members.[18]

It was the same with the Sunday School: 537 children on East Parade's books in 1875, with another 179 at Woodsley Road, the more active of its two branches; 282 in 1890, with 407 at Woodsley Road;[19] and the same again with finance. In 1888 Dr Conder's salary was £600; in 1891 it was £525. Giving to the London Missionary Society declined from £561 in 1875 to £245 in 1890. In 1889 the church's total income was £1,944; in 1890 it was £1,469, and the most significant drop was in pew rents, which fell from £673 to £518.[20]

These figures conceal considerable and sometimes dramatic fluctuations, which testify to the church's vitality but make it clear that the church's decline was the more inexorable for being so unsteady.

Conder stamped it with his personality until the end. When the chapel was renovated in 1877, it was a matter for congratulation that there was 'no idle waste in gaudy ornament'. Two years later Conder belaboured the woolly young ministers who rocked the Congregational Union with their Leicester Conference. He warned East Parade of 'the thick-skinned pertinacity of those who will not go out from us, though it is manifest they are not of us, and the exuberant charity of those who are willing to give ecclesiastical house-room to everybody who asks for it'.[21] He told the Yorkshire Congregational Union: 'You have no more right to think as you please than to act as you please. Truth has the same imperial claim over the intellect as duty over the conscience. There are laws of thought as well as of conduct, and true liberty lies in intelligent and willing obedience.'[22] There spoke Edward Baines's father-in-God and son-in-law, whose own pulpit would soon enough be occupied by the thick-skinned pertinacious.

Conder's conservatism was strong because it was flexible. Prayer, promptness and mission continued to characterize it, helped now by temperance. He urged promptness with the force of a manual for etiquette: 'To be late, even at a dinner-party, is justly blamed as discourteous. . . . If we had tickets of admission to a meeting at which our Sovereign was to be present, every one would take good care to be early. Do we think less of our Lord's presence?'[23]

There was equal efficiency in his concern for worship, softened now by family words: the congregation used Henry Allon's *Congregational Psalmist* because it was a 'family book', and he once described a church as 'a free brotherhood'. In the last years of his ministry the Young People's Guild, the Choir's Sacred Cantatas, the Band of Hope's Fruit Banquets, the Sunday School's 'Robin's Treat' and the Sale of Work with its entertainment in 'representation of the breach of promise trial, "Bardell v. Pickwick"', not to mention Conder's 'five minutes' sermon for little people', at morning service, showed that East Parade differed little from other busy chapels. 'If it cannot be said that the masses filled his church, yet men and women of all conditions in Leeds were among his hearers.'[24]

The alertness to evangelism foreshadowed in the earlier 1870s became a feature of his later years, and so did the interdenominationalism which it fostered. He found the Anglican Leeds Mission and the Wesleyan-led United Mission of 1875 at once business-like and brotherly and the Moody and Sankey mission of 1883 delighted him with its simplicity and sincerity. It cannot have been coincidence that East Parade received forty-six new members on profession of faith in 1875, and forty-eight in 1883.[25]

Temperance evangelism accompanied this. East Parade's Band of Hope was formed in 1872, a Total Abstinence Society followed in 1875. Both societies flourished, with Edward Baines as President of the Total Abstainers, followed by his son-in-law, Wrigley Willans, but the echoes of compulsion which closed Baines's parliamentary career and divided his supporters eventually penetrated East Parade. The chapel's communion wine was at issue and Conder, concerned in his Baines-like way at the threat to liberty of conscience, found it 'the severest strain of pastoral anxiety . . . during forty-three years of ministry'. The church evolved a compromise: it held two monthly communions, one for fermented and one for unfermented wine, thus avoiding the expedient used elsewhere of separating the pews into fermented and unfermented sections. It was an unsatisfactory solution, but Conder rejoiced in the temper which produced it: 'I never felt more conscious of the presence and power of the Holy Spirit.'[26]

Conder greeted the church's jubilee with the phrase, 'we have lived into a new world'.[27] By 1880 the chapel was a Sunday oasis in a weekday world of commerce, drawing its members from miles around.[28] Removal was inevitable. That it took so long reflected the age and sentiment of East Parade's leadership, as well as its dogged sense of duty. It also reflected the fact that East Parade's social and political leadership among Congregational churches had passed to the daughter church at Headingley Hill.

Headingley Hill was spacious, suburban and prominent. Its architect was Cuthbert Brodrick, of Leeds Town Hall. Within ten years of its foundation, its minister's stipend was £500. Its membership drew upon the prosperous families of the central Leeds chapels. From East Parade it attracted a Baines as one of its deacons, T. R. Leuty who was M.P. for East Leeds from 1895, Obadiah Nussey who chaired the Leeds Textile Committee from 1875, and Wemyss Reid. It differed from East Parade in one interesting respect. Despite the large families who worshipped there for two or three generations, it was not a 'family church' in the same cousinly way.[29] This was a change of direction, as well as generation, a reflection not merely of chapel's integration into Leeds life, but of the widening of that life. There was less need now for chapel to be a voluntary exercise in social control, but the character of its ministers and the vigour of its leading members enabled Headingley Hill to survive the transition without bothering unduly about new bases for a Christian church.

East Parade was less fortunate. There seemed to be a flexing of memory in 1891. Free Churchmen were using the seventeenth century to brace them for the twentieth. In April Edward Butler, church member since 1846, and chairman of the Leeds School Board from 1882 to 1888, died: he lived in a house called Hampden Villa, and was descended from Oliver Cromwell. In July a sermon on 'World Questions' was preached by Dr Bradford, who was descended from William Bradford, the Pilgrim Father. Conder's own puritan ancestry embraced the Ejectment, but who should be his spiritual descendants? He offered to forgo £150 of his salary to provide for an assistant, but the search was as fruitless as the attempts to sell East Parade.[30]

Writing to his deacons shortly before his retirement Conder urged them to call a man 'in full vigour, and in touch with social movements — able to work in such fresh lines as wisdom may indicate'. This was all very well, but Charles Lemoine, Conder's successor, was a restless force. The chapel's cricket club joined the Leeds Nonconformist Cricket League, free-will envelopes replaced pew rents, new members joined at the rate of over thirty a year and the chapel was lit by electricity. 'Jesus Christ is not a mere energy, he is a *presence*, a *comrade*.'[31]

So whirlwind a style had its effect. 'We have come to the last year of the greatest of the centuries', Lemoine wrote in the 1900 *Church Book*, 'The year 1900 should end in LOVE'. It ended in compromise: Lemoine resigned, his future was uncertain beyond a lecture tour in the United States. The deacons were concerned at this, but his decision was a mercy. Perhaps he lacked dignity. He certainly lacked safety. His resignation preserved East Parade's reputation for harmony and avoided the rupture threatened a few months earlier when a group of members petitioned for his removal. Above all it ensured that the new building should begin in unity.[32]

In the *Church Book* for 1899 Lemoine warned his people that 'we must soon be engaged in an economic struggle for life'. That year an offer for £30,000, quickly raised to £31,000, was made for East Parade. It nearly doubled one made in 1897 and it was not refused.[33]

The final services were held at East Parade on 23 July 1899, and the old chapel was demolished in 1900, giving way 'to the resistless march of the business enterprise of a great city'. Its replacement on Woodhouse Lane, towards the University, was opened in October 1902. It was called Trinity and was built by G. F. Danby in 'Perpendicular Gothic, somewhat freely treated'. It was commandingly sited and beautifully furnished; nave, chancel, transepts, centre aisle, tower and spire, suites of ample rooms behind it. It cost over £24,000 and it was Leeds's finest Congregational Church.[34] It was also the least Congregational in appearance, its Gothic free but nowhere skimped.

Yet the site was as inappropriate as it was commanding, in an area already served by Presbyterians and the Blenheim Baptists, and on the direct road to Headingley Hill. It seated 800, which was fewer than East Parade, and it never needed the galleries for which there was room. It opened with 300 members, a Sunday School of under 200 and a minister's stipend of barely £350. It was a stunning misdirection of faith.[35]

Trinity was not a Baines church. Baines cousins and descendants contributed handsomely to the fine stained-glass windows, but this was an act of remembrance. Mrs Conder, the last Baines to remain in membership, lived in Kensington. One of her sons was an Anglican clergyman, and most of the other Baineses had become Anglicans. In 1880 twelve were in membership; the number halved in six years.[36] Edward died in 1890, his brother Frederick in 1893, his son-in-law Wrigley Willans moved to Harrogate. Edward's daughter Florence transferred to Headingley Hill in 1894, resigning her membership there in 1899: she would appear to be the last Baines in active membership at either of those churches.[37]

The music at Edward Baines's funeral delicately recognized his knighthood with an old East Parader's hymn, George Rawson's 'Captain and Saviour of the host / Of Christian Chivalry'.[38] Something of that strain continued in his grandson Herbert and his nephew Talbot, whose lives close this study.

Herbert Stanhope Baines joined Headingley Hill in 1884 and entered the *Mercury* office in 1890. Although it is not clear whether he maintained his membership he seems to have been the last male Baines to combine his family's Liberalism and journalism with something of their Nonconformity. His children were baptized at Headingley Hill in 1894 and 1896; he became the *Mercury*'s editor in 1895, and in the July election he was the Gladstonian candidate for Leeds North, Headingley Hill's constituency. He lost, and died on a health cruise to Africa in the following May.[39]

His cousin Talbot Baines, Frederick's son and Sir Edward's nephew, was the first Baines to go to Rugby School, two years before the publication of *Culture and Anarchy*. For twenty-two years, from 1875 to 1897, he worked for the *Leeds Mercury*, but he worked as a mirror image of his uncle and grandfather. He was an Imperialist and a Liberal Unionist. While his first wife, an Ulsterwoman, was active at East Parade, he turned to the Established Church, its schools and its rights. During the Great War he became a bureaucrat and worked for the Political Intelligence Department of the Foreign Office.[40]

Nonetheless, as his uncle and grandfather wrote on the textile industries of Yorkshire and Lancashire, so he wrote about the industrial north, and he died in Leeds. He also brought about a linking of dynasties which Sir Edward Baines would have relished. In 1891 he married Caroline Agnes Talbot, daughter of the Tory M.P. for Oxford University. The second Mrs Talbot Baines was thus a grand-daughter of the Lord Wharncliffe to whom Sir Edward had addressed open letters in the 1840s; she was also a niece of Edward Talbot the powerful and powerfully loved Vicar of Leeds who was attracting several Baineses to his pews and his Church, and she was a great-niece of Mrs Gladstone. A brother-in-law became Bishop of Chichester and two cousins became Dean of York and Bishop of Pretoria. Edward Talbot of Leeds became Bishop of Southwark, Rochester and Winchester. There could not have been a more bracing infusion of all that was vital in England's Established Church and established order, or a sweeter enactment of Sir Edward's Golden Wedding Address to his family when, recalling the advantages of a pious ancestry, 'on both sides', and the happiness of kinship with 'an unusual number of truly Christian families', he ended in the hope 'that the remembrance of them will be a continual motive to spotless virtue, to intellectual culture, to Christian usefulness, and to the carrying down of the line of piety to a remote posterity'.[41]

Chapter 5

Pacemaker or Crotcheteer? —
The Impact of a Strolling Agitator:
A Study of Edward Miall

It was one day in the summer of 1839 that my father, whom we had supposed to be travelling abroad, came suddenly upon us as the Church was in imminent danger, and civil and religious liberty was trembling in the balance, to bid us be ready to accompany him to London in an hour's time.

(A. Mursell, *Memories of My Life*, 1913, p. 14.)

Edward Miall disliked the Scots for their dirty habits, coldness and religious intolerance, but he liked Ireland. His love of cigars reconciled him to German thought: 'I suppose in that land of universal smoking the clear sharp outline of a face is never visible, and all things are seen through a hazy medium. Perhaps, indeed, German mysticism is to be traced to this cause. . . .' His life was prayerful, private and disciplined, passed chiefly in Tufnell Park and Forest Hill, lightened by music and his family:

Till then, good-bye, love and kisses to the children, and for yourself the heart of
Your most affectionate,
Edward.[1]

He belonged to a difficult but intelligent class of Victorian, the Nonconformist minister who had left the stated pastorate, floating thereafter in a limbo of almost-layness. His departure from the ministry was in obedience to the same stern quality of logic which impelled the younger Edward Baines. It owed nothing to intellectual unease and he seldom moved in intellectual circles, which was remarkable for so rigorous a journalist. Perhaps this was because he was a relatively poor man and in poor health, perhaps because his particular notoriety could only embarrass established men of intellect. His intellectual power, therefore, was a mystery save to fellow Nonconformists.

Free of pastoral responsibilities he became a peripatetic speaker and sermon-taster, sitting under the more thoughtful sort of preacher.[2] He was particularly impressed by the extraordinary Norwood Baptist,

101

Samuel Augustus Tipple, the 'Wordsworthian Pantheist', of whom Ruskin approved but Lloyd George had never heard, who attracted a small, interdenominational auditory of prosperously intellectual Londoners whose principles allowed them to use public transport on a Sunday.[3]

Edward Miall, who kept a quiet Sunday but disliked Sabbatarian humbug, was that sort of sermon-taster. Indeed he was himself an unexpected sermonizer. He was the quintessential Dissenting parson — 'you can see he has been brought up in a divinity college; he has all the prim and unfashionable air of youths reared in such secluded spots' — yet he read his sermons. He achieved that actor's rapport with his audience which was the secret of pulpit power, yet his was a cold appeal, 'seemingly void of all animalism — a rock with a gleam of sunlight on it — an incarnate idea. . . .'[4]

His character fitted the outlines of his career better than its realities. He was born in Portsmouth in 1809 and died in Sevenoaks in 1881. He was a Nonconformist minister in Ware and Leicester from 1831 to 1840 and the founder and editor of a London weekly from 1841. He was a Liberal M.P. for northern constituencies between 1852 and 1857, and 1869 and 1874, and he stood unsuccessfully for a motley collection of boroughs on six other occasions. Like too many prominent Victorians he was an author, chiefly of works critical of the State Church, but also of a volume of theology and one of editorial musings. He was involved, as a minister turned politician and author was likely to be, in great causes, and to judge by the memories of other Nonconformists he was a man of great effects.

In 1849, when he was still a man of impractical radicalism, he appeared to a Unitarian commentator to represent all that was most hopefully progressive in a transformed Congregationalism, freeing itself in theology, orthodoxy and social spirit. It was a triumph of education.[5] A few years later James Travis, a young Primitive Methodist, contemplating Miall's candidature for Rochdale, 'was led to believe that Mr Miall . . . was bent on closing the churches and destroying religion, and that if he got into Parliament every kind of evil would follow . . . but when given to understand that Mr Miall was a good man and only wanted the Government to treat the Anglican Church as it did the Primitives and other dissenters, I joined those who shouted for him'.[6]

It was James Ewing Ritchie, converted like Miall from the ministry to journalism, who identified that mixture of man and mind which enabled Miall to appeal to such opposite types as the Unitarian or the Primitive Methodist: Miall was 'an abstract principle embodied — that man is everything, that the human being is divine, that the inspiration of the Almighty has given the meanest of us understanding'. This was a

Bible-based principle. It led to a rejection of ecclesiasticism, and therefore to disestablishment, and to an advocacy of the equality of men who are equal before God, and to suffrage reform. It was, so Ritchie felt in the 1850s, a rare personal success since disestablishment and complete suffrage were far-away causes, but this lent enchantment since Victorians were connoisseurs of personality. Principle made a man of Miall, endowing him with a style clear and cold as ice, yet with the power of speaking directly to the poor. No wonder theological students and young ministers hero-worshipped him.[7]

Alexander McLaren, thinking of his first pastorate at Southampton in the late 1840s, recalled an enthusiasm which owed as much to long rambles and 'hours of heart confidence' as to Miall's infectious flouting of convention.[8] R. W. Dale, at Spring Hill College, Birmingham, in the same decade, succumbed with the other students: 'they regarded him as a master; they were trained in his school; they perpetuated his thought; and they carried on the great controversy with the Established Church in his spirit.'[9] Guinness Rogers, at his first church in Newcastle-upon-Tyne in the late 1840s, played host to Miall and so 'learned to respect and honour him; and today, as I realize better the depressing influence of the atmosphere amid which his work was done, I simply marvel at the spectacle of moral heroism which he presented, and thank God for the amount of quickening influence which he exerted. For his was distinctively a religious influence'.[10]

By 1881, the year of Miall's death, McLaren, Dale and Rogers had become household names, and not just in Baptist or Congregational households. McLaren, now in Manchester, Dale, still in Birmingham, and Rogers, now in Clapham, amply expressed the moral, intellectual and political force of Nonconformity in a way which had only just become conceivable in 1841, the year when Miall took to successful journalism. Edward White of Kentish Town, another notable Nonconformist, was not far wrong in attributing to Miall the revolution that had taken place in the general estimation of Free Churchmen and their principles.[11] Miall once disarmingly presented himself as a 'strolling agitator';[12] his career, with its strolls from London to Birmingham and Manchester, or Southampton and Newcastle, was a tribute to the ennobling effects of agitation.

Miall's was a life of single-minded intensity and multiple significance. It was rooted in his war to disestablish the English Episcopal Church. This apparently ecclesiastical war might entail the upending of the English ruling classes, their education and their property as well as their Church, and it therefore committed Miall to a succession of battles for educational and electoral reform. The long battle for the abolition of church rates, which turned Miall into a combatant in the first place and which he barely outlived, took him beyond English chapeldom to the outposts of establishment in Ireland and the Empire. It provided him with an army in the shape of the Liberation Society, although he was merely one of its generals, never its commander-in-chief, and it led to pacts with other armies of radicals, Irishmen or labour aristocrats. As a strategist Miall had the strengths as well as the faults of the single-minded, and must be seen as an architect of the Gladstonian Liberal coalition.[13] Arthur Miall, Edward's son and biographer, felt in 1884, unwittingly on the eve of that unlikely coalition's greatest test, that Edward and his associates did 'more than any other party . . . towards the formation of that Liberal majority in the House of Commons which at the present time upholds the strongest reforming Government this country has seen since the Common-wealth'.[14]

Thus so negative and divisive a cause as the disestablishment of the national church, had its chief effect in cementing the progressive party in the first age of the mass electorate. It is here that comparisons are called for with that other edgy apostle of fusion, moderation and cool reason, Sir Edward Baines.

Baines and Miall shared generation and denomination. Both were backbenchers during Gladstone's happiest administration. Both stood for a freedom which their reason carried beyond reasonable bounds: indeed, Miall chiefly offended in this, since he stood for the dismantling of a church which was already part of the national fabric, while Baines tried to prevent the further extension of the state into the minds of its citizens.

Baines, however, would have been notable regardless of his Noncon-formity: he was a newspaper proprietor, the son of a provincial M.P., and the brother of a cabinet minister. Miall would have been nowhere. He emerged from the fringes of the middle classes, for whom the Dissenting ministry offered the likeliest path of social advance. All other openings involved luck: the ministry was merely a matter of vocation. Let a man be called to the ministry, and his spheres of influence were immeasurably widened.

It depended, nonetheless, on the call and Nonconformity had its own ways of testing this. Miall's career as pastor, journalist and politician was a consistent response to his call.

Here there is a further point of comparison with Baines. Baines's prominence was assured, but it was shaped by the church at East Parade. Miall's prominence depended on his Nonconformity but it was sustained neither by the 'family' life of a great Congregational church nor by the camaraderie of the Congregational Union, with its committees and May Meetings and Autumnals. His career would have been impossible without Congregationalism but he was much less of a Congregationalist than

Baines. It was this which allowed him to escape his denomination's enticing mediocrity and to remain almost as important a radical as he was a Nonconformist.

As a minister he was flung into leadership. In a country town like Ware he could not be other than a symbol of opposition. In a town like Leicester, full of Baptists, artisans, and small manufacturers, ministry became a radical matter, with none of the stateliness attaching to it in prouder mercantile cities. He was in neither place long enough to become an institution or to merge into his congregation. He was long enough in London to do both, but as a political journalist whose words were deeds, in competition with established denominational practitioners, radicalism came naturally, preserving his detachment from Congregational minutiae. It was this, perhaps, which R. F. Horton had in mind when he commented that Congregationalism was better served by Miall's *Nonconformist* than by denominational papers.[15]

Yet Miall's career, no less than Baines's, was limited. With Baines, for all that most of his life was spent in London, he could be dismissed as the essence of provincialism. With Baines, for all his protestations of large views, he announced sectarianism. With Baines too, for all that he was a southerner, he seemed to stand for the north and for Manchester School machinery. With Baines he was an urban man.

This was inevitable, for with Baines he was middle class. His desire for a fusion of classes was real enough and it comprehended rural labourers as well as urban ones. Rural Nonconformists were more uniformly the victims of injustice than townees and Miall wished to harness this experience of shared oppression. There was to be a movement of town and country, middle class and working class, a new politics. As W. R. Ward has suggested, this harnessing of discontents was as unlikely after the 1840s as before, because the rhythms of British industry and agriculture were separating, the short-term movements of industry no longer dependent on the movements of agriculture.[16] Only in the 1880s would there be a systematic attempt to exploit the countryside for the cause of progressive politics, and then it could not be fully pursued.

With the urban lower classes, and for all his wide powers of sympathy, Miall's failure remained one of imagination. He shared with Gladstone that best of faults, an addiction to principle as the root cause of social betterment, a preference for justice to bread and butter. It is an attitude which may be impractical, but never impertinent and seldom condescending. It had its limits, as a letter written by George Howell in 1871, suggests. A Working Men's Committee for the promotion of disestablishment, had been formed under Howell's chairmanship, but the Liberation Society was stingy in servicing it: any expenditure above £10 a month had to be specifically sanctioned. Howell spelled out the implications:

1 shilling for bus fare is nothing to some of these men but to some of our men it is material. . . . Is it not wonderful how some men of what is called the middle class expect us to more than equal their contributions, not by work only, but by petty expenditure caused by that very work. More than ten per cent of my income, in addition to labour, has been devoted to this kind of work for more than 20 years. I wonder how many can say the same. . . .[17]

Howell's grumble of 1871 has its value. It might serve as a footnote to the thesis of *Culture and Anarchy*, a voice of the future condemning the thirty year reign of middle-class Miall-biased Nonconformist philistinism which Matthew Arnold believed to have ended with the Second Reform Act. Or it might be set beside a later assessment, Whig interpretation though this may be; for Haslam Mills of the *Manchester Guardian* believed that 'it was about the year 1871 that England, considered as a middle-class paradise, reached perfection'. This perfection flowed from the 1868 election, when the country divided 'on an unmaterial issue. The newly-enfranchised trooped to the polls in their thousands in the character of Erastians or anti-Erastians; and, lest anybody should be troubled by even the ghost of a personal interest in the direction of his vote, circumstance would have it that the church whose disestablishment was in question should be the Irish Church, with the English elector a stranger at once to its sacraments, and its soup and blankets. All the politics of the time turned indeed on creed, and when they did not turn on creed they turned on conduct.'[18]

Mills and Arnold would have agreed in one thing: 'the times were a paradise of the Dissenting middle class, and the observation is the more true because paradise would not be paradise without a grievance. And there were many grievances!'[19]

Mills's account is a celebration of the middle class, all justice, and abstract principles, spiced with grievance. It was as much Miall's doing as anybody's. He, like the middle classes, was a great English fact of the mid-nineteenth century. Facts are finite. Religious principles are not.

The teetotalers have built a hall called the Good Samaritan Hall, on Saffron Hill. It is a low neighbourhood. It is surrounded by the dwellings of the poor, and it is erected there as a light for that dark spot, by means of which the drunkard may emerge into a higher life. The last time I heard Miall was there: the room was full. On a table, dressed in an old blue great coat, stood Miall, preaching to men and women, gathered from the highways and byways, from the crowds for whose souls no one cares.[20]

There was more to Miall than dressing up the lower orders to look like good bourgeois.

Matthew Arnold was a devastating adversary, all slippery sweetness and darting light, shifting his ground where it suited him, confusing the effects of Presbyterianism and Independency, faintly praising the Puritan contribution without bothering his mind as to whether the constraints upon latterday Puritans were self-imposed or Anglican imposed. Miall personified an age of machinery, and Arnold in his educated Anglican way lacked the sympathy to perceive that Miall represented a life which was as comprehensive as Anglicanism. Arnold saw only its limits. 'Look at the life imaged in such a newspaper as the *Nonconformist*, — a life of jealousy of the Establishment, disputes, tea-meetings, openings of chapels, sermons; and then think of it as an ideal of human life completing itself on all sides, and aspiring with all its organs after sweetness, light, and perfection!'[21]

These were Nonconformity's occupational hazards and Miall disliked them. They said little about the source of Miall's life, without which his career would be an unpleasant nonsense. In England's strange religious structure Nonconformity provided a built-in opposition, cushioning the Establishment from the extremes of nastiness, steadily dissolving the Establishment's pretensions, but doomed itself to dissolution the more nearly it approached the Establishment's heart. Or rather, it was less Nonconformity than its social and political expressions which were doomed as it approached its goal. Nonconformity's base was religious. It offered alternative forms of churchmanship to the Established Church. It offered an alternative Christian society. This was the positive side of Nonconformity, and Miall championed it. For all the exceptions to the rule, men were not Nonconformists for convenience or fun. Nonconformity did not live by social pressures alone.

Nonconformity was bred on deprivation. Victorian England faced the consequences of a system which had kept a sizeable and articulate section of Englishmen from their rights for two hundred years. The first of these consequences was that the excluded classes were profoundly sceptical about government. Because they had been excluded on religious grounds, their suspicions did not include opposition to religion as such, but merely to its established, imperfect, form. Indeed, it often meant commitment to religion: secularism was a very slender thread in the fabric of nineteenth-century English society.

A second consequence was that the excluded classes and the established classes had in common the very thing which divided them: a basic religious experience, Protestant and usually evangelical. There was thus all manner of contact, on committees, in philanthropies; exclusion was never total.

It may, therefore, be true that Victorian England's freedom from revolution owed much to its religious structure. It is equally true that the alternative society offered by Nonconformists, could never achieve political shape. There was never any possibility of a Dissenting *party*. There could never be more than that amorphous thing, a Dissenting *interest*. Edward Miall's career, grounded in his religion, was a demonstration of this. The causes which alone gave him political influence could never give him political power.

Nonconformity was the marrow of his being. It made possible the self-made man and fused him with the God-made. His father, Moses Miall, was a general merchant who ended up in North London as a schoolmaster with too large a family for his means. Its members fended early for themselves as hack schoolteachers like their father. For Edward this meant ushering at private schools in the eastern counties.

One thing kept their heads above water: their evangelical faith. Moses exhorted Edward to the patient path of excellence and there came the time, dated precisely to Tuesday morning, 8 May 1827, his eighteenth birthday, when he followed countless Puritan youths and consecrated himself to God: 'By the blessing of God, and under his Divine assistance, I, Edward Miall, solemnly dedicate myself, soul and body, unto the Lord. . . . Witness my signature, Edward Miall.'[22]

Miall suffered all the agonies which an individualistic faith can induce. He recalled them in the old, touching, jargon at his ordination four years later. 'I took no step towards reformation. I continued to live without hope and without God in the world . . . conscience sank into a state of torpor' and only Providence saved him 'from the grossest extremes of immorality'. But Providence showed him two books. One, which he read on the Sabbath, was a play of Foote's, which disgusted him; the other, from his mother, was Buck's *Christian Experience*, which set him thinking:

like an electric flash, my past ingratitude, my present degeneracy, my future prospects, shot across my mind. I instantly retired to my chamber, and wrestled with God in prayer. I entreated in agony of soul that this emotion might not prove transitory. I devoted every leisure moment to the hearty pursuit of God. My impressions were deepened, my desires increased. . . . A glow of love to the Redeemer pervaded my heart.[23]

He determined to enter the ministry.

It is important to grasp this experience. It was common to many thrusting boys. Three of Miall's brothers felt it, and two of them entered the ministry. It is also important to see where this experience led. Edward Miall, the struggling schoolmaster, was nobody, but Edward Miall, the college-trained pastor was another man entirely.

Wymondley, where he was trained from 1828 to 1831, gave him friends, connexions and his sole dose of intellectual discipline, which meant sermon classes, a debating society and a self-imposed course of Gibbon, Locke, Dugald Stewart, Mackintosh and Adam Smith, as well as Bishop Butler and Jonathan Edwards, taken daily for two hours before breakfast.[24] At Ware from 1831 to 1834, and Leicester from 1834 to 1840, this young man without prospects became the acknowledged leader of self-sufficing communities of tradesmen, professional men, widows, servants, and hangers-on: solely because of obedience to God's call. The world was his; and in 1835 he toyed with going to South Africa as a missionary.[25]

His upbringing among the Micawber classes, Wymondley's books and Leicester's radicalism, set in the context of the 1830s — he was converted on the eve of the Test Act's repeal and ordained amidst the Reform Bill's turbulence — determined some other mission field. He became intimate with the radical, missionary, Baptist, Mursells; he was deeply interested in Scottish voluntaryism and got to know Scotland and Wales first hand from holiday rambles. He expressed himself publicly about Establishments. It was towards the close of Melbourne's shabby Whig administration and the Bond Street flock was restive. Miall resigned his pastorate in the autumn of 1839, remaining until 1840 on a part-time basis. He was clear that he must become a missionary in the cause of religious freedom. There followed the turmoil of a further conversion, in which he was guided and persuaded by his minister friends, J. P. Mursell the Leicester Baptist, and David Lloyd of Harleston, Norfolk, his companion since Wymondley days. There must be a weekly paper, in London, with an editor.

Miall was neither the immediate nor the natural choice, but he became the only one. Mursell told him so, on a platform of Rugby railway station. It was a proper beginning for the journalistic career of one whose mission was to expose the dishonour of a Church turned into 'a mere political engine', although the suggestion hardened into decision in the different atmosphere of Lloyd's manse at Harleston, in the rural heart of Puritan England, urged on by John Childs, the rugged popularizer of literary classics.[26]

The result, after an intensive and painful fund raising campaign, was the *Nonconformist*. Its first issue appeared on 14 April 1841:

The modern Independents have a newspaper, the *Nonconformist*, written with great sincerity and ability. The motto, the standard, the profession of faith which this organ of theirs carries aloft, is: 'The Dissidence of Dissent and the Protestantism of the Protestant religion'. There is sweetness and light, and an ideal of complete harmonious human perfection![27]

The *Nonconformist* lasted from 1841 to 1884 when it merged with the *English Independent* to become the *Nonconformist and Independent*, to all intents a denominational journal. Edward Miall was its sole genius, although his son Arthur took over the commercial management in 1862. The fireworks died with Edward. By the end of its first year the circulation was 2,000 and by 1853 it reached 3,200 copies weekly. In 1854 more stamps were issued to it than to any other Dissenting journal, the Wesleyan *Watchman* included.[28] Its finances were sound without being easy, largely sustained in the early years by the Birmingham Quaker, Charles Sturge, and his family, with whom Miall was in natural sympathy.[29]

The *Nonconformist* was well-timed. It appeared in the first real railway decade. The weeklies owed much of their influence to the fact that they were standard reading on long railway journeys. Serious middle-class families could often only afford and perhaps only desired one weekly which should be religious. Thus the religious weeklies provided a varied and secular diet, of a type inconceivable to their latest posterity. The *Nonconformist* offered shrewd political commentaries, well-informed foreign coverage and a literary department under G. B. Bubier of Cambridge and Salford which showed, or so Guinness Rogers felt, 'that Dissenters were not insensible to the charms of culture'.[30] It was also fortunate that it emerged amidst a *cause célèbre*, which ensured its notoriety, determining its tone and thereby its radicalism.

In November 1840 William Baines found himself in Leicester County Gaol. With twenty-six other parishioners of St Martin's, Leicester, he refused to pay the church rate. The case came before the Court of Arches. Baines refused to have anything to do with it, since that sort of ecclesiastical authority was not in Scripture; hence his imprisonment. His disputed rates were £2.5s.0d.; his costs were £125.3s.0d.

The affair was no more exasperating than similar cases scattered throughout England and Wales in the late 1830s and early 1840s. Baines, however, was a Bond Street notable. Mrs Baines was in 'a critical state of health' (which suggests pregnancy) and Edward Miall was a personal friend. Perhaps Baines's own solid name ensured his wider fame, although there was no connexion with Baines of Leeds.

Miall whipped up local feeling, chaired local meetings, sent books to the comfortably imprisoned Baines — 'Get Thomas Carlyle's *Lectures on Heroes* and read — especially those on Luther and Cromwell — it will brace your mind like spring-water.' — and with the *Nonconformist* under way never rested until Baines was at liberty, mentioning him in every leader until the wretched man was freed late in June 1841.[31]

This set the tone of the *Nonconformist*, which Arthur Miall hopefully recalled as 'bold but courteous'.[32] Its purpose was twofold: to unmask the Church and to brace Dissent. Where the Church was concerned, boldness soon outstripped courtesy. 'A State Church! Have they never pondered on the practical meaning of that word? Have they never looked into that dark, polluted, inner chamber of which it is the door? Have they never caught a glimpse of the loathsome things that live, and crawl, and gender there?' And he captured the rhetoric of Popish medievalism: 'The Establishment a Counterfeit Church — An image carved with marvellous cunning, tricked out in solemn vestments, a part woven by human fancy, a part stolen from the chest of truth.'[33]

When it came to Dissent he left sham romance for pinched Dickensian domesticity. 'They are just like poor relations living upon the cold charity of a well-off uncle, half-obsequiousness, half-irritability, in conduct very meek, in disposition somewhat sly, who seldom speak above a whisper . . . in whom there is waging incessantly, but unnoticed, a conflict between desire and habit'. No wonder he braced students but devastated others bearing the name of the journal which they dared not read. 'With us, moral heroism is impossible, and we go about the world with a label on our backs, on which nothing more is written than the word "Fool". Nobody hinders us, we may walk where we please; but the brand is upon us. . . . We become ashamed of ourselves, ashamed of our principles; and look, and speak, and act as though we were ordained to be despised and have made our calling sure.'[34]

The language was radical, the impact political, and Miall exploited it. There was more than an unmasking of the Church and a bracing of Dissent behind his brisk dismissal, in the *Nonconformist*'s second issue, of the results of the Great Reform Act: 'cold iron and brickwalls — good police establishments and triple-guarded union-houses.'[35] This captures the effect of Miall's *Nonconformist*: it brought into the open an articulate, broad-bottomed Nonconformist consciousness. Yet it was a vital agent in the dissolution of that consciousness as a purely Nonconformist thing. Its fate was that of all educators.

Edward Miall had been a schoolmaster and was a schoolmaster's son. As minister and editor he remained an educator. Education was tied up with factory reform, parliamentary reform and the State Church. It was an intensely political issue. It gave Sir Edward Baines's career much of its cohesion, and in the public eye Edward Miall's attitude was scarcely less consistent. From the 1840s to the 1860s he was a voluntaryist: state education confirmed the State Church in its privileges, and smelt of coercion and jobbery. It was at once condescending and debilitating since it deprived self-respecting working men of their rights and opportunities.

You could not be independent in a state system. State schools would be Church schools, dotting the country as garrisons of privilege, outposts of parish church and manor house, manned not by teachers but by state policemen.

Graham's proposals of 1843 were easily seen in this light,[36] and the uproar which they caused contributed powerfully to Miall's credibility as a Nonconformist spokesman, and to the formation of the Anti-State Church Association. He extracted a similarly loaded moral from Russell's proposals of 1847: 'the connection between Dissent and Reform-club Liberalism is at an end.'[37] From 1858 to 1861 he served on the Newcastle Commission, his voluntaryism unabated and indeed strengthened by Robert Lowe's doings.[38]

Perhaps the Newcastle Commission worked on him as the Taunton Commission later worked on Baines. It brought him into the closest contact with men of affairs; it even revealed Newcastle as a thoroughly affable Duke.[39] By 1867 Miall's views on government interference in education had changed, like Baines's views, though he placed a characteristically radical gloss on them. They had changed because 'government is passing away now — passing away from one class chiefly into the hands of another class'.[40]

It was inevitable that Forster's Act, so partial to the State Church, should disappoint him. Most prominent Nonconformists disliked it, although the nature of their dislike varied bewilderingly. Miall felt now that state education should be secular education, but he was careful to distinguish the secular from the irreligious. School boards should be secular as railway directorates were secular.[41]

Forster's Act marked the closing of Miall's public career rather as Graham's proposals had enlivened its opening. It provoked a clash with Gladstone which Miall gamely dismissed as a lover's quarrel, but which spurred him into his last attempts to make disestablishment a key issue; and it complicated his relations with his constituency, Bradford, where Forster was his running mate.

As to education, R. W. Dale, who had parted company with Miall years earlier on the matter, felt that Miall still rather regretted abandoning the voluntary principle.[42] For all the radicalism there remained limits to his imagination. He continued to oppose compulsory elementary education, and his most notable educational success — his support in 1853-4 for ending religious tests for first degrees at Oxford — he valued chiefly as a symbol. Oxford was dangerous for young Nonconformists.

The Liberation Society, founded in 1844 as the Anti-State Church Association, was Miall's chief agency in the missionary, educational, task of freeing the 'religion of Christ secularized'.[43] It is tempting to regard the Society as Miall multiplied but it had its own organization, served by men of character and ability, and its journal was not Miall's *Nonconformist* but the *Liberator*. It was radically conceived but it moved, as any successful organization must, to occupy a middle ground.[44] It is significant that when Miall stood for Southwark in 1845, with every taint of radicalism, the Anti-State Church Association did not fully support him.[45] Nonetheless Miall's genius permeated the movement and this, given form by the executive abilities of Carvell Williams and the persistent enthusiasm of F. A. Cox and the barrister Dr Foster, preserved it from the fate of mealier-mouthed predecessors.

The Anti-State Church Association issued from a conference held late in April 1844 in London's Crown and Anchor Hotel. It was attended by 700 delegates, mostly provincials, only three of them leading London ministers, and it was a huge success, 'like a dream to us — a lovely and majestic dream'.[46] It crystallized what had long been in Miall's mind but its immediate style was determined by the twin excitements of the Graham proposals and the Scottish Disruption. What was happening to the Church of Scotland was profoundly suggestive, even if the disrupters came involuntarily from their national church. There resulted an abrasiveness fostered by the propagandist needs of the new movement which displayed the narrowness that Miall was at pains to dispel. He was concerned that the movement should embrace all reformers, and the change of name to 'The Society for the Liberation of Religion from State Patronage and Control', in 1853, after prolonged debate and as one of Edward Baines's happiest suggestions, was an earnest of this.[47] In 1862 Miall was particularly careful to see that Liberationist enthusiasm for the bicentenary of the Great Ejectment should not be an excuse for celebrating the heroic 2,000 as founder members of the Liberation Society.[48] There must be nothing sectarian about what too easily appeared as the ultimate in sectarianism.

Whatever its tone there was no doubt as to its efficiency. The care which had gone into the Crown and Anchor Conference — a committee of 200 had elected an executive of twenty who then corresponded with the provinces to ferret out likely delegates[49] — marked the Association which grew from it. At the Crown and Anchor a Council of 500 was chosen, who in turn elected an executive of fifty. The Council and the Executive met each other annually, but the supreme authority lay with Conference which was to meet triennially. Links were maintained with provincial associations by area registrars. This cumbersome mechanism was to avoid the presumed illegality of having provincial associations corresponding directly with a central executive. Eventually the executive was given national authority while local committees were made responsible for local activities, paying any monies raised into the central treasury. A rhythm developed of pamphlets, deputations and lecture tours. In March 1846 John Kingsley was appointed full-time lecturer, and in the following year John Carvell Williams, Congregationalist and London Welshman (he became a member of the church at Surbiton), was appointed full-time secretary.[50]

By 1847 the movement had its own momentum. At first Miall acted as minute secretary and the committee met weekly on the day after the *Nonconformist*'s publication.[51] It throve in the heroic atmosphere of ostracism and persecution, fostering its image of provincials beating London at its own game.

There was some truth in this. In the Association's pre-history it was provincial impatience which made the running. It became a matter for fond recollection that no London bank would receive their account and no Westminster chapel would give house room for their lectures, that railway bookstalls banned their pamphlets and that the large industrial cities were scarcely less cold.[52] Nonetheless the Association was London based and London organized and it needed London money, even if its members came from elsewhere. This indeed explained its success. Its efficiency was nationwide — upwards of 198 registrars by 1847[53] — drawing on the obvious sources, but also exploiting other veins of opinion.

Thus the Association was not initially strong in Lancashire, and it was only in 1847 that the Leeds Bainesocracy swung Yorkshire over in public support, but from the start it captivated the imagination of country churches and it attracted the young and the Baptists.[54] This gave it a vigorous basis, democratic inasmuch as it depended on the groundswell of opinion among local churches, articulate, shading towards the lower edges of the middle classes, especially where Baptist support was most pronounced, but seldom touching the industrial working classes. By capturing the ordinands of the 1840s it made sure of the pulpits of the 1860s. By capturing Baptists it ensured a flavour of evangelical radicalism. It was thanks to Baptist support that the cause began to penetrate not merely Lancashire, but Liverpool.[55] In Northamptonshire support was powerfully voiced by the county's Baptist Association in the 1870s as in the 1840s. It was no coincidence that J. Turland Brown, an old Leicester friend of Miall's and a consistent Liberationist, was minister of College Street, Northampton, one of the largest midland churches, for fifty years from 1843.[56]

By 1856 the organization had an income of £3,208, and by the end of the decade it claimed 5,500 subscribers from 517 places.[57] It was now a prime source of Nonconformist opinion; as a large London Congregational church put it many years later: 'The Congregational body has long since been educated up to a thorough belief in both the rightness and practicability of the aims of the Liberation Society.'[58] It was also now a political power. As the *Eclectic Review* expressed it in 1855: 'What was once reproached as political dissent is now acknowledged as dissenting politics.'[59]

Its political ambitions were almost as old as the movement itself, and Edward Miall's political career was inevitably, but not entirely, bound up in them.

In the summer of 1845 the executive committee resolved to field at least six candidates in the next general election, and to make no contribution to their expenses. Almost immediately there was a by-election in radical, Dissenting Southwark. Miall was urged to stand. He polled 353: the victor and official Liberal, Sir William Molesworth, polled 1,942.[60]

Miall's candidature embarrassed the Anti-State Church Association, but he did little better when he stood for Halifax two years later with their full support. It was a strange campaign, in a sound Nonconformist town, with three weeks of confident spiritual electioneering: 'My committee is composed almost wholly of religious men, who make every day's work a matter of prayer. I have had much talk with the different electors almost wholly upon spiritual subjects.'[61]

It did little earthly good. Miall split the Liberal vote, coming well behind Sir Charles Wood, the jittery but notable Whig candidate, and letting a Tory creep to the top of the poll who was so inarticulate that his victory speech collapsed into a rendering of 'Hearts of Oak'. For Miall there were only the vicarious satisfactions of seeing over sixty Nonconformist M.Ps in the new House, of knowing that twenty-six M.Ps were Anti-State Churchmen, and of having the young Charles Reed hail him as leader: 'If we cannot secure his return to Parliament this time, let us at least make it known, that he is the *adopted candidate of the Dissenters, to represent them as a body in the House of Commons.*'[62]

In the 1850s the cause perfected its political techniques and parliamentary strategy, changing its name and widening its basis in the process. In 1856 it appointed C. J. Foster as the salaried secretary of its Parliamentary Committee, and it developed after careful scrutiny of division lists and judicious choice of issues what amounted to a parliamentary whip. Miall himself entered Parliament for Rochdale in 1852, not merely one of a dozen Congregational M.Ps, but one of thirty-eight M.Ps representing a fifth of the electorate: a portentous statistic for reforming Nonconformists.

Miall was concerned as to his reception at Westminster, which was not a sympathetic place for middle-aged Nonconformists, and he confided in Henry Richard, who found him 'rather nervous about his first effort in Parliament, which he means — I think wisely — to postpone as long as he can, in order to understand the tone and spirit of his audience'.[63] No notorious political Nonconformist ever quite mastered that unique club's tone and spirit, but in one sense Miall need not have worried.

One of the notable parliamentary features of the years of equipoise was the amount of time spent debating ecclesiastical issues. Between the opening of the new session and Easter 1854, twenty-six out of fifty-four divisions on public matters were on ecclesiastical topics.[64] This reflected less the extent to which the ruling classes were at ease among themselves than their subjection to constant, principled scrutiny at their most vulnerable point. Equipoise does not mean repose. Miall set himself to a discreet exploitation of such issues. When he spoke it was on admitting Dissenters to Oxford or secularizing Church property in Canada or abolishing church rates. In the busily ecclesiastical session of 1854 he concerned himself with the Ministers' Money (Ireland) Bill, the Parliamentary Oaths Bill, the Colonial Clergy Disabilities Bill, the Episcopal and Capitular Estates Bill, the Church Building Acts Amendment Bill. He recovered in Switzerland.[65]

Above all he brought disestablishment into the sphere of serious politics. On 27 May 1856 he moved the consideration of 'the temporal provision made by law for religious teaching and worship in Ireland'. He spoke for two hours. The resolution was mistimed. It coincided with the Crimean victory celebrations and it had already been once postponed in favour of the Victory Review at Spithead. It was inevitable that it should fail, but to lose by 93 to 163 was marvellously encouraging. Great reforms had begun on less.

Miall's defeat in the 1857 election checked such hopes. It was only in March 1869 that he was again returned to Parliament, for Bradford. In between the Liberation Society celebrated its coming of age, and considered that it had secured the defeat of J. D. Coleridge, the Liberal candidate in the 1864 Exeter by-election, because he was unsound on church rates. But this was a negative thing, and so was Miall's return for Bradford, at the third attempt.

He was defeated at a by-election in October 1867 and at the General Election in November 1868. He was only successful following the unseating for bribery of one of the victors of 1868. Bradford Nonconformity had Baptist and Congregational theological colleges to give it backbone. The senior candidate in 1868 was W. E. Forster, an ex-Quaker equally opposed to disestablishment and educational voluntaryism.

Forster was strongly supported by the *Bradford Observer*, whose owner, William Byles, was a deacon of Horton Lane Congregational Church. There was a crypto-Tory candidate, H. W. Ripley, also once a pillar of Horton Lane. It was Ripley who was later unseated for bribery. Miall was the outsider, although his half-brother, James, was minister of Bradford's second Congregational Church, Salem, where the Byleses were also active.[66]

Thus the Bradford elections encompassed every shade of Nonconformist personality and politics, but they were primarily party political elections, with the standard ingredients of violence, drink and mud. Miallism was a gloss, devoted though its Bradford adherents were. They could not be ignored and they very properly made life miserable for Forster in the 1870s, but, should matters be pushed to conclusions, theirs was merely a destructive power.

The moral was driven home in Gladstone's first administration. On 9 May 1871, at tea time in a crowded House, driven to such action by the implications of Forster's Education Act, and after a series of rallies in large cities, Miall moved to disestablish the English Church. The Irish Church had fallen in 1869, its future the object of wide enthusiasm at the preceding General Election. Gladstone had engineered Irish disestablishment because it was politically imperative, but the Liberationists had brought it home to Westminster in the first place. They must do the same for the English Church. Miall envisaged an annual motion leading up to the next General Election at which the matter would be an unavoidable issue, rather like Baines's borough franchise motions of the early 1860s.

The 1871 debate was encouraging: packed front benches, speeches from Gladstone and Disraeli, for once in alliance, and from Henry Richard. As Miall rose to speak George Hadfield, the Congregationalist who sat for Sheffield, whispered, 'Miall, fear God, and you need not fear any man'. Thus braced Miall spoke to his belief that 'conscience and faith can no more be restrained within limits drawn around them by the law of man, than the dreams of childhood can be preserved under a glass shade'.[67]

He lost, of course, by 374 to 89. He lost again in 1872 by 295 to 96, and again in 1873 by 396 to 61. At first it looked as if the tactic might work. In 1871, 144 Liberals had absented themselves, unpaired, from the division and in 1872 only a third of Liberal M.Ps opposed him, the rest abstaining or voting with him. It really did seem, as *The Times* believed, that the Church of Cranmer and the Prayer Book would be a memory by the century's end. Yet the efforts were counter-productive. They did not reveal any political imperatives to Gladstone, and they provoked an effective response from the Church Defence Association.[68] Miall's health told increasingly against him and in 1873 he decided not to stand again at Bradford. By the end of 1874 he had effectively retired from politics.

Miall and the *Nonconformist* had done their work too well: they had left the Liberation Society high and dry. Not merely had Dissenting issues been brought into Westminster, Dissenting men had come as well. They were becoming accustomed to Westminster politics at the very moment that Westminster politics was beginning to accustom itself to the implications of a wide electorate and the accumulated legacy of decades of piecemeal legislation. Nationwide intervention on the part of government was now a fact. Miall's sharp insistence on first principles had done much to prepare Nonconformists for this and there were now fresh generations of theological students, their search for first principles excited by higher criticism, scientific advance, and the social need which these new vistas seemed also to reveal. The Liberal party was there for such men as Liberals as well as Nonconformists. They were tied to it. So, therefore, were the Liberationists: their cause was no longer a crotchet, but neither did it any longer set the pace.

And Miall had always been a full-bodied Radical. A measure of radicalism was built into the Liberationist stance, inasmuch as many Liberationist M.Ps were Manchester School men sitting for Manchester School seats. Miall himself sat for Rochdale, that most suggestive of constituencies, between 1852 and 1857. Whatever their views about the Church, such men were not to be ignored but largely because of those views they helped to bring two other groups into the coalition which masqueraded as Gladstonian Liberalism.

Miall played a significant part in enlisting the sympathies of Irish Catholic M.Ps in the struggle for disestablishment. The Maynooth controversies of the 1840s and 1850s did much to crystallize Miall's views about this. As a good voluntaryist he opposed the government grant to that Catholic seminary, but he disassociated himself from the campaign's crude no-popery, for Irish Catholics too suffered from the Anglican Establishment. When Irish disestablishment became a live issue in 1856 there was liaison with Irish Catholic supporters of the measure through J. O'Neill Daunt. Arthur Miall carefully referred to them as 'well-known Irish patriots of loyal disposition', but the liaison had more parliamentary significance for Liberals and Liberationists than this might suggest.[69]

There was also movement in Wales. In the autumn of 1862, as part of bicentennial enthusiasm, and again in the autumn of 1866, in the immediate context of the struggle for Reform and the longer context of twenty years of English Nonconformist concern and curiosity, Miall, Carvell Williams and Henry Richard visited Wales to further Liberalism and Liberation. At the General Election of 1868 Welsh parliamentary politics were transformed. Tory equality was turned into a Liberal preponderance, and if only three of the twenty-three victorious Liberals were Nonconformists, one of them was Miall's old crony, Henry Richard, who was elected for Merthyr Tydvil. Richard stood for the Peace Society in the public eye rather as Miall stood for disestablishment. They were both former Congregational ministers.[70]

There was more to Miall's radicalism than doing a good turn for up-to-date Liberalism by way of the Irish and Welsh, let alone Manchester School men. 'British Christianity is essentially the Christianity developed by a middle-class soil. . . . It aspires to be genteel rather than irresistible. . . . Its charity prefers foreign objects . . . it strikes one as an almost impenetrable mass of conventionalism.'[71] Miall aimed to penetrate the mass.

His views have been described as 'class-conscious Nonconformist Radicalism'.[72] So they were. He believed that the English middle classes held the key to the future, for they would have to decide whether to throw in their lot with the aristocracy or the people. 'The oligarchy must fall. It is with us at the present moment to determine whether it should fall by peaceful or by violent means.'[73] Violence lay with the aristocracy, and in the 1840s he was second to no Manchester Radical in his contempt for the old order, the 'Cardigans and Waterfords, the Palmerstons and Sibthorpes, the soldiers and the lawyers, the gamesters, duellists, and blacklegs of the upper and lower Houses of Parliament'.[74] Peace lay with the people. There must be fusion between the middle and working classes; and he expressed a sense of middle-class guilt not so very different from the confessions of sin voiced forty years later by Arnold Toynbee and his friends: 'whilst we attribute to the working men evil *designs*, they can charge us on evidence not to be pushed aside with evil *doings*.'[75]

His views on the fusion of classes, inspired partly by observation and experience, and partly by the firm conviction that an established church was a mere aristocratical engine, whose dismantling must have the widest implications, led him to espouse complete suffrage, sympathize with the Chartists, and fret at the inadequacy of the Anti-Corn Law Leaguers. 'The question is no longer one of party. With more than half of our population it is one of life or death.'[76]

His views about complete suffrage precisely indicated his radicalism. He believed that the vote was a natural right attaching to able-bodied men, not to property. He also believed that franchise extension on this level was an all-embracing issue which could appeal to working men on their own terms, offering a genuine basis of union between classes. Of course the result would be a virile public opinion braced by the more dynamic middle-class virtues, for all would be middle class now. So it was that Miall could be as voluntaryist as Edward Baines when it came to education, and as suspicious of the Ten Hours Movement as John Bright when it came to factory reform. These were incidental to his fundamental search for justice. He could also oppose capital punishment, advocate care and humanity in the punishing of delinquent children and condemn prohibitionist faddism. Not only were these matters incidentals in his search for justice, but they involved aspects of coercion which he found as repugnant as compulsion in education.[77]

The political expression of this was the formation of the Complete Suffrage Union in 1842, and the adoption of the *Nonconformist* as the suffrage movement's official organ. In 1845, when he stood for Southwark, it was his views on the suffrage together with his espousal of the other five points of the Charter which frightened away supporters: the addition of disestablishment as a seventh point did not mollify them. In 1848, when the virgin enthusiasms of the Charter and Complete Suffrage had long exploded, he concerned himself with the short-lived People's League.[78]

In the 1850s his radicalism, Church and State permitting, became more conventional, better judged by his support of specific issues than by a large perspective. He still supported suffrage reform ('Help forward the suffrage wherever you can, help forward the separation of Church and State ... but if you cannot do both, help forward the suffrage, and the other will be secured'),[79] he embraced financial reform, to which he added a far-away concern for India. The missionary enthusiasm of his denomination, the commercial interests of his constituents, the complex problems of religious equality in so tangled a continent, and the opportunities thus presented for bad government by the hangers-on of aristocratic England, made it a classic case for moral politics. Miall was among the thirty or so radical parliamentary supporters of the Indian Reform Society, established in 1853 and largely defunct by 1857. So were Apsley Pellatt, who had urged him to stand for Southwark in 1845, and George Hadfield, who whispered encouragement to him in the disestablishment debate of 1871. So was John Bright.[80]

It was on such issues that he was closest to Bright, with whom perhaps the public always associated him despite his feelings about the Anti-Corn Law League, and like Bright, he was defeated in the 1857 election. This was hard since his attitude to the Crimean War had been one of loyal distaste: if the thing had to be fought, it might as well be fought properly.[81]

He failed to fuse the classes. It did not prove possible in the 1840s to use Complete Suffrage as the means of reconciling Chartists and

Anti-Corn Law Leaguers. In the 1840s his views were sanguine for he was convinced that they were founded on natural justice. There was also an element of fear in them, and this hardened in succeeding years. In the 1840s he was sure that a cataclysm was upon us, and he found the prospect exciting. The Year of Revolutions was proof of this, and he visited Lamartine. The young R. W. Dale was particularly grateful for such an example.[82] In the 1870s Miall was no less certain of approaching crisis, but now he was less sanguine about the inevitable tornado, and his support of Reform during the whirlwind months in 1866-7 of the Liberal and Tory Reform Bills was conditioned by fear of explosion, or at least of working-class aggressiveness,[83] doubtless understandable when it is realized that between 1867 and 1868 his Bradford electorate bounced from 6,000 to over 20,000.

He was still radical enough. In 1866 he contributed to the *Commonwealth*, a working man's journal in which his son Arthur had an interest, and early in 1867 he chaired an unsectarian conference about artisans and the churches convened at the London Coffee House by Edward White, one of the rare occasions on which Miall came into contact with such men as Dean Stanley and F. D. Maurice. His victory at Bradford in 1869 was the excuse for the presentation of an address from 1,500 Bradford working men, and a library from Bradford women.[84]

The vigour, however, had gone. Radicalism had overtaken him and at Newcastle in 1871 he urged working men to turn to disestablishment, for they should expect little more social reform. 'We in this country are material enough. . . . There will be nothing so improving to the great working classes who have been brought into the fresh enjoyment of the franchise as to set them at once in pursuit of an enterprise that will lift their minds a little above wages and such like, and place them upon principles of higher value. . . .'[85] With this we are back to Haslam Mills's recollection of 1871 as middle-class England's brief encounter with paradise.

A recent scholar has commented that by the 1870s Miall's views of the relations between the middle and working classes had become very similar to his views of the objectionable relations between Whigs and Dissenters in the 1840s, with the working men now as the poor relations.[86] If this reflects a hardening of Miall's political arteries, it also reflects the extent to which he had become part of Gladstonian Liberalism, however tumultuous the lovers' quarrels.

Miall early admired Gladstone's high qualities. He admired his mastery of detail, and his eloquence. 'Nothing comes upon him unawares . . . even in committee, he often rises into eloquence', he felt in 1853.[87] If Mr Gladstone's patience and strength equalled his purpose and heart he would be the politician of the future, and nearly twenty years later, as M.P. for Bradford, Miall expressed the view that 'loyalty to Mr Gladstone, constituted, after all, the strongest weapon which the Government could command in their assault upon the strongholds of prejudice, injustice and ignorance'.[88]

Miall's was the most interesting accession to the Gladstonian camp, and despite rapid disillusion, he remained in that camp. Rebellion was for younger, healthier men. In September 1867 he felt that Gladstone's 'insights into the wants of the age may be trusted, we think, for correcting the prejudices of the school from which he emerged'. If events failed to bear him out, he still felt that Gladstone was more sinned against than sinning, and in November 1874 he blamed the Liberal defeat largely on 'the overbearing tone assumed by Trades Unions, the extensive strikes which have crippled many industrial interests: and the exclusive pretensions of various organizations of the working people'.[89]

Edward Miall's political career shows the extent to which any Nonconformist leader was tied willy-nilly to Liberalism. Nonconformist involvement at Westminster is difficult to assess. Members of Parliament who happened to be Nonconformists, and were most often Liberals, were tied to the party conventions appropriate for the times, yet the fact of their Nonconformity set them apart: it conditioned their thinking, and made them vulnerable to certain political pressures. M.Ps who were stridently Nonconformist were scarcely less tied if only because the successful pursuit of their particular crotchet normally demanded compromise with established forces. Either way they were best seen as representing an interest, in the old-fashioned parliamentary sense, one, moreover, which represented as many shades of opinion as there were Nonconformists. Miall's electoral experiences at Bradford were sufficient proof of that.

There could thus never be a national leader of Nonconformist politics. In many ways Miall approached this, and he was not replaced. Neither was he adequate in the role, for the very issue which made him prominent was too partial — and too demanding of his time and intellect — to give him wide influence. The same applied to Henry Richard: there were too many crotchets in the Peace and Liberation Societies.

Perhaps there were too many crotchets hidden in the Nonconformity of any Nonconformist M.P., but plenty of other factors made it unlikely that Nonconformists would ever find a satisfactory parliamentary leader. A political career demanded a large income, and many of the best-known Nonconformist M.Ps were men whose formative years had been spent in business, and who came late to Parliament. They had been given a sound commercial education but the abilities which made for commercial fortunes were not best suited for Westminster politics. It was a classical education which caught the spirit of parliamentary debate. Classically educated M.Ps possessed the rounded ease of amateurs; the rest were merely amateurish.

Personality, age, education and Nonconformity combined with ill-luck, because at least one Nonconformist politician flickers bravely as an 'if' of history. From 1867 to 1873 Henry Winterbotham was M.P. for Stroud. He was a young man, soundly educated for a professional career, a barrister with a reputation at the Chancery Bar. He was the son of a provincial banker, the grandson of a Baptist minister who had been imprisoned for sedition in the brave 1790s. He belonged to an active family of Baptists and Congregationalists, whose contacts placed him at the heart of orthodox Dissent. Winterbothams were prominent in the chapels of Stroud and Cheltenham and Kensington.

In Parliament he made his name as a radical and Nonconformist, active in criticizing Forster's Education Bill. In March 1871 he became Undersecretary of State to the Home Department; at the age of thirty-four he had the prospect of an assured political career, accumulating experience in high office. These were opportunities denied to most Nonconformists. Little came of it. He overworked, and died in December 1873. In Rome.[90]

Winterbotham belonged to that mainstream section of Nonconformity whose religious loyalty was a matter of personal, evangelical, commitment. It was a question of conversion. Bright and Chamberlain, the two most prominent Nonconformists in Victorian politics did not belong to mainstream Nonconformity, and perhaps this would have precluded John Bright from assuming the role of leader of political Nonconformity, even had his personal decision not come into it. As it was he made an indifferent politician when it came to high office, with his patchy education, his temperament and his ill health. Similarly Joseph Chamberlain, as a Unitarian, lacked that evangelical compulsion which might have given him a fuller understanding of his Nonconformist constituency, and a personal cohesion. There was more to Nonconformity than radicalism born of social discrimination, and an ability to organize.

At the core of Edward Miall's life, however, was his conversion experienced as an eighteen year old in 1827. However worldly the wing of Nonconformity which he represented his own passion was religious first and last. How could the Evangelical's encounter with God be fully realized amidst the constraints of an Establishment? How could one support an established church as essential to faith if it took an episcopalian form in one part of the British Isles and a presbyterian form in another? How could one contemplate raising the daemon of the people without faith in God, and what other than faith would permit the moralizing of such a people? Miall's public life was an answer to these private questions.

Miall's family life provides another answer, for it shows the extent to which the minister was a social catalyst. The Mialls came from the middle classes' lower edges, but Edward married the niece of Dr Morell, his college principal, which placed him firmly within the ministerial classes: at least nine of his wife's immediate kinsmen were Congregational ministers.

The ministerial classes were also the teaching and communicating classes. Edward Miall's brother Charles, his son Arthur, and his son-in-law H. S. Skeats were literary Nonconformists of mild note; a nephew was Professor of Biology at Yorkshire College, Leeds, a great-nephew worked on the *Leeds Mercury* and another was a parliamentary candidate in 1906. The links become more enticing. Edward's brother, James Goodeve Miall, ministered at Salem, Bradford, from 1837. In 1861 he was Chairman of the Congregational Union and he retired from Salem in 1875, the year after Edward ceased to be Bradford's M.P. James Miall likewise married into the ministerial classes: three of his wife's immediate connexions were Congregational ministers. She was also an aunt of Sir Morell Mackenzie, the fashionable — indeed notorious — surgeon, a great-aunt of Compton Mackenzie the novelist, and a first cousin once removed of John Addington Symonds and Mrs T. H. Green. Kinship brought the Mialls strangely close to the Arnoldian world of sweetness, light and Oxford. Indeed, Mrs Edward Miall's cousin, J. D. Morell, was an inspector of schools from 1848 to 1876, his appointment preceding Matthew Arnold's by three years.[91]

Such connexions lend weight to Maynard Keynes's feeling, based partly on the early Anglican life of Mary Paley Marshall and partly on his own respectably Nonconformist background, that 'perhaps no one who was not brought up as an evangelical or a nonconformist is entitled to think freely in due course. . . .'[92]

Chapter 6

Connexions and Consequences.
A Country Election in 1885

Now boys this is Mr Cozens-Hardy and we mean to return him to Parliament, he will say a few words to you and we will give him 3 cheers.

(The Master of Hevingham Reformatory addressing his boys during the election campaign of November 1885.)

The General Election of 1885 has been overshadowed by more famous contests, rather as the Third Reform Act, of which the 1885 election was the first test, has yet to receive the attention accorded to its predecessors. Yet this Reform Act had profound implications for British politics and the election should have suggested the pattern which would emerge. Indeed it would have done so had not Home Rule for Ireland, in its coincidence with particular personalities and tendencies, twisted politics for the next four decades. However, this should not detract from the interest of the election or from its individual contests. One of these might be selected for its textbook quality: it should have been a pattern for other places and subsequent occasions.

This particular contest was in a new, completely rural, division. The result hinged on the new voters, most of them farm labourers. What sensitive Victorians long feared had happened: the classes were swamped by the masses. Save that it was not like that. The franchise was still based on property. There were still millions of able-bodied voteless men. The working of the electoral system still discriminated against truly popular politics, and perhaps against Radical politics.[1]

Yet in one respect Liberal politics, whether or not it was Radical politics, did not suffer. The people who benefited most from the Second and Third Reform Acts were those caught between the middle and lower middle classes. Proportionately they were a powerful segment of the electorate, but their real importance lay in their position as political initiators at the local level. It was here that Nonconformist Liberalism almost came into its own. If the Liberalism of the middle classes was not always to be counted upon, that of middle-class Nonconformists was

125

more dependable and so their place in local Liberal hierarchies was assured. These were the men who made Miallism a force in Bradford in the 1870s, or formed the bulk of Leeds town councillors in the 1890s. These were the office-holders of the large chapels of London suburbs. Even in country areas, even before county councils, such men came into their own. This was the substance of that celebrated mirage, the 'Nonconformist Conscience', the phrase coined in a correspondence to *The Times* during the Parnell affair, and seized as his own by Hugh Price Hughes.[2]

It was, nonetheless, a mirage. Like any other act of Parliament the Reform Act of 1884 was the product of circumstances prevailing at the time in Westminster. It was the product of 'high politics', perhaps of the alliances and dispositions of several hundred politicians, certainly of a few dozen of them. The implications of this were less narrow than might seem at first sight, since parliamentary sessions were shorter in the 1880s, and parliamentarians led expansive lives. Even the Westminster pursuits were not to be entirely divorced from the softer obligations of clubs or the duties of Society.

None of this, however, left much room for Nonconformist considerations. This was manifest enough in the next two decades of Westminster politics, whatever the skirmishings over education or Welsh disestablishment, because at Westminster party lines had been conveniently deflected by the impact of Ireland. When Westminster's Irish ripples reached the shores of an electorate, irritated but not unduly put out by Irish squabbles or Parnell's immorality, it was as if an unusually unkind trick had been played on Liberalism's Nonconformist activists.

The favourable circumstances of the 1885 election were not to be repeated until 1906; then alone was the Third Reform Act vindicated. In between, despite twenty years of Free Churchmen's activity on town councils, county councils, parish councils and school boards, there had also been twenty years of Conservative parliamentary preponderance, of economic change and international pressures, of social gospels and novel theologies. The electorate was twenty years larger and twenty years more working class, and society was twenty years wider. The ambitions and strategies of late Victorian Westminster translated to electoral level contributed to an atmosphere which was as favourable to new movements as to the steady work of buffeted Free Churchmen. In any case buffeted Free Churchmen were no more than a collection of perplexed, if professionally sentient, individuals. They were as fully capable as any other articulate individuals of adapting to new circumstances, but they no longer had the advantage which should have been theirs in 1885. The next Reform Act — which came in 1918 — or a cataclysm — which came in 1914 — would show this beyond any shadow of doubt.

If this means that the election of 1885, at which an interesting number of Nonconformist politicians were blooded, was merely a museum curiosity, it also means that it is important in assessing the extent of Nonconformist prospects. Hence the interest of one of the contests of that election, and the value of setting it in the context of the Third Reform Act.

There was an inevitability, no doubt misleading, about franchise reform in the 1880s. Ever since the 1867 Reform Act had brought the towns into their political own, the position of the counties had been grotesquely anomalous, and the publication early in 1884 of the 1881 census returns added fuel to the fire. The anomalies were pointed out. The old, careful, balance of borough seats and county seats was seen to be a careful imbalance. It was also clear that population changes were such that any reform would be a complicated business necessitating a considerable redistribution of constituencies.

Between 1883 and 1894 five Acts, four of them Gladstonian, accomplished this reform.[3] Their cumulative effect was profound, not least, although least investigated, on local politics.

It is arguable that party politics turned more rapidly into class politics; that provincial English politics gave way to centralized English politics, but that Celtic politics was temporarily strengthened. The politics of suburbia was certainly strengthened, and one-tenth of Commons seats were now for London's suburbia. The Irish and Radicals were immediately satisfied, although Parnell and Chamberlain had at first seen little benefit in further franchise reform. The Whigs almost disappeared, although Whiggishness in politics is indestructible.

All this is arguable. What is certain is the physical impact of the Acts of 1884 and 1885. The Representation of the People Act, 1884, established a uniform household and lodger franchise throughout the United Kingdom. This meant, if they troubled to register, two million new electors. The following year's redistribution of seats ensured that seventy-nine small boroughs lost their seats; that thirty-six moderately small constituencies lost one of their two seats; and that almost all of the remaining two-member constituencies were carved into single-member *divisions* roughly equal in size.[4]

The implications were tremendous. It was not merely that there was now a mass electorate with a working-class base, although universal manhood suffrage was still over thirty years off and there were still millions of unenfranchised males. It was certainly not simply that town and country were now on an equal footing, since what had really happened was that at Westminster their roles were reversed, and town was king. It was rather that the electoral system had been re-created. Constituencies were now *divisions*: the very word had an artificial sound. These divisions were angled towards Westminster and they required a similarly angled political organization. Nothing in the structure was specially designed to foster traditionary or local influences. It was this which makes the legislation of 1884-5 important in its own right.

But how had the game (for so it is at Westminster) been played to produce this result? In a waspish, commonsensical, illuminating book Andrew Jones portrays the Third Reform Act as the result of a match played according to the subtly shifting rules of a purely political Westminster game by a group of select and dexterous professionals, uncomplicated by spectators, and not unduly hampered by symptoms of team spirit.[5]

At least this explains the cliché about Parliament being a superb club. It puts into words what gentlemen do in clubs once past the porter and of an active turn of mind. For this is how any Bill, whether for plumbers or peers, actually emerges.

The game began with Gladstone's victory in 1880, with over a third of Liberals in the new Commons having mentioned Reform in their electoral propaganda. Reform was no longer a crotchet. It had become inevitable. Neither its timing nor its nature, however, was inevitable, for Reform was best not seen as an *immediate* goal since tactics suggested that the close of Parliament, a political eternity away, was the sensible time for it. It would be a prelude to the next General Election.

Thus the conventions of the game were formulated, and a Franchise Bill was introduced in February 1884. Its most obvious feature was that it applied uniformly to the United Kingdom. This time there were not to be separate, carefully arranged bills for the Celtic fringe, and Ulster was treated with happy disregard. Ireland's place in the Bill was its most portentous aspect, and yet the measure had a curiously tranquil passage in a Commons which had been overburdened with Irish matters, and conflict with the Lords was avoided, after some rather stagey skirmishing, by tea-table negotiations with the Tory leaders, chiefly over the timing and extent of that redistribution of seats on which Conservatives now relied for comfort.

It was cleverly done. The crotcheteers, the men of conscience and principle, were encircled and Gladstone's dexterity as an old parliamentary hand was seen at its spryest. He isolated Hartington, the Whig leader, he satisfied Parnell and Chamberlain, he impressed the bishops. He captivated his backbenchers with his visions of a truly conservative reform which he then characterized as radicalism of purest essence. He did this at the tail-end of an administration since regarded as a melancholy succession of misadventures. The achievement was remarkable, not least when described in its own language: politics.

Most games depend on the personalities of the players, all of whom sooner or later, if only at general elections, are at the mercy of real life. At some point issues must impinge and in the 1880s there were issues and to spare. This was made clear in a scurrilous, enjoyable piece of Tory propaganda, printed in Tory red by William Blackwood and Sons: *A Diary of the Gladstone Government*, Fortieth Thousand, Price sixpence.

It began with a motto: ' "Liberalism is a policy of noble sentiments, of superfine professions, of exalted motives, of plausible platitudes. It appeals to the ear alone; it professes to believe that the world is better than it is, and that we are better than the world. It does little and costs much", *and it may be concealed beneath an umbrella.*'[6] That umbrella was the *Diary*'s motif. The pamphlet was illustrated by cartoons featuring two villains. Joseph Chamberlain was one. The other was Mr Gladstone, usually clutching an ill-furled gamp.

The parliamentary party, which on 1 April 1880 — All Fools' Day — flocked under that umbrella, was a strange coalition of Whigs, Radicals and Irish Home Rulers. Together they swamped the Tories, but togetherness was not their chief virtue. Nonetheless this coalition was reflected in an outstanding administration — any government which at various times included Gladstone, Dilke, Harcourt, Fawcett, Rosebery, Bright, Hartington and Chamberlain was a remarkable concoction — unless like the *Diary*, one applied Harcourt's dismissive phrase: 'a mere chaos of fortuitous atoms.'[7]

The preliminaries over, the *Diary* went to town on Egypt, the Sudan, South Africa, Ireland, and Charles Bradlaugh the 'atheist', all heaven-sent opportunities for Tory apologists. Wherever possible it relied on a misuse of Liberal words, exploiting the loquacity of the Gladstonian age. Gladstone himself was fair game, that Gilbertian

> . . . grand and verbose old man
> A spout as-he-goes old man
> A highly sophistical,
> Non-atheistical,
> 'Come-under-my-Gamp' old man.[8]

His absence in August 1884 from the Jubilee of the Abolition of Slavery allowed for the resurrection of the Gladstone family's slave-holding connexions and an apt quotation from the Grand Young Man: 'Are not Englishmen to retain a right to *their own honestly and legally acquired* property?' There was happy play with his exuberant verbosity: 'Last session Mr Gladstone was on his legs 178 times and his speeches occupy about 180 columns of *The Times*. In single column they would reach to the top of the Monument.'[9] By association they compared him to the Channel Tunnel ('Another big bore shut up'[10]); and there were statistics to display.

It was, for example, noted that if Gladstone's Liberal Cabinet and Salisbury's brief Tory Cabinet of 1885 contained an equal number of peers (eight in each), the 'people's' peers held more church livings, their families extorted more pensions and their estates engrossed a higher rental than those of the Conservative peers.[11] When Gladstone spoke of the improved state of Irish affairs it was noted that between January and March 1880 (that is, in the last months of Disraeli's government), there had been 294 Irish murders and outrages, while from January to March 1882 there were 1,417.[12] When Chamberlain celebrated British prosperity it was noted that in five years of Disraelite government, from 1875 to 1879, only 622,515 British subjects emigrated, while in five Gladstonian years, from 1880 to 1884, the number was 1,312,207.[13]

Parliamentary reform was absent from this fun. It was doubtless no business of Tories to draw attention to Liberal vote-catchers; and the fact that the whole business ended in a Liberal deal with Tory leaders was no part of partisan electioneering. So the *Diary* contented itself with a restrained comment for February 1884: 'After four years' delay, the Franchise becomes a good umbrella to hide foreign muddles.'[14] Reform appeared merely as a run of the mill incident in an administration already rocked by catastrophe, and when the Government fell in June 1885 the event was portrayed in purely political terms as the Grand Old Skipper scuttling the ship in the absence of the crew.

Thus the politicians and the propagandists; at what point do they coincide with the people? One answer is at the point of a general election. The Franchise Bill received the Royal Assent on 6 December 1884. Five days later a Parliamentary Commission began to investigate the constituencies as the prelude to a Redistribution Bill, which in turn received Royal Assent on 25 June 1885. Two days before that, following a Liberal defeat on an amendment to the budget, the Conservative leader, Lord Salisbury, had accepted office as head of a minority administration. In November, when the new registers were ready, a general election was held.

Here there would certainly be dialogue between politicians and 'the people'. Hitherto there had been little dialogue: any popular agitation about the Bill or the peers' opposition to it had been late and rather contrived. At election time, however, games and realities must coincide. Politicians emerged from Westminster to confront other politicians who were new to the game or had long been excluded from it. None could discount the electorate. If the form of the Third Reform Act depended upon 'the subtleties of political persuasion practised by men whose life was this art',[15] then the implications of that Act, channelled through the vulgar language of election politics, would determine the future subtleties of electoral persuasion.

In 1885 a few things at least were clear: new registers must be compiled; the larger part of the new voters would be agricultural employees; there must be an adequate organization to deal with this. The parliamentary game becomes lost in the bustle of an election in which the lives of men — and women — as yet unblessed by the light of retrospect are intimately involved. And what if among them were Nonconformists, part of a connexion of attitudes seldom grasped even by their chosen leaders at Westminster, and not easily reflected in redistribution acts, let alone Tory propaganda?

North Norfolk was entirely rural, a pleasant landscape of large farms and politically amiable landowners. There were no large towns, although places like Holt or Aylsham contained that leaven of respectable schools, circulating libraries, professional people and tradesmen which distinguished urban life properly understood. There were no factories. The coast line provided the chief sources of variety: fish and fashion. The fishermen of Wells and Cley and the genteel visitors to Sheringham and Cromer lightly complicated any electoral calculations.[16]

The division had been part of a larger North Norfolk, one of the county seats created in the wake of the Second Reform Act. This North Norfolk had been steadily Tory although Sir Fowell Buxton, the Liberal candidate at by-elections in 1876 and 1879, attributed his defeats to Yarmouth Toryism outweighing village Liberalism.[17]

In 1885 the constituency was much truncated. Its easterly portions fed the new divisions of Yarmouth and East Norfolk, and what remained was merely one of the six divisions into which the old Norfolk county seats had been distributed. The electorate of the new North Norfolk was 9,924. Its population was 51,072. What had formed part of a county seat, once regarded as the chief repository of freeborn opinion, but latterly preserved as a bulwark of the landed interest against the pretensions of a new and bourgeois society, now became simply a country seat; a division like any other, which happened to be rural, while Yarmouth, for example, happened to be urban.[18] The political content of this division was, as yet, guesswork.

Yarmouth was supposedly Tory. So, it was considered, were the fishermen and fashionables elsewhere on the coast, and the closed little society of Aylsham.[19] The labourers, however, were anybody's guess. Mr Gladstone had protested that their deferential vote would balance the roaring democrats in the cities. Norfolk retained a residuum of Liberal landowners. The Earl of Kimberley was in Gladstone's Cabinet. Others, like Lords Leicester and Suffield, tended to be non-political. That is to say, they exerted no improper pressure on their tenants. What held for the peerage held also for lesser grandees, particularly in North Norfolk. Already Fowell Buxton's agent had found that the villages were Liberal: he meant farmers and village tradesmen. What of the labourers?

Fortune favoured the Liberals. The division was already controlled by shrewed party managers, who might rely on the deference of the tenants of Liberal landlords and hope for bloody-mindedness from those of Tories. Above all there was the comfort that chapel was Liberalism at prayer. In North Norfolk chapel was strong and remained so despite the pressures of agricultural distress and emigration.

In Norfolk chapel usually meant Methodists. In North Norfolk the varieties of Methodism were strikingly significant for a rural area. The Primitive Methodists were probably most numerous; their strength lay traditionally among the labourers. The Wesleyans were the longest established and the weakest; they had not recovered from the disruptions of mid-century. The edge was provided by the United Methodist Free Churches, children of the disruption, who in Holt were the dominant Methodist society, articulate as disrupters should be and in the more general sense political. There were also a few very small Methodist societies which had remained aloof from the United Methodist Free Churches.

If membership totals are taken together, they would of course form a small proportion of the electorate: after all, subtract the women and how many remained?[20] But the strength of Nonconformity could not lie in its stated membership. Rather it offered an alternative establishment whose attitudes it articulated; and established attitudes permeate. This was the importance of Nonconformity and especially of Methodism, which was here less moulded by Wesleyan inwardness, in North Norfolk.

The ideal Liberal candidate for such a division would be an unlikely fellow. He would be rich, for there could be little guarantee of expenses paid; of the landed interest, preferably with local connexions; sensibly radical, with an eye to the labourers. He would need to be a Methodist, but well inclined to the rest of Nonconformity.

Such a man was swiftly found. Herbert Cozens-Hardy was a London barrister living in Ladbroke Grove, with a growing practice at the Equity Bar. His father, W. H. Cozens-Hardy, was squire of Letheringsett, one mile from Holt, and owned nearly 3,000 acres.[21] His elder brother, Clement, farmed at Cley Hall, four miles away, on the coast. A younger brother, Theobald, farmed extensively near Norwich. Herbert Cozens-Hardy was both sensible (he was, quite simply, a nice man, and he remained so) and sensibly radical. He was no longer a Methodist, but his parents and Clement were Free Methodists while he had moved towards Congregationalism. His wife came from a Baptist family.

On the Hardy side his family came from Yorkshire. On the Cozens side they had farmed for generations in Norfolk. They had lived in Letheringsett since the late eighteenth century, and the complicated accidents of birth, marriage and death had resulted, as with the Pattissons of Witham, in the accumulation of a considerable property. What had started as a capitalistic enterprise — a village brewery with a few dozen acres of land — became a sizeable agricultural estate. Letheringsett assumed the aspect of an estate village. The surrounding hills were planted with trees, the Hall was dignified by a ponderous Greek colonnade, and the road through the village was diverted to enlarge the mansion's pleasure grounds. A bridge was built. Cottages were improved. In the 1820s the scene delighted William Cobbett. By the 1880s the estate was in its prime.

With the big house close to the churchyard wall and the parish church with the round flint tower and its Butterfield porch all as it should be, there was nothing to suggest that the family at the Hall were ever other than pillars of the order so carefully established in Church and State. But they were Nonconformists, their Nonconformity distinguishing them from County Society as then conceived. They were not isolated from it in any superficial way, but they did not marry into it. The Cozens-Hardys were part of a small, almost unclassable, group in county life largely ignored by the historian: the Nonconformist landowner.

They had moved to Letheringsett in the 1780s. So had Wesleyanism. With the connexional disruptions in the 1850s, however, W. H. Cozens-Hardy emerged as a leader among the seceders: for the rest of his life he sat on the Connexional Committee of the Methodist Free Churches. He dominated the Holt Free Methodists and he was chiefly responsible for their chapel, an inescapable building in streaky-bacon Gothic, which commands one entrance to the town as the parish church commands the other.[22]

William Hardy Cozens-Hardy was a man of pronounced opinions. He had succeeded to the various portions of his kinsmen's properties and consolidated them. He was prominent in his denomination and a man of note in his locality. He epitomized the political classes.

The family had once supported Coke of Norfolk at county elections. In the 1790s Cozens relatives, who were Baptists in Norwich, had been ardent reformers.[23] By the 1840s William Cozens-Hardy was a Dissenter for the new age, hot and strong against the establishment. In 1847 his name appeared on a list of possible Dissenting candidates compiled before the General Election.[24] The enthusiasm was transmitted to his children. All save Agnes, the spinster daughter, married into families with Nonconformist connexions, present or passing, and so encompassed horizons beyond the confines of local County Society. The boys went to Amersham Hall, the Baptist school near Reading in the tradition of Carver's at Melbourn or Barbauld's at Palgrave, with a reputation for humanity, learning, and that freedom which comes from a proper understanding of discipline.

Clement, the eldest, was to inherit the bulk of the Hardy estates and to continue the brewing connexions. Theobald, the third boy, took over the old Cozens property at Sprowston. They were Liberals and Dissenters, cricket-loving men, devoted to shooting and rural pursuits, active on the Bench and, when it came, the County Council. Both married Huddersfield girls, Wrigleys, so forging links with Free Trade, wool trade, doctrinaire Liberalism. Sydney, the youngest son, embodied the teetotal spirit more usually associated with Nonconformity. He built up a strong solicitor's practice in Norwich and played an honourable part in the exuberant public life of that cathedral city. His wife's family were Mancunians who had moved out to Wilmslow. In them cotton balanced wool: their circle included the Armitages, Rigbys, Haworths and others of Manchester's 'cottontots'.[25]

Of the girls, two, Cecilia and Kathleen, strengthened the Huddersfield connexion. They in turn married a woolstapling kinsman of the Wrigleys, James Willans. Kathleen's marriage, in Switzerland, contravened English law, but marriage to a deceased wife's sister was an illegality condoned by many Free Churchmen prosperous enough to afford a ceremony abroad. For some it assumed the aura of principle. Willans collected butterflies and stood for an advanced shade of Congregationalism. His father and an elder brother had been parliamentary candidates and his nephew, Herbert Henry Asquith, by 1885 had already refused invitations to stand in the Liberal interest.[26]

It was Caroline, the eldest daughter, one of those enviable women whose appearance is lost in personality, who married most advantageously. In 1856 she married a family connexion, Jeremiah James Colman, head of the Norwich side of the mustard and starch business. A Baptist until the 1870s, when he became a Congregationalist, he was intimate with the national leaders of those denominations. As the leading figure in the chapel and business life of Norwich and Norfolk, it was natural that he should lead in its political life. Since 1871 he had sat for

Norwich. At Westminster he was an unswerving Gladstonian. In Norfolk he was worth more to the cause than any of those peers or country gentlemen who still added an apparently indispensable gloss to local Liberal politics.

It is here that Herbert Cozens-Hardy's candidature assumes its chief interest. Herbert had been unusually close to 'Cary' Colman in his formative years. Subsequently an affinity had developed with his younger brother, Sydney.

Sydney had practised in Norwich since 1873. From 1877 he acted as Joint Registration Agent for the old North Norfolk constituency, and in 1880 he was Jeremiah Colman's election agent in Norwich. He had an unassailable reputation for honesty. It was natural, therefore, that the attention of Jeremiah and Sydney should turn towards Herbert, with his London connexions and legal reputation.

Jeremiah broached the matter in the spring of 1879: Herbert should stand for Ipswich, which had a strong Nonconformist interest, though no family links. Herbert was attracted. His wife, Maria, was 'by no means opposed to ambitious views and would gladly see me in the House'. There was no political difficulty. 'My convictions as a Liberal and as a Dissenter are growing year by year more deeply rooted.'[27] But there were financial obstacles, and he turned it down.

Herbert's was a recent prosperity in 1879. His first years at the Bar, since his call in 1862, had been suitably spartan. When he married and set up house in one of Notting Hill's duller roads, his professional income amounted to little more than £100, supplemented privately.[28] By 1870, however, his professional income reached 1,000 guineas and ten years later it approached 5,000 guineas. Herbert was a prudent man; 'We have never lived up to our income, and the last few years I have been able to lay aside considerable sums.'[29]

He believed, however, that he could not enter Parliament without taking silk, which was a gamble likely at first to entail loss of income.[30] He was not prepared to take this step, let alone the worry of a constituency where, in addition to his election expenses and the necessity of heading the subscription lists of every good (and Liberal) cause, he would have to pay an agent for the annual registration of electors, a vexatious burden in rural or contentious constituencies.

He took silk in 1882. His practice did not suffer[31] and the Corrupt Practices Act of 1883 with its limit on election expenditure smoothed the way for those with strong views on such matters.

At this point the story is best told by his wife, a cultivated Londoner, nicknamed Vesuvius by her family,[32] whom a late marriage had preserved from a nervy spinsterhood. 'Early in the year 1885, we, i.e. my husband and myself, were startled one morning at breakfast by receiving a letter from Sydney.'[33] Its burden was a request that Herbert stand for North Norfolk. Sydney had deftly brought Maria into the picture, 'for my husband said that he could take no important step without my consent'. Herbert accepted, subject to a unanimous invitation.

The initial steps were soon over. There was a visit to Warlies, the Essex seat of Sir Fowell Buxton, who waived his prescriptive right to the candidature explaining that he could not stand against his cousin, Samuel Hoare, the Tory candidate.[34] Then, in May, there was a visit to the constituency to stay at Bolwick Hall with the leading local Buxton and to be vetted at Aylsham by the Liberal Hundred. 'Of Disestablishment he said, that by birth, by education and by conviction he was a Nonconformist and in favour of disestablishment but that he should not vote for it, until it was brought forward as a government measure — this is the view now generally taken by Liberal candidates.' Such safe straightforwardness gratified the Aylsham Liberals who selected him unanimously.

The campaign began properly on 15 September with a Reception Meeting in Norwich. The Cozens-Hardys stayed at Carrow with the Colmans. 'Herbert spoke well.' There followed three months of electioneering less to attract old faithfuls or reassure wavering notables than to educate the new electors in the mysteries of the ballot, to take care that the Corrupt Practices Act was not infringed and to see that the electors knew where they stood about intimidation. Apart from a break at the end of October and early in November and, of course, Sundays, meetings were now a daily occurrence: at Binham, Corpusty, Kelling, Hindolveston, Bawdeswell, an endless litany of Norfolk place-names. But there was a pattern to it all.

The traditional courtesies of an election campaign of the more decent sort continued unquestioned, and a round of visits to the still numerous Liberal gentry accompanied each meeting. The Buxtons headed the list. Sir Fowell, for all his delicacy about standing and his reputation for being a platform 'wet blanket', came up from Warlies and spoke or chaired meetings with the best of them. So did his brother Francis, who could be so long-winded that Fowell had to tug at his coat tails. The most agreeable Buxtons were the Louis Buxtons at Bolwick: 'they are very pleasant simple people — the simplicity of everything struck me very much — no grand dinners, everything studiously quiet and in good taste. Mrs Buxton is a clever woman and very particular about her children. . . . The house is nice — there is a large carpetted hall as you enter where prayers are always held every morning. The garden is well kept.'

The most formidable Buxton was the Dowager Lady Buxton, of Colne near Cromer. By birth a Gurney and daughter-in-law of Emancipator Buxton, she 'trusted that whatever the result of the election all would be for the glory of God'. Luncheon with her was simplicity itself: a tiny piece of roast mutton, stewed plums from the previous day's meat tea, and a pudding. The ramifications of her clan were endless. J. H. Gurney of Hill House, Southrepps, was visited, and chaired a meeting. The Joneses of Cranmer Hall, near Fakenham ('very pleasant simple people') were particularly accommodating, and there was Hugh Barclay of Baconsthorpe and old Mr Upcher of Sheringham. But it was from beyond this circle that the most notable accession and some irritation came to the cause.

The irritation came when Lord Wodehouse, the Earl of Kimberley's heir, who was due to take the chair at Mundesley, telegraphed that

he had missed his train . . . of course we knew that it was an intentional missing. Lord Wodehouse has acted very strangely about the candidate for E. Norfolk — having been very candid about Mr Lee Warner, and then suddenly turning round and saying he could not vote for him so that Mr Lee Warner was not chosen by the caucus. Then Lord Wodehouse brings forward a candidate whom no one knows. Mr P. Falk, a German who cannot speak English at all hardly or at least well. The whole Buxton clan are very angry.[35]

Despite this aristocratic caprice, and the wind and rain which battered a rickety tent, the meeting ended heartily, with cheers for Mr Gladstone, Mr Cozens-Hardy, and '3 for Mrs Cozens-Hardy'.

The accession came from the new squire of Felbrigg. The Kettons of Felbrigg were Tories, but now Robert Ketton came forward as a Radical full of sympathy for the agricultural labourer. Early in October the Cozens-Hardys dined with him and his sister. His drawing-room was adorned with Liberal bills while his gateposts were painted Liberal blue. Later in November Maria heard him address 500 people at Aldborough: but Ketton was 'either twirling his moustache or twiddling his coat button the whole time as usual. I should like to send him Miss Edgeworth's Frank'. Perhaps these were signs of that nervousness which developed into eccentricity and seclusion. Mr Ketton's energetic Liberalism came to little.[36]

It was of course the candidate's own family and connexions which gave the campaign its distinctive edge. Maria and her sister-in-law Agnes tirelessly attended the meetings. The presence of ladies at such times was a delicate issue and Maria noted that the presence of Buxton ladies at Runton overawed the audience who 'were too silent, too well-behaved'. Their children were another matter. Hope was too young but Katharine and Edward were brought up from London whenever school permitted

137

and Willie, in his final year at University College School, entered fully into the delights of electioneering. He spoke at village meetings, often with his grandfather Cozens-Hardy — a neat contrast — and he explained the intricacies of the ballot 'very well indeed with ease and clearness a good many remarks were made about it afterwards'.

At the other end of the scale old William Cozens-Hardy, with Clement and Theobald, and James Willans and one of the Wrigleys from Huddersfield, played their part. Maria fretted about her father-in-law. He liked to fight the ruder battles of earlier years and Maria had to talk to him about it. Clement on the other hand, whose wife inclined to the Church and modelled her politics accordingly, bore up admirably. At Cley he was naturally in his element.

'The granary on the Quay was very nicely decorated with flags, and evergreens, and sunflowers, the latter rather a Tory colour. Clement took the chair. He spoke very well, but long, and in such a funereal tone, that it nearly made me laugh. We teased Helen, and asked her how she could listen to such doctrines as Disestablishment — exclusion of Bishops from the House of Lords etc. Indeed she was heard to hiss once.' It was a splendid meeting, with jokes about Joe, the local 'character', who had paraded Cley during the 1880 county election in his donkey cart, with the beast resplendent in Tory colours. As he explained, 'only donkeys wear those'. Billy Bastard, a retired sea captain, and a liability at such times, started up a loud 'for he's a jolly good fellow'.[37]

Two barrister friends of Herbert Cozens-Hardy came down from London. Nathaniel Micklem, President of the Oxford Union in Asquith's decade, had read in Herbert's chambers: he was to be one of the Liberal M.Ps of 1906. W. H. Gurney Salter, of the family of Parliamentary Shorthand Writers, had been at Amersham Hall with Herbert, and later became a fellow member at Kensington Chapel. They came from that group of metropolitan Baptist and Congregational families to which Maria belonged. Inevitably they added to the Nonconformist bias in the campaign.

Salter spoke at Oulton in the Congregational Chapel whose origins recalled the times when Cromwell's kinsmen, the Fleetwoods, lived in the neighbourhood. The party had to provide their own candles for the little brass holders on top of the pews. 'It was an old chapel some wooden inlaid work on the wall at the back of the pulpit, like my secretary [i.e. secretaire] at home, the pews high and square we all sat in the table pew. . . .'

Salter was 'much struck with the good English used by the speakers two of whom were working men and local preachers the third a small farmer. They referred to Herbert as a God fearing man — to the knowledge they had of his family and their belief that the candidate was a chip of the old block'. It was at such times that gold was struck: the small men, beloved of the self-helpers, the men made articulate by Nonconformity, devoid of clap-trap, after whom the newly enfranchised masses were less worrying for moderate folk. At Foulsham militant Dissent had been represented by Mr Freeman, a Baptist preacher who spoke energetically. At Aldborough it was Maria's turn to be impressed by the working men, their good English breaking through their Norfolk brogue. She attributed it to the influence of Methodist local preachers, and at supper she sat amongst such a family: 'thoroughly superior people.'

There were few jarring notes. At Baconsthorpe, where 'the audience were requested not to applaud with their feet, lest the room should descend', Herbert was hailed as the working man's choice, at which a heckler said he stood solely to ensure a judgeship. At Hindringham 'Mr Elgar made an injudicious speech, denouncing trade unions etc.', but, by contrast, at a meeting chaired by old Mr Cozens-Hardy the tone 'did not please me — there was too much talking against the parsons, too much exaltation of the people, as if the latter were to override everyone and everything. . . .'

On the whole it was a smooth campaign. If the Wesleyans were unable to allow the use of their premises for political meetings, the Primitives were more open-handed. If the Matlaske village school was not available, the schoolmaster made it quite clear that this was an arbitrary decision unsanctioned by the School Board; and in Roughton National School three cheers were given for the sympathetic new rector. At Buxton, Mr Sewell, 'son of the authoress of "Mothers last words",' brother, therefore of the authoress of *Black Beauty*, took the chair. At Hindolveston Joseph Arch, the labourers' leader and Primitive Methodist, 'spoke very well' and at Hevingham the master of the Reformatory instructed his boys to give three Liberal cheers. It was a Sunday and to recompense the unsabbatical cheers they sang Moody and Sankey hymns. Maria found the lads bright and pleasant and 'very few had a low criminal type of face'. At Wells Herbert faced, and impressed, the teetotalers; elsewhere he endured an old woman's reminiscences: 'Ah I remember my grandmother used to buy ½ oz of tea for 8*d*. and that had to last her a fortnight — if the Tories come in we shall have all that back again.'

The excellence of local Liberal organization was increasingly apparent. The Norfolk constituencies, helped by good train services, were in easy contact with each other. Their candidates spoke for each other and there were morale boosting trips to Norwich to hear famous Liberals and to stay at Carrow with the Colmans or in Bracondale with the Sydney Cozens-Hardys.

By the middle of November the campaign reached its peak. The election results were staggered between 24 November (Yarmouth) and 5 December (South-West Norfolk). By 16 November rumour credited Herbert with a 1,000 majority, although his father insisted that the Tories would win. A week later it was reported that a stone had been thrown at Samuel Hoare who had been cut by it. Herbert immediately wrote to express his regret and with equal promptness the Hoares called at Letheringsett Hall where Maria was in bed with a cold.

On the 26 November news of the Norwich result reached Maria. She was disappointed. Jeremiah Colman had been re-elected, but he came second to Bullard the Tory, after a contest in the rough old style.[38] Agnes, Cary, and Theobald's wife, Saranna, had attended the declaration of the poll, but Cary had foolishly ventured on to a balcony to be greeted by stones and oyster shells. The news had some impact on North Norfolk. The Tory ladies of Holt became vocal. Mrs Waldy of Letheringsett Lodge, backed by Mrs Rogers of Holt Hall, assured one of Agnes's friends that, come Disestablishment, 'I shall leave the country, I must live where there are Christians'. On the Liberal side a voter from 'near Hunstanton has written to say that he wishes to record his vote, he will get leave of absence and will start at 4 a.m. on Tuesday morning to be in time. It is hard that no one may *give* him food; he must buy it himself'.

On the 28th news came of the Unitarian Francis Taylor's victory in South Norfolk: the majority was 940.[39] 'Father in high spirits and Mother clapped her hands at the news. Father says we shall get in by 1,000.' That evening Herbert addressed a noisy meeting at Cromer. 'Mr Hoares' a gentleman — he's a gentleman', shouted Mr Cremer's drunken steward. 'One of the Miss Hoares was there,' Maria noted. The 30th was devoted to the making of rosettes: 'all the brewery horses are to have them. . . . To-morrow Herbert, Willie, and Katharine and I start in the Letheringsett carriage and post horses for round.'

The round took place on polling day, 1 December. At Billingford the Hudsons of Beck Farm had assembled the best turn out of all, with their waggons (one with a banner, 'Hurrah for the Grand Old Man') and three fine horses gay with blue and white streamers and rosettes. So to Reepham full of Tory red where there was a cart with a 'nigger' singing a pro-Hoare song to drum and banjo. In the hot little committee room at Cawston there were worries at stories of local intimidation. At Aylsham there was concern that a hundred illiterate voters had already polled, but at Aldborough where Robert Ketton was working busily there were assurances of a 500 majority. And so to Holt, to join Sir Lawrence and Lady Jones and the William Cozens-Hardys. Here Herbert voted. The polling station was in the school and the children had been given a holiday. There seemed to be more commotion here than anywhere else, with people standing at their front doors, women clapping and waving blue ribbons, and a little boy shouting 'Hallelujah!'

Next morning Herbert left by train for the count at Aylsham. The rest of his party followed later, to assemble for luncheon with the Dowager Lady Jones and the Misses Jones, the Louis Buxtons and Miss Buxton. Then the rival parties went to the Town Hall. Maria greeted Mrs Hoare: 'we had a little talk, but it was not very favourable for conversation.' After an interminable wait, or so it seemed, the door opened and the Under Sheriff appeared, with the candidates and their agents. Herbert nodded at Maria and Sydney was beaming with pleasure, but Maria stifled all hope until the Under Sheriff reached the words: 'Cozens-Hardy 5 . . .' at which there was cheering. The majority was nearly 1,700 and unexpectedly large.[40]

After that the party dispersed by train. Herbert and Maria went first to the Colmans in Norwich, accompanied for part of the way by Mrs Louis Buxton who told them of Tory bitterness at a victory connived at by Trade Unionists to bring England to the eve of revolution. Then 'home, finding Edward and Miss Wilson expecting us, a banner hanging in the hall of welcome to the M.P.'.

Maria felt grateful to the labourers who had 'behaved splendidly, many of them came long distances and refused a ride though offered it'. Others had worked without meals so that they could leave to vote early. There had been very few Liberal spoilt papers, thanks to their care in explaining the ballot. And their letters included a happy one from a legal friend: 'A new phase of our lives is beginning: one which will, I hope, bring happiness to all of us — an untried path, but one in which I trust and hope that we may have that guidance, which alone will help us in the right.'

Meanwhile William Cozens-Hardy and Clement had returned to Holt which, according to Mrs Cozens-Hardy, was in the throes of Tory reaction. Only at 'young Howes' house' did Liberal spirits revive with

a number of Letheringsett people who shouted and told Robert to get off the box. They then put on ropes and dragged us to the Hall door. Clement and Edith [his daughter] had to walk, so Robert put in his horses again and met them and the horses were again unyoked and the same process gone through. It really seemed too bad not to give the men, who had worked as horses, some beer and we had told Wagg he might, but when Clement came, he said it must not be. It might void the election. So it was not given. But I think they quite expected it. The next day after Mr Hoare's entry and speech at *Holt* beer was given to his men.

The Conservatives were poor losers and there were stories that a neighbouring squire had told a Liberal blacksmith that he would turn him out *and* send his horses elsewhere if he did not deal with his son for joining Willie Cozens-Hardy's ballot-explaining forays. It was said that bad language had been used at the squire's family, and that a publican had given a Liberal stonemason notice to quit, and that Mrs Rogers of Holt Hall had informed her Liberal newsagent that she no longer required any periodicals. Mrs Cozens-Hardy feared for such conduct. 'In fact the Tories seem to wish to succeed by bringing in a reign of Terror. Agnes' old women were indignant at the . . . affair, but having to turn off a son and quit your home or work must have an affect in many cases at another election.'

The Norfolk results were encouraging. Three of the four urban seats went to Conservatives but four of the six rural divisions fell to Liberals and the Tory majorities in the remaining two were slender. Since the towns polled first the results tended to disprove the 'snowball' theory applied to staggered elections. Four of the Liberal M.Ps — Colman, Cozens-Hardy, Francis Taylor and Joseph Arch — were Free Churchmen. North Norfolk remained safely Liberal until the Great War, although the Liberals never gained a higher percentage of the vote than they did in 1885.

Samuel Hoare entered Parliament in 1886 as one of the members for Norwich, which he represented for twenty years. Herbert Cozens-Hardy sat for North Norfolk until 1899. Although he disliked Gladstone's Home Rule Bill (but who did not?) and abstained in the critical division, he remained in the Gladstonian fold, popular and reliable in the House and consistently successful at the Bar.

In 1899 he became a judge of the Chancery division. As Lord Halsbury, the Lord Chancellor, expressed it, he was recommending Cozens-Hardy 'notwithstanding your abominable politics'.[41] He was knighted by the Queen at Windsor. 'She looked very old.' His law was good without brilliance, which means that it has lasted. In 1901 he became a Lord Justice of Appeal and in 1907 Master of the Rolls. In June 1914 he received a peerage: Baron Cozens-Hardy of Letheringsett. He was at once amused and regretful since he found pomps and peerages irrelevant. 'It is a relic of the past, and I do not suppose it will continue for many more years.'

As for the North Norfolk election of 1885, its spirit was embodied in the marriage in August 1892 of Herbert Cozens-Hardy's daughter Katharine to Silvester Horne, the Congregational minister who later sat for Ipswich, which Cozens-Hardy might have represented thirty years earlier, had he been a richer man.[42]

Book III

The Culture of Anarchy

Chapter 7

Dissenting Gothic

> ... the architect has not hesitated to adapt the flexible architecture of the fourteenth century to the requirements and uses of modern Nonconformist church service. Hence, iron is adopted in place of stone. . . .
>
> (Broughton Congregational Church, Salford, by Thomas Oliver jnr, described in *Congregational Year Book*, 1857, p. 234.)

The Congregational Year Book for 1847 contained architectural descriptions of eleven new chapels, five of them in variations of the pointed style. Of the others, one was 'Italian', one was in the 'Roman or Basilic style', one was 'Grecian'; the remaining three were merely tasteful and commodious.[1] This was symptomatic of a trend in chapel-building which so delighted the *Year Book*'s editor that he prefaced his annual account of new chapels with an essay about it.[2]

Naturally his concern was to unite taste with Congregationalism. He began, therefore, with a history of religious architecture, ranging from 'the edifices to which our Lord and his fellow-countrymen resorted to perform acts of public worship', to the works of the Middle Ages. It seemed to him 'that regular architecture had appeared under two general forms, and associated with two potent systems of false religion; the Grecian architecture identified with the temples of Minerva and Jupiter, and all the abominable idolatries of a classical mythology; and the Gothic or pointed architecture adopted to the shrines, and high altars, the sacristies and Lady chapels, of Popish superstition'. He illustrated the consequent Puritan reaction in favour of a 'religion of Barns' by describing the meeting-houses of New England and so he returned to old England and the preaching boxes of the Methodist revival. He dismissed George Whitefield's Tabernacles in London as masses of architectural deformity; Wesley's Chapel in the City Road 'scarcely possesses an architectural character'; Rowland Hill's Surrey Chapel was 'little better than an architectural eye-sore'. It was only with the Grecian chapels of the past decade — East Parade Leeds and Great George Street Liverpool among them, all pillars and porticoes — that he discerned quality, and even then 'architectural proprieties are sacrificed in almost every instance, to seeing and hearing'. His argument now began to bite. To be

145

architectural a building must obey a style, whether Grecian or Gothic. He even admitted that 'if an edifice is to possess any architectural pretensions whatsoever, the requirements of sight and sound must not be rigidly enforced'. Yet, the vital question remained: which style best suited Protestant Dissenters, for whom 'the pulpit, not the altar, the teacher, not the symbol, must be conspicuous'?

Although he called Christopher Wren to his aid, it was to the Gothic or, as he carefully put it, the *English* style, that he leaned:

> . . . we need not regard its symbolic mysteries, or adopt those ornaments which we know have been prostrated to purposes of superstition. We have our Protestant character to maintain in its integrity; and in these times of fearful apostacy to the church of Rome, it would afflict many honest Christians in other denominations, as well as in our own, if they should see our taste leading us to questionable conformities. But let us avail ourselves of those attractive forms, which are most agreeable to the eye, and are so flexible as to permit the erection of organ lofts, schools, lecture rooms or vestries, in harmony with the general edifice. This the Grecian style will not often allow. . . .[3]

His Protestantism thus established, the editor turned to the materials which should be used. Here he used the Cambridge Camden Society as his authority, although earlier he had ridiculed their fancies about architectural symbolism. With them he condemned brick and urged the use of stone; where transport allowed he, too, advocated Bath stone, with Caen stone for walls and windows and Purbeck marble for piers and shafts. If oak proved too costly, then let pulpit and pews 'be stained by the modern process', and varnished. This would be cheap, pleasing and efficient. His conclusions were clear: '. . . we have no need to *build* barn-like places of worship. When money is to be spent for the service of God, we are bound to use it with taste and judgment, so as to attract, rather than repel persons of intelligence and respectability'.

It was hard to avoid the language of respectability, and inevitably this was sometimes misunderstood. The editor began his essay by remarking that 'in those quarters least likely to be moved from the pattern adopted by their forefathers, we now witness a conformity to ecclesiastical models which is to us as unexpected as it is agreeable'. The phrase 'a conformity to ecclesiastical models' suggests mere copying of the parish church, but the architectural responses of Nonconformists were more complicated than that. No doubt an increasing number of chapels from the 1830s were a fair imitation of Commissioners' Gothic, and a few, as early as the 1840s, were faithful copies of the real thing,[4] but where they were genuine responses to the needs and prejudices of their congregations they should be judged accordingly, in their full context. This was vernacular architecture, not Gothic but English.

Naturally much of this was a keeping up with the Anglican Joneses. Nonconformists were growing richer and freer, and there were more of them. They needed to express this in their buildings, which were now public buildings, and the obvious point of comparison lay with the State Church. Hence the protestations of respectability to be found in every account of a new chapel, together with a nervousness, frequently overcome, about lavish decoration. The nervousness was justified. Nonconformist display was hampered by fear of popery, though less than might be imagined; it was hampered by inadequate funds, and therefore by reliance upon architects who at best were competent second-raters; and it was hampered by new techniques and materials which were applied with too brash an enthusiasm. The result was Dissenting Gothic.

But Dissenting Gothic commands its own perspective. Whether the chapels were built in new suburbs, new holiday resorts or in the new towns of the north, they were built to express the spiritual dimensions of men who had grown with their towns: they had moulded them. They were proud of an achievement which compared with any in the great cities of medieval Italy or the Low Countries, and their villas, banks, warehouses, town halls, Y.M.C.As and Mechanics' Institutes were re-creations of Florence or Milan, perhaps Antwerp or the Rhineland, sometimes Istanbul or Samarkand. Halifax is a restless Renaissance city, with the Crossleys of Square Chapel as its Medici; Huddersfield, a few miles away, is a colder, processional city, a foretaste of Edinburgh. Their builders may have been hard men but they had a growing sense of responsibility to their surroundings. The emergence of civic pride among people long deprived of the means of exercising it is a moving thing. This is the context in which to place Victorian chapels, seldom worthy in their own right, but sometimes invaluable because they complete the civic scene, enhancing urban vistas, their spires giving point to shopping parades or suburban terraces.

Neither were the chapel-builders fools. The chapel must be a credit to its neighbourhood, which is the credit side of respectability. It must be built according to a strict budget, to accommodate men and women listening to the word of God, read, sought and expounded. Its seats, therefore, must be the right size, the right shape and in the right place. There needed to be carefully integrated ancillary buildings to serve as Sunday Schools, parlours, kitchens and lavatories. This implied a new dimension of church architecture. Mere copying was out of the question, for there were too many novel problems to be solved. Given a limited amount of money, and therefore a limited choice of material; given the needs of a self-conscious, self-contained congregation, and the prejudices of its building committee, some of them fresh from foreign holidays, and the answer is Gothic, less because it points heavenward — though that will come — than because it combines cheapness, flexibility and dignity. When the Altrincham British Schools were rebuilt in 1860, the building committee determined upon 'the Early Pointed as the most effective and economical style'.[5] Fourteen years later S. M. Daukes's proud Congregational church in Broughton Park, Salford, was so planned that the arcading which decked its walls could be pierced with windows to provide more light, while what to the passer-by might seem to be chancel and side chapels in fact contained vestries, lecture hall and parlours. Broughton Park was expensive, but it was highly practical.

The *Congregational Year Book* cannot have had a large circulation in the 1840s. Assuming that delegates to the Congregational Union's annual assemblies were more likely to have access to copies than others, it becomes relevant that the delegates at the 1847 May Meetings in London should have included John Tarring, and that at the York Autumnals they included Charles Pritchett.[6] Tarring was a London architect with a growing reputation for chapels and houses. He was a thoroughly solid practitioner, at his best with Early English spires: his Grecian Park Chapel, Camden Town, of 1843, had been damned with faint praise in the 1847 *Year Book*.[7] Pritchett belonged to a family of architects with large practices in Yorkshire and the north-east. Their main offices were in York and later in Darlington, but from 1843 to 1862 Charles P. Pritchett was a member of Ramsden Street Congregational Church, Huddersfield, and as such he attended the York Autumnals in October 1847.[8]

Whatever architectural character Huddersfield possessed by 1847 was largely in the Pritchett mould. The parish church of St Peter had been rebuilt and the church of St James, Meltham Mills, had been built, between 1834 and 1838; the delightfully Gothic Huddersfield College faced the New North Road by 1839, and the railway station, as grandly columned as a country mansion or a palace of justice, was under way by 1847. Thereafter every rail traveller to Huddersfield arrived in state.

The Pritchetts were competent in Gothic and Grecian, and their earlier Nonconformist buildings tended to the latter. James Pigott Pritchett, the senior partner,[9] was responsible for the restrainedly classical, stone Ramsden Street Chapel in 1825, and for the similar but mean and brick Nether Congregational Chapel in Sheffield three years later. In 1839 his chapel for the original Airedale College, Bradford, one of two Congregational theological colleges in Yorkshire, was again in pilastered and pedimented Grecian. Huddersfield College, however, built at the same time as a boys' school, with Nonconformist backing, was freely Gothic, and thereafter the Pritchett chapels tended to be Gothic too. Pritchett of York's son and namesake, Pritchett of Darlington, developed a workmanlike specialism in them which came into its own by the 1860s. There was a pattern-book air about the younger Pritchett's chapels, as if they had been assembled from a kit, with optional extras depending on the money available, but including wherever possible, as their trademark, a corner tower made conspicuous by a spire, and invariably in shades of Early English.

Among the delegates at the 1847 May Meetings was a Huddersfield woolstapler, William Willans. Willans had been secretary to Ramsden Street Chapel's building committee in the 1820s and members of his family were concerned with the building of two other Congregational chapels in Huddersfield: Hillhouse in the early 1860s and Milton in the early 1880s. Each of these chapels was the creation of men who had formed their town, reflecting the tensions appropriate to successive generations. Each resulted from a partnership between the architect and the community whose needs he interpreted. Each reflected different stages in the progress of chapeldom. Indeed, Ramsden Street expressed the last stages of Dissent; Hillhouse was a tribute to Nonconformity, and Milton celebrated Free Churchmanship. It was Hillhouse which stood best for Dissenting Gothic.

Ramsden Street's stonelaying took place on Bastille Day, 1824. 'The inhabitants of Huddersfield are generally interested in the object now before us', Edward Parsons of Salem, Leeds, informed the 1,500 gathered on Back Green in his stately way, 'The sanctuary to be erected on this site will add to the respectability of your town; will be viewed as a new proof of its increasing population and prosperity; and which is the chief consideration, will contribute to the increase and security of its religious welfare'.[10]

Ramsden Street was an amicable but impatient break-away from Highfield Chapel. It was a young man's church in a young man's town. William Willans, the secretary of its building committee, was in his early twenties. Huddersfield was still small and haphazard. In 1801 its population was 7,000. By 1821, just before Ramsden Street was built, it was under 15,000, smaller than Bradford, a third the size of Sheffield and a sixth the size of Leeds. In 1861, just before Hillhouse was built, its population was almost 35,000; and in 1881, when Milton Church was formed, it was 87,000.

Congregationalism in Huddersfield was a product of the Evangelical Revival, no more indigenous than Wesleyan Methodism, whose spacious chapel in Queen Street testified to local Wesleyan importance. Highfield, the mother church of local Congregationalism, dated from 1772, formed by people awakened by Henry Venn at the parish church and unable to continue there with his successor.

Congregationalism was at its height in Huddersfield between 1840 and 1880. Ramsden Street, particularly under Richard Skinner, minister from 1845 to 1877, was the more aggressive church, remarkable for its Sunday Schools. Highfield, particularly under Robert Bruce, minister from 1854 to 1904, was the more exclusive. Both churches testified to the importance and influence of the northern pulpit when allied with a thrusting and interrelated people. Both were invigorated by a constant influx of newcomers to the town.

The peak was reached in 1874 when the Congregational Autumnals came to Huddersfield. Bruce of Highfield summarized the position in a paper prepared for the Assembly: 'until fifty years ago only one congregational church, until nine years ago only two. The date of our origin is so recent that very many now living distinctly remember the first Independent minister'. But now there were six chapels, holding nearly 6,000 people with room for 3,000 Sunday scholars; their premises had cost over £40,000; the eighteen church members of 1772 had become 1,150 by 1874. 'We have not in a single instance multiplied by division.'[11]

Ramsden Street was the impulse behind the expansion. At first it overreached itself. Pritchett's chapel of 1825 with its central pilasters and pediment, well placed for what was bound to become the centre of Huddersfield, was built as a preaching centre to hold 1,400. The first subscription list raised £1,305.11s.0d. from fifty-three people, thirteen of whom gave £1,000. On the strength of this they engaged J. P. Pritchett. Inevitably the cost outran the estimate: the total bill came to £6,514.11s.4d. Four lives were lost in the course of construction. The debt was not paid off until 1845.[12]

The elements of growth and division were equally present in the early years. Eagleton, the first minister, was thought to support the Ten Hour Movement and known to be a millenarian, and John Thorp, his successor, demonstrated the vanity of mere pulpiteering.[13] From 1836, however, first under Richard Knill, the famous foreign missionary,[14] and then under W. A. Hurndall, the church's energies became disciplined. The contradictory gospels of self-help and personal fulfilment, of peace, retrenchment and reform, of freedom in church, trade and schools, carried overseas and intensified at home, became as institutionalized at Ramsden Street as in any other successful chapel. Huddersfield's Dissenters had become Huddersfield's Nonconformists and under Richard Skinner their story became 'a romance of religious achievement'.[15] Hillhouse, on the Fartown side, was the prime consequence of this.

By the 1850s Huddersfield was developing its own network of suburbs, to the east at Moldgreen, and at Fartown to the north, with solid and roomy terraced houses for artisans and shopkeepers. The woolmen's villas were steadily climbing out of the town beyond Highfield Chapel and along the New North Road towards Halifax. To keep pace with this movement Ramsden Street organized District and Cottage Meetings and engaged a Town Missionary. The first fruit of his efforts was a mission chapel in South Street, on Huddersfield's west side. William Willans laid the foundation stone on 29 May 1856, amidst the victory celebrations for the Crimean War.[16]

It was Fartown, however, that nursery for self-help, which chiefly attracted the busy spirits at Ramsden Street, Willans at their head. The area was spiritually destitute. The remedy began in 1862 with a meeting at Willans's house on West Parade, attended by the Highfield and Ramsden Street ministers and half-a-dozen laymen, of whom Willans's brother-in-law, Charles Henry Jones, carried most weight. They decided to build a chapel and Sunday Schools at Hillhouse.[17]

They met again at Willans's house on 8 January 1863, with Bruce of Highfield in the chair. This time they formed themselves into a committee. They were all men of substance, Willans as a woolstapler, Jones as a director of the Midland Railway. William Hirst, the building committee's secretary, was a wool merchant. A subcommittee was appointed to view an eligible site; it was agreed that they should have in mind a church which would seat 700, but be capable of enlargement, with schoolrooms for 400 and space for a caretaker's house. £1,068 had been promised in addition to Willans's own contribution of one quarter of whatever could be raised locally.

There began the routine natural to such committees. At their third meeting, on 12 January, they set their own house in order, fixed upon a quorum (five), elected a Vice-Chairman (Wright Mellor, a deacon at Highfield) and agreed to begin all meetings with prayer. They also agreed not to commence building until £2,000 had been subscribed, and they drafted a letter to the ground landlords: 'if we did build, we should erect a place that would do Credit to the neighbourhood and be the means of improving the Estate'.

Style and plan now became of paramount importance. They consulted the plans of other new chapels, and particularly liked the Gothic of Queen Street, Oldham, built in 1855. By the 26 January they had decided upon 'a Gothic Chapel with spire capable of seating 700 with a possibility of enlargement to 900'. The cost must not exceed £2,000, and the building must be practical: 'comfortable seats to be provided. Enquiries to be made as to the space required for this purpose.'

There remained the question of the architect. The chapel was to be the subject of a competition, and on 29 January William Hirst was empowered to write to a series of architects known for their chapels. Within the next fortnight six firms had agreed to compete – Pritchett of Darlington, Kirk and Sons of Huddersfield, Lockwood and Mawson, and Mallinson and Healey, both of Bradford, Paul and Ayliffe of Manchester and R. Moffat Smith of Manchester, the architect of Queen Street, Oldham. The committee sent them their instructions: 'all obstructions to the effective hearing and seeing of the Preacher to be avoided'; sittings to measure three feet from back to back, save for 200 which were to measure two feet nine inches. The closing date for entries was 18 March 1863.

As it happened only three plans were submitted, of which the committee favoured 'Labor et Spes'. This promised a church for £2,000 with a spire for £200 and a choice of schoolrooms under the church for £300 or behind it for another £400. Already the costs were mounting.

The decision lay with Willans, who was abroad trying to recover his health: as chairman of the committee, initiator of the venture and largest subscriber, his agreement was essential. By 20 April this had been secured and Willans expressed his confidence in the committee's choice, 'Labor et Spes' by Pritchett of Darlington, the son of Ramsden Street's architect with whom he had worked forty years earlier. A week later conclusions were reached with young Pritchett: 'if the tenders for the Church should exceed the Architect's Estimate by £500 no charge whatever is to be made for Commission', and if they exceeded it by £200, then the committee were to be free to abandon the scheme, on payment of £50 to the architect. At the same time consolation prizes went to the two runners up in the competition. 'Propriety and Adaptation', the second choice, received £10.

For the next six months the committee's energies were concentrated on the subscribers and the architect. With the former they were on stronger ground. There was a ready-made cousinhood of wool men, merchants or manufacturers, most of them Congregationalists, chiefly from Ramsden Street. In May 120 likely subscribers were listed, almost all from families whose local Congregational connexions would span the century. There were ticks against eighty-seven of them, perhaps because Willans and C. H. Jones had already visited them, perhaps because they had already subscribed. By the end of May £1,793 had been promised and a further thirty-three names added. By the end of June £1,845 had been promised and there was a list of thirteen 'parties who had promised to give but had not named any definite sum'. An estimate of £219 was pencilled against these.

The architect needed different treatment. The committee were determined that their church should above all things be comfortable, and they examined other new chapels with this in mind. Pritchett had already built for the Wesleyans at Sheepscar and for the Congregationalists at Darlington. In May Charles Henry Jones spied out the land at Sheepscar and was 'very much pleased with it', though the pulpit, water-closets and chapel-keeper's house were too small, the gallery stairs too narrow, the gas lights too near the roof, the spire too squat and there were too many doors into the church. Two months later Willans himself went to Sheepscar with Pritchett. It disappointed him. 'We must have a more suitable edifice both more comfortable and more proportionate.'

Darlington was altogether better, comparable in size and price, with 'seats wide enough to satisfy the most fastidious followers of modern fashion', slanting back, oak stained and varnished. The pillars of the arcades had caps of gilded foliage and the church was gas lit by two large coronae suspended from the roof each with thirty jets: the gas fittings were painted blue and chocolate and gilded.[18] The Huddersfield visitors were 'generally well pleased' with Darlington and were sure that with a few improvements it 'would do very well as a model'. They wanted, however, a platform instead of a pulpit, no pew doors but rounded pew tops (as at Lockwood and Mawson's new chapel at Harrogate: Bruce of Highfield later advocated trefoil ornamenting), larger water-closets than at Sheepscar, and stained glass in the window borders.

By the end of August they were ready to accept the builders' tenders, standing at £2,410.15s.0d. This was Willans's last meeting. Within a fortnight he was dead; the new church was his memorial.

Once building had begun in the autumn of 1863 (completion date was to be 1 August 1864) fresh worries assailed the committee. There were arrangements to be made for the stonelaying. Willans's youngest son, James Edward, was added to the committee, although he was barely twenty-one. Willans's eldest son, John Wrigley, who was a wool-broker in London, was to lay the foundation stone so a 'handsome mallet' and a silver trowel (it cost six guineas) would need to be selected for him. It was important that John Crossley, the most dynamic of the Halifax family of carpet manufacturers, should be present, and two of the committee waited upon him 'to show him the plans, contracts, specifications etc., with a view to obtaining a subscription'.

The stonelaying was on Saturday, 7 November, in pouring rain at three in the afternoon. The cavity beneath the stone contained coins of the realm, suitable newspapers and a photograph of the late William Willans. The rain kept the proceedings short and to the point, but two days later the real celebrations were held with 400 taking tea at 6d. a head in the Ramsden Street Schoolrooms, and 700 cramming into the chapel for a public meeting chaired by Crossley of Halifax.

The meeting had its desired effect. The treasurer declared that £2,012 had been promised to date; £130 more was promised on the spot and Crossley gave £50, while William Willans's four sons, John and William from London, Thomas from Rochdale and James Edward in Huddersfield, announced that they would give the spire in memory of their father. Naturally there were reminiscences of William Willans, and J. Wrigley Willans 'explained the principles of congregationalism, which he maintained were of primitive origin, and the best calculated to develope [*sic*] the whole man'; another speaker noted that there was no Congregationalism in the slave states of America, 'to whose interests and institutions he presumed it was thoroughly inimical'. It was all immensely satisfactory, down to the account of the Puritan divines ejected from their livings in 1662.

Relations with the architect and builders were less satisfactory. There was wrangling about the space under the church. Pritchett blamed the surveyor for any miscalculations, but when he insisted that classrooms 11 feet high could still be built the clerk of works contradicted him: they could only be 8 feet 10 inches high. It was felt that Pritchett had become dilatory, and he had to be asked to come monthly to view the site. These difficulties were compounded by a joiners' strike between June and September 1864, which left the roof vulnerable to wet weather and delayed the opening. The August date turned into September, then October, then Christmas. Finally it seemed that all could be ready for 26 January 1865: until this became 15 February.

The committee's minutes became increasingly hectic. There was a sudden shortage of funds, which they tried to meet by canvassing at Highfield, and in the streets around the new chapel. There were decisions to be made about the decorations and fittings. The chandeliers at Blenheim Baptist Chapel, Leeds, were inspected, and approved; so was the iron work at the Unitarian Chapel. Sharp letters were written about delays in installing the windows and warming apparatus. Then the pulpit was found to be too narrow, and the architect insisted that the Blenheim Baptist fittings would be quite unsuitable and urged Darlington's instead. There were further disagreements over the colour scheme. The committee decided upon ochre and light red tints for the walls, and French grey and light blue for the roof, but they were convinced that Pritchett wanted far too dark a stain for the woodwork.

By January 1865 there was a proliferation of subcommittees. Miss Willans and her cousin Miss Jones were to help select carpets and window blinds. The *New Congregational Hymnbook* was to be purchased, and a harmonium. The precise colour of pulpit and pew cushions needed to be determined.

This was routine, exhausting no doubt, but since May 1864 there had also been delicate negotiations as to the opening preachers which the building delays completely frustrated. A shortlist of fifteen pulpiteers — Newman Hall, Henry Allon, Alexander Raleigh, R. W. Dale, Baldwin Brown, together with the Baptists, Brock of Bloomsbury and Alexander McLaren — was drawn up, in order of preference. The procedure was useless. Eventually, after a complicated correspondence and a round of visits, promises were secured from Baldwin Brown of Lambeth and Thomas Jones of Camden Town, both of them outside the run of chapel openers, Brown because of his controversial books,[19] Jones as the preacher who delighted the Brownings.

By the beginning of February the arrangements were well in hand. It appeared that the total cost of the enterprise would be £3,605, of which Pritchett's fees were £160; three members of the committee gave £100, and a final canvas of a further fifty-four friends secured £300. As for the opening services, James Willans had ordered 2,000 circulars (there had been debate as to whether 500 or 1,000 would be the proper number) and a subcommittee was to organize dinner for 100 notables and tea for fifty more. Another subcommittee, with an eye to when the last echoes of Jones and Brown had died away, decided that students supplying the pulpit should be paid 30 shillings a Sunday, and ministers £3.

The morning of Wednesday, 15 February 1865 was 'beautifully fine but intensely cold'. Over 300 listened to Thomas Jones, who was 'most beautiful and impressive'. He was again 'very good', but less powerful, in the evening. On Sunday the 19th — 'one of the most inclement of the season, snow and driving wind the snow melting so that it was most uncomfortable walking' — Baldwin Brown addressed comfortable congregations, and £45 was collected. Two days later, J. P. Chown, the Bradford Baptist, preached excellently to a church which was half filled, and £8.14s.0d. was collected. So it continued. Sunday the 26th was 'rather wet', but Robert Balgarnie of Scarborough preached impressively to a church 'crowded in every part some having to go away not finding room'.

The climax came on the 27th when 350 sat down to tea and then joined those who were already filling the church for the public meeting. The Willans family were to the fore, and the chair was taken by Edward Baines of Leeds, who was Wrigley Willans's father-in-law. Again there were reminiscences of William Willans and Baines saw in Hillhouse a triumph for voluntaryism. He hoped that schools would be rapidly built, and that the church's motto would be 'Purity, unity, activity'. John Crossley echoed him, and John Hanson, the Baptist minister, made happy jokes about the Jordan being the only barrier between them, and how he wished that he could pull the Congregationalists in.

More to the point, the debt had been cleared: the Willans family had given £600, with a further £260 for the spire. If two-thirds of the cost had been met by barely thirty individuals, most of them from Highfield and Ramsden Street,[20] nonetheless £150 was in hand for Sunday School buildings, and 293 sittings had been let. Willans's determination had been justified. A church of thirty-nine members, sixteen of them from Ramsden Street and eleven from Highfield, was formed on 1 June, with William Hirst of Ash Villas as one of the first deacons.

The building committee continued until January 1867, when trustees were appointed. There were still problems to resolve: the sun shone too brightly through the west windows, and there was difficulty over Pritchett's commission. The Sunday and Day Schools, which were opened in October 1867 at a total cost of nearly £2,000 were the preserve of a new committee.

The Willanses maintained their interest in the cause. Five of them gave £345 to the schools; a further £155 came from William Willans's sons-in-law and £60 from his brothers-in-law. James Willans was treasurer of the fund and on the management committee. Twelve years later he gave £50 towards an organ for the church; he was meticulous in contributing to Hillhouse's special efforts.[21]

Baines was right: Hillhouse was a tribute to voluntaryism. It stood at the junction of two residential streets to the west of the road to Bradford, its corner spire tapering delicately, 120 feet high. It was built in local stone and a diagonal pattern of blue and green slates coloured its roof. Inside it was roomy, the preacher unobscured by the iron-columned arcading. The woodwork was deal, dark stained and varnished; there was cathedral tinted glass in the window and large gasoliers hung from the roof.[22] It was a Pritchett chapel, distinctive, convenient, its Gothic too spindly for elegance. It was more expensive than Pritchett's chapel at Darlington, on a par with those at Ripon, Pudsey and Knaresborough, less luxurious than at Holywell Green near Halifax, where the pulpit was Caen Stone, and the arcades were in moulded stone with pillars of polished granite.[23]

Like all vindications of the voluntary principle Hillhouse was the work of a community, representative alike in style, decade, origins and intentions. It was Early English of the 1860s, veering towards the Decorated, a symbol of the tensions implicit in an age of equipoise. It expressed the missionary aggressiveness of a town whose Nonconformity was as recent as its growth: so it harked back to the traditions of 1662. It was intended for the lower middle classes by men who had moved into the professional and mercantile middle classes, members of a large, quarrelsome cousinhood who saw their lives as celebrations of self-help when in fact it was mutual-help which had got them where they were.

Hillhouse's architect, James Pritchett the younger, was such a man, about to make his mark in a profession which was now almost gentlemanly. Between 1851 and 1871 the profession of architect was growing rapidly, although many architects were barely distinguishable from surveyors. It offered much to men at the edges of the professional classes, the sons of parsons perhaps, or attorneys' sons (Pritchett's grandfathers were a country clergyman and a country attorney). The Hillhouse commission was won by Pritchett in competition, a popular method in the provinces, helpful for young architects.[24]

Yet Pritchett was no more self-made than most other self-made men: he had family backing and useful connexions on both sides of the ecclesiastical fence. He was indeed no more self-made than Hillhouse, or Hillhouse's subscribers those Wrigleys, Shaws, Hirsts and Willanses recurring at every point of Victorian Huddersfield's life.

Edward Baines remembered William Willans from Leeds days when they had both worked for the Leeds Juvenile Missionary Society. Willans's Leeds kinsmen, the Willanses of Willans and Nussey, prospered, prominent with the Baineses at Salem and East Parade, active in Leeds politics and commerce. William, however, had struck out for Halifax and then for Huddersfield, where he set up as a woolstapler in 1825. From 1833 he was a deacon of Ramsden Street, alert in every Congregational work; from 1838 he was a power behind Huddersfield College, and the standard bearer of Bainesite voluntaryism in Huddersfield. He worked in every general election, most notably for Richard Cobden in 1857, and was narrowly defeated on the sole occasion when he stood for Parliament in 1852. From 1861 he was President of the local Chamber of Commerce, and when he died his funeral was on a scale novel to Huddersfield, its route carefully arranged to give the ladies of his family an opportunity to see the long procession.[25]

So it was with his kinsmen. His brother-in-law, Jones, was Huddersfield's first mayor, in 1868; one son-in-law, Freeman Firth of Heckmondwike, where he made carpets, became a Dissenting baronet, and another, William Shaw, became Chairman of the Rochdale School Board. Of William Willans's sons, John Wrigley eventually worked for his father-in-law Baines on the business side of the *Leeds Mercury*. William Henry, of Islington and Kensington, stood as Liberal candidate for Frome in 1874; Thomas Benjamin was Mayor of Rochdale in 1869 and James Edward, the youngest, named after the Yorkshire preachers, James Parsons of York and Edward Parsons of Leeds, continued in Huddersfield. He became President of its Chamber of Commerce in 1908 and Chairman of its Education Committee in 1909, incidents in a life filled with religious, philanthropic and commercial endeavour. When he was made an Honorary Freeman in 1918, the schoolchildren were given a half-holiday in celebration, 'that they might in after years be interested in public service'.[26]

Each of these men was active in a Congregational Church, although W. H. Willans later conformed to the State Church. Each, save James Edward and Thomas Benjamin whose wives were Free Methodists, married into Congregational families. Their fame was provincial: it spread with the third generation. Among William Willans's great-nephews was the Liberal theorist, F. W. Hirst, about whose marriage to Helena Cobden, Richard Cobden's great-niece, there was a charming Manchester School symmetry. Willans's best-known grandson was Herbert Henry Asquith, whose earlier career makes little sense without some knowledge of the uncles so briefly alluded to in *Memories and Reflections*.[27]

Hillhouse celebrated the Nonconformity of the 1860s. Milton heralded the Free Churchmanship of Edwardian England. It cost more than Ramsden Street and Hillhouse combined, the Huddersfield expression of tendencies of taste and culture described in the next chapter. It also marked an explosion of Dissenting dissidence, dividing the Willanses, with Jones and Shaw of Rochdale against James Willans and the Hirsts. It was a classic affair: a clash of generation, language, personality and doctrine.

Three years after the Huddersfield Autumnals of 1874, at which Bruce of Highfield had rejoiced that Huddersfield Congregationalism was nowhere the fruit of division, Skinner of Ramsden Street retired. Charles Jones, presiding at the farewell, repeated the boast that Ramsden Street had mothered no schism and that its daughter churches were tributes to the voluntary spirit: 'therefore there had been no jealousy, and nothing to cause anxiety amongst them.'[28]

Skinner's successor, J. T. Stannard, was a man whose thought and eloquence were very much in the modern style. The change of pastorate occurred in the year that the notorious 'Leicester Conference',[29] convened during the denomination's Autumnal Assembly by a group of younger ministers, brought suspicion of the modern style into the open for Congregationalists. Most of the Ramsden Street congregation and Sunday School regardless of age or standing warmly admired Stannard, but some accused him of violating the doctrinal provisions of the trust deed. It was the language of the 1870s against that of the 1820s. Brought to law in January 1881 the language of the 1820s won, and Stannard and his supporters seceded. Ramsden Street never again set the pace of Huddersfield Nonconformity.

The seceders, worshipping temporarily at the Victoria Hall, formed themselves into a separate church on 5 May 1881.[30] It bore all the signs of success — a readymade Sunday School of 520, most of whom had followed their teachers from Ramsden Street, and a church membership which had reached 253 by May 1882 and included most of the families who had made Ramsden Street notable, a large proportion of whom had helped build Hillhouse in the 1860s. James Willans played a leading part, aided by the Hirsts and the Woodheads, a family of Quaker origin who were to dominate the new church's life for the next seventy years. The Woodheads of the *Huddersfield Examiner* were another Congregational Yorkshire newspaper family to be added to the Byleses of Bradford, the Leaders of Sheffield and the Baineses of Leeds.

It was very much a Free Church in language and enthusiasm. Its name — Milton, chosen after Victoria, Wycliffe and Christ had all been rejected — expressed this. So did its pulpit supplies: John Hunter of Wycliffe, Hull, later to achieve a wide reputation as minister of Trinity, Glasgow; P. T. Forsyth, the future Principal of Hackney College; and Asquith's brother-in-law, William Wooding, a Congregational minister who taught mathematics at the City of London School, and was progressing steadily towards Unitarianism.[31] J. T. Stannard's own language compounded the freshness and vigour of the new cause. In the Church's *Year Book* for 1881 he urged his people that 'Independency, like every other type of Church polity, is itself but a means to the highest of all ends, viz: the nearer and nearer approach to the true ideal of a Christian Church — a spiritual brotherhood whose band and centre is the Living Christ. . . .' Two years later he called for freer preaching, to prove that 'Christianity is a religion which seeks to save society as well as individual men. It is the true social science. It is also the true secularism, having the richest blessings for the life that now is as well as for that which is to come'. The accompaniment of such preaching must be greater social freedom: the social element 'is to our Church life what the fireside is to our home life. It tends to produce the almost unknown quality of which so much is said in the New Testament, and so little known in the Church — *fellowship*; a sort of joyful inspiration at the sense of a "fellow" by your side. . . .'[32]

Milton became a great place for fellowship, with its cantatas and conversaziones, its swimming club and a cricket club whose seven performances of the Operetta 'Robin Hood' raised over £100 for the Church Building Fund in the spring of 1884. It is this which suggests that it was more a matter of language than of doctrine, for Milton was admitted to the Yorkshire Congregational Union and on great occasions it attracted denominational elder statesmen to its pulpit, and local notables to its platforms. It was Huddersfield's Mayor, Wright Mellor of Highfield Chapel, who performed Milton's stonelaying ceremony, and it was

159

everybody's kinsman, the Yorkshire M.P. Edward Crossley, John Crossley's nephew, Sir Edward Baines's son-in-law and Wrigley Willans's brother-in-law, who opened the great Building Fund Bazaar.

This was reflected in the building. It was still a town-centre church, its site in Queen Street South leased for £100 a year from Sir John Ramsden, on whose estate much of Huddersfield had been built. The requirements were a church to seat 600 with gallery accommodation for a further 200, and ancillary buildings for the Sunday School, now 634 strong. This meant twenty-six classrooms and a central hall, with an adult lecture hall, parlour, library, kitchen and caretaker's apartment. The cost of the church must not exceed £5,000; that of the school, £4,000. In the summer of 1882 a building committee was established, with James Willans as Vice-Chairman. By January 1883, 142 subscribers had promised £5,360.[33] There was nothing new in chapel-building.

In the event the buildings cost £14,000, of which £600 were for the Conacher organ.[34] They were of a completeness new to Huddersfield Congregationalism. The architect, Healey of Bradford, belonged to a firm which had been invited to compete for Hillhouse in 1863. The style was still Decorated Gothic, but heavier and rather dour outside, its period becoming later and freer as the school buildings were encountered. Unlike Hillhouse, Milton was more tower than spire. Inside it was clearly a church, with chancel, transepts, central aisle and side pulpit. The arcades were stone, not iron and wood, and the chancel wall was hung with tapestry curtains given by James Willans. The services were self-consciously liturgical; by February 1887 it had been agreed to adopt the 'Commandments' and 'Beatitudes'.[35]

Milton had not merely replaced Ramsden Street, it had become part of Huddersfield's public life. At its Jubilee in 1931, Charles Hirst, last of the founders (James Willans had died in 1926), estimated that 'nearly 1,000 persons have been associated with the Church as members, and upwards of 3,000 young people have passed through the Sunday School'.[36] Outwardly the church represented changes in Congregationalism best personified by C. S. Horne,[37] reflecting a religious progressivism which was the exact counterpart of the political progressivism apparently engaging the Liberal party of which James Willans's nephew, Herbert Asquith, was the exemplar. Yet Milton was not a new cause, like Hillhouse, and its membership never exceeded that of Ramsden Street in its palmy days, neither did any of its ministers compare with Richard Skinner or Robert Bruce.

In its freshness and variety Milton's is a more appealing story than that of other Huddersfield chapels, but it was the first Congregational church in the town to start by living on capital. The care and money lavished on its buildings no doubt obscured this, while the nature of those buildings testified to the vigour of their users. The buildings were still Gothic.

Years later the Governor of the North-West Provinces of India, Sir Harcourt Butler, ruefully surveying the incongruous Gothic arches of Naini Tal, his summer residence, noted: 'The arch springs, it is in motion, never at rest. It is difficult to rest in a room all arches.'[38] That sense of unresting quest, overlaid in too many parish churches by the comfy good manners of generations of established Christianity, was the supreme achievement of Dissenting Gothic, whatever its Victorian period.

Chapter 8

The Shores of Philistia: A Perspective of Late Victorian Nonconformity

These essays are edited from the heart of Philistia. In other words, their author belongs to that region of *esprits bornés*, and of intellectual density, connoted by the terms Protestant Nonconformist. To enter here will be, doubtless, to many cultured persons, an adventure as serious and unwonted as to traverse the realms of

Antres vast and deserts idle,
Of anthropophagi and men whose heads
Do grow beneath their shoulders.

If any such make the venture we can only wish them a safe and happy issue out of it. Should they emerge alive it may perhaps, be with the tidings that the tales of intellectual savagery in vogue concerning its inhabitants owe, like some of Othello's stories, a good deal to the imagination of their authors.

(J. Brierley, *From Philistia: Essays on
Church and World*, 1893, quoted in H. Jeffs, *'J.B.' J. Brierley,
His Life and Work* n.d. (*c.*1915), p. 116.)

Educated Nonconformists were deeply wounded by *Culture and Anarchy*, for Matthew Arnold was better placed than most of his class to know what he was talking about. His duties as an Inspector of Schools had taken him into British Schools, their schools, and he was on friendly terms with such models of puritan culture as Dr Reynolds of Cheshunt College or Dr Allon of Islington. Yet he had coined the word 'Philistinism' — the very word was alien — to express their attitude towards life and literature.

Twenty-four years after the appearance of *Culture and Anarchy*, Jonathan Brierley, a retired minister who was building a second reputation as a religious journalist, produced *From Philistia*, essays in defence of the Nonconformist values of a suburbia whose density had multiplied since Arnold's day. Most of Brierley's essays were written from Neuchâtel, but when in London he lived at 'Helensleigh', Willesden Green and he worshipped in Hampstead at Dr Horton's Church. A Boston journalist had felt that R. F. Horton was Matthew Arnold turned Salvation Army captain,[1] so there was some aptness in this Dissenting apologia from one whose horizons extended from the Alps to Willesden

Green, taking in the spiritual peaks of Lyndhurst Road on Sunday mornings.

Suburbia was a fact of late Victorian life. It was also a fact of late Victorian Free Churchmanship, as churches like Henry Arnold Thomas's Highbury Chapel, Bristol, or R. F. Horton's Lyndhurst Road, Hampstead, bore witness: in them suburban man was transfigured.

Suburban man was the distillation of Victorian civilization. J. M. Richards, suburbia's most refreshing apologist, has described suburban man with a perception unmisted by sentiment. He sees him as the distributor in society, the stockbroker perhaps, or the commercial representative: 'the man with a bias towards distribution is . . . an extrovert — a materialist, in contrast to the mystic [who is the producer in society]. The mystic enjoys his sport, the materialist his *sports*.' So suburban man is sketched as 'the life-long games player, the "hearty" who judges everything by its physical perfection, whether motor cars, film stars, or his own kind, in whose good-fellowship he indulges so irrepressibly. The ball-game cult coincides with his rise into prominence, and he is the embodiment of the team spirit.' Yet his sociable instincts tend 'all towards anarchy. This applies equally to his political instincts, though these are often disguised as liberalism (or, when he is thwarted, as Fascism). His system is *laisser-faire*, his ethics enlightened self interest and his philosophy the survival of the fittest. . . . His art is one of *pastiche*, and his architecture that of fancy dress.'[2] He prefers 'reproduction' furniture.

Richards's suburbia grew lushest between the wars, but its pre-history is nineteenth century from Nash's scene-painting in Regent's Park, nature and builder intermingling, past Norman Shaw in Bedford Park to those villas of Voysey, or Baillie Scott which broke, almost by accident, 'into a looser, more casual arrangement of plan, a more informal grouping of roofs, initiating the process of linking house and garden together'.[3] It was a transition from grand opera to provincial repertory, but it was of European significance.

Suburbia has been shaped by its contradictions. It is 'an accumulation of happy accidents', and yet contrived and accounted for down to the last geranium. It is a psalm to individualism, if not to anarchy, yet all is well for that individualism is family-centred and reflected in safety and tradition. It is even indivisible since no individual suburban item bears examination else 'the scene itself would disappear'.[4] Its architecture may be fancy dress, but it is nonetheless vernacular, the creation of men 'perpetually on the fringe of change', wherein 'even its shortcomings — its snobberies, its self-deceptions, its sentimentalities, the uncertainties of its objectives — are evidence of this closeness to everyday life'. Indeed because its foundation is anarchy and its builders are at the mercy of change (and of mortgages), it aims at permanence: 'Architectural styles have to be reinterpreted as social symbols. An elaborate code has grown up ... by means of which family circumstances are depicted ... in architectural language. ... Advantageous alliances are reflected as clearly in a fructification of shrubberies and bay windows as they are in elaborate quarterings.'[5]

Such is suburbia: a celebration of paradoxes. It is the product of an urban civilization housing people dependent on that civilization, and yet it is sub-urban. It is a monument to amateur inspiration, and yet the speculative building which characterizes it is uninspired and there is a daunting professionalism about the suburban conspiracy of estate agents and builders. Neither were the heroes of its architecture, Webb, Shaw, Voysey, Lutyens, amateurs although their plagiarists demonstrated what poor architects they very nearly were.

There is, in short, a problem which needs resolving: that of discovering the true creators of the suburban setting, men reared in it who remained faithful to it, linking the speculative builder's suburbia with that inspired by the writings of John Ruskin, the designs of William Morris, and the buildings of Charles Voysey. To put it another way, the search is for men who were nourished by the Pre-Raphaelites, lingered over *Art Nouveau* and yet opted for Jacobean.

There is a further dimension. If suburbia's surface is scratched a stratum of Puritanism is revealed. In the late nineteenth century this was isolated and identified as the 'Nonconformist Conscience', the political and religious bed-rock for tennis clubs and literary societies, encompassing Unitarian refinement and Methodist 'mateyness'. It enfolded teachers, general practitioners, administrators and shopkeepers: the distributors of society, among them some creators of the suburban setting.

The chapels disciplined the anarchy of suburbia while demonstrating the autonomy of the religion practised within them. Sometimes they refined the intermingling of buildings with surroundings. Morley Horder did this at Cheshunt College, Cambridge, an easy alliance of Tudor college and manor house for an uneasy alliance of Congregationalists and Lady Huntingdon's Connexion. Percy Worthington did this for the Unitarians at Ullet Road, in Liverpool's Sefton Park. Edgar Wood perfected the intermingling for the Christian Scientists at Daisy Bank Road, in Manchester's Victoria Park. At its best suburbia was intensely moral. In 1909 T. Raffles Davison, artist and architectural journalist, son of one Congregational minister, whose Christian names perpetuated the memory of another, spoke for that 'large class who desire the comfort and something of the luxury which all people of refined taste enjoy, but who nevertheless have very small means', and whose hope lay 'in a rigid determination to accept simple conditions and genuine honesty of purpose'. He liked houses and gardens which 're-act on each other' but he knew that 'the strong air of honesty and simplicity' was a contrived air: 'it is the mission of the architect to supply Art. . . .'[6] The rhetoric is chapel rhetoric — 'honesty', 'simplicity', 'purpose', 'mission'. The aim is suburban — contrivance. The method involved initiative, imagination and aspiration. The result, unless chapel intervened, was deception.

Chapel, however, frequently intervened as the following web of connexion might suggest. The suburbia concerned is that of Manchester and Liverpool and the families concerned centre upon that of Elkanah Armitage, a Congregational minister who was a close friend of R. F. Horton of Hampstead, and an intimate friend of Arnold Thomas of Bristol.

> On Monday Mar. 23. I went to London to set out for Italy. I joined the party consisting of Rev. Thos. Green and his wife, Mr and Mrs Newton (Waterhead) and Mr and Mrs A. Dodgson (Oldham) and we travelled together as far as Pisa. They then went to Rome and I to Florence where Mr and Mrs Bulley, Ella and Nanny came.
> I became engaged to Ella, and after a visit to Venice I joined her at San Remo, and came back to England with her. We reached London Sat. May 2nd. and I came North by a night train, getting to Waterhead on Sunday morning. . . .[7]

So noted Elkanah Armitage, minister of Waterhead, a church on the outskirts of Oldham, in the spring of 1874. There is nothing unusual about it. Italy fascinated cultivated Victorians, and if Rome and the moonlit Coliseum exerted its spell in the 1830s on the young Gladstone and Catherine Glynne, there was no reason why Florence in the 1870s should not hold similar romance for a Manchester cotton-spinner's Gladstonian son and a Liverpool cotton-broker's daughter. Italy was inevitable for readers of Ruskin and Browning, followers of Gladstone, admirers of Garibaldi. To the villa dwellers of New Brighton and Altrincham it announced freedom.

Further freedoms were announced in the 1870s. 18 May 1874: 'Went up to Cambridge for the opening of the new chapel there on the 19th. Dr Raleigh preached. Lady Reed and many more were at Cambridge. Annie and Amy and Caroline Bulley at Merton.'[8] This entry is less innocent. Armitage was a Trinity man with a first in Moral Science; Dr Raleigh was a prince of the London pulpit, whose son became Professor of English Literature at Oxford; Lady Reed was the wife, daughter and sister of Liberal and Dissenting grandees, and her son wrote schoolboy yarns; Annie, who was Elkanah's sister, and Amy and Caroline Bulley who were

Ella's sisters, were pioneers at what became Newnham College — Ella, indeed, had been one of the first five students there.[9] All of them, Raleighs and Reeds, Armitages and Bulleys, were family friends of long-standing, active in that breaking of barriers which so exhilarated English Nonconformists in the 1870s. The chapel whose opening they celebrated sanctified such a breaking of barriers.

Emmanuel Congregational Church, Trumpington Street, stood amidst the colleges, confronting Pembroke and overshadowing Peterhouse, symbol of the abolition of university tests. Its building committee employed a prominent London architect, James Cubitt, and contributions were expected on a national scale for it was to be a University Free Church, spiritual home of future generations of educated Bulleys and Armitages, Raleighs and Reeds, and its architecture was to express the culture of Puritanism renewed:

> The design presents itself outwardly as a rather lofty church, with a conspicuous clerestory; and its front is formed by a massive tower, flanked by an octagonal turret of considerable size. . . . Satisfactory outline and proportion have been the first objects sought for in the architecture, and the decoration is of the rather severe sort which prevailed in the earlier part of the thirteenth century. Except in the wheel window . . . there is nothing approaching to tracery. . . . Internally, there will be somewhat more of ornament, still, however, of a rather reserved and simple type. . . .[10]

Fifteen years after this Cambridge victory Elkanah Armitage, now a minister in Rotherham, was in Oxford for a grander breaking of barriers. 14 to 16 October 1889: 'Opening of Mansfield Coll., Oxford. All the money had been got. Most stirring meetings. . . . Ella and I stayed . . . at the Randolph Hotel.'[11]

The barriers to be broken at Oxford were at once cultural, educational and religious. Ever since the early 1870s and the abolition of university tests it had been a chief desire of leading Congregationalists to move Spring Hill, their most advanced theological college, from Birmingham to Oxford there to celebrate the proper place of Dissent in the nation's religious and intellectual life. After years of preparation the building was begun in April 1887, and it opened, as Mansfield College, in a blaze of Nonconformist jubilee in October 1889.

It was a Nonconformist *tour-de-force* beating Oxford at its own game, exquisite in its library and chapel, sufficiently ponderous in its dining-hall and common rooms, its full-blooded Collegiate Gothic reflecting here the Reformation of Edward VI, there the Reformation of John Wycliffe, but nowhere the Reformation of Henry VIII, a morning star for causes which Oxford would not be allowed to lose.

Its furnishings reflected this. Everything, down to the J.C.R. and the professors' sitting-rooms, fitted these Lollards of the new age — easy wicker chairs, oak rush-seat chairs, Goldsmith chairs, tables, a bookcase, three 'Crome lounges' and a Turkey carpet for the J.C.R; an Anglo-Indian carpet, rush-seat and wicker chairs, pedestal writing table, and two bookcases, for a professor, with 'Rush seat Settee with cushion to fit seat and pillow cushion' and an 'old oak chest for papers and occasional seat'.[12]

Mansfield College was all this and more, for it was, perhaps, the Manchester School's main religious triumph. Despite the fact that the scheme, prompted by James Bryce and T. H. Green and moulded by R. W. Dale, had chiefly originated in Birmingham, and that the £50,000 raised by February 1890 had come from Congregationalists everywhere, it remains true that Lancashire and Manchester in particular, had played a vital role in this. If the larger subscribers are gathered into cousinhoods the largest sum, over £6,000, came from a group of Manchester textile families, Armitages, Haworths, Rigbys and Lees: Elkanah Armitage's kinsmen.[13]

It was a well-orchestrated campaign. The cousinhood furnished committee members as well as money. Elkanah's brother-in-law, Jesse Haworth, the yarn merchant, gave stained glass for the chapel, and his brother, Faulkner Armitage, contracted for the bulk of the furnishings. Even the choice of architect was turned to account when the Manchester School's Oxford triumph was completed on home ground in the shape of Liverpool's finest gift to Manchester.

The Mancunians, or at least the Haworths, had wanted the Liverpool born Alfred Waterhouse to design the new college.[14] The grander parts of Lancashire, some chapels and recent additions to Lancashire Independent College included, as well as Balliol and the Oxford Union and Pembroke and the Cambridge Union, were stamped in his image. Accordingly he produced a design for Mansfield. Mercifully for both Oxford and Manchester, he was in competition and his tired piece of French Renaissance was rejected in favour of the design of his younger and lesser-known competitor. Basil Champneys was the son of W. W. Champneys, a Low Churchman much admired by Free Churchmen, who became Dean of Lichfield. Like Waterhouse he had worked in Oxford and Cambridge. He was best known for his charmingly suitable 'Dutch Domestic Revival' buildings erected since 1876 for Newnham College. At Mansfield, Oxford, he switched styles with results which entranced Congregationalists. His library particularly impressed Mrs Rylands, of Stretford.

Enriqueta Augustina Rylands was a Liverpool woman, the third wife

167

of that least obtrusive but most opulent of merchant princes, John Rylands, and she was recently widowed. She had contributed liberally to Mansfield and now she determined to give Manchester a fitting memorial to her husband. It was to be a library. It was to be Gothic and Champneys was to be its architect.

Champneys accomplished the impossible. On a restricted site in the commercial heart of Manchester he produced a medieval collegiate library, far larger than any medieval college library had ever been, with electric light, lecture rooms and committee rooms such as no medieval library would have, and he did this flexibly and airily, playing dramatically with space and stone without ever forgetting that he was providing a memorial for a mercantile city, testifying to the mercantile virtues as well as to the broadest values of religion, reformed and liberated by scholarship.

Thus Oxford settled in Manchester. On 6 October 1899 the Rylands Library was opened, ten years to the month after Mansfield College. The inaugural address, delivered 'for nearly fifty minutes, without a note, and apparently without an effort', was given by Principal Fairbairn of Mansfield College. With great felicity he added Manchester to the tradition of mercantile learning — Alexandria, Florence, Venice, 'it will be, as it were, a spiritual exchange'.[15]

What was the nature of this northern mercantile civilization and the families who promoted it, for whom Oxford and Mansfield College, Cambridge and Newnham College, industrial pastorates in Oldham and Rotherham, suburban villas in Bowdon or New Brighton, and medieval libraries with Renaissance electroliers and dust excluding bookcases were part and parcel of freedom and eternity as well as assertions of propriety?

Part of the setting must be late Victorian Manchester itself, the city of Waterhouse's Town Hall and Owens' College, a city of some philanthropies and much music where 'the name of Hallé was already written large across the sky of every Thursday night in winter', and where 'in streets like Cecil Street and Acomb Street the soft hats and violin cases and the chamber music which was audible on Sunday nights made the district look and sound like Prague'.[16] It was also a city with a well-developed suburban confederacy of villas, parks and chapels, for the living, enjoying, and worshipping of that great Victorian fact of life, the urban middle classes. At one of the chapels, Waterhouse's Rusholme Congregational Church, on the edge of the business-like fantasies of Victoria Park, in August 1877, H. H. Asquith, a young barrister whose career was already a consummation of the suburban virtues, married the daughter of a local doctor, Frederick Melland.[17] Two years later, in September 1879 and in the same chapel, her younger sister Josephine married Samuel Rigby Armitage, younger brother of Elkanah.[18]

'One of the main difficulties of an historian of Manchester is with the family of Armitage. There are as many Armitages in the history of Manchester as there are Scipios in that of Rome, and the confusion which must inevitably result from this is confounded by the habit to which the Armitage family were prone of naming their sons after a small-favoured circle of Old Testament heroes.'[19] There were three chief strands of Manchester Armitages, descending from three brothers, Elijah, Ziba and Sir Elkanah. Each strand was cotton. Together, with unexpected romance and some panache, they expressed that many-faceted thing, Nonconformity.

The eldest brother, Elijah, had varied a prosperous commercial life by spending over fourteen apparently unsuccessful years in the South Pacific as an artisan missionary for the London Missionary Society, teaching the islanders of Moorea and Rarotonga the cultivation and manufacture of cotton. He had returned to Manchester's friendlier cotton industry in 1836, bringing what has since been recognized as one of the most important of surviving Polynesian sculptures.[20]

The youngest brother, Sir Elkanah, lived more publicly and more politically. His family's houses at Pendleton — Chomlea, Sorrel Bank, Hope Hall — were nerve centres for Salford Liberalism. Their cotton business was one of Manchester's largest and Sir Elkanah's largesse dignified a string of Congregational chapels. He sat on Manchester's first Council and had stood for Parliament, unsuccessfully, for Salford in 1857. He had been knighted for his conduct as Mayor of Manchester during the Chartist troubles of 1848, and John Ruskin conferred a further accolade when he dubbed him 'one of Nature's aristocracy'.[21]

There was a verve about him, suggesting the stage at which Nonconformity and commerce merged into a more spanking world. He has been described as

a merchant prince and conducted himself as such. The horses and carriages with which he served the office of High Sheriff of Lancashire in 1866 were probably the most dashing and sumptuous that Manchester had so far seen. But then, all the great Manchester men of the age . . . were, as the saying went, 'very particular about their horses', and considerable colour and movement were added thereby to politics, and not only to politics but to Nonconformity where colour and movement are not usually looked for. . . . There were many Congregational and Unitarian Chapels in Manchester and Salford and the smaller Lancashire towns, to say nothing of Bowdon, in which the arrival in the street outside of carriages drawn by horseflesh in its most mettlesome examples betokened with certainty the approaching end of the sermon and was indeed as much part of the order of worship as the collection or the concluding hymn. Many of these horses underwent unheard-of trials of the spirit on nights of victory or defeat at the poll. They were embedded in torchlight processions; they were snatched from the traces in the public street. It brought about a curious conversion not to say sanctification of the horse.[22]

'To say nothing of Bowdon. . . .' Bowdon was where the Ziba Armitages lived. Unlike his brothers Ziba Armitage never became his own master, save in self-respect. From 1836, however, his only son, William, became the dominant partner in the cotton firm for which his father and uncles had first worked. Renamed Armitage and Ward, in one of those subterranean mutations of family connexion necessary to an understanding of the Victorian business scene, and then, from 1860, Armitage and Rigby, the concern prospered abundantly. By the 1850s it had weaving sheds in Ancoats, large mills at Warrington and a warehouse in the middle of Manchester and its specialisms were all that made Lancashire textiles notable: ticks, flannelettes, denims, ginghams, drills, ducks, dooties, cottonades, towels, lustres, suitings and jeans. By the 1870s the warehouse was in Portland Street, and William Armitage had joined his uncles as a prototype northern manufacturer, teetotal, Liberal, Nonconformist, philanthropic, and with the authoritarianism which often accompanies those qualities. He had also become a banker. Observers, however, remained satisfied with the stock picture of such a man: 'He was a self-made man, and never attempted to throw off or gloss over his innate home-bred qualities.'[23]

In 1853 he purchased Mount Pleasant and six acres of land, where Bowdon merges into Altrincham. Over the years, enlarged and renamed Townfield, it became a solid, rambling, restrainedly Italianate villa of the kind best seen at Folkestone. Each New Year for over forty years it housed monstrous clan gatherings and it offered a haven throughout the year for visiting preachers and missionaries newly on furlough.

The Armitages moved to Bowdon at the time of its major expansion. Nine miles from the centre of Manchester, but tied to it since 1849 by the railway, it demonstrated the contradictory qualities of Victorian England's most distinctive contribution to civilized living, suburbia. It exhibited both anarchy and conservatism, perpetual change as well as minute control of each blade of grass. Its gardens, trees and glass-houses intermingled. It was synthetic. It was dramatic. It was at once romantic and Puritan. It was suburban.

It was manifestly neither town nor country. In the 1850s it had no public supplies of gas or water. There was no parcel delivery and letters were delivered once a day. Such simplicity was compounded by the Earl of Stamford's ample parklands at Dunham Massey. Any feudalism at Bowdon, however, was merely a carefully contrived atmosphere. Lord Stamford was no doubt an outpost of Cheshire's Tory landed interest, but in fact much of his income derived from real estate in the cotton towns and from the villas of the Bowdon cottontots discreetly crowding the edges of his plantations along the Dunham Road. Indeed Bowdon's pleasure grounds emphasized how contrived it all was, for the avenues, the drives and the walks belonged not to Lord Stamford's Dunham Massey but to Hurst Dale, Highfield, Racefield, Fern Lea, Fair Lea, Park Gate, Glebe Lands, Woodlands, Woodside, Westacre, Hill Crest, Green Bank. Even Stamford House and Dunham House, Dunham Lodge and Dunham Woods, were cottontot houses.[24]

By the 1880s Bowdon was Manchester's most relaxed suburb, relatively soot-free, outpacing Victoria Park and Broughton Park. It was boasted that Green Walk, Bowdon, housed as many millionaires as Park Lane, London. There was this difference, however, in that Bowdon retained its Puritan stratum. It was well-chapelled and despite the presence of fine parish churches this was not a question of Dissenting traps stopping by the lych-gate when they turned into carriages. The Wesleyans and the English Presbyterians had burst out in Dissenting Gothic, flamboyant and dubious in the case of the Methodists, predictable and dubious in the case of the Presbyterians. The pace had been set by the Congregationalists on the Higher Downs.

Their church was set back from the road, its site carefully laid out in 1848. A gate led into a carriage drive which ended in a circular sweep in front of the chapel for the better positioning of the cottonmen's carriages. Semi-detached villas for the families of professional men flanked the drive. In 1878 'Festus' of the *Warrington Examiner* found it a fine building, cruciform yet never quite Anglican, expressing tensions natural to rich Puritans in a suburb. The trees glimpsed through its high windows recalled the medieval idea of nature caught in tracery and stained glass. It was roomy and comfy and colourful, 'for on the rafters above there are designs in red, blue, and white paint; the organ pipes are decorated in semi-barbaric splendour, while all around are brightly varnished seats, red cushions, and red curtains'.[25]

The marks of culture accompanied the comfort and colour. In subsequent years the fine stone pulpit was joined by a communion table of cedar wood from Lebanon and olive wood from the Mount of Olives, and the fine stained glass was joined by panels reproducing Luca Della Robbia's *Singing Boys*. Together they indicated the fusion of the taste and aspirations of the minister and his people.

Italy, the Florence of Della Robbia, sanctified by John Ruskin who purged it of earthly passion, was the minister's eternal passion. In the Nonconformist world there was no influence so pervasive as that of a pulpit prince. Alexander Mackennal reigned at The Downs from 1876 until his death in 1904. He was a power among Free Churchmen and in the councils of Mansfield College and the Rylands Library. He was stalwart and ruddy, his features announcing the virtues of mental energy and analytical power without the faults of intellectualism. A university man, he lacked the oddities of some Dissenting preachers. He was dignified in his demeanour, with music in his voice and polish in his accent, 'untainted by provincialism of any kind'. He read his sermons, and at times there was the poetic line, perhaps from Tennyson, and sometimes there was a dramatic sharpening of phrase, as when he depicted the man pursuing wealth and stricken by a 'greedy pallor, the very colour of the gold he toiled for'. Mackennal had been a schoolfellow of Edward Clarke, the advocate, and Henry Irving, the actor.[26] The livelihood of all three depended largely on their power of accent.

The context of the parson's sermon was his people's service. At Bowdon they were musical. The organ was played 'with great taste' and the singing was intelligently done, for parson and people were at one. Like them he was a distributor. His stipend reached £1,000; his son went to the school to which their sons increasingly went, which was Rugby School; his children married the grander chapel families; his sister ran an exclusive girls' school in the midlands.

This was the community – a fusion of pulpit and pew; Florence, the Mount of Olives and the Pilgrim Fathers; parson, cottontots, a first generation of university graduates and a strange generation of Dissenting public school boys, and their sisters, future wives for them all – of which the Townfield Armitages were part, and since none of William Armitage's children and only one of his children-in-law, reacted against their Nonconformity, an understanding of it has been necessary.

Eleven of William Armitage's fourteen children flourished into the prime of life, largely free from the ill health which galloped in many comparable families and which had dogged his own life since mid-century. All his children married firmly into commercial families save one son who married the daughter of a Congregational minister. Three sons entered the family firm, Armitage and Rigby. A fourth, Elkanah, became a Congregational minister but strengthened the family's textile connexion's by marrying Ella Sophia Bulley, daughter of the Liverpool cotton-broker employed by the firm since 1852. Only one of the boys went to Cambridge: it was Owens' College for the others. The youngest son, alone, went to a public school. The choice was the recently founded Clifton College. The younger girls were sent to Laleham School in Clapham, established by that redoubtable Manchester Methodist, Miss Pipe.

It is with one of the sons, George Faulkner Armitage, two of the sons-in-law, Arthur H. Lee and Richard Harding Watt, and the brother of a third son-in-law, Arthur Kilpin Bulley, that the remainder of this chapter is concerned.

Armitage, Lee and Watt had much in common. They were Congregationalists and chapel deacons. They were men of means, Watt as a glove manufacturer with interests in South African gold mines, his brothers-in-law by virtue of their family cotton businesses. They were well-travelled men who knew Europe intimately. Lee developed business connexions in the United States; Armitage had travelled to Brazil and Argentina; Watt's variants of the grand tour were a youthful voyage to Australasia and one in later years to the Middle East.

Here the similarities end. The Bulleys, for example, nurtured their idiosyncracies. There was a social edge to their concerns and a tendency to leave Congregationalism for agnosticism. Perhaps this was a measure of the difference between Manchester and Liverpool, but there was also an elusiveness about Watt. He wished to marry Mary Ethel, the youngest and one of the prettiest of William Armitage's daughters, in 1882, but the marriage was not arranged until 1906 when Ethel was forty-five and Watt was sixty-three. The reasons for this romantic delay do not go beyond surmise.

Armitage, Lee, Watt and the Bulleys represent the tendencies expressed in the Rylands Library, Mansfield College and Emmanuel Church, Cambridge, as well as in the villas and chapels of Bowdon or the Wirral. They were men of taste without aestheticism, of intelligence without intellectualism, whose scholars were antiquarians rather than historians, whose parsons were preachers rather than theologians, whose thinkers were doers, whose poet was Browning. They were the distributors of society, denizens of J. M. Richards's castles on the ground, at once moral and theatrical, fancy dress yet close to daily life, and perpetually on the fringe of change. Indeed, they were among the creators of that world, Armitage and Lee as gifted amateurs who became professionals because they made taste their business, A. K. Bulley as an amateur whose temperament and social imagination combined to turn his hobby into business, Watt as eternal amateur who overstepped them all in a brief burst of anarchy as patron and scene painter of genius.

The length and innocence of Faulkner Armitage's life obscures the significance of his work. He was too easily seen as Altrincham's Grand Old Man, survivor of more liberal days, driving to the last in his brougham. Even his name recalled the heroic age: George Faulkner after the Quaker manufacturer who had befriended William Armitage in his pioneering days and had persuaded John Owens to leave his fortune for educational

173

purposes.[27] Inevitably the causes represented at Faulkner Armitage's funeral and alluded to in his obituary notices suggest a man in the mainstream of municipal benevolence: J.P. from 1894; Chairman of the Bench from 1930 to 1934; Mayor of Altrincham from 1913 to 1919; President of the local Liberal Association and presiding therefore over the 1923 election victory, among the first of a long line of suburban Liberal rebirths; a supporter, too, of hospitals, education, temperance, the Brotherhood Movement, and bowling as a healthful recreation.[28] There was no trace of intellectualism about him, and there were few books in his otherwise carefully furnished house.[29] The positive side of his character was guilelessness, humour and unsnobbishness; the negative side was that facile optimism which sometimes accompanies Liberalism and is the baffling attribute of many good men. However, these are not the obvious attributes of a successful interior decorator turned architect and his movement into those burgeoning professions remains obscure.

He was William Armitage's fifth son and was born in 1849. By his own account prolonged ill health — he was a short man encircled by tall brothers and his genial wink was in fact a nervous spasm caused by a wasp sting — shaped his education and led to a period abroad where he acquired a knowledge of art.[30] Doubtless this and his upbringing in a Manchester whose taste was formed by Ruskin's *Two Paths* and kept to the mark by the visits of William Morris, amidst cottontots whose villas were ready to succumb to the Domestic Revival of Tudor brick and Cheshire half-timber, dictated his future. As Raffles Davison put it in the *British Architect* in 1891, bracketing Armitage with Morris:

He has studied and *worked* in workshops and factories in England, France, Switzerland and Italy, and spent nearly two years in study of wood-carving on the Continent. He practised wood-carving as a speciality in England for some time, and then took to designing and modelling, and thereafter to decoration and furnishing at which he has worked for the last fourteen years until he has developed a business (or practice or whatever you like to call it) of which he may be proud. His studios and workshop are side by side and the design and execution of wood, metal, plaster, etc., go on fairly hand-in-hand, the only items of work at present being executed for him away from his own place being stained-glass and carpet weaving. His draughtsmen have been educated out of the material to be found in the ordinary day school and which usually develops into shop-hands.[31]

He had started as a woodcarver in the 1870s, taking a room at Townfield, with a derelict shippon as workhouse. By 1878 the business was on a serious footing and with his youngest brother, Joseph Frederick, and his cousin, John Rigby, there developed a flourishing partnership. A large property, Stamford House, which had been a coaching inn and a school, and stood opposite Altrincham Parish Church, was purchased for offices and workshops. When the business expanded into showrooms in John Dalton Street, Manchester, and Clifford Street, London, with further workshops in Altrincham, it became Faulkner's private house. In 1879 he married John Rigby's sister, Annie. The marriage of her sister, Lily, to Arthur Haworth and Faulkner's eldest sister, Marianne, to Arthur's uncle, Jesse Haworth, partners in James Dilworth and Son, reputedly among the world's leading yarn agencies, emphasizes the respectability of Faulkner's position.

Interior decorators who turn into architects are hard to place. They are at the mercy of fashion. Their work is synthetic, scene-setting. It is suburban. At its worst it is hack work, and at his worst Faulkner Armitage displays all that is embarrassing in late Victorian taste: furniture too large for its setting and comfortless; electric fitments used with more enthusiasm than understanding; Jacobean woodwork distorted for purposes of which no Jacobean dreamed; no wall without shelving or cupboards; no billiard room without its frieze of fibrous plaster or its painted panels of fishing boats in a Dutch mist. At his very worst he is simply insensitive, sticking '1890ish' Elizabethan on to a pleasant Regency frame or planting a limp copy of Bramall Hall by the shores of Lake Windermere.[32]

At his best, however, there is a liveliness which anticipates *Art Nouveau*, especially in his metal work and his designs for glass. Sometimes there is a feeling for shape and purpose which explains his Manchester agency for the firm of William Morris[33] and always there is a magpie originality, a quality of workmanship and a search for integrity. He deserves to be remembered as a moulder of the Domestic Revival, interpreting it for his sort of people.

Armitage worked from the 1870s to 1914. Save in details he advanced little in that time, moving amiably across the Renaissance centuries, pausing frequently at a flavoured Jacobethan of the ingle-nooked kind. He reached his peak in the 1890s and battled in 1895 with nearly fifteen commissions.[34] By 1914 he was old-fashioned.

Apart from his architectural work, which was chiefly the extension of existing buildings, but which included private houses and a charming — and thoughtful — children's home near Rochdale, his commissions fall into four main types: ecclesiastical, exhibition, domestic and public. He carved a pulpit for Wycliffe Congregational Church, Warrington,[35] a roodscreen for Rainow Parish Church, and three choir stalls and an altar table as part of the restorations which transformed Chester Cathedral into a Victorian treasure house.[36] His exhibition work included interiors for the Manchester Jubilee Exhibition of 1887 and the Paris Exhibition of 1889, where his Council Chamber for the British Commission was awarded a gold medal for its strength and skill. It was certainly a judicious mixture of Jacobean mansion and Victorian mayor's parlour, a precise evocation of the political realities of English society, affording proper counterblast to the Eiffel Tower, meeting the frolics of modern engineering with the roast beef of Old England. His public work included the heavy redecoration of the classical Liberal Devonshire Club in St James's Street, and the smoke rooms of the Liverpool Reform Club and the Oxford Union Society.[37]

His chief work, however, lay in furnishing the bedrooms, bathrooms, billiard rooms and drawing-rooms of the Forsytes of provincial England: Brockhampton Court, Herefordshire, for one of the Fosters of Black Dyke Mills, subsequently put to architectural shame by Lethaby's revolutionary parish church nearby; Pull Woods, Ambleside, for William Crossley the Manchester engineer, put to equal shame in the same decade by two of Voysey's best houses, further down the lakeside; Abney Hall, Cheadle, for James Watts, whose father rivalled Sir Elkanah Armitage in his Congregational largesse and the core of whose house distilled all that was most Puginesque in English interior decoration of the 1850s. Or there was the billiard room of Stoneleigh, Huddersfield, 60 feet by 39 feet, its billiard table with automatic electric markers, its fibrous plaster frieze of shields painted with the arms of twenty-four Yorkshire towns, and its fireside where 'elaborate stained glass panels, form the backs to low cushioned seats on either side . . . and below the level of the baluster work in the upper part of the screens is a gilded ceiling pierced for the passage of warm air from the fire . . . the combination of rich and refined detail in wood, metal, plaster, and glass, make this interior of more than ordinary quality'. Altogether it formed 'a saloon such as no good country house should be without'.[38]

Yet there was always integrity; a concern, however thwarted, for harmony of colour and shape, for health, and for improvement. In 1890 he completed a commission which expressed all of these, when he converted a dull Sheffield mansion into the Ruskin Museum: 'Such a museum for our artisans as they have not yet dreamt of; not dazzling nor overwhelming, but comfortable, useful, and — in such sort as smoke-cumbered skies may admit — beautiful . . . the interior a working man's Bodleian library, with cell and shelf of the most available kind, undisturbed for his holiday time.'[39] We are back in the world of Mansfield College, the Rylands Library, and the breaking of barriers.

Textiles were in their bones, and both Faulkner Armitage and John Rigby designed fabrics, exhibiting them at Arts and Crafts Exhibitions in the early 1890s.[40] In 1890 Faulkner's Macclesfield Satin, 'Japanese Sunflower', pure white blossom on a light yellow ground, was exhibited in New Bond Street as part of a collection of artistic silken fabrics of English manufacture.[41] This concern for textile design was instrumental in the development of A. H. Lee as a manufacturer of furnishing fabrics.

On 21 August 1878, Arthur Henry Lee married William Armitage's third daughter, Caroline, at Bowdon Downs Chapel.[42] The Lees, from the Broughton side of Manchester, were like the Armitages in their business, Tootal, Broadhurst and Lee; their politics — Arthur Lee's father, Henry Lee, was Liberal M.P. for Southampton in the 1880s; their municipal verve — Sir Joseph Cocksey Lee, was Chairman of the Manchester Ship Canal Company; and their Congregationalism. Their Broughton Park Church, however, opened in 1874 by Dr Raleigh whose sermons had opened Emmanuel, Cambridge, a few months previously, lacked Emmanuel's restraint. It was unashamedly rich in its Decorated Gothic of the fourteenth century.[43]

For ten years Arthur Lee worked in his family's Bolton mill. In 1888, however, tired of plain weaving, he set up on his own account to produce choice fabrics and fine tapestries, using a shed in the Warrington mills of Armitage and Rigby. Twenty years later, by which time his three sons had joined him and a selling company had been developed with offices in New York, he removed to a purpose built factory in Birkenhead. The firm of Arthur H. Lee and Sons Ltd, had assumed its final shape.[44]

Faulkner Armitage provided many of the early designs, but Arthur Lee went beyond Armitage and Rigby for them. He had sufficient imagination both to design his own fabrics and to use the work of contemporary artists, Walter Crane, Charles Voysey and A. H. Mackmurdo among them.[45] His training enabled him to apply their designs skilfully and profitably to the exigencies of machine techniques. Until the Great War there was an adventurousness about his choice of artists and it is this, as well as the technical quality of his goods, which lends significance to his work.

He specialized in furnishing fabrics, notably tapestries, woven on Jacquard looms which he used with considerable ingenuity. In an age when technique outpaced design he strove to bridge the gulf, conscious that his designs set the standards for mass-produced wares. He occupied a delicate place as founder of a business sprung from the great age of industrial Lancashire, which yet resolutely turned its face from a mass market.

He shared Faulkner Armitage's concern for the underlying principles of design and good workmanship. These were the principles of William Morris after his discovery of the textiles of late medieval Italy, and of the Arts and Crafts Movement as reflected in the interlocking guilds of the

1880s, from the Century Guild of 1882 to the Arts and Crafts Exhibition Society itself, of 1888. When it is recalled that Lee's work included commissions for the Century Guild and that Walter Crane, a unifying figure in all this guildery, designed for Lee, the interest of this intensifies.

The Century Guild tried to preserve art from the tradesman, so restoring it to the artist. Arthur Lee was a tradesman who performed yeoman service for the artist, and it was perhaps his mingling of business with art which enabled his firm to take a step from which Arts and Craftsmen recoiled: he made use of *Art Nouveau*, using such designs in 1904 on a new technique for Jacquard-woven and hand-blocked tapestries.[46] In the light of retrospect such progress seems admirable. At the time it might have suggested a failure of integrity inherent in any machine-based business when it came to true craftsmanship. Business and art can be enslaved by fashion.

The firm's subsequent development bore this out. There were no more opportunistic jumps, doubtless because the complexity of techniques made it difficult to keep abreast of contemporary design. Instead there was a concentration on traditional work, marked by an interest in needlework and explained accordingly: 'the vitalizing hand of William Morris appears to have overlooked this old and essentially English craft.'[47] It was this which gave the business an international reputation, thus ensuring its conservatism. The expense of their techniques restricted their fabrics to prosperous clients and, as Arthur Lee's youngest son reflected when contemplating his 'international public of taste and means': 'Designs are mainly traditional — perhaps because those who can pay the prices have generally reached middle age.'[48]

This tendency was entrenched before 1914. An American's request for tapestries adapted from antique embroideries marked a turning of the ways: their longest-lived designs included one of 1906 based on the Tree of Life, or one of 1917 of horsemen and peasants and trees, from an embroidery in the Victoria and Albert Museum. Their Adam and Eve tapestry, from an antique petit-point, led to a demand from dealers for reproduction work.[49]

The accolade came with commissions for the 'Queen Mary' and a vast panel for the Board Room of Lutyens's Midland Bank, in London. As with Faulkner Armitage, rich clients had exerted their compromise. William Morris had turned into Jacobean and it could not have been otherwise. Among Walter Crane's most delightful designs for Arthur Lee was a tapestry called 'England and France', full of chivalry and vigour, but stylized to the point of *Art Nouveau*. Crane became a Fabian, dedicated to good design for mass markets, yet, as a commentator has put it: 'his world is a world of elegance and grace and fantasy and all things inaccessible and expensive.'[50]

'There is a plant in our rockery that entirely puzzles me and my gardening friends. I wonder if you gave it to me!' wrote Mrs Arthur Lee to her brother, Ziba Armitage of Newton Bank, during the Great War. 'Its foliage in appearance is rather like the greenhouse spirea but not glossy and it has the sharpest red thorns up its stem. Its flower is something between a wild white rose and an autumn anemone. It grows in little odd independant shoots about 1 ft to 1½ ft. Does this description convey anything to you? I cannot find it in Robinson. . . .'[51]

One of the marks of the English Domestic Revival, and certainly a mark of suburbia, is the synthesis of house and garden. The first great age of the professional interior decorator was also the first great age of genteel professional gardeners, of whom Gertrude Jekyll is the best remembered. A passion for gardens was the mark of an Armitage. Elkanah Armitage was devoted to his gardens at Easthill, Rotherham and Westholm, Rawdon, the latter with its split levels, its terrace flanked by creepered turrets, its roses and its wood across a steep path. Ziba Armitage had a fine rockery at Newton Bank, near Warrington, and Faulkner's house was softened and coloured by a profusion of flowers. It was the Bulley connexion, however, which converted the garden into an object of social engineering.

The Bulleys were Liverpool to the Armitages' Manchester, cotton-brokers as opposed to cotton-spinners. Liverpool cottonmen were gentlemen, not cottontots. There was almost a romance about the Bulleys. They had been Newfoundland traders forced by the incursions of Bonapartist privateers to leave Poole for Liverpool and the Atlantic trade for cotton-broking.[52] They provided Liverpool with one of its first aldermen, Great George Street Congregational Church with one of its leading families and its minister, the fabulous Dr Raffles, with a son-in-law.

By the 1850s they had moved to the suburbs, across the Mersey to New Brighton where their church in Rake Lane stood like The Downs or Broughton Park, Puritan, Gothic and with its due portion of Italian mural sculpture.

They were an individualistic family: Caroline Octavia married John Cox, the Cambridge physicist who had been Asquith's closest school-friend; Edith married a lecturer in classics and Leonora a Congregational minister twice her age. Amy Agnes combined women's rights with books on comparative religion and Mrs Raffles Bulley wrote *Life. A Pamphlet for Girls and Boys of 14* and *A Talk on Questions of Sex. For Young Men and Girls of 18*: brave work for a deacon's wife in 1911.

Of the men of that generation, two became agnostics and Faulkner Armitage built houses for both of them. Marshall left cotton-broking for Hindhead, that Alpine part of Surrey so attractive to the late Victorian upper middle classes. At West Down, on the Portsmouth Road, the Marshall Bulleys settled with their paintings, their music, their daffodils and pine trees, and their Cheshire manor house transplanted to the North Downs, with a narwhal horn over the music-room fire.[53]

Arthur Bulley also left cotton-broking and Congregationalism. In 1898 he removed to Ness where Faulkner Armitage built Mickwell Brow for him, a hard-faced house in red Ruabon brick, on a sandstone hill facing south across the Dee. It was a site for a frontiersman and there, over the next forty years Bulley converted a windswept sixty acres into gardens: but there was a clear purpose to it. He used his fortune to scour the world for plants — he has been called 'the first of the great twentieth-century patrons of plant collecting'[54] — and he turned part of his estate into a commercial nursery, Bees Ltd. Thus, from 1909, some of the new species could be made available to the public. Bulley's public, however, was not to be the nurseryman's traditional carriage trade: his intention was to provide cheap seeds for the lower middle classes, to provide delphiniums for the semi-detached, a breaking of barriers for which established nurserymen could not easily forgive him.

Such social engineering took him into politics. In January 1910 he stood for Parliament, for Rossendale, under the auspices of the Lancashire and Cheshire Women's Textile and Other Workers' Representation Committee. He was in opposition to the sitting Liberal and the local Labour Party stayed neutral, but he polled 600 votes, necessarily male.[55]

Victorian agnosticism was strongly religious and the inspiration behind Bees Seeds was little different from the hymns which Arthur Bulley's sister, Ella Sophia, wrote about gardens or the flower services which her husband, Elkanah Armitage, held in his churches.

There remains Richard Harding Watt. Faulkner Armitage summarized the 'incredible Mr Watt's'[56] achievement with an understatement bereft of understanding: 'Later in life he became deeply interested in Architecture and built a number of houses, etc., reproducing in Knutsford something of the South European style which he so much admired in Italy.'[57]

Posterity has been less reticent: 'Legh Road can boast the maddest sequence of villas in all England. . . . The beginning . . . is harmless enough, just Italianate, reminiscent of 1840 rather than 1900. But then the Witches' Sabbath starts, incredible top crestings where the chimneys are, and stone-domed turrets and Italian villa towers and harmless Ionic porches.'[58] Knutsford's Witches' Sabbath began when Watt moved from Bowdon and built a large but inoffensive house called The Croft. It lasted for a dozen years. Thereafter the cauldron merely simmered.

The flight from normalcy, however, had been long a-brewing. Watt had entered Bowdon life in 1879 when he joined The Downs, of which he became a deacon six years later. He was a travelled young man of means, cultivated but mysterious. His figure suggested an obstinate kindliness and his cosmopolitan life could not entirely remove the traits of a *parvenu*. Many of his tastes were predictable — bottled water from the Biblical seas, and travel albums. His love of animals verged on the extravagant.

In 1883 he remedied a curious gap in his travels, and visited Italy. Recently rebuffed in his love for Ethel Armitage, he fell on the rebound for Italy. It best expressed his aspirations. It set the seal on his education. He had become the Hebrew perpetually tantalized by the Hellene, and when he moved to Knutsford in 1895, a prosperous, artistic glove manufacturer, a middle-aged bachelor, a chapel deacon and Liberal, a man of influence and culture in an area where such improbable combinations were not uncommon, his frustrations demanded an outlet.

The result was predictable: his villas on the Legh Road, with their suburban names — The Croft, Moor Garth, The White House, The Round House, Breeze, Broad Terraces, High Morland, Chantry Dane, Aldwarden Hill — were speculative housing for the professional classes. Three of them had motor houses. They were inadequately heated and their bathroom provision was conservative, but their accommodation was appropriate for houses staffed by resident servants. They were sufficiently convenient, with too many doors, and if their lighting fluctuated according to the demands of picturesqueness such was often the case with suburban houses. Their gardens were carefully built round them.[59]

Equally predictable were the public and service buildings which he gave to Knutsford: the Laundry in Drury Lane, the Ruskin Recreation Rooms, the King's Coffee House in the main street, with its reading, concert and refreshment rooms and its Old English furnishings and the Gaskell Memorial Tower next to it. This was clearly the inspiration of a landlord concerned for the improvement of his inferiors, as the mottoes from Cromwell, Ruskin and Gladstone on the walls of the Coffee House and Recreation Rooms proved.

Even his choice of architects was predictable. Two of the four whom he employed became wholly acceptable northern architects. John Brooke, architect of The Croft, had recently completed Albion Chapel, Ashton-under-Lyne, that costliest of provincial Congregational cathedrals, with its Burne-Jones glass. Harry Fairhurst, architect of the

Laundry, was a fellow Congregationalist who developed a leading Manchester practice with a specialism in commercial and university buildings.

Yet here reason cascades into fantasy. This generous landlord used his architects lavishly but mercilessly and drove his builders to mutiny. An instinctive architect and competent draughtsman, he was unable to read elevations — the ultimate frustration for so compulsive a patron. He was forced to rely on an exasperating empiricism and his wide experiences had to be interpreted by local professionals whose competence inevitably outran their sympathy.

The result was inescapable. Legh Road's Italianate gardens; the Laundry's Damascene water-tower and its interior of turquoise, cream and red; the deep verandas and strange turrets and boundary fences; the walls pitted with nesting boxes, were without doubt 'all-in' architecture, and Watt's habit of using materials from demolished buildings added dash and timelessness to the scene, as well as a puritan, if ineffectual, touch of economy.

And the correct assessment of it all? When it came to styles, Watt refused to classify himself: 'This is British, yes, British architecture.'[60] That is just what it was not. There is no evidence that he knew directly of the contemporary trendsetters in British architecture, whether Lutyens, Voysey or Mackintosh — although The Croft looked across a shallow valley to a pleasant Baillie Scott house of 1895, Bexton Croft — and Watt's presence at the opening of Mansfield College was merely that of a northern subscriber. He was, in a strict sense, architecturally illiterate yet some have found in him the English Gaudí: 'His motifs mix wildly, Classical, Italianate, Byzantine, and Unprecedented, he likes towers of jagged outline and domes, and his fenestration is as random as any brutalist's today.'[61]

In 1940 the Tatton Browns were impressed by his concern with spatial relations and his freedom from academic conventions, qualities which transcended his naivety.[62] They also discerned qualities which suggest that after all he remains within the suburban tradition of his brothers-in-law, merely reminding us more forcefully of the anarchy which it usually holds in check. His houses were built for distributors, intermingling with their grounds, with all that intense theatricality, that scene-painted lack of depth which marks suburbia. Even to their use of second-hand materials, they were synthetic. The Tatton Browns felt each house to be a backcloth to the next in a ninefold stage set, and even the Coffee House, built for the working people of Knutsford, was no more 'than a pleasant tea-shop for the well-to-do'.[63] As if the set were for a matinée performance only: in 'Cranford'.

On Thursday, 29 March 1906, Elkanah Armitage wrote in his diary: 'Today at Bowdon I married Ethel to Richard Harding Watt who 24 years ago first asked her to be his wife! Beatus hodie fidelis! She is 45 he is 53. A happy family gathering about this *quiet* wedding (No presents etc). They are to live at Watt's house at Knutsford.'[64]

Thereafter Watt's compulsive architecture died away. They travelled abroad, their journeyings little more architectural than those of any Armitage. In a final gesture Watt designed a club house and manse for the Congregational Church supported by the Armitages in Partington. 'The buildings . . . are of a simple Spanish type. . . . The walls are of brick finished in cement and lime whiting, and there are red corrugated Italian tiles on the roof.'[65] The anarchy was checked, but there was a tower.

In March 1913, Elkanah Armitage, holidaying near Naples, noted: 'Richard Watt thrown from carriage and killed. Thursday March 13.'[66] It is thought that the horse shied at paper blown by the wind as Watt was standing up, the better to see his houses in the Legh Road.

Watt was the first of the brothers-in-law to die. In 1914 Faulkner Armitage retired, although after the war he designed Altrincham's war memorial, added a sensitive memorial porch to The Downs Church and carved for Chester Cathedral a fourth misericord of St George slaying the dragon. He used his secretary as a model for the saint, who was to represent the League of Nations.[67] He died in November 1937, from a cold caught when attending a memorial service for 'Dick' Sheppard, his nephew by marriage. His business survives in Manchester as Wolff and Alexander. Arthur Lee died in 1932, and rising costs forced the closure of his firm in July 1970: the premises have since become Status City, a do-it-yourself discount centre. Arthur Bulley died in 1942. Bees Seeds survive in different hands, and the gardens at Ness have been given to Liverpool University.

The firm of Armitage and Rigby survived the Second World War. Elkanah Armitage's son, Godfrey, became its chairman and his wife and first cousin, Margaret Bulley, achieved the perspectives which had eluded Faulkner Armitage. She had lived in Bloomsbury and known Roger Fry, and her house in Didsbury was revived with white walls and African fabrics. Her pictures included a Rouault and a Picasso. There were no picture rails, corner couches or friezes, but the moral purpose remained in her books — *Art and Counterfeit* (1925), or *Art and Everyman* (1952).[68] She became a Christian Scientist.

Of them all Richard Watt had offered the strangest perspective. A product of Calvinism, he was a creator in an environment where nothing is left to chance, but where the best expression is nonetheless a happy accident and where the message expressed in his houses in Knutsford no less than in Emmanuel Church, Cambridge, Mansfield College, Oxford, the Rylands Library, Manchester, as in the lives of his textile kinsmen, is that from Ruskin's *Proserpina* which Faulkner Armitage stencilled on the library frieze of the Sheffield Ruskin Museum: 'Every noble life leaves the fabric of it interwoven for ever in the work of the world.'

A postscript is necessary. In a moment of private politics Asquith dismissed Bonar Law's establishment as being in the manner of Altrincham.[69] No doubt he had the families of his mother and first wife in mind, but his recollection was selective and insensitive. The Willanses and Mellands were part of the Armitage connexion: they were among Faulkner Armitage's clients. The Armitage connexion suggests a development of taste which would be of little surprise had it emerged from an established Unitarian cousinhood; its significance lies in the fact that it was a facet of dissident Dissent, teetotal, evangelical, industrial, Radical.

Faulkner Armitage and Arthur Lee are types of the middle men of taste, the distributors. Between Armitage's robust eclecticism and the trendsetters there is a firm enough link: in the late 1880s Armitage's staff included Armitage Rigby, a brother-in-law of Faulkner's, who became a successful architect in the Isle of Man where his houses have been confused with the work of Baillie Scott, and Barry Parker, the future partner of Raymond Unwin.[70] It was Parker and Unwin, the architects of much at Letchworth and Hampstead Garden Suburb, whose *The Art of Building a Home* (1901) furthered the transformation of suburbia into a land of cheap and artistic semi-detacheds, all nooks and pretty bays.

Architecture, in short, had become suitable for boys from Nonconformist families. The Bulley cousinhood could point to Raffles Brown, who had a respectable mid-Victorian practice in Liverpool, and Hargreaves Raffles who had a pleasant way with 'Pont Street Dutch' in the Home Counties. J. Medland Taylor, the quirkiest and naughtiest of late Victorian Manchester architects, and a 'Taylor of Ongar' by descent, was a connexion by marriage of Faulkner Armitage's partner J. F. Armitage. Outside the cousinhood, at the top of his profession, was Morley Horder, son of a musical, suburban, Congregational minister, and architect of Congregational churches, university buildings, and important branches for Boots the Chemist, but first known for his houses, gabled and ingle-nooked, at one with their gardens.[71] In this respect he was part of that tradition which also produced J. A. and Lawrence Gotch, Norman Jewson ('his buildings look as if they had grown naturally from the ground')[72] and Ernest Weaving, all from Baptist families.

The tradition which they represented was an artificial one, the more so for its striving after the natural. It was the distillation of a suburban civilization. The search for integrity could become precious and brittle, fringing the inter-war world of A. A. Milne — whose wife, Dorothy de Selincourt, came from a London Congregational family — which 'still took servants for granted, educated its male children at public schools, made an art of polite conversation (but banned sex, politics, shop, and religion as dinner-table topics), played amateur cricket, patronized musical comedy. . . .'[73]

At its best, it was a consummation of the Puritan virtues: for the achievement of integrity demands grace combined with reserve and a sense of discipline verging upon repression. It is contrived: it speaks of that service which is perfect freedom. Between the Puritan and Art there is tension but no incompatibility.

Book IV

From Nonconformity to
Free Churchmanship

Chapter 9

'No Quest, No Conquest'.
Baldwin Brown and Silvester Horne

What I dread is the drift of a current, not the action of a will.

> (J. Baldwin Brown in 1878, quoted in Elizabeth Baldwin Brown,
> *In Memoriam: James Baldwin Brown, B.A.*, 1884, p. 28.)

I have just come away from seeing the Varsity play the Preston North End team. . . .
At the Milton Club last Monday we had a glorious debate on Socialism.

> (C. S. Horne to Mrs Charles Horne, 26 November 1888,
> in W. B. Selbie, *The Life of Charles Silvester Horne*, 1920, p. 61.)

Art and Puritanism are not incompatible since art is merely a means to the end. If Nonconformists became deft in their use of this means it was as much through the influence of their prime distributors, the ministers, as through any irresistible tendencies in society. The minister's role was complex, but in the world's eye it was defined by the pulpit. The minister transmitted the Word: but the transmission depended upon his own spoken word and the artistry with which he projected it. The minister was an actor.

If he stayed the course, and a mutuality developed between himself and his people, then art — and artifice — remained properly subordinated to the Kingdom. It is in those who stayed the course that the real interest is to be found. Many bruised and fascinating souls left the ministry for a more general fame. Those who remained, sharing their views though with blunter minds, had the greater influence on their kind. Turns of phrase, shades of ritual, types of ornament, would appear, suggesting a mere ecclesiastical keeping up with the Joneses, but in fact reflecting profound intellectual development. One man's theology became another man's rhetoric: this was a process of development not degeneration. The minister was the intermediary in this and his success a delicate balance between artistry and integrity.

This was a role peculiar to the Nonconformist minister, and even among Nonconformists the mutuality between parson and people was peculiar to Baptists, Congregationalists and Unitarians. Methodists could not share in it because of the circuit system. Methodist ministers were more of an order than their Free Church brothers: for them the mutuality was with Conference.

This role, the diffusion of theology into rhetoric, the balancing of artistry and integrity, to achieve movement, is clearly illustrated by the careers of two London Congregational ministers, James Baldwin Brown (1820-84) and Charles Silvester Horne (1865-1914). Their lives show the power of the pulpit and the potential of the gathered church. They also show the extent to which the Nonconformist ministry became the perfect profession for able, moderately ambitious, young men from the middle classes.

Baldwin Brown and C. S. Horne were lured by the art of preaching. For Horne art turned into romance, and his last essay in the craft was a course of lectures on the romance of preaching. For Brown art turned into passion. He recalled the mastery of John Leifchild in the 1830s, who 'lit the flame of zeal, of love, I might say of passion, for the ministry. . . .'[1]

These preachers were educated men. In them the intellectual discipline imposed by university education confronted the indiscipline inevitable to heavy pastorates. Perhaps only good second-class minds could meet the challenge: Silvester Horne sailed through his courses at Glasgow and Oxford; Baldwin Brown was one of the earliest graduates of University College, London, and took his degree at the earliest permissible age. There was an intellectual facility about such men which John Stoughton, one of Horne's stately predecessors at Kensington Chapel, expressed in a story which he would tell against himself. It concerned a conversation with Dean Stanley, to whom Stoughton confessed, 'You know I am not a person of great learning'. 'No,' said the Dean, 'Matthew Arnold tells *me* the same thing. You are not a man of great learning, he says, but you are a man of extensive information.'[2]

Men of extensive information, however, care for education. Silvester Horne's children went to boarding schools, and a daughter was a scholar of Lady Margaret Hall, Oxford; one of Baldwin Brown's daughters was the sole Dissenter attending F. D. Maurice's Harley Street lectures and his son, Gerard, was the first Nonconformist to be elected to an Oxford Fellowship after the repeal of university tests.[3] 'I remember', said Garrett Horder, one of Brown's disciples, 'on one occasion to have asked him why he had chosen Oxford rather than Cambridge for his son's University. He replied that, in his judgment, Oxford furnished a more comprehensive culture than the sister University.'[4]

The search for a comprehensive culture by these men of extensive information underlines their position as distributors, leading their congregations, moving with them, and advancing socially in the process. The ministry was a social as well as an intellectual lightning conductor and Horne and Brown were preaching gentlemen as well as preaching scholars.

'Christian Gentleman' was a phrase dear to obituarists. It was dear to Dissenters fresh from their first novel, their first Cook's tour abroad, or their first detached villa in Streatham. It implied breeding, despite everything, and masculinity, in an age of ritualism. It enhanced their sense of spiritual superiority, and gave it a social clothing. Silvester Horne was among the last and greatest of the breed: 'In dress, in manner, in approach of speech he was a simple Christian gentleman, unconventional to a degree. . . . If he had asked for cheers for Jesus Christ he could have got them.'[5]

It was, however, a side entrance to gentility. These assured preaching scholars and gentlemen were nonetheless inferior, caught in the continuing fight for recognition. They were, therefore, Christian soldiers, indeed they were Christian commanders, perfect knights, and their congregations were their men, spiritually assured, socially edgy. The perfect word to describe them is 'self-conscious'.

The mingling of such ministers with such people was a chancy matter and there were frequent explosions. At its best, however, the relationship was without compare and an understanding of it helps explain the attraction which the voluntary principle held for so many Victorians. Silvester Horne was called to the pastorate of Kensington Chapel, a church remarkable for its weighty ministers, while he was still an Oxford undergraduate. Was he too young? 'We want a young man, we have a number of competent people who will rally round him and take the burden off his shoulders' and Thomas Walker, their senior deacon and an editor of the *Daily News*, promised him: 'We will surround you with our affection and our diligence.' Horne responded accordingly: 'And now one pauses and holds one's breath and thinks of what one is committed to, and hardly dares look the whole thing fully in the face, but puts one's hand in God's. . . .'[6] And towards the end of the partnership he wrote:

> Latterly the feeling has been growing upon me that I have done all I can with this congregation. Last Sunday evening, for instance, I harangued them on Temperance. I had the sense then, which I so often have, of talking things, which to me are almost life-blood, to those who are just a little amused at my impetuosity. In other words, I think the large majority at Allen Street do not believe *with* me. They are here because they believe *in* me.[7]

To Free Churchmen this speaks of the reality of the Spirit at work among them. To anybody it is a tribute to the power of personality. It suggests what was vital in Victorian Nonconformity.

London 18 June 1856: 'Our last day at Cousin James'. Miss Evans, Cousin James, and the Leifchilds, went down to the Crystal Palace to the opening of the large new fountains in the grounds. . . . In the evening we went . . . to St Martin's Hall, Long Acre, to hear Rossini's Stabat Mater, and Mendelssohn's Lob-Gesang. . . . Cousin James came in time to hear the Lob-Gesang: he took us home.'

19 June: 'Mary and I left Cousin James, after a stay of three weeks and went down to Aunt Wilson's at Tunbridge Wells. . . .' 21 July: 'Mary and I left Tunbridge Wells for London our visit being now ended. . . . We went to Cousin James' house again.

'Cousin James is very ill now. He sat in the drawing room in the evening. Mr Frank Leifchild was there. He can talk extremely well, and is privately most immensely conceited.'[8]

These are entries from the holiday journal of Ella Sophia Bulley, then an alert teenager from New Brighton with a taste for music and an eye for description, visiting her southern relatives, the Joshua Wilsons of Nevill Park, Tunbridge Wells, heirs to the benevolence of Thomas Wilson of Highbury. Frank Leifchild belonged to Cousin James's wife's family, and Cousin James was James Baldwin Brown, on the verge of the ill health which issued in his most controversial book, *The Divine Life in Man* (1859). The journal, therefore, is less an account of the middle classes at leisure than of the *Nonconformist* middle classes at leisure.

Baldwin Brown would not have equated leisure with recreation, as Frank Leifchild recalled:

> I remember walking with him through Derbyshire, . . . and being struck with his pertinacity and dash in examining for himself every point of interest along the rocky beds, and the abrupt hill-sides of the Dove and the Derwent; but this scrutiny accomplished, there was no loitering by the way, no dalliance with nature, no dream, no indulgence; we were, as I used to think, in bondage again to the plan marked out for the day. No one, however, paid sincerer homage to those fortunate spirits who, as they wait or wander by the way, are drawn into secret communion with Nature — that is, if result of this secret communion were forthcoming in poetry and art. But for him a purpose was necessary. . . .[9]

He was tall, with erect carriage and rapid walk. Like so many olympian ministers he was a gardener and a mountaineer. 'In his youth he was a famous runner and jumper, and had all a Londoner's love of boating' and throughout life he was 'intellectually always on some enterprise or excursion, or newly arrived from one'.[10]

He was a gentleman. There was no doubt as to the quality of his religious descent for he was a nephew of Thomas Raffles of Great George Street, Liverpool and his wife was a niece of John Leifchild of Craven

Chapel, London. Raffles, Leifchild and John Angell James of Carrs Lane, Birmingham, took part in Brown's ordination in 1843: contemporary Congregationalism could not have produced a grander trio.[11] He was, therefore, a connexion of Sir Stamford Raffles of Singapore and a brother-in-law of H. S. Leifchild, a sculptor known for his statuary on Biblical and classical themes.[12]

His parents were a nervously energetic couple, his father a barrister from Bloomsbury, 'rarely to be seen, even at meal times, without a book or pen in his hand',[13] the author of poems, a life of John Howard and an unsuccessful venture into quarterly journalism called *The Investigator*. The elder Brown was prominent in the 1820s and 1830s in the increasingly political activities of metropolitan Dissent, working with Thomas Wilson and Josiah Conder. He was a Whiggish man, but the title of a pamphlet which he wrote in 1821 foreshadowed issues which made dissidents of the most Whiggish Dissenters: *An Appeal to the Legislature and the Public, more especially to the Dissenters from the Established Church, of every Denomination, on the Tendency of Mr Brougham's Bill for the Education of the Poor, to augment the Poor's Rate; to interfere with the Rights of Conscience; and impinge on the spirit of the Toleration Acts, with some Remarks on its probable Effects in injuring Sunday Schools.*[14] The twin worlds of Edward Baines and Edward Miall were well in the making.

Baldwin Brown's career followed uneasily upon that of his father. He was educated in London at University College School, and then at University College. From 1839 to 1841 he was at the Inner Temple, reading for the Bar with one of his Raffles cousins. He then changed course. To his father's annoyance he deserted the law to plead for eternity and entered Highbury, the theological college endowed by the Wilson family.

His first charge was at London Road, Derby, new and Corinthian-columned, already housing the nucleus of an influential congregation: Thomas Wilson had contributed a tenth of the cost.[15] Brown was its first minister.

He was too ignorant of jargon, too critical of Calvinism, too vigorous and London for Derby: 'I very well remember the affair with old Mr —: it was at a meeting of the Sunday School Union, at which most of the preachers of the town were assembled. When Mr Baldwin Brown had nearly finished his very interesting speech on the best method of training the children in our Sunday schools, he cautioned teachers not to be always harping on the fact that the children were such great sinners, and then he spoke of subjects, like the Fatherly love of God, which they might dwell on instead. As soon as Mr Baldwin Brown had concluded, Mr —

arose, and after making us all know what miserable sinners we were, delivered with much emphasis his judgment as to the proper instruction in Sunday schools. "If you ask me what you ought to teach the children, I say, firstly, teach them that they are sinners. If you ask me what you should teach them secondly, teach them that they are *sinners*" — and then, with still more emphasis, "If you ask me what to teach them in the third place, I answer, teach them that they are SINNERS".[16]

In London, however, his pastorates at Claylands, Lambeth and in Brixton were partnerships ended only by death. His pulpit style was direct, his voice clear, but throbbing: 'A living man, with a fire burning in his heart, stood forth, and nearly always before he finished, an almost sobbing voice told us that in the heart of the Great Father there was room for the farthest and saddest wanderer to find peace.'[17] Much of his effect depended on soft contradictions: 'Life from the birth is a dying daily. . . . This black thread runs through the whole texture of human existence; it is the key of its sinful unity. . . . Life is imperfect till death completes it. It is that end of the work — the daily dying — which crowns it.' And it is Christ's touching of the black thread with a golden lustre which has made 'the royal thread of our existence'.[18]

Like Thomas Binney, with whom he was sometimes compared,[19] he gathered round him a church full of young men, pluming themselves on their thoughtfulness. His congregation included John Doulton, the potter, journalists like Lucy of the *Daily News*, theological students like the young P. T. Forsyth, politicians like Henry Richard and legendary missionaries like Robert Moffat. Edward Miall occasionally sat under him.

They were not, however, allowed to escape with mere sermon-tasting: there were night schools, penny banks, provident societies and district visitations to be organized. Darkest London had to be probed from the Moffat Institute. The whole was welded together by a self-conscious urge for culture: 'The guests were invited by the City Missionary from every house in turn, in all the streets of the district; tickets were left for each person in the house, and no inquiries made about them, and the delight and astonishment of some poor outcasts at being thus recognized as "neighbours" may be imagined . . . "why he put his hand on my shoulder as if he was my brother!" The wealthier members of the congregation were invited to come and make tea for the poor people, and to bring microscopes, photographs, and whatever else they had of interest, to show them afterwards; but, above all, to bring *themselves*, their kindliness, their intelligence, their refinement, to make the evening brighter. The musical members of the congregation, some of whom had a very rare gift, were asked to sing their best, and they took great pains to practise for these occasions. He and his wife gave readings from the classical poets — Shakespeare, Wordsworth, Burns, and others — as well as from Dickens and the Lancashire poet Waugh, of whom he was very fond; and the evening closed with "family prayer".[20]

This was more than an early example of a type of meeting common to most large chapels by the 1890s, for it began at Claylands in 1859, the year of Darwin and Mill on Liberty; the year too when Brown published his *Divine Life in Man*.

The book was the product of his sick room, the first major work of the most prominent of the younger London ministers. It created a furore. Leading Baptists condemned it, and so did Joshua Wilson. It conferred upon its author an isolation and a notoriety which he exploited. But he did not leave his denomination and he was not disowned by his congregation; he continued with his writing, he persevered with his raising of awkward questions at annual assemblies and he became a hero to succeeding generations of young ministers. His combination of denominational prominence and doctrinal boldness ensured him a greater influence than if he had followed his first inclination and left the ministry. Indeed, because his flavour of heresy enforced his Independent stance, it gained him a hearing in unlikely places: 'If the official guardians of orthodoxy refused to countenance him, his ministrations were eagerly welcomed in country districts and among ministers who, though of the old school, lived far from controversies.'[21]

His significance was that Nonconformists could reach F. D. Maurice, or F. W. Robertson, through him. John Hunter assured the Brixton people that Brown 'had done for their Nonconformist Churches what Maurice had done for the English Established Church'.[22] For Brown the chief Christian fact was the Incarnation: 'as we drew near through Christ to God, we found that our hiding-place was an infinite human heart.'[23] Christ was the Representative Man claiming and consecrating all that concerned his brothers: and the family concepts of brotherhood, and therefore of fatherhood, with all their charm for family-conscious Victorians and with all their social and political implications for Radical Liberals, became a part of the Nonconformist stock-in-trade, irresistibly voiced by the last of the Independents.

P. T. Forsyth, grandest of Congregational theologians, expressed it in a memorial sermon:

His chosen and special field was history. He had the historic sense. . . . Everything centred in the Incarnation, in the historic God . . . in his deep, deep sense of God in the present, God there in these worn or imbruted or helpless men and women, God in this great nation and society of which they were an indispensable part. . . . They were an integral part of a society which had its right and power to exist only in virtue of the indwelling and inworking of the Redeeming Son of God. It was not condescension to bring these people the Gospel. It was brotherhood. . . . There was no going *down* to them; it was stretching a hand *across*. . . . The more the Incarnation becomes a human fascination the more will it be realized as a divine power. . . . That seemed to me how it worked in the greatest Independent of our time. . . . There is nothing makes such men as the faith that God is man.[24]

The social implications of such brotherhood were immediately apparent to Brown: there was nothing self-contained about the agencies which he promoted at Claylands or Brixton. The Claylands buildings sheltered the Kennington Y.M.C.A.; the Moffat Institute was run on an undenominational basis; he was concerned with sanitation, and with the university extension movement, and with Henry Solly's Working Men's Club and Institute Union. In 1853 he supported the Sunday opening of the Crystal Palace ('the utterance of the mind of the Church upon this great question will probably determine the character of its relations to . . . society for some years to come'),[25] and while his lax views were condemned by Edward Baines and Angell James, they contributed towards the emergence of that easy 'social sabbatarianism' which mainstream Nonconformity assumed. In the winter of 1866 to 1867 he was active with Edward Miall, W. W. Champneys, F. D. Maurice, Tom Hughes, Goldwin Smith and Ludlow in the meetings at Anderton's Hotel and the London Coffee House which Edward White of Kentish Town had initiated to discuss artisan alienation from Christianity.[26]

These concerns were taken up in Brown's year as Chairman of the Congregational Union in 1878, when the passions of thirty years caught fire. In his address *The Perfect Law of Liberty* he contemplated imperialism, 'that bastard of empire', and he attacked rearmament. And then he looked at the Proletariat, 'a class now grown to portentous magnitude in all Christian States'; he considered the prospect of class warfare — 'a vast chasm everywhere but in England, and here the gap is fearfully wide, separates the classes, the one body of Christ' — and he reached his climax: 'Brethren, if history has taught me anything, it has taught me this, that there is no way out of such a state of things as Christians have been content to tolerate in Christendom, but by fierce struggle and terrible pain.'

It was a middle-class failure — 'that class which is the stronghold of commerce, morality, and religion' — and 'it is the turn of the democracy next. You may already hear its tramp in America and Germany . . . and we or our children shall witness a great democratic experiment to establish . . . some fair image of the Kingdom of heaven. And it will fail like the rest; inevitably it must fail. But one shudders sometimes to think what the effort may cost the world.'[27]

Six years later, Forsyth reflected that Brown 'always carried about with him the sense of what civilization and progress costs'.[28] In 1878, however, he was unable to transmit that sense to his hearers. He begged them in vain to look from their 'comfortable homes and churches, on the lairs, the rags, the miseries of the poor, Christ's poor,'[29] but they were more concerned at tendencies inside their comfortable churches which his Chairmanship of the Union appeared to magnify. The result was a confrontation which Baldwin Brown used with magnificent irresponsibility. In so doing the Brixton Independent served the interests of his denomination and its officers, and the wider implications of his addresses could rest unread between the *Year Book*'s boards.

Brown's election to his denomination's highest office serves to recall that he was, despite everything, a Dissenting grandee, the sort of minister to whom Gladstone ought to be introduced, and in 1875 and 1877 he attended the useful functions arranged by Newman Hall for Gladstone to chat painlessly with Nonconformists about popery, disestablishment or the Eastern Question.[30] He was also in demand as a preacher for anniversaries and openings, and he was a magnet for sermon-tasters. In January 1868 the schoolboy Asquith described to his mother a Sunday diet of Samuel Martin at Westminster Chapel, Dean Stanley at Westminster Abbey, and Baldwin Brown: 'All very good . . . Baldwin Brown, whose was the best of the three, on the Ministry of Scepticism to Truth.'[31]

It was this which made him unassailable, transforming him into Congregationalism's chief lightning conductor. He was instrumental in getting the strangely advanced P. T. Forsyth settled at Shipley in 1876 and then at St Thomas's Square, Hackney in 1878. In 1865 he had preached at the opening of Hillhouse Church, Huddersfield and in the early 1880s he was keenly interested in the progress of Milton Church, Huddersfield and in its minister J. T. Stannard at whose ordination in February 1880 a host of the advanced had gathered: Principal Simon, Forsyth, John Hunter and Baldwin Brown.[32] In 1882 Milton Church's *Year Book* contained 'helpful words for the times'. These included quotations from Baldwin Brown and T. T. Lynch, a suggestive combination.[33]

The combination was especially suggestive because in 1856 Brown had been active in that influential London ministers' fraternal whose support of T. T. Lynch did much to turn the *Rivulet* controversy into a *cause célèbre*. Perhaps only Brown's chronic ill health in the late 1850s prevented him from rushing to the forefront of the battle with the verve which he displayed twenty years after at the time of 'Leicester'.

In the light of retrospect the Leicester affair of 1877 seemed a muddled business. It concerned the attempt of a group of woolly ministers to hold a meeting in Leicester in October 1877 for all 'who value spiritual religion, and who are in sympathy with the principle that religious communion is not dependent on agreement in theological, critical, or historical opinion'.[34] Because the conference coincided with the Congregational Autumnals, also in Leicester, the heresy hunters sniffed long and deep. By 1878 it was the issue of the hour.

Brown was not sympathetic to the views of the Leicester men, which he found insubstantial: as P. T. Forsyth later put it, they too well reflected 'the age of impressionism, now dying'.[35] He was sympathetic, however, to the men themselves: Forsyth, Stannard and J. A. Picton were his sort of man — Forsyth had sat under him in his student days and there were other links with Picton, whose father, like Brown's brother, was a prominent Liverpool architect. Picton, indeed, was a type of that educated Nonconformity which too seldom sent its sons into the ministry. Moreover, Brown was committed to the cause of young ministers:

> I speak for my young brethren, whose work is very difficult, whose battle is very hard, harder than many of you know. . . . Brethren in Christ, let me appeal to you as one who has been for a full generation in the very midst of the conflict; do not fire into the troops who are bravely fighting your battle; do not blight with your distrust the men who are struggling hard, through many errors and failures no doubt, but still with honest and truth-loving hearts, to discover and disclose the harmonies which *must* subsist between the word of Scripture and the deepest needs, experiences, and convictions of the great world of men.[36]

Consequently his role in 1878 was straightforward. Despite the clear opinion of most delegates to the May Meetings, and the disapproval of denominational statesmen, who felt that he was abusing his position as Chairman, he championed the minority. The motions reaffirming denominational orthodoxy were passed, but the abiding memory was of Brown's support for the less orthodox, and the masterly way in which he built it upon a plea for all that was substantial in the traditions of his denomination.

The Autumnals were in Liverpool, and Brown delivered his address in Great George Street Chapel, where his uncle Raffles had ruled for fifty years, and where he himself had been invited in 1858 with a view to the succession. This was not lost on his hearers, as he compared Raffles with the ritualizers and sentimentalists of latter days,

> I look at the number of hysterically-sentimental hymns in our new Supplement; I mark the nature of the most potent and trusted influence in current revivals; I see a county town placarded with the notice that a minister 'will preach and sing the Gospel', and then I recall the men, in the place of one of whom I stand . . . who did not sing the Gospel, who did not paint or carve the Gospel, who did not dress the

Gospel, who did not incense the Gospel, who did not parade the Gospel in procession, but who preached the Gospel, with all the fervour of an intense conviction.

And he trembled for the 'contempt into which many of our childish methods are bringing the Gospel in honest minds and manly hearts'.[37]

Among the honest minds and manly hearts of Brown's audience was Elkanah Armitage, who was staying with the Marshall Bulleys at New Brighton. Armitage's recollection was brief: 'Mr Baldwin Brown (chairman) renewed his attack on the May resolutions, but most people were agreed that what he said would do good.'[38] The internal war was almost won: he made no mention of a class war.

Baldwin Brown died in June 1884. His last days were spent botanizing in the Surrey woods. He died from a stroke. 'It was as when one walks doubtfully through the windings of an obscure wood and suddenly comes out upon the light!'[39] There was a striking note about the memorial tributes. Again and again they used the language of chivalry: 'a true minister, valorous, intrepid, sanguine, his face was ever towards the dawn'; 'the veteran hero whose banner floats above them as they ride forth from the camp'; 'one of the noblest, most chivalrous . . . men I have ever known'; his 'gentilesse'; 'so full was he of spirit . . . of that specially English quality, pluck'; 'He was intensely chivalrous'; 'an almost unresting force . . . in the ardour of his Championship . . . by a kind of chivalrous instinct'; 'a chivalric soldier of conscience'; 'as a friend, he was as true as steel'; 'what chivalry'.[40]

The age of imperialism and rearmament was also the age of the Christian soldier, Elkanah Armitage was called 'Kay' by his family, and so left the Old Testament for King Arthur's Court, the world of Tennyson and Burne-Jones stained-glass. Even Dissenting Gothic bred chivalry and twenty years later Dorothea Price Hughes would turn her father's biography into a manual for Free Church, catholic, chivalry. Baldwin Brown had endowed that language with a grammar, before it joined the other jargons. It was Arthur Mursell, the Baptist *enfant terrible* and licensed jester, who captured the achievement: 'To see Baldwin Brown, lithe as a panther, and graceful as an antelope, bound down the steep of Box or Leith Hill, and clear a five-barred gate, at fifty years of age, "without turning a hair", was to see the outward and visible sign of the inward and spiritual grace which dominated and pervaded a "whole-souled" man.'[41]

The virtues which Arthur Mursell perceived in Baldwin Brown were consummated in Silvester Horne. The chivalric imagery was there: 'what a

199

Sword of Spirit he was, with a point and an edge, and a flash, and a laugh', 'the gaiety of the troubadour, combined with the valour of the knight in the lists'; '. . . a knight pilgrim . . . our Galahad home now in the city he sought'; 'This gay and gallant cavalier of the Cross, this chivalrous knight of the Holy Ghost. . . .' But the Arthurian legend had coarsened into the world of Henry Newbolt: 'to him life was a gorgeous adventure — a vagabondage in quest of the infinite'; 'he was, in the old Elizabethan sense, a great adventurer'.[42]

Horne was the son of a country minister, who left the ministry to edit a provincial newspaper owned by his wife's family. The manse at Cuckfield or the offices of the *Newport Advertiser* differed only in degree, however, from the Bloomsbury drawing-rooms of the Brown family, and like the Browns the Hornes had family connexions with Merseyside. Horne, like Brown, was invited to the Great George Street pulpit but refused it. In his undergraduate days at Glasgow, Horne sat under Dr Goodrich of Elgin Place, at the very time that Goodrich refused a call to succeed Brown in Brixton.

These were links natural to a denomination which depended for its cohesion on a mixture of personal beliefs and personal relationships, and Horne's country-town background and relatively modest means placed him among the general run of ministers. The early pattern of his career, for example, approaches that of Alexander Mackennal of Bowdon: the same edged, politically articulate upbringing, followed by a Scottish university. Mackennal was at Glasgow in the early 1850s; Horne in the 1880s. Both coasted through their courses, both were active in the Dialectic Society, and in student Liberal politics.

The difference of generation, however, was important: Mackennal was a contemporary of Edward Caird's; Horne a pupil. In Horne's time university politics meant agitating for a students' union and a students' representative council, as well as disestablishment of the national churches. In Mackennal's day the election of Macaulay as Lord Rector was the political issue of the hour. Mackennal moved on to a London theological college: Horne was one of the first students at Mansfield College, Oxford — 'what the High Churchmen here are pleased to call the "Dissenteries" '[43] — with Mackennal on the interviewing board.

Horne was, therefore, one of a new breed. He fell for Oxford as undergraduates should, speaking in the Union to radical motions about Ireland, Sunday Closing, Disestablishment or Education, promoting the Milton Club for Free Churchmen (at Glasgow he had been secretary and promoter of an Independent Association); walking in Bagley Woods or rowing on the river; playing cricket or being photographed with the Ruskin Society or conducting mission services. It was all fine fun.

It was also fun which marked him out for a fine pastorate, Kensington Chapel. It was not the largest of the London churches — its membership hovered around 500: it could offer a stipend of £6-700 — but it was the most solid. It had the inestimable advantage of a continued existence in an area which had changed in character but not in respectability. Consequently it depended less than many churches on the attractive powers of its ministers, although they had been men of great weight. There had been no schisms. The membership in the 1880s and 1890s offered that mixture of prominence and ballast which had characterized Dr Allon's Union Chapel, Islington, a little earlier, and which would shortly characterize Dr Horton's Lyndhurst Road, Hampstead. Between the 1870s and the early 1900s the members and seatholders included businessmen like Asquith's richest uncle, William Willans the wool-broker; retailers like Toms of Derry and Toms or the Harrod of Harrods; inevitable Dissenters like a branch of the paper-making Spicers, or descendants of the Conders of Leeds, or a son-in-law of Sir Titus Salt; country Dissenters with London houses like the Cozens-Hardys or the Fordhams of Melbourn Bury; legal families like the Winterbothams; visiting M.Ps such as Rowland Barran, Sir Robert Wallace, Sir Dods Shaw, T. Arnold Herbert; Mrs Rylands, when in London; even, for a short time, the fashionable artist De Laszlo. Clara Butt belonged to a Kensington Chapel family, and sometimes sang there, loved and formidable beneath the pulpit in white dress, white gloves, white picture-hat and 'a profusion of arum lilies'.[44]

Inevitably the minister of such a church was a power among Nonconformists, particularly when they were searching to replace the older generation of pulpiteers and (who knew?) to cross into the political world which still eluded them, but which now seemed empty of sound men. Horne sprang into note at a time of carefully fanned missionary enthusiasm with his speech on Free Church Principles at the Southport Autumnal of 1891, and his advocacy of a Forward Movement at the first International Congregational Council held in London the previous July. He became known as a racy author and propagandist. His novel, *A Modern Heretic*, was a pale shade of *Robert Elsmere*; 'the struggle of a young squire who felt a call to be a Divine Teacher, and yet could not honestly subscribe the Articles. Of course Dissent was the only alternative'.[45]

There was nothing new about novel-writing ministers: but it was published anonymously. The tensions to which Horne was subject in the 1890s were significant however hidden. Doctrinal problems never arose. Horne had grown naturally into his faith. He found no difficulty in accommodating himself to a 'far truer perception of the majesty of Paul's view of predestination', as he put it in 1894.[46] His hearers testified to the spiritual quality of his conduct of worship, whether the electric stillness of his mission services or the charm and 'instinctive rightness' of his Kensington sermons, or his flexibility at Whitefield's: 'The simple Communion Service was a joy from beginning to end. To me in that he was always at his finest. From then on for the rest of the day he was absolutely a free-lance. The level in the afternoon and evening was always high, but free, with the freedom he loved so passionately. He never descended in anything . . . it was simply a change of movement.'[47]

Neither was his way of life constricted, for he lived like a comfortable London professional man. He was fond of the theatre and Gilbert and Sullivan, of cricket and that new game, golf. He took strenuous holidays, sometimes abroad, and frequently at The Bluff, Sheringham or The White House, Church Stretton, family retreats made possible by the generosity of his father-in-law, Herbert Cozens-Hardy, the Liberal lawyer. He enjoyed motor-cars and bicycles, and was 'Charlie' to his family.

The tensions, other than those caused by overwork, were more general. They concerned the nature of the ministry as understood by a late Victorian Congregational Church. The church at Kensington was stolid but not unimaginative. It was possessed of immense resources of ability and goodwill, as well as money, and Horne tapped them to the full. The trust between his people and himself was complete. But was such a pastorate really the culmination of Christian endeavour in the world's largest city: large, thoughtful, loving congregations, backed by a mission in Notting Dale chiefly begun at their pastor's prompting when he realized that his people sustained nothing of that sort, thirty years after Baldwin Brown had pointed the way in Lambeth? He expressed his predicament in that rare tribute, already quoted, to the strength — and weakness — of the Congregational ideal, written at the end of 1900 amidst the prospect of removal to a fashionable Edinburgh church: what was he to do with men and women who believed *in* rather than *with* him?[48]

Among those who believed both in and with Horne was Mrs Rylands. She used her wealth sensitively: Horne had holidayed abroad at her expense; she contributed to the Notting Dale mission; and in 1899 Horne, as befitted a Mackennal-picked Mansfield man, stayed with her for the opening of the Rylands Library. She was among those who made possible what seemed to many to be the answer for city Congregationalism: a Congregational Central Hall.

Congregationalists and Baptists were as ill-equipped to cope with the growth of cities as they were well-equipped to cater for the suburban civilization which that growth threw out. The Independent Church required intelligence as well as a level of affluence. Its misleading dependence on the powers of its minister sometimes masked this. City chapels, bereft of a well-loved and long-lived minister, frequently found themselves without congregations (for their hearers were suburbanites who now turned to suburban chapels), with a church inadequately grounded in churchly principles and on both counts without the means of existence. The usual answer was removal to fresh pastures, thus justifying Anglican criticisms that gathered churches could not meet the spiritual demands of those who most needed them.

Free Churchmen tried to meet the criticism and when Baldwin Brown's people moved from Claylands to Brixton, a section remained behind to continue an aggressive work, while the rest opened the Moffat Institute. Brown considered that every suburban church must be engaged in such a venture. Thus Kensington prospected the ground in Notting Dale.

Another solution was to build churches at the point where districts changed character, their spires reflecting the consecrated wealth of the villas to westwards, and the consequent mission for the terraces to eastwards. There remained the tenement dwellers, and in the largest cities there was the problem of successive waves of expansion as districts changed character with distressing frequency. Arthur Mursell, of Stockwell Baptist Church, drolly compared this chapel in the late 1870s, 'begirt by gardens, villas and orthodoxy', with the same place ten years later, 'squeezed between hawkers and heathen'.[49] As it happened, he made a going concern of the hawkers and heathen.

Even so, such congregationalism was the merest impressionism, quixotic rather than knightly. Horne's removal in 1903 to Whitefield's Tabernacle in the Tottenham Court Road suggested the extent to which Congregationalism could become concerted, its knights part of a chivalric order: 'During the last few years a new spirit has come over Congregationalism — an evangelistic temper, aggressive, and altruistic, with enthusiasm for souls as its dynamic, and calmly reasoned methods as its machinery.'[50]

The impetus was Wesleyan, the inspiration of Hugh Price Hughes and his West London Mission of the late 1880s. In the early 1900s Baptists and Congregationalists enthusiastically adopted the idea, the Baptists most centrally at Bloomsbury Chapel, under Thomas Phillips, and the Congregationalists at Whitefield's.

It was not, however, a new idea for Congregationalists, who had been searching for a practical expression of their 'Forward Movement' since the early 1890s. It had been thought that Westminster Chapel might provide the answer, and there had been strenuous attempts to lure R. F. Horton from Lyndhurst Road to lead the venture. In 1902, the year of Hughes's death, the chairman of the London Congregational Union, W. H. Brown, a banker who admired Hughes, initiated the revival of Claremont Chapel,

Pentonville, as a Central Mission. Claremont was followed by Whitefield's in 1903 and Crossway, south of the River, in 1905. It was Whitefield's which seized the imagination as 'one of the most phenomenally successful central missions in England'.[51]

Yet even this extension of the Congregational ideal revealed as many limitations as strengths. Chief among them was the impact of Horne himself. The necessary money was rapidly raised, not least through the generosity of Mrs Rylands whose £4,000 cleared the debt on the Institute. When the Mission was opened, in September 1903, the platform was dark with pulpiteers and politicians, even a progressive peer, Lord Carrington. At the Institute's stonelaying in May 1904, Asquith, kinsman of Mrs Horne's Willans connexions, was the speaker. When the Institute was opened the speaker was Augustine Birrell, kinsman of Mrs Horne's Pilkington connexions.

Such prominence was easily maintained. It was less easy to reconcile the gathered church at the core of the venture, whose members were drawn from the residential squares nearby, with the clerks and shop girls who filled Tottenham Court Road in the weekdays, let alone with the people of the slums and brothel land which jostled the squares and business houses. There was nothing new in the problem, but the panache with which the mission was launched suggested that the solution would be new, sophisticated, and Congregational, or, as Horne intended, 'based on common sense, courage, and unconventionality'.[52]

The reconciliation of such disparate elements was an alliance rather than a fusion. The morning service, seats let, dignity enthroned, was the church's preserve. The afternoon was consecrated to the men's meeting and the evening to popular services. There was nothing inherently Congregational in it, other than the emphasis on freedom, but Horne's control of it was a distillation of the pulpit master's arts. James Holmes, Horne's factotum and stage manager, described it as a daring experiment turning Horne, that 'democrat of democrats', into a 'sort of autocrat with a small bureaucracy of governors; but those who lived closest to him and understood the workings of his mind, and the dreams he dreamed, and the visions he saw, followed him all the way with unimpaired confidence'.[53]

The Mission was to be a big business house for Jesus Christ, a workshop for him, meeting and beating every business in the Tottenham Court Road, using methods hitherto reserved for bodies like the Y.M.C.A., and then only in favoured places. 'The electric light is unsparingly used, and before the great arc lights outside the illuminations of gin-palaces hard by pale into yellow insignificance.' Once inside, there was the Institute, 'as cosy as a West End Club', or the Toplady Hall, whose easy lounges and cosy corners and Sunday afternoon teas made it a 'veritable drawing-room'.[54]

At this level Whitefield's Mission, like that of the Y.M.C.A., was for those on the social borderlands: assistants, clerks, young people 'in business', or respectably in service. The Sunday men's meeting was there for them in the afternoon, followed by social teas for both sexes, which merged in turn into the evening services. Here, 'preceded by half an hour's excellent music from a capable orchestra', Horne was in his element, speaking 'as a big brother speaks to his young brothers and sisters', holding up Christ 'as their Saviour from sin and their Ideal in life', impressing at least one of his hearers by praying with his eyes wide open. A final hour of 'genuine brotherly fellowship, over a cup of coffee', in the Toplady Hall closed the proceedings.

The pattern was established, save that it was not a pattern. A journalist who described Whitefield's in 1905 was convinced that there were new fields to conquer, and that 'Mr Horne is the kind of man who will find some, or make some — somewhere'.[55]

In the event this proved as risky for his health as for the tolerance of his mission council. In Baldwin Brown's last years there had been a suggestion, carefully muffled, that Brown and his deacons were not at one. It was the same with Horne at Whitefield's: his experiment proved too broad, and this first serious tension in twenty-five years of ministry met him unprepared. In 1914 he resigned the pastorate at Whitefield's.

The principal cause was an aspect of his life which he had seemed most triumphantly and naturally to have tamed: politics. It seemed to many that Horne had converted all that was negative about political Dissent, into all that was truly progressive. His success misled many into believing that there really was a definable political power called the 'Nonconformist Conscience'. If it ever existed, which is doubtful, it was between 1906 and 1910. The trouble with a power, however, is that it can be assessed and then dealt with. Nonconformity was rumbled the moment that it took itself seriously as a political power and its long accumulation of influence (a very different thing) was unnecessarily and prematurely dispersed. Silvester Horne's political career is as much a testimony to that, as it is to any coming of age of Political Dissent.

Horne entered Parliament for Ipswich — the constituency which his father-in-law had turned down thirty years previously — in January 1910. There was nothing haphazard about the timing: it was Horne's year as Chairman of the Congregational Union, and the political twist was the result of careful prompting by denominational leaders. Practical men with long parliamentary experience, like his father-in-law Cozens-Hardy, were dubious about it. It was hoped that he would silence Lord Hugh Cecil;

that he would be the latest Rupert of debate (an unfortunate analogy). The combination of his candidature and the political crisis of 1910, with its overtones of Free Trade, People's Rights and Peers' Privilege, expertly handled by what was, despite constant betrayals, a Free Church cabinet, was irresistible. What was more, Ipswich had a place in electoral lore akin to that of Vermont or Maine in the United States: it was among the earlier constituencies to poll, and its results pointed to the rest. Since Horne's senior partner in the contest, Daniel Ford Goddard, was also a Congregationalist, from the Tacket Street Church, the morals to be drawn seemed unusually clear.

Horne was not the first Nonconformist minister to sit in the House of Commons: Henry Richard, Edward Miall, James Allanson Picton and W. J. Fox had all held pastorates, and Richard and Miall remained convinced members of their denomination. Neither was Horne the first minister in good standing to be a candidate: in 1886, for example, R. F. Horton had been urged to stand for Hampstead and he was in a long succession. But he was the first minister in charge of a church to be elected and must be distinguished from Charles Leach, the M.P. for Colne Valley, who had left a highly successful ministry in 1908.[56]

Horne was immensely conscious of being the first Congregational minister in full charge to be a Member of Parliament since Cromwell's day, and his historical sense, already breathlessly communicated in his *Popular History of the Free Churches* (1903), explains both the smoothness of his transition to politics and the stage at which the hollowness of 'Nonconformist politics' was revealed. He venerated Cromwell,

> with his powder dry for the sceptred lie
> and the mitred pride of power[57]

and he held services at Kensington to commemorate him. 20 April 1899:

We are going to have a unique Cromwell service on the 30th. I am printing a special Order of Service. We are going to sing Cromwell's psalm (117) in the old Scotch version, to Bangor, the tune to which Carlyle says it was sung. Then Andrew Black is going to sing, and we have chosen 'Is not His Word like a fire?' from the *Elijah*. You remember how the Lord whets His sword and breaks them in pieces like a hammer! Oh, very Ironsidy. He will also sing 'Why do the nations?' with the lovely bit about the Kings and Rulers of the earth setting themselves against the Lord's anointed![58]

At Whitefield's in 1908 and 1909 the Men's Meeting held a Gladstone and a Lincoln Centenary, and a Milton Tercentenary, with lavish programmes amply illustrated. Fifteen years earlier, for the Tercentenary of the martyrdom of the Separatists, Barrow and Greenwood, Horne addressed an open letter to the Congregational youth of London: 'Will you undertake in your various Districts to organize yourselves into battalions, and to obtain promises from all whom you can influence, both men and women, to come to the Park on the afternoon of the 8th. of April next, and show that you are on the side of Truth and Freedom still?' And he quoted Dr Fairbairn: ' "Wherever the Independent has planted his foot, he has prevailed". . . . . Our traditions are all of victory.'[59]

For a latterday Independent the romantic conclusion must be 'that there is no Church meeting held in this country that is more constantly and practically concerned with living religious problems than the House of Commons'; and the struggles of 1910 recalled John Hampden and Ship Money, that crucial stage in the battle against Stuart autocracy. 'No good Independent could be outside that fight.'[60]

When it came to practical politics, however, romance wore thin. Milton tercentenaries could easily be translated into the traditional issues of education, temperance and disestablishment. These were matters of fundamental importance which remained as fresh in the 1900s as in the 1840s, and only superficial commentators could regard them as *vieux jeu*. Such issues, cemented by the spiritual facts of Sunday worship and the family facts of life, still made it natural for Free Churchmen to protest at the 'amiable delusions of Tory Politics'.[61] Such issues, however, were no more aired in a vacuum in the 1900s than in the 1840s, and few Nonconformist electors outside the ministry saw them in a vacuum. They had to be balanced with questions of authority, international morality and social tension, for which there was never a clear answer, and they had always, at the appropriate stage, to be juggled against the inevitable compromises of Westminster politics.

The Nonconformists, like all ill-defined but self-conscious minorities, were strongest as an influence rather than a power. Their tragedy was that at the General Election of 1906, when their sort of issue seemed fresher than ever, and their ministers — who, in the public eye, were their leaders — were men of transparent vigour and ability, it looked as if their influence really had become power: 223 Nonconformist candidates, of whom 92 were Congregationalists; 185 Nonconformist M.Ps of whom 73 were Congregationalists, all save six of them sympathetic to the government;[62] a cabinet teeming with Nonconformist connexions. It was the millennium.

For a while they behaved as if they were a power, but the failures of successive ministers to solve the education issue revealed the hollowness of their position. At the very moment that the baselessness of their power was revealed, profound shifts were taking place in the nature of British politics. Individual Free Church politicians were better placed than most to adapt to these shifts; as a group, however, Free Church politicians were cumbersome, easily divided, and out-manoeuvred, and their rank and file were as uncertain about the newly insistent questions of society as anyone else.

The Nonconformist rank and file were numerous, but their electoral effect was elusive. England's chapels were unevenly spread, and by the time that the women and youths and disenfranchised men were discounted, who remained to provide the Nonconformist vote? Were they Wesleyans, Congregationalists or Unitarians? In Birmingham, Manchester or Eastbourne? The questions are important, for they mean that no more can be assumed than that throughout England, often strongest in the least likely places, there would be groups of people for whom chapel was the foundation, who tended to think alike, who were articulate and prosperous enough, who could never be discounted as opinion-formers but who could be outflanked, who were most vulnerable when most clearly defined, because then they could be taken for granted. In a shifting society their potential influence was immense: unfortunately society was shifting at the very time that they were most clearly organized. Their influence had hardened into power; and the clothes of this particular new emperor were revealed for what they were at the worst possible moment, the eve of total war.

It is said that when, in 1906, the Bloomsbury Baptists found themselves frustrated in their attempts to purchase the freehold of their buildings, their negotiator threatened the Commissioner of Woods and Forests with questions in the House. 'Don't forget, this is a Free Church Parliament.' If he had been more keenly aware of the divided enthusiasms which the chapel 'Parliament' had shown on the issues of the hour (the 'Liberal Ministerial Statement' carried only by a casting vote: in 1906), he might have rephrased his annoyance.[63]

Silvester Horne's political career epitomizes the conflict between influence and power, and the year of his election, 1910, accentuates this. He was elected as a sign of Free Church power when such power had gone but when Free Church influence might have been at its most telling.

He was at his best at elections, for it was then that Free Churchmen were best seen as opinion-formers and organizers. His platform reputation was at its height, and Horne, with or without motor-car, was in incessant demand, speaking zestfully for friends and connexions in 1906, and for himself in 1910. His accounts of the glorious excitement of 1906 — 'Thousands were frantic in the Tottenham Court Road' — and the Ipswich triumphalism of 1910 — 'one seething host of triumphant men, who had many of them risked everything to save liberty' — remain incomparably fresh. 'Hasn't it more than atoned for all the misery and suffering of these last years to see the soul of England awake at last?'[64]

As long as it remained thus, all was well and Lady Wimborne could appeal to him from the hinterlands of Poole, 'to come and give us a helping hand here where we are fighting a desperate fight against the power of landlordism, the drink and tariff reform'.[65] But the fact that the Liberal candidate for East Dorset was so uneasy an opponent of landlordism, drink and tariff reform as Freddie Guest suggests the point at which compromise began. At Mansfield in the 1880s Professor Elmslie had thrilled Horne in an Old Testament Class by suggesting, as an analogy of divine revelation, that Parnell might be a man of God, compromising himself to get his message across. What was thrilling in a seminar was harder to sustain at Westminster, and this was shown on the issue which had most alerted Free Church opinion: education.

Free Churchmen had coped as best they might with the open wound left by Forster's Act. Elementary education became compulsory in 1880 and free, in fact if not quite in theory, from 1891. In many urban areas school boards became powerful, progressive bodies. Although the limits of their competence were unclear, they experimented with secondary education, becoming fair game for the organizing abilities of Free Churchmen, reared in the tactics of Victorian pressure politics, ingenuously marshalling their forces under the banner of 'non-sectarianism'. In most rural areas, however, Free Churchmen remained at the mercy of a voluntary, and therefore Anglican, network which was now inextricably part of the national system.

The question of secondary education, with its dark implications for local rates, was an open and therefore explosive one. The question of fair education in country districts became an urgent one upon the extension of efficient local government into the countryside, with county councils after 1888 and parish councils after 1894. Conservative predominance at Westminster, Anglican vitality in the country and Free Church expertise on school boards, mingled with administrative turmoil as school boards proliferated and voluntary schools vociferated and pressures for secondary education accumulated (and the Cockerton Judgment of 1901 exposed the legal inadequacy of the system to meet those pressures), to turn the education issue of the 1890s and 1900s into a minefield as dangerous as any of the 1840s.

The needs were clear: a rationalized system making proper provision for secondary education. The issues at stake were the same as they had ever been: the right place of the voluntary schools in a system dependent on public money. It was a question of the right use of public money. It was a question too of the life blood of Free Churchmanship, for what of Nonconformist children in rural, single-school, Church-school areas? Or what of Nonconformist teachers, as likely as not debarred from schools throughout the country? What, for example, was the future of Methodism, let alone of Liberalism in North Norfolk? As in the 1840s it was a question of freedom, but this time the Free Churchmen opposed the voluntaryists, whom they preferred to see as clericalists.

The armies formed. The voluntaryists gathered under Lord Hugh Cecil and Bishop Talbot of Rochester, formerly Vicar of Leeds, whose nephew by marriage, Talbot Baines of Leeds, became Secretary of the National Society in 1905 and at the heart of the battle's later stages. The Free Churchmen counted on John Clifford the Baptist and Hugh Price Hughes the Wesleyan, backed in the provinces by men of ferocious principle. In the north since 1896 Free Churchmen of the extremer sort had been enthused by the Northern Counties Education League, dexterously managed by James Hirst Hollowell, a Rochdale Congregational minister, connected with some of Asquith's Rochdale cousins.

Of the major battles the Free Churchmen won that of 1896, when a Tory education bill was withdrawn. They lost that of 1902, when A. J. Balfour introduced his celebrated measure. This Act, which has since been praised, provided a unified elementary system and led to an adequate secondary system. It met the needs, but not the issues. It made away with the old school boards in favour of County and County Borough Councils. These now were the local education authorities. It confirmed voluntary schools, rate aided and privileged, in the public system. Quite simply, Anglicans had preserved their advantage while Free Churchmen had lost whatever they had secured in the last thirty years.

Horne was a leader in the campaign against Balfour's Act but his account of a meeting in March between thirty ministers and the Liberals, Campbell-Bannerman and Herbert Gladstone is instructive.[66] The Boer War, Home Rule and Liberal splits were the chief topics of discussion, the ministers were hopelessly divided in their preferences, and Campbell-Bannerman easily handled them. Horne was sickened. He feared that 'the surges of Imperialism would not be allayed'; and, perhaps unconsciously, he testified to divisions among Nonconformists which were profounder than any unity aroused by the education question.

On Free Church platforms, however, education healed all splits and suggested the way in which Free Church principles might infiltrate Parliament. The lure of a Nonconformist Party, as loosely tied to official Liberalism as the Radical groups which had come and gone at Westminster since the 1830s, was almost irresistible.

According to the journalist, Arthur Porritt, he and Horne were playing golf at Mitcham when Horne asked: ' "Don't you think the Free Churches ought to put up a hundred candidates at the next election?" "I suppose you mean to make sure of getting a good Education Act," I replied. "Exactly," answered Horne, "if we are not represented by our own people we may get 'let down'." ' And the idea was taken to Herbert Gladstone, the Liberal Chief Whip.[67]

The upshot was that Free Church M.Ps were outmanoeuvred and their powerlessness revealed on the very issue which had brought them to Parliament. Birrell, McKenna and Runciman, for all their Nonconformist connexions failed to satisfy them. A solution was never reached.

Even as an influence Horne was a disappointment in Parliament. The charm of his voice had aged into platform hoarseness. His interventions, on the Congo or Welsh Disestablishment, were those of a useful backbencher as his last speech, on Ireland, made clear: 'The whole point of the Irish situation is simple. You have a large body of people who, on the score of their industry, of their integrity, and their commercial genius, are deserving of all respect, but on the other side of their nature, on the side of their theological and ecclesiastical opinion, they are the victims of a pure hallucination.'[68] It needed an English Puritan to speak thus of Ulstermen.

R. F. Horton felt that, given ten years, Horne 'would have been a member of the Liberal Government'.[69] In 1910, however, Horne had written to Arthur Porritt: 'I do not believe the House of Commons need unmake one spiritually nor Whitefield's unfit one for things secular. If these things, which all my life I have believed, prove to have no foundation, the bottom is out of my creed.'[70]

In 1914 he resigned from Whitefield's, and he was in two minds about resigning his seat. There remained one outlet in which he might find fulfilment: the Brotherhood Movement. In this 'he saw the machinery for Christianizing democracy and infusing the idealism of Jesus into the working men of England'.[71]

The Brotherhood Movement had grown from the Pleasant Sunday Afternoons inspired in 1875 by a midlands draper, John Blackham. In their most characteristic expression of free and easy men's Sunday afternoon meetings, bound together by free and easy organization, they seemed to offer a future for churches in the democratic age, a socialism without Socialism. 300,000 men meeting on church premises Sunday by Sunday suggested a power which the nebulously social and political content of much Brotherhood religion seemed to confirm. Although it was an impressively interdenominational movement, it spoke particularly to Congregationalists, to whom it offered fresh facets of churchmanship.

The concept of brotherhood was integral to Baldwin Brown's Independency. To him, suggested P. T. Forsyth, the great Church was 'the fraternity of the emancipated, the redeemed, the realized'.[72] One of

Baldwin Brown's earliest pamphlets had been *The Brotherhood of the Church: being a plea for Christian Union*, and the same themes informed Horne's address to the Congregational Union in 1910. Horne, however, tried to expand the theme of church fraternity to cover the whole social fabric. It was his conviction that the Free Churches, with Congregationalists in the van, were predestined to achieve a social reformation; their organization and their sympathies were open to it.[73] In November 1907 he told Salem, Leeds, reopened as an institutional church, and famous for its men's meeting:

> The purpose of an institutional church was to reconstruct human society on the basis of brotherhood. . . . It was a church for bringing the influence of Jesus Christ to bear on every side of a man's life, so as to transform him. It was more urgent to reconstruct society than to reconstruct theology. . . . The cardinal point in institutional methods, second to a tremendous belief in the fatherhood of God and the saviourhood of Jesus Christ, was the belief in the sacredness of man.[74]

Increasingly, however, Horne saw that the 'dynamic of righteousness' which brotherhood presented lay in the Brotherhood Movement itself. In 1914 he was president of the National Brotherhood Council, hailing it as the New Protestantism.

He did not live to see his faith in Brotherhood as misplaced as his zest for politics, or even for Whitefield's. The movement's vigour did not survive the Great War: it was merely the latest agent in the secularization of Nonconformity, and the social Gospel which it presented marked at best 'the baptism of the Labour movement into the Christian spirit',[75] but not into the Christian churches. At its best it was fresh and socially varied, reaching sections of the working classes with marked success. At worst it was as empty and well-meaning as William Ward's portrait of it in 1911, *Brotherhood and Democracy*. At best and worst it was what a recent historian has called it: the religious equivalent of Liberal Progressivism.[76] The Great War revealed how insipid were the freshness and originality of brothers and progressives.

In the spring of 1914 Horne was at Yale to deliver his lectures on the 'Romance of Preaching'. He crossed into Canada, in the course of a journey over busy with engagements. He had several times felt unwell. 'As the boat entered Toronto harbour he was walking on the deck with his wife when he suddenly fell.'[77] He was dead.

The Toronto *Globe*'s main headlines were 'Silvester Horne Drops Dead; Tragic End of British Puritan' and 'Duke of Argyll Dead: A Notable Career. . . . Married Daughter of Queen Victoria'. Its language was jumbled, journalistic and moving: 'On the upper deck, alert, alive, aware, stood a great English preacher ... leader of the World's new democracy.'[78] P. T. Forsyth refined these sentiments: 'He went as the lightning flashes from this earthly end of heaven to the other. He went with a pure apostolic haste. ... There is in Padua a fresco by Giotto of Christ's Resurrection in which He seems almost shooting upward from the tomb, His face impatient to leave the world and return to His Father. And we can think of this soul now.' Then, recalling the Whitefield's banner of an armed and armoured knight, burdened with a wounded companion but still climbing to shining towers, and correcting its motto of 'No quest, no conquest', he added: 'Here his life was ... a divine, sleepless importunacy. ... But all that now gives way. Quest ends in conquest.'[79]

R. J. Campbell of the City Temple considered that the Free Churches had sustained no greater loss since the death of Hugh Price Hughes in 1902.[80] It is perhaps pointless to separate one man from the mass of those who 'think in individuals', but Horne best expressed what Free Churchmen hoped to see in themselves. Hugh Price Hughes was a greater statesman, and had fewer scruples: he was an ecclesiastic. They shared intellect, political zest, social passion, love of Cromwell, concern for 'the democracy' and they announced manliness. People used the language of chivalry to describe them.

Campbell himself affords an instructive comparison. Despite the doctrinal controversies which pursued him, he was admired among Congregationalists. Free Churchmanship, however, was merely a phase — although the finest phase — in his career. Horne was forty-nine when he died, his future Congregationalism less obvious than it might be; Campbell was forty-nine when he left Congregationalism.

Of the London ministers, R. F. Horton was unchallengeable in spiritual and intellectual power, but there was a fineness about him which was a less faithful reflexion of Free Churchmen in the street than the vigour of Silvester Horne.

Such comparisons serve to prove that the most representative men are incomparable, suggesting thereby the attraction of *family* ties — God's Fatherhood, Christ's Sonship, man's consequent brotherhood — for convinced individualists. 'The Congregationalist ... finds himself committed to a creed of even awful and lonely splendour which only men and women of some strength of individuality, and the developed instinct of personal religion, can dare to believe or aspire to preach.' The base, and cure, for such high commitment lay in the Church, as by *grace* established.[81]

Chapter 10

'The Church as By Grace Established': A Christian Imperialism

Question: What are the reasons which lead you to believe you are called of God to missionary work among the Heathen, and what is your encouragement and inspiration in the face of its prospective difficulties and dangers?

Answer: I am going in obedience to Christ's command when He said: 'Go ye into all the world and preach the Gospel to every creature'. For centuries this command has been sadly neglected and it is only during this century that the Church has been awakened to her responsibility. As one member of Christ's Church I am seeking to obey the command, which for so many ages had been thus neglected. . . .

(From the Ordination Service of Oliver F. Tomkins,
Norwich, 6 December 1899.)

'I ventured to point out to you in May,' said Baldwin Brown at the 1878 Autumnals,

how the training of our church life tends to set our members on the right side, the progressive side, in political affairs. And I venture to prophesy that from our churches will come the most constant, strenuous, and intelligent protest against that bastard of empire — Imperialism; which tends to substitute the arm of force and the hand of menace for that lofty, intellectual, and moral influence which it has been the distinction of England to exercise through the civilized, and no small part of the uncivilized, world.[1]

Brown was doing more than voice the stock responses of a type of Liberal. Indeed, he was demonstrating the views which such sentiments demanded. It was imperialism which he condemned, not empire. In the succeeding generation C. S. Horne's mistrust of imperialism was seen when he opposed the Boer War, but his imperial vision was suggested by his history of the London Missionary Society (1895) and by his blithe confusion of the roles of missionary and agitator: 'What we want always and everywhere is *missionaries* — what Aunt S. disapproves as "agitators"! These causes can only be won by people who will agitate for them, I now regard you as having definitely joined the ranks of the agitators!'[2]

There was no real confusion in such views, although their development was less simple. Nothing is more easily misrepresented than the attitude of Nonconformists to 'abroad'. Because Nonconformists appeared to flourish most among the lower middle class, it seemed sensible to view them as Little Englanders, the essence of a nation of shopkeepers. So they were, which meant that they were open to the possibilities of an industrial society, the opportunity to travel and its consequences chief among them.

The implications of this can be illustrated by the Y.M.C.A., a body rare among major Christian movements in Britain in that it is truly international. It was not coincidence that its founders in the 1840s were a group of young men in the London drapery trade, each of them with the prospect of a shop of his own, most of them Nonconformists, and the most representative of them, George Williams, a member of the King's Weigh House Congregational Church.

Williams was born into the rural middle classes and died a member of the urban and commercial upper middle class.[3] Emigration was a fact of life for his sort, a safety valve widening the horizons of countrymen as far as the colonies or the United States. For those who prospered, holidays became further facts of life, providing another sort of safety valve, widening their horizons as far as the mountains or spas of fashionable Europe. By the early twentieth century the web of Williams family connexion included Australians, Canadians, Americans, as well as Frenchmen and the family of Thomas Cook, the pioneer of convenient travel.

The rag trade, on which he depended, relied on America, India and Egypt for its raw materials, France for its fashions, colonials for its customers. There was nothing odd about the imperial horizons of the world's foremost nation of shopkeepers. In George Williams's case the activity inherent in successful drapery was extended and disciplined by the activity natural to a City church. The Weigh House's conviction of mission extended from London's slums to the Caribbean and South Seas, to India, Africa, China and to Siberia. Thus an adventurous evangelical dimension was added to the prospects of emigration, the enticements of holidays and the calls of business, all pressing upon young men whose vision was as boundless as their shop counters. Imperialism of all sorts came naturally to these products of the lower middle classes, and the great missionary societies transmuted this into a Christian Imperialism.

For Williams the chief Christian issue from this accumulation of activity was the Y.M.C.A., whose remarkable development owed much to the fact that the fusion of commercial opportunity and missionary imperative achieved by the Weigh House in the 1840s was equalled in chapels throughout England. By the end of the century it was a commonplace for chapel 'distance lists' to contain members in New Zealand or South Africa, or India. In July 1899 Williams, now Sir George and an Anglican of over forty years standing, laid a foundation stone for the renovated Paddington Chapel, one of innumerable such occasions. Inevitably the chapel's members and seatholders included some of his missionary connexions.[4] Inevitably too its organizations contributed to missionary societies and took pride in missionaries who had grown up among them. There was nothing new in this. In 1815 Henry Townley declined the pastorate of Paddington Chapel so that he might go to Calcutta. As he explained: 'The claims of Paddington of Ireland and of India have severally demanded the most careful examination I could give them. . . .'[5] Thereafter the tradition was unwavering.

It was, however, a very complex tradition. The facts of lower middle-class life gave it vitality and urgency, and the expertise of the missionary societies disciplined it, but there was nothing inevitable about its form. From the 1830s Paddington Chapel's seatholders included the Moulton Barrett family, whose fortunes depended on their Jamaican properties; from the 1890s the seatholders included the Berry brothers, editors of the chapel's *Monthly*. No firm conclusions may be drawn about the missionary attitudes of a church whose supporters included such former slaveholders as the father of Mrs Browning or such future pressmen as Lords Camrose and Kemsley. All that can be said is that their horizons were extensive.

An appreciation of the strength behind this missionary impulse, and of its complexity, is vital to an understanding of nineteenth-century Nonconformity. Evangelical Christians in an imperial nation were irretrievably committed to foreign missions. Neither the missionaries nor their supporters were always successful in distinguishing between the claims of empire and the entanglements of its bastard, but they were open to the curious influences of the communities which they sought to convert and had first to understand. In the context of the intimate links fostered between missionaries and their supporters on the home front, many of them artisans who might come to know more of Madras than of Merseyside, the startling developments of perspective and leaps of imagination which had to be made became natural. The exercise was one of sympathy and the consequences were unimaginable. Where Free Churchmen were concerned imperialism was always tempered by missionary conscience, and when, in an unfortunate moment, the Wesleyan M.P., William McArthur, declared that 'Imperialism without Liberalism is Jingoism, but . . . Liberalism without Imperialism is Parochialism',[6] it might be urged that he was not so very far from Baldwin Brown speaking twenty years earlier.

A sense of the intertwining of inherited evangelical responsibility and commercial opportunity is conveyed by the Congregational Missionary Forward Movement of the 1890s, the counterpart of similar movements among Baptists and Methodists. Inevitably there were imperial overtones, but the movement's inspiration was quite distinct from the imperialistic pressures of Edwardian England. The centenaries of the Baptist and London Missionary Societies fell in the decade; the London Missionary Society was in financial difficulties and its morale was wavering — a Forward Movement was a natural response.

Its genesis, however, was significant. On 1 October 1890, Elkanah Armitage, who had recently moved to Bradford, to become tutor in philosophy and comparative religion at Yorkshire United Independent College — the paradoxical title reflected the recent union of the former Rotherham and Airedale Colleges — wrote in his diary:

> Missionaries (Sadler, Macfarlane, and Hadfield) came to the College and addressed the men. They afterwards dined with me as did 6 students and tutors.
> At dinner Sadler pleaded for missions, but all seemed to resist us. Painful impression. Sadler deeply distressed.
> At night the public L.M.S. meeting at College Chapel (Holborn's).
> Sadler and I spoke about our afternoon experience to Mr T. Craven who is a zealous man, and *he* again spoke to Dr Anderson and to Mr Williams and these all came up here to supper and afterwards remained here in earnest conversation till 1:15 a.m. We were brought to sign a document pledging ourselves to pray that *100* missionaries might be called out from our churches!![7]

The College was not an easy place in the 1890s. The staff were theologically divided and the students were restive. In July 1890 they had 'protested that they were not being satisfactorily fitted for their work in the ministry in any department', and although they withdrew their complaints, an atmosphere of difficulty remained.[8] Their lack of commitment, conveyed to a man of Armitage's temperament and background, had profound consequences.

His missionary concern was not a matter of chance. On 19 May 1821, following the decision of the London Missionary Society to send out artisan missionaries capable of transmitting their skills to native converts, two members of Grosvenor St Chapel, Manchester, Elijah Armitage and Thomas Blossom, sailed with their wives for Tahiti. Blossom remained in the South Seas until 1844, Armitage until 1835, returning to Manchester in March 1836.[9] Armitage, who was Elkanah's great-uncle, had been head of the putting-out room in the Manchester cotton manufactory controlled by a Quaker, George Neden. His years in the South Seas were steadily unsuccessful, but the missionary perspective thus engendered remained with his family and accompanied the marked success of its various branches in the Lancashire cotton industry.

His missionary exploits entered family lore: in Moorea he amputated the leg of a British sailor, using a meat chopper and gold tie pin.[10] His letters to his former employer, at least one of them taking twenty months to arrive in England, were kept. 'Dear Friend' he wrote in October 1824, '... with respect to these islands I cannot give you a more full and particular account than the one published by Captain Cook. ... I have not yet been able to make cloth from the native cotton, but I hope before many months to be in full operation. The reasons I have not been able to get on far are various, but chiefly the Idleness of the people. Every individual here is as independent as an Esquire in England, from the child of five years old to the man of sixty'. He signed it, 'Your old fellow servant'.

Three years later, in May 1829, he wrote: 'My dear Old Master ... for the first six years of my residence I laboured hard and succeeded with my own hands in getting the manufactury endway, and wove from six to seven hundred yards of calico and check. But after all it is really uncertain whether they will follow it up.'[11]

There can be no doubt as to the significance of this aspect of Manchester School education. Elijah's nephew, William Armitage of Altrincham, developed the firm of Armitage and Rigby from part of George Neden's business. Like Elijah, William belonged to Grosvenor Street Chapel. He was treasurer of the Manchester Auxiliary of the London Missionary Society, presiding sometimes at its meetings in the Free Trade Hall, giving annual missionary breakfasts, and entertaining famous missionaries at Townfield.[12]

By the end of the century his firm's prosperity depended on its colonial markets. When William's son, another William, voyaged to South Africa in 1905 to salvage his health, it was inevitable that the sightseeing should include business visits, that the missionary connexions of his contacts should be carefully noted and that a visit to a Zulu village should elicit sympathetic comments on African dress and morals. He, at least, did not seek to reproduce English gentlefolk on the Westminster model.

It was inevitable too that the wake of the Boer War should remain to perplex him. On the voyage out he noted amidst the delights incidental to first-class travel on an Edwardian steamship that 'Major Lombe and others are expecting trouble with the natives in S. A. some day, and thinks a thorough rising of them will be the best thing for drawing the English and Boers together'. On the voyage back, the passengers included 'a Miss Marie Botha sister of General Louis Botha and her niece ... on their first visit to Europe'. The ladies entered gamely for the fancy-dress ball, the niece as a Zouave and Miss Botha as Dover Castle. Armitage's own view of the situation may be deduced from the newspaper cutting which he preserved with his travel journal. It concerned the fear that the Transvaalers might pass class legislation when the opportunity allowed: 'This is a faint echo of the real racial question of the future in South Africa.' Naturally, there were limits to the liberal view: 'We do not mean, of course, that the native should have the franchise, or anything of that kind . . . class legislation need not be degrading, and may even be beneficial, such, for instance, as prohibiting of the sale of liquor to natives.'[13]

In a cousinly society it was hard not to have missionary connexions. The enthusiasms of Elkanah's father and brother, derived from their uncle Elijah, were reinforced by those of Mrs Elkanah Armitage's family, the Bulleys. Her grandfather, Raffles of Liverpool, was first cousin to Raffles of Singapore; her brother-in-law, William Stallybrass, had been born in Siberia, whither his father had been sent by the London Missionary Society in 1817.[14]

Like the Armitages, the Stallybrasses had been Dissenters since the seventeenth century. With their Nonconformity expanded by Siberia and the South Seas, and fuelled by a host of ministerial and mercantile connexions the force behind Elkanah Armitage's despondent missionary prayer meeting of October 1890 becomes apparent. Just as the success of the Y.M.C.A. had depended on its relevance for young men already caught up in the mission of numerous chapels, so the success of the Missionary Forward Movement of the 1890s depended on their appeal to the inherited and intertwined consciences of countless chapel communities. The answer to prayer was already there; it had only needed the prayer for the work to begin.

Armitage's campaign for the 100 ministers got under way. Encouraged by a further visit from Sadler, the Amoy missionary, Armitage spent the days before Christmas 1890 enlisting the aid of Arnold Thomas, his closest friend, R. F. Horton and Charles Berry. Alexander Mackennal promised his support. The ministers of Highbury, Bristol, Lyndhurst Road, Hampstead, and Queen St, Wolverhampton were automatically men of weight; Horton and Berry, moreover, were pre-eminent among the younger Congregational ministers.

In April 1891 the four of them issued a letter calling for the 100 missionaries and this was followed in the autumn by 'Preparing to Go Forward. A Call to Prayer', drawing attention to an all-day prayer meeting for women at the London Mission House, in Blomfield Street. It was, however, the Congregational Autumnals at Southport which really launched the movement.

The Southport meetings were memorable in several ways. The Chairman was John Brown, of Bedford, Maynard Keynes's grandfather and an elder statesman among Congregationalists. There was an attempt to urge Alexander Mackennal into the vacant secretaryship. C. S. Horne and J. D. Jones, later of Bournemouth, first made their denominational name there. Altogether the meetings 'reached a kind of high water mark of spiritual power. First came Dr Barrett's searching sermon on "Sin". Then came the most moving missionary session I have ever known, with speeches by Ward of St Helens and Elkanah Armitage of Bradford — the effect of which was to give a tremendous impetus to the great Forward Movement of the L.M.S.'[15] Armitage's own comments were similarly thankful: 'A memorable meeting! Introduced and sustained by much prayer and waiting before God. Somebody has said of our Congregational churches at this time. "The 7,000 are finding one another." We owe much to Horton.'[16]

Thereafter his diary is filled with the Forward Movement. The delegates at Southport had been greatly moved at the offering of Lavington Hart, a Fellow of St John's College Cambridge, and his brother Walford, a member of Horton's church, for service in China.[17] On the Sunday following the Autumnals, Armitage preached at the Laisterdyke Chapel anniversary, in Bradford, and noted that three of its young men 'wish to become missionaries and go to India'.[18] In 1892 came the remarkable news that R. J. Ward, minister at Ormskirk Street, St Helens, for nearly thirty years, had offered for India. His reason? 'To save the British Empire.' The St Helens Church was an important one, not least because of the Pilkingtons. Armitage had preached there in January, and again in October.[19]

Ward was one of five ministers to leave their pastorates for the mission field. In the autumn of 1892 they had addressed an appeal to their fellow ministers: 'I think that several are eager to respond.' Late in November Armitage was in Liverpool to see Ward sail for India aboard the S.S. Peshawar.[20]

A particular interest attached, however, to one of Ward's companions, William Thomas, who had volunteered for Central Africa, 'because Africa had a great future'. Thomas was Armitage's successor at Waterhead, Oldham, which had been Armitage's first pastorate, and Waterhead's sparse records convey the providential excitement of the decision, and its impact on a small community.

In March 1892 it was agreed 'that we join the Forward Movement of the London Missionary Society in holding a prayer meeting on Monday night next'. In June, it was minuted 'that our minister be requested to urge our young men to stay and worship with us on the Sunday mornings instead of going to the Forward Movement'. In August the results were clear. On the 3rd the minister announced his resignation, so that he might go to Central Africa, and on the 24th, twenty-eight people, eight of them men, joined the church. The following month 400 filled the infants' schoolroom for tea. A cheque for £35 4s.0d. was presented to Mr Thomas ('not the gift of the rich; it came out of the hard earnings of loving hearts') and there was a profit of 11s.6d. on the teas.

The senior deacon found it 'like the answer to a long felt wish that they might not only send their pence but send a man'. Thomas, in his reply, expressed his pride at being one of Professor Armitage's 100 missionaries: 'they stood in special relations with the missionary cause.'[21]

By the time of the Bradford Autumnals of 1892, seventy-two of the 100 had offered themselves. Horton and Arnold Thomas stayed with the Armitages, and there was a 'specially memorable' valedictory meeting for twenty-six missionaries at the St George's Hall.[22]

Thereafter the movement lost momentum, but its main purpose, the alerting of the nation to the call of the mission field, had been achieved, and in 1895 Armitage could write:

This is L.M.S. 'Founders' Week' and great meetings are being held all week at the City Temple. Ella presided at an afternoon meeting and I did so on Wednesday night.

Some have of late lost heart in the 'Forward Movement' which aimed at sending 100 fresh missionaries into the field before the end of the Centenary year.

I called on the Society to adhere to its purpose, and later both Horton and Arnold Thomas did so also.[23]

It is clear from Armitage's diaries that many considerations intensified the urgency of the mission call. In 1891, for example, the first International Congregational Council meetings were held in London at the new King's Weigh House Chapel, near Grosvenor Square. The meetings reflected the sense of belonging to a world community which Methodists had already expressed in the previous decade, and which Baptists would echo in the following one. It was a transatlantic internationalism, orchestrated on the English side by Mackennal, and Armitage was among the delegates.[24]

There was nothing new about links with American Congregationalists, but such meetings provided structure as well as excitement, adding point to their common mission, as when a visitor from Princeton assured a group of London theological students that '*6,200* students of the American Universities are pledged if God opens the door to go out as missionaries'.[25]

Other doors were also opening. In November 1890 Armitage read William Booth's *Darkest England*, and four days later the General breakfasted with the Bradford students.[26] At Rotherham in the 1880s Armitage had persuaded his congregation to read Henry George. In Bradford in the 1890s he noted the doings of the Independent Labour

Party, and occasionally tasted the worship at Labour Churches. Yorkshire United was a College with a radical streak in politics as well as theology, and while Armitage remained Gladstonian and orthodox, he was nonetheless a man of broad social sympathies. The Forward Movement was to bring social as well as spiritual freedom to the foreign mission field: darkest England and darkest Africa were to share Congregational loyalties.

Closely allied to these freedoms was freedom for Christian women. It was in the 1890s, perhaps at the Bradford Autumnals of 1892, that women delegates were first admitted to the annual assemblies of the Congregational Union.[27] The Yorkshire Congregational Union paved the way. When Ella Sophia Armitage instituted a Women's Conference at its Dewsbury meetings in 1891, and formed a Women's Guild of Christian Service, she was clear that women's Christian service extended far beyond ladies bountiful. She was already known as a forceful platform speaker, and now she began to preach: 'This evening Sunday April 26 Ella for the first time fully took a service and preached. It was at Girlington and she took the service in order to liberate me for Ilkley.'[28] This was a decisive stage for Congregational women: and if the ordained ministry remained closed to them until the First World War, the mission field offered their boldest vocation.

These concerns were cemented by the renewed spiritual power which Armitage sensed within himself. 'Come Armitage', said a Bradford minister, 'you have something that we have not. Just kneel down and pray for us'.[29] This was a deepening which he shared with Horton and Arnold Thomas, and which brought him into touch with Silvester Horne. In Armitage's case it was partly a reaction against the this-worldly stance affected by some of his students and inculcated by certain of his colleagues,[30] and it was partly a development of Keswick teaching.

Leading Congregationalists mistrusted the teaching of Keswick Conventions. They found it flabby and unintellectual, but they admired its spirituality. Some of them felt that R. F. Horton's books provided an alternative, a sort of Keswick with brains. In the late 1880s and early 1890s Armitage stayed at Keswick, and supported meetings on Keswick lines at Bradford. He found deep personal renewal at them, and the knowledge that several Bradford Congregationalists loudly opposed 'Conventionism' added the spice of combat. Most important of all, was the impact which Keswick had on foreign missions. It was 'Keswick teaching' which had sent R. J. Ward from St Helens to Madras.[31]

Keswick also played its part in determining the career of the missionary who best expressed the spirit of the Forward Movement of the 1890s:

Oliver Tomkins, from Norfolk.

Tomkins and his younger brother Leo entered the service of the London Missionary Society, Tomkins in New Guinea, and Leo Tomkins in China. Their decision issued from several years of steadily growing conviction, fed by the atmosphere of a large and missionary-minded Congregational Church and by occasional deepenings of spirit, at Keswick, or a Moody service. There was an almost romantic aptness in Oliver Tomkins's commitment caused partly by his singular freshness of character and partly by his place at the very heart of what gave life to Congregationalism. Tomkins's father, Daniel Tomkins, had left the Nonconformist rural middle classes — the Tomkinses farmed near Bristol — for the urban middle classes when he settled in Yarmouth in 1847. He became one of Yarmouth's leading Nonconformists and Liberals, in a town as noted for its Methodism as for its electoral corruption. As a private schoolmaster he was at once a businessman and a professional man. As proprietor of Yarmouth College, to which his wife added Sutherland House for Girls, he made the running in the town's middle-class education. As a Congregationalist, he became the leading layman in Norfolk's second largest Congregational Church, with over 400 members in the 1890s, among them six justices of the peace. He married into one of the chapel's families, and in 1876 he was elected to the School Board, of which he became chairman, and to the Borough Council, on which he was at first the only Evangelical Nonconformist. For thirty of his fifty years in Yarmouth he was the leading Liberal, President of its Liberal Association.[32]

This was the background of the eleven Tomkins children, politically thrusting, intellectually open, adequately prosperous, edged with something of Yarmouth roughness, bound by their common Nonconformity. In Oliver's case it meant schooling at the College and then in Switzerland, before filling a position in Norwich at the Colman Carrow Works and joining Prince's Street, the Colman church.[33]

That was the key. Prince's Street was the largest Congregational Church in East Anglia and its minister, Dr Barrett, was a national force in the manner of Dr Mackennal; indeed he too had been suggested for the Secretaryship of the Congregational Union in 1891 and actually became its Chairman in 1894. He was associated with the Missionary Forward Movement, and at the Spring Meetings of 1892 he preached the annual Missionary Sermon — at which Elkanah Armitage led the devotions — while at the Southport Autumnals in the previous year his sermon on 'Sin' had contributed so powerfully to the expectancy of the hour.[34] Oliver Tomkins joined Prince's Street in 1890, when he was seventeen, and others of his family worshipped there when they moved to Norwich on

Daniel Tomkins's retirement. Their letters testify to the impact of Barrett's sermons.

It was a strenuous church and there was nothing formal in the act of joining it. Oliver and Leo Tomkins had made their first Christian commitment in 1889. 'My dearest Leo,' wrote Oliver from Switzerland,

I dare say you will be rather surprised at my writing to you as you have a poscard [*sic*] from me every week, but I want to tell you something that I could not well put on the postcard. I think Mother told you sometime ago that since I have been here I have been saved. It is about that that I want to write just a few words. Mother and I have been praying for you ever since that God will open your eyes to see what a great salvation He has prepared for all of us. Sooner or later the Holy Spirit will come to you (perhaps now) to ask to give yourself. . . . Do not be afraid to tell dear Mother all about it. . . .

Eventually the reply came:

My dearest Oliver,
    Thank you very much for that letter you sent me some time ago. I am now going to answer it.
    This afternoon Mother spoke to me about it and then we knelt down and I saw that I need only to come to Christ and simply trust Him.
    Do go on praying for me that I may not go back from Jesus.[35]

Oliver's sense of Christian direction intensified at Prince's Street. He taught in the Sunday School of the branch church at Trowse, and he shone in the Y.M.C.A's Missionary Parliament, whose reporter felt he could best describe him 'by calling him a true *Christian gentleman*'.[36] There was the Moody sermon on the Holy Spirit which the brothers heard early in 1893, and which convinced Leo that he ought to become a missionary, and later there were Keswick Conventions with their emphasis on the indwelling Spirit, which Oliver felt had purged him 'of a constant sort of self-reproach and consciousness of failure and weakness, which I used to have, and which used to make me sometimes afraid I should not be happy abroad'. Oliver urged Leo to spare a summer week for Keswick.[37] No less sensibly there had been missionary trips with the North Sea fishing fleets, in the care of a skipper who was an old Yarmouth College boy.

For Oliver the point of missionary decision came in the late summer of 1895, when he applied for immediate entry to the missionary Harley College, East London. Leo was the first in his family to be told, and to be asked for his special prayers. 'I cannot exactly describe to you what prompted me to do this but somehow I felt I was obeying God's will.'[38] He was ordained on 6 December 1899 at Prince's St with Dr Barrett presiding. Just over a month earlier the London Missionary Society held its own valedictory services in Kensington Chapel for twenty-two missionaries, half of them new workers, fourteen of them women, bound for China, India, Africa, New Guinea and Samoa: Silvester Horne presided. There was an air of celebration which transcended the high emotion born in singing 'God be with you till we meet again'. Some of the Prince's Street service sheets were printed in gold, with a motif of honeysuckle and bees, also in gold.[39]

The celebration was natural. The old century was closing with war in South Africa, and in the Imperial Parliament there were dissensions in the party of movement. At Prince's St, Norwich and Kensington Chapel, however, it was closing with the certainty of missionary endeavour, for Oliver Tomkins was bound for New Guinea to serve with James Chalmers the missionary (Tamate to the natives), whose opening of that complicated territory to the light of the Gospel ranged him in Christian esteem with Robert Moffat and David Livingstone.

Chalmers, 'as big as a church', 'restless as a volcano, and as subject to eruptions', who fascinated Robert Louis Stevenson and captivated missionary auxiliaries throughout the British Isles, had served the London Missionary Society since his ordination at Finchley in October 1865. The rest of his life was spent in the Pacific. From 1876 he was in New Guinea, hero of numberless escapes from death, a living missionary vindication of all the yarns that G. A. Henty ever dreamed of for his boy readers.[40]

The combination of such distinct types of manliness as Chalmers and Tomkins was indescribably appealing. Chalmers had laid the foundation for a Christian work whose issue could not now be in doubt, and the offering of Tomkins suggested a truly apostolic succession, a foretaste of eternity at the gate of the new century. It was natural, therefore, that the sense of celebration was invaded by jubilant indelicacy. The way in which evangelical joy is easily blunted by mere jocularity was shown by George Clarke of the *Home Magazine*, whose 'Missionary Band' provided much of the money for Tomkins. Clarke described Tomkins for his readers with the racy ease of popular religious journalism:

> When he entered my office, I beheld a nice, fresh-looking young man, 6 feet in height at least, and about 26 years of age. After shaking hands with him, I said: 'Well, you are going out amongst the cannibals.' 'Yes', he replied; 'at least, to the few that are left'. I could not help remarking, in a jocular way, as I looked at his jolly English face and honest blue eyes, 'I hope you will be somewhat wasted away before you get out there, for I am afraid the cannibals will think you are a very tasty dish!'[41]

Little jokes like this crept into the farewell services, coming naturally to Englishmen reared on tales of Chalmers's charmed life and convinced that cannibalism was dying with the century. The *Home Magazine* told its readers a great deal, not least of the effects of white men's clothes and drinks and illnesses on natives, and its snappy style added a dash of immediacy: 'We are providing Mr Tomkins with a camera, and he has promised to write us from time to time, and send us pictures . . . so that we may be all kept thoroughly in touch with him.'[42]

However, it could not convey the vastness of the work in New Guinea, or the danger of the Fly River, whose estuary fed the Gulf of Papua, where Chalmers was devoting the last stage of his service. There was always a vital gap between the knowledge of the missionaries and the expectations of even their best informed well-wishers at home. It was in this gap that the cruder manifestations of missionary consciousness grew, and empire became imperialism.

Until the end, however, Tomkins's missionary career vindicated the jauntiness of his sponsors. The power of his letters to his parents, his sister Dora, and his brother Leo, lies in their ease. Tomkins knew that his letters would be public property, passed on to the branches of his family in Norfolk and Yorkshire and through them to Sunday Schools and mission auxiliaries. He was also concerned to reassure his parents, now that his father was in frail retirement; and his aunts, who had given him a box of homeopathic medicines, needed a particular reassurance about the climate and his diet. Their pride and love was to be sustained. Perhaps it was this family mutuality which ensured that his letters should remain personal however public their contents. The picture which they convey of steady work unmarred by doubt or ill health, must be taken at face value: the face is too honest for any other interpretation to be possible.

Together the letters form a small, unspectacularly helpful archive of missionary endeavour. Into them come the overtones of a world more complex than evangelical enthusiasms sometimes admitted. They show the great test of sympathy confronting all missionaries from their first arrival on the field, and for which no training can be adequate. From them come the morals to be translated for the mission bands and watchers' guilds at home.

The tests began on the outward voyage. Amidst the seasickness there were services and Bible readings to be arranged, steerage passengers to be mingled with from a multitude of nations (Tomkins was travelling second class), and fellow missionaries to be assessed and accommodated. Tomkins could find common ground neither with a High Churchman called Ward, nor Havers, an American with whom 'total abstinence and non-smoking are essential to church-membership'. The three Christians contented themselves, therefore, with the amiabilities imposed by December travel abroad the 'Orizaba'.[43]

At Naples and Port Said there were glimpses of alien civilizations. It was Sunday at Naples, and the boat loads of singing, mandoline-playing, fruit-selling men and women worried Tomkins who contrasted the teasing beggars in the streets with the quiet earnestness of young Mr Topley in the Sailors' Rest. 'It made one pray "May God deliver England from the Continental Sabbath". It really seems no Sabbath at all.' Port Said came almost as a relief: 'Even Mohamedanism does not seem to have such a degrading effect as Roman Catholicism seemed to in Naples, altho' they say Port Said is one of the most wicked places on earth.' The 'Orizaba' coaled at Port Said and the sight and noise of hundreds of Arabs working through the night with their baskets of coal, their faces as dusky as their Christless souls, brought out the missionary yearning in him. It was easier to bear in Egypt than in Christian Italy. The first remoulding of opinions had begun.[44]

Port Said was another world, yet nowhere was Tomkins free from the opposing standards of other white men. The Boer War cast its shadow everywhere. As the Mediterranean fleet passed them in the Straits of Messina 'one felt a sense of British supremacy to see these English vessels, prowling about in Italian seas, and to know that behind these pretty illuminations were guns enough, probably to sweep the whole Mediterranean, if necessary'. In go-ahead Sydney, so full of trams, people seemed to be 'very keen on the war — more patriotic than some of us English people, I think'.[45]

Tomkins's own patriotism was muted. He belonged to a class which, while it traded and settled abroad, neither fought nor governed abroad, and he was sometimes mystified by those whom he met from the fighting or governing classes. Once in the islands beyond Australia in the Torres Straits he was struck by the solitary white men who had settled there, owning boats or employing natives to dive for pearls, men driven there by the advance of civilization. They were poor men, drinkers like Yankee Ned of Masig, who had run through a fortune, or well-connected in the English sense like the university man with four small cutters or the two ex-public school boys on Mabuiag. At Daru, in New Guinea itself, there was a white community which included two young Australians, a Frenchman, and the resident magistrate, the Hon. Mr Murray, 'quite a young swell. . . . His brother is M.P. for Midlothian'. Tomkins feared that the natives might not make the necessary distinction between the encroaching forces of Law and the pervasive force of the Gospel, when both were brought by white men, and he had already seen enough of Chalmers to realize where lay the greater knowledge of everyday matters in the South Seas.[46]

The meat of the missionary life lay in the interplay of Law, Gospel and trade. Tomkins was on Mabuiag at the end of January 1901. On the 27th they held memorial services for Queen Victoria, the native deacon selecting for his text 'She hath done what she could and verily wheresoever the Gospel shall be preached this that she hath done shall be spoken of for a memorial of her'. A pearl fisher had brought in a pearl thought to be worth £800: 'This led our thoughts in the afternoon to a "Pearl of great price" ', and then, on the evening of the 27th, a Samoan came 'like Nicodemus, more anxious about his soul's salvation than any native I have ever seen so far. He . . . might become a teacher some day. Let us pray for him.'[47] Thus Tomkins brought his family into the heart of his evangelism, and through them the people of Prince's Street, and aunts and cousins in Yarmouth, the older brother in Leeds, and Leo, now at Cheshunt College: the rhythm of prayer had been caught in England.

Tomkins's relationships with Chalmers were unclouded. There was perfect accord between them, and growing accord with the Christians on the mission stations. The language problem was intense. Pidgin was complicated enough — in April 1900 he delighted his sister Dora with a letter in Pidgin — but with the dialects nearest to hand there was the problem of conveying a Christian understanding of love, when the language made no allowance for the concept, or of conveying a sense of number when it was impossible to count above two. Even football was a problem. ' "Run" is "siororowagurumo", "kick" is "aramosiodoi". Before you have time to tell the goal-keeper to run and kick, the goal is scored!'[48] Indeed the very idea of football was novel to the natives, who rolled in delight at their first sight of it.

Such revelations of first principles were hard to meet. When Tomkins gave a lantern show he caught the full blast of native simplicity, for 'the best slide I have ("Ecce Homo") was in their ignorance greeted by laughter, happily checked however by the better informed. But I am sure the pictures do good and let a lot of light into the sadly darkened minds of many of them. They will talk about them for weeks after.'[49] Such a response was fatherly rather than paternalistic; the situation demanded too great a leap of imagination for mere paternalism to enter into it, and there was mutual sensitivity in the relations between the missionaries and their converts.

'No doubt the "hardships of the Gospel" will come in good time, but they have not come yet with me.'[50] Tomkins throve in the tiresome climate, almost ashamed at his robust health in the face of so many intimations of mortality. Mrs Chalmers died in October 1900, and in December he read the biographies of two English Congregationalists who had recently died in their prime of life: Charles Berry of Wolverhampton, who had helped to launch the missionary Forward Movement, and Frank Crossley, the Manchester engineer and mission worker who had been one of Mackennal's deacons at Bowdon. From China there was news of missionaries threatened in the Boxer Uprising.[51] Yet in New Guinea the threat posed by the climate failed to materialize, and the crocodiles could be laughed off.[52]

There was always, however, the Fly River. Chalmers had no illusions about its dangers. It is possible that he wished to shield Tomkins from too early a knowledge of them, and perhaps Tomkins in turn shielded what he knew from his family, especially his mother. It could not be done. In August 1900 he told his parents of the 'great work to be done up the Fly River', at the same time writing — not entirely as if of past heroism — of Tamate's miraculous escapes from death. A month later he described a missionary reconnaissance along the estuary of the Fly River, telling of the tidal bore — the only thing Chalmers feared in New Guinea — and of a recent brush between the resident magistrate and villagers from the very district that the missionaries hoped to visit. At one village the chief begged for a teacher, but at another a teacher had been attacked not long before. 'Today for the first time I have been actually face to face with Heathen darkness. How helpless one feels.'

At this his mother was thoroughly alarmed, and in November he wrote: 'No, Mother, but I am quite safe in the Fly River, since I believe it is where God wishes me to be and if so, I should not be safe anywhere else.' He then described a district on the northern estuary where the Government magistrate had recently fired on natives while apprehending a murderer.

> That is just the district, which Tamate is anxious to open up next. . . . That sort of thing does not frighten him at all.
> But what are these troubles compared with what the missionaries are going thro' in China? I have been deeply touched in reading of their trials and sufferings, some of them even to death. They need our prayers.

And he ended, promising a better letter next time, with 'best love to Aunts and all and much for yourselves'.[53]

On 27 March 1901 he wrote one of his best letters, explaining towards the end that 'if the weather keeps fine, I am going with Tamate tomorrow in the "Niue" across to the Fly River district'. It was to be a long journey and some time might elapse before his next letters home. 'Anyhow you will know that I am in the safest and best keeping.'[54]

Their first destination was not the Fly River but Goaribari Island in the Aird River delta further north in the Gulf of Papua. Chalmers, for once unwell, Tomkins, and some native students formed the party. On Easter

Sunday, 7 April 1901, Tomkins pencilled in his pocket diary the only entry to be other than a list of letters sent or provisions received:

We had been sailing in the open sea since Good Friday morning and this afternoon we drew towards our destination viz Risk Point (we anchored at 3 o'clock in a fine harbour and we're just having a short service with the crew). This district has only been visited once before, and that was 5 years ago when the Government steamer came here and tried to civilize the native by the gentle persuasion of the rifle. So we did not know what sort of a reception we might get. . . . Before the service was over several canoes appeared in the distance coming towards us. They were all small canoes, some with one man only others with three or four. As they came nearer the wonder was how they balanced themselves standing up in less than half of the trunk of a tree hollowed out and no outriggers to keep them steady. By this time there must have been 20 or more. They hesitated as they got nearer to us, till we were able to assure them that we meant peace. Gradually one or two of the daring ones came closer and then alongside till at last one ventured on board. Then in a very few minutes we were surrounded by canoes and the vessel was covered with natives. One of my earliest impressions of missionary work was gathered from a picture of the missionary jumping ashore with a book presumably the Bible in his hand from which, the picture leads one to suppose, he is forthwith going to instruct the natives who are to be seen crowding round. I have wondered since, if this depicts the missionary's first visit to some heathen tribe, and if so in what language the Bible is written and how the translation was obtained. On this our first visit we were able to do really nothing more than establish friendly relations with the people. They stayed on board about three hours examining everything from the ship's rigging to our shirtbuttons.

They tried hard to persuade us to come ashore in their canoes, but we preferred to spend the night afloat and promised we would visit their village in the morning.[55]

They went in the morning, to Dopima, on Goaribari Island.

On 22 April a Reuter's telegram appeared in the British press, subsequently confirmed by a telegram from the L.M.S. agent on Thursday Island: 'News from Daru states Chalmers and Tomkins, with twelve students, murdered on Aird River; tribal fight at time. Chalmers landing, tried to make peace. Society's agents at Daru looking after Mission. Governor-Resident wired Brisbane asking permission to render assistance.'[56]

The details were pieced together in the course of the next few months. It was in February 1902, however, that the Tomkins family were told all that they really needed to know:

I do not think that either of them expected much danger when they went ashore on that Monday morning, though I think Tamate did not quite like the look of affairs, for he tried to persuade Oliver to stay on board.

Bob [the native skipper of the 'Niue'] says they had quite an argument as to whether Oliver should go or stay, and he settled it by getting into the boat and saying 'If you go, I go. If you stay on board, I stay on board.'[57]

It is no longer easy to picture the shock which the news caused. It committed Congregationalists to an interest in New Guinea which has continued with its emergence as a sovereign state, the latest instalment of that lengthening of horizons entailed by evangelism. It confirmed Leo Tomkins more firmly to the missionary cause, and he was ordained at Prince's Street in September 1903 for service in Central China.[58] When Lovett's biography of Chalmers was published in 1902, R. F. Horton noted of it: 'They were clubbed, and *eaten*. In this way they were allowed to give their flesh, like the Master, for the life of the world.'[59] Elkanah Armitage made no reference to the murders in his diary. In 1886 he had heard Chalmers who was then on missionary deputation, and in the spring of 1890 Armitage had given a series of addresses to his Rotherham congregation on 'Victories of the Cross'. The first of these had been about the cannibals of New Guinea.[60]

Armitage's concern for the mission field, however, grew into the new century. He spent the winter of 1902-3 in India, visiting mission stations, and witnessing Lord Curzon's state entry into Delhi, while Ella Armitage stayed in Bombay with a University ladies' mission to the Parsees.[61] In 1902 he had told the Yorkshire Congregational Union that 'every true soul looks out upon Reality and sees something of it. . . .'[62] His visit to India afforded him space to test the breadth of this conviction.

The extent to which Armitage, or those like him, passed such tests must remain a matter for debate. Perhaps missionary endeavour was no more than a weird Puritan phenomenon.[63] So comfortingly rational a thought fails to meet the quality of the enterprise, or the nature of the leap from imagination into faith. When the Bible Christians, Free Methodists and New Connexion Methodists united to form the United Methodist Church in 1907, the representatives of the constituent denominations were listed alphabetically according to circuit. Thus China appeared between Chesterfield and Chorley, and Sierra Leone between Shrewsbury and Southport (Duke Street).[64] The Uniting Conference was a heady business, held at Wesley's Chapel in the City Road, and marked by civic and imperial pomp, as United Methodist mayors and lord mayors filled the platform for the visit of Lord Mayor Treloar and the Sheriffs of London. The visit closed with the National Anthem. 'But', said the President of Conference, 'we have another King, one Jesus. Let us sing one verse of "All Hail the Power of Jesu's Name".'[65] The listing was odd and the choral spontaneity undignified: but no other perspective would have been tolerable.

Chapter 11

Christ's Choice of a Battlefield?

Give me to see the foes that I must fight,
    Powers of the darkness, throned where Thou shouldst reign,
Read the directings of Thy wrath aright,
    Lest, striking flesh and blood, I strike in vain.

(From a hymn by Henry Child Carter, 1875-1954, Minister of
Emmanuel Congregational Church, Cambridge, 1910-44.)

You'll find Cambridge a strangely different place next term if, as I fear, this
ghastly war still continues. But unless we want to see our womenfolk under the grip
of the German soldiery there is nothing for it but a fight to the finish.

(Letter 28 August, 1914, in records of Cambridge University
Nonconformist Union.)

'Look round you on Christendom, the realm of the Prince of Peace!
4,000,000 of men under arms form the peace establishment of the
Christian nations; you must raise it to 12,000,000 in time of war.
£4,000,000,000 is the sum of the public debts of Europe, of which all but
the smallest fraction has been spent in armaments for the swift
destruction of mankind.'[1] Thus Baldwin Brown at the 1878 Autumnals.
His fear of armaments was a natural one, with Russians and Turks at each
other's throats, and it issued from a close knowledge of Europe: he had
been in Italy in 1859 and seen the battle for liberty at first hand.

Nonetheless his was a Nonconformist response, natural to men who
traded, travelled and prayed, but who neither fought nor governed and
were not diplomatists. Men who prayed, as well as traded and travelled,
were professionally articulate. What happened when their language
assumed the colour of their surroundings, and Christian chivalry was
blooded?

This had always been a Quaker problem, although it took the First
World War for the Quaker peace testimony to assume its present shape.
Since 1816 their response had been institutionalized in the Peace Society
which was not a Quaker organization. In Henry Richard, M.P. for Merthyr
from 1868, and Secretary of the Peace Society from 1848, the movement
had a leader of national repute.

The Crimean War had been its first test, and it caught Nonconformists at sixes and sevens. So did every martial involvement thereafter although it might seem that the disinclination for entanglement shown by subsequent Liberal governments marked a belated victory for those who had testified in the 1850s. In the last quarter of the century, however, the armaments race could no longer be wished away, and the language of war kept pace.

There was nothing new for Nonconformists about such language. Their hymns were all of war. Protestant life was one of perpetual conflict with the world, and when the Victorian Puritan began to celebrate it in the chivalry of stained-glass, this was merely a fresh stage in the old battle between Hebrew and Hellene. But whose was the victory?

The Cromwell tercentenary brought something of this out. All Free Churchmen were Ironsides now, even the Wesleyans of the *Methodist Times*: 'Cromwell not only laid the foundation of our Colonial Empire and our mighty fleet, but in five short years he gave England for the first time in her history the mastery of the seas, and made this little island the most powerful kingdom in Europe. Never since, not even in our own time, has the voice of England been so potent throughout the civilized world.'[2]

This meant, however, that the epics of Christian endeavour would be compared and often confused with the epics of nationhood. In the spring of 1901 Dr Barrett of Prince's Street reminded his congregation at Oliver Tomkins's memorial service of the volunteers recently returned from fighting in South Africa 'as we believe, for righteousness and liberty. And as I looked on their faces I thought of that good servant of Jesus Christ, Oliver Tomkins.'[3]

Silvester Horne's death also inspired talk of volunteers. Lynn Harold Hough wrote a Sunday School story about Jimmy Ellerton, son of an American 'self-made captain of industry', and a latter-day prodigal who, though 'he had managed to escape the coarser vices . . . had elected pleasure as his major in the university of life'. Then, one dull Sunday in the Tottenham Court Road he followed a crowd into Whitefield's. Alas for his impulse, he found himself at a memorial service: and thus he learned of the man whom they commemorated, Silvester Horne, and of his 'majestic energy', the 'gay human zest with which he swung through life'. At the end, overwhelmed, young Ellerton 'threw back his head. The message of the music and the message of the sermon had come to the citadel of his soul and had captured it'. He prayed, passionately: 'O God, one of the captains is gone. I can only be a common soldier. But if you have a place for me I am ready to enlist.'[4]

The language of enlistment changed dramatically within the next three years. When war broke out in August 1914, men enlisted. From January 1916 men *were* enlisted. It is arguable whether conscription achieved anything that volunteering had not already done but the change of attitude which it both forced and reflected was unalterable.

The war was an immense and bruising affront to all Liberals and Free Churchmen. In the light of retrospect it might seem strange that it did not provoke more protest from their leaders, and indeed it was not at all clear up to the moment of declaration how they would react and what the response of their press, their organizations, or their likeliest parliamentary spokesmen would be. What would have happened had Mr Lloyd George come out against the war?

The answer is that probably nothing would have happened. At the level of immediate response there was nothing in the concept of war, honourably undertaken, which was more alien to Free Churchmen than to any other Churchmen. Indeed it is probable that in the summer of 1914 the concept had unusual immediacy since there was the prospect of civil war in Ireland.

When the war came, however, it presented Liberals and Free Churchmen with a multi-dimensional vastness for which they could not have been prepared. Within five years the inadequacies of their theologies and the naiveties of their social responses — which had long been under siege — were cruelly revealed. At the same time the sort of politics to which they had best adapted was transformed. At both levels the transformation, which in some form was inevitable, took a shape which was not predictable, because of the unnatural rapidity of the process.

Free Churchmen found themselves at war when, diplomatically at least, England was nowhere in dispute. They found themselves at war with Germany, a country for which many of their spokesmen felt particular *rapport*. The expense and complexity of the war was unimaginable to them, and demanded prompt solutions for which they were not equipped. As to their prime ministers, Lloyd George was the politician tarred with victory and therefore the man whose policies made mincemeat of the prerogatives and responsibilities of any individual life. He was also the man most in tune with Free Church rhetoric: he had been reared among the Disciples of Christ and he never repudiated his adherence to the Baptists, who were closest to the Disciples. Asquith, whom admirers have liked to see as a Liberal of purest essence, was the man who introduced conscription, the symbol of the new order. He was connected with some of the chief names of Victorian voluntaryism — indeed he was a nephew of the Bainesocracy.[5] He had been born into the heart of northern Congregationalism, and was once a Congregationalist by conviction as well as birth.[6] The ironies were stupendous.

Most Free Churchmen could greet the war with certainty. All of them, however, were prey to a mistrust which for many accumulated into betrayal. Politically the victim of this resentment was the Liberal Party, whose parliamentary disintegration could easily be attributed to the unworthy clashes of defective personalities. At the chapel level there was no victim other than the Master whom they served. Recognition of this demanded a redefinition of attitudes as profound as that demanded of their Separatist, Ironside, Ejected or Wesleyan ancestors: and since transformed men are still men, the result was no less ragged.

Silvester Horne's death secured Jimmy Ellerton's enlistment in Christ's war. Horne's father-in-law, Herbert Cozens-Hardy, greeted the Kaiser's war with the resignation of one unlikely to experience much beyond it. Despite his peerage he was still a radical lawyer, rather old-fashioned now, still living in Ladbroke Grove. The war brought inconveniences. The Hall at Letheringsett was used by staff officers for several months and soldiers were billeted in the village. His chauffeur, gamekeeper, gardener and carpenter were all in the army by 1917, and he became economy conscious.

The implications went deeper than inconvenience. One son was in the Admiralty and three nephews had volunteered: and this in a family which had neither cultivated nor desired a military tradition. As the war proceeded his concern mounted at the emergency legislation passed without adequate scrutiny, yet invariably affecting the rights and properties of individuals. 'Money is being spent like water, and a huge debt is being contracted,' he wrote in August 1915,

When this war is over ... we shall undoubtedly witness great changes. The supremacy of the House of Commons will be weakened — old party lines will disappear — state socialism will be extended — the reign of the Manchester School will be ended — we shall think more of sailors and soldiers — and our colonies will be given a definite part in the direction of Imperial policy. But all this is prophecy, and I daresay foolish prophecy.[7]

It was neither foolish nor unique. The Armitage confederacy reacted similarly. 1914 was marked by an increasing round of deaths among friends and family. It was also marked by wider recognition in their spheres of usefulness. Cozens-Hardy was offered his peerage by Asquith shortly before the King's Birthday on 22 June; Elkanah Armitage retired from Yorkshire United College on 24 June, and was presented with his portrait. 'Heaps of kindness', he noted.[8] Early in July he was in Norwich staying with the Sydney Cozens-Hardys.[9] The family diaries became suitably summery, noting the hot weather ('almost fainted in chapel'[10])

235

and preparing for holidays in Cornwall. On 15 July the Faulkner Armitages arrived in Liverpool from America. On the 28th William Armitage noted that 'Austria declared war on Servia' before itemizing further holiday arrangements. Two days later the William Armitages were in London for a family wedding. The ceremony was at Kensington Chapel, and the day closed with a theatre visit while the newly-weds set out for Switzerland, 'via Germany'.[11]

The sheer affront of the war, and its vastness, became most apparent in such a context. It occurred amidst family celebrations and holidays, weddings and funerals. The Armitages were politically committed, but their diaries were for family and church, not politics, save for echoes of startling doings. William Armitage made little reference to the divisive domestic politics of 1914 beyond feeling that Asquith was 'splendid'; Elkanah merely noted that he heard Asquith and Grey speak at Leeds in the winter of 1913, and Lloyd George at Huddersfield in March 1914. 'We are all very proud of our Liberal Administration.'[12]

The war, however, after a piquant delay, became ever present. Latterly Elkanah's diary had been irregularly kept: 'It is the mournful outbreak of a great European war into which we have been drawn that moves me to resume it.'[13] For William the family holidays continued, but in the atmosphere of khaki as sons and nephews volunteered: another family assimilated to a military tradition.[14]

Bradford and Manchester had sizeable communities of German origin; their chapel communities were cosmopolitan, surnames and business ramifications testifying to links with central and eastern Europe hardly less than with the outposts of the Empire. They were cultural connexions as well as commercial ones. Elkanah Armitage spoke German and knew Germany; he had been at school in Stuttgart in the late 1850s and since then he had walked, cycled and studied there. He felt an affinity for the country: holidaying at Taormina in 1913 he had happily stayed 'at the modest Pension Schuler which was full of agreeable Germans'.[15] The war was heartbreaking, the overturning of affections which it entailed was complete. It was the first war-time leap of imagination.

'But *we* are satisfied that Grey, Asquith, and our whole Liberal administration has *strenuously* pursued peace and though Morley, Burns, and Trevelyan have resigned, the Liberal party stands firmly by them.'[16] It was the invasion of Belgium which made this conviction possible. Stories of German beastliness and Belgian dignity were quick spreading and the burning of Louvain compounded them.

We are persuaded, the world over, that Germany has exhibited a brutality and vileness more terrible than that of Huns or Red Indians. Poor little Belgium is now *stamped out* in blood and iron and fire, with orgies of bestiality in which pillaging troops have been egged on by their officers. The catalogue of her crimes can never be told, but she is formally indicted by visits to Washington (as the great neutral State) of a select Belgian Committee.[17]

It seemed that German cunning had been foiled: the Irish and Indians upon whose rebellion the Germans counted, had rallied with the 'utmost enthusiasm about the old country. Not only Canada and Australia but actually Boers and others from South Africa and above all India is marching to our help'.[18]

Such a scale of enthusiasm was within the bounds of comprehension: so was the more human scale of Belgian refugees, of whom twenty-five or so were housed in a neighbouring villa, thanks largely to the Armitages' efforts. The Armitages' own Belgian guests cloaked their emotions with 'courteous self-restraint and pleasantness'.[19]

The cumulative impact, however, transcended all imagining. By November 1914, thirteen nephews had volunteered, eighteen by New Year. In 1915 the first family deaths in action were reported from Gallipoli. There was the reorganization of business and administrative affairs for the war effort. There was nervousness about the reactions of Labour — 'Difficulties with the Labour Party arise continually, especially with colliers', (Elkanah noted that the German Socialists were 'solidly loyal to the Kaiser's action') — and there was regret about the fall of Asquith, 'bowled out' with 'all the strong Liberal members of the recent Coalition Government'. The manufacture of armaments and the appalling indebtedness generated a terrible momentum. Elkanah commented on the thousands of wealthy and refined women in munitions factories, and on the girls of the Armitage confederacy busy in depots and canteens. It foretold a new society. 'Vast changes of a socialistic kind are being effected as war-measures: — we are by this time accustomed to our military conscription, save that every week a finer comb is used to drag up men; but the Government is taking control of transport. . . . And everybody seems to say "*Go on*"!'[20]

The momentum did not cease with the end of war in November 1918. Peace ('The armistice terms are *hard* HARD HARD!') came with almost as dramatic a suddenness in 1918 as war in 1914. At least twenty-three nephews had served in the armed forces, eighteen of them abroad. Eight had been killed. No family could survive such mortality with its values unaffected. Early in 1917 Elkanah had noted: 'Revolution in Russia! Almost bloodless. It is found that the Romanoffs were playing Germany's game!'[21] By 1919 it was more than clear that revolution was endemic in Europe, that it was as murderous as war, and that unrest at home could not be divorced from it. 'Sad *Labour Unrest* in Britain as in much of Europe. Wild schemes of revolution in the air, the workmen refusing control.'[22]

Elkanah now commented regularly in his diary on political and social tendencies: such things were no longer to be taken for granted. The war had aged him, demanding too changed a perspective for a man in retirement. Armitage remained alert, but with an old man's alertness. He never ceased to be an Asquithian Liberal. Yet in August 1914, his Christian hope impelled him to face the new perspective: 'The one happy gleam is found in the deep expectation that the conscience of the world is today at the point of feeling the *criminality* of militarism and the rule of brute force. Men are daring to hope that this awful war must issue in a new order of political conceptions and a fuller realization of the unity of man.'[23]

Christian men and women survive like anybody else: the question which faced Free Churchmen, beneficiaries of a particular social and political structure, with their values formed within it, dissenters indeed but from within the system, was whether they could face the new perspectives with a realism to equal their faith.

There is no single answer, but the interplay of tensions and responses is seen in the records of the Bowdon Downs Congregational Church. The Downs had become a mother church for the Armitage clan, symbolized at their annual parties, first at old William Armitage's house, Townfield, and then at Stamford, where Faulkner Armitage lived. Between sixty and 100 of them, of all ages and denominations, would return for this family reunion, at whose core was the New Year's day early morning prayer meeting at The Downs Chapel. For the Elkanah Armitages the New Year Armitage party at Altrincham often followed a Christmas Bulley party at New Brighton.

The Downs, however, was more than a spiritual point of reference for one large extended family, or Manchester cotton at prayer. It combined several roles. As has been seen, it spiritualized the suburban ideal;[24] it was a family church, of which the Armitages were only part; it was a civic church whose membership included people of note in the public life of south Lancashire and Cheshire; it was a missionary church, upholding local missions and contributing large sums each year to foreign missions; and it was a Dissenting church – every adult who worshipped there was in some measure protesting at the values of society. This was as true of The Downs as it had been of Edward Miall's Bond Street, Leicester: indeed there were family connexions between the Bowdon people and William Baines, the church-rate martyr. These roles were not easily compatible, but the tensions which they created made for vitality. The nature of The

Downs was revealed most tellingly in war time.

The Boer War served as a dress rehearsal. For Elkanah Armitage at Rawdon the winter of 1899 was 'one of the gravest in the history of our country that I have ever known. *War with the Boers*'. He took a moderate line: 'The Liberals have as a whole upheld Lord Salisbury and Mr Chamberlain in the prosecution of the war, as having been inevitable, though there has been a peace party which has called it a cowardly war.'[25] Dr Mackennal belonged to that party.

Alexander Mackennal was a seasoned supporter of the Peace Society. In the 1850s and 1860s he had justified the Crimean and American Wars as conflicts issuing from generous impulses. There was no generosity about the Boer War which he saw as a dismal reflexion of a world grown small and embattled. Mackennal had done as much as any man through the Congregational Union, the International Congregational Council and the Free Church Council, to articulate a Nonconformist voice: the Boer War suggested the slight effect of his efforts. 'It is a sorrowful fact', he wrote in 1901, 'that those of us to whom the sinfulness of this war appears so clear that it is a duty of a solemn order not to trifle with the conviction, are reduced to the necessity of private communication, and that too, when we believe that there is an unavowed feeling of the same sort in many of our churches which does not let itself be aroused.'[26] The Downs was such a church. Exception was taken at some of his sermons and there was a little pamphlet war. The formal view of the members, however, was expressed in April 1900: they upheld Mackennal, 'believing, as we do, that your responsibility is not to us, but to Him who has called you'.[27]

This, amidst more pressing tensions and sharper personalities, was the view to which they clung in 1914. The Downs in 1914 was sufficiently flourishing. Its income, which never quite met expenditure, was up; its collections for the London Missionary Society were nearly £600. Its membership was slightly down.[28] The Chapel Literary Society, whose meetings had included sessions on Women, Socialism and 'Evolution and War', held for its 1913-4 winter programme, a debate which Faulkner Armitage opened, on 'Has Suburban Life an Adverse Influence on Character' and another, which his brother-in-law, Arthur Haworth, chaired urging 'That the System of Compulsory Military Service for Home Defence should be adopted in this Country'.

The impact of war was immediate. By January 1915 The Downs Roll of Honour stood at 102 serving men. The Boys Brigade noted that over fifty of its past or present members 'are serving in the navy or army'. The Girls' Club introduced ambulance classes. The branches were equally active: Hey Head collected for a family of Belgian refugees and sent money for soldiers' comforts; Partington also knitted woollen comforts, their enthusiasm kindled by a lantern lecture on Belgium; Broadheath feared that there had been no spiritual deepening in response to the crisis, and estimated 'that forty-five young men connected with us in one way or another have offered their services to our country'.[29]

There was a surge of leadership. Faulkner Armitage became Mayor of Altrincham in 1913 and Arthur Haworth, recently a Manchester M.P. with a brief achievement of junior office, succeeded C. P. Scott as President of the Manchester Liberal Federation. During the war, while his wife organized a War Hospital Supply Depot, Haworth commanded the 1st home battalion of the Cheshire Regiment. In May 1915 he became Chairman of the Congregational Union, the sixth layman to hold that office: it was the summation of civic, political and religious leadership.

Nonetheless it was a Dissenting summation. In his Spring Address, 'Some Thoughts on the War and the Church', Haworth was at pains to speak as a Free Churchman. He found the situation in August 1914 'extraordinarily simple and clear': a matter of Belgian integrity and British honour. It was also a matter of German philosophy, and he talked of Nietzsche, Treitschke, Bernhardi and the State. In this guise the war was 'redemptive in its aims', and he spoke of ennobling qualities, and the spirit of unity. Here he took Edward Miall as his guide and gathering in the experience of the Empire's Free Churches he concluded: 'Unity, but not uniformity, of the Church in England is a noble ideal to aspire to, and worthy of our best. It can only be obtained through Disestablishment. That will come; and it will come through reason, and not by violence.'[30]

This was the authentic voice of Edwardian Congregationalism, and Haworth returned to the battle in October 1915, when he spoke of 'Liberty *versus* Government, or Liberty and Government'. He quoted Henry Allon at the 1881 Jubilee; he recalled the Pilgrim Fathers and the Elizabethan Separatists and he declared that 'Freedom and self-government have made the Empire'. And he worried at the problem of liberty in wartime. What was the balance between individual and social liberties? Was there not too much reliance on government in our ordinary affairs? He dwelt, shudderingly, on 'the question of State compulsion of military service'. His views were clear: in the absence of proof that voluntary enlistment failed to maintain the fight for liberty (and he believed that there would be no such proof) he was sure that 'to compel a man to fight, and possibly lay down his life for his country, is the greatest infringement of liberty, and ought to be strenuously resisted as such'.[31]

Haworth was self-consciously the Dissenting Baronet, but there was no humbug about him and while he gave no answers he stated the case as Free Churchmen tried to see it. There was piquancy in this because his own minister was a notorious pacifist: Haworth spoke from a conflict which was waging among the pews at The Downs.

The Downs had been without a minister for much of 1914, suffering a series of candidates who came to preach 'with a view'. William Armitage, who was on the selection committee, commented tersely on them in his diary. On 10 May, however, 'Rev. Leighton [*sic*] Richards late of Melbourne preached at The Downs. Created rather a sensation'. The selection committee was bowled over by Richards, and a church meeting was unanimous in its approval. William Armitage was a shade regretful, wishing that there had been an opportunity to assess Nathaniel Micklem, a young Mansfield College man whose visit had been postponed because of tooth trouble;[32] but on 22 May he was at the Manchester Reform Club, inviting Richards to settle among them. The appropriate church resolution had been proposed by Sir Arthur Haworth, and seconded by Rigby Armitage, Asquith's former brother-in-law.

Leyton Richards was a boldly suitable choice. He was thirty-five, with pastoral experience in Scotland and Australia. Like so many ministers he came from a family poised uncomfortably between the middle and lower middle classes. It was his fortune to belong to the last of those few generations of bright Free Church boys who, when faced with politics, the pulpit or journalism, could choose the pulpit without incongruity. The generosity of his church in Reading sent him to Glasgow University in 1900, where he followed in the steps of Mackennal in the 1850s and Horne in the 1880s, immersed in the Liberal Club and Dialectic Society. He was known as a Pro-Boer.[33] Like Horne, he moved on to Mansfield College and was marked out for note among Congregationalists. His wife, Edith Pearson of Somerville College, was from a background as assured as his own had been edgy. Her father, Samuel Pearson, had ministered at Great George St, Liverpool in the 1870s and Broughton Park, Manchester, between 1892 and 1907.

At this point, however, the boldness rather than the suitability of the choice becomes apparent. The intensely political undergraduate carried his politics into his pastorates. At Peterhead in 1909 he criticized Liberal foreign policy, which would lead to war,[34] and in Australia, at Collins Street, Melbourne, he led a campaign against compulsory military training, preaching on 'Compulsory Military Training and the Duty of the Church. A Plea for Liberty of Conscience' to a congregation which included the Minister of Defence and some of his officials.[35]

His Australian pastorate lasted from 1911 to February 1914, long enough to add an imperial dimension to his pacifism, which accorded strangely with the imperial experience of many in his next congregation, at Bowdon. It was while holidaying in Tasmania in 1913 that he came across naval officers who talked convincingly of the inevitability of war with Germany, and on his return in 1914 he stopped in South Africa where a Pearson brother-in-law was helping Gandhi's first non-violence campaign. In the nine years between William Armitage's visit and his own the South African pattern of race relations had hardened. There was nothing obscure about the pre-history of apartheid and Richards was convinced that the Boers had emerged as the true victors of the Boer War: 'Present methods are merely a foolish amalgam of selfishness and drift, and some day there must be a terrible harvest.'[36]

Richards arrived in England in April, preached at The Downs in May and began his stated ministry in September. William Armitage's diary is brief and to the point about it. The pastorate began amidst the novel swirl of war. The first Belgian refugees had arrived, two of them staying with the William Armitages at Beech Hurst, while there were wounded Belgian soldiers to be visited at Ancoats Hospital. On 1 November Citizen Sunday was marked by a Civic Service at The Downs, with Faulkner Armitage attending it for the second time as mayor, and William Armitage singing in the augmented choir. 'Leyton Richards preached a splendid sermon.'[37] On 25 December William cycled with Leyton Richards to Warford: 'we sat amongst the soldiers for some time.' Three days later one of William's fellow deacons called 'with a copy of resignation by the Rev. Leyton Richards in consequence of a meeting at Arthur Haworth's'.[38]

Almost immediately he was urged to withdraw his resignation, thus starting an honourable tug of conscience between himself and The Downs which lasted until July 1916. Richards's opposition to the war had been public knowledge in Manchester since its beginning, and it received a wider publicity in the Christian and daily press. His sense of isolation was dissipated by this, and by a Cambridge conference which he attended in December 1914 from which issued the Fellowship of Reconciliation. This strengthened his resolve and he became a focal point for pacifists in the area, in contact with Quakers and the Manchester branch of the No-Conscription Fellowship.

The strain of ministering to a church which was habitually in the public eye, whose people were greatly attached to him but whose commitment to the war effort was complete, told upon him. The Downs' natural patriotism was immeasurably strengthened by its links with young volunteers. Free Churches had never before been so directly and intimately linked with the emotion of war, and the pastoral tensions which resulted have been movingly described by Edith Richards.[39] The church contained a small group of pacifists and others were attracted, but many members could no longer in conscience attend. Arthur Haworth worshipped at St Margaret's parish church for the duration of Richards's ministry: he cannot have been mollified by the views of its incumbent,

Hewlett Johnson, the future 'Red Dean' of Canterbury.[40] William Armitage, whose three sons had volunteered, and whose daughters were active in war work, remained staunch. He cycled with Richards, and he sat through the more explosive sermons: 'Leyton Richards preached a great sermon Luke XXII 38 "Behold here are 2 swords. And he said unto them 'It is enough' "; Leyton Richards preached a tremendous sermon on passivism . . . a wounded officer from India, to supper.'[41]

Late in July 1915, with news from the Dardanelles flooding in, the tug of conscience recommenced. Richards again resigned and again he was urged to reconsider it, 'only three voted against in a room full; some did not vote'.[42] By now the business was newsworthy and accounts of this meeting appeared in the local press. For a while the routine of church life continued. In October 1915 Mayoral Sunday was once more observed at The Downs ('Faulkner's 3rd appearance in chains') with Richards as the preacher: 'What shall I do with Jesus.'[43]

The pace was now altering. In November and December William Armitage was busy recruiting 'under Lord Derby's Scheme'. What Arthur Haworth had deplored at the Congregational Autumnals was almost upon them, and on the second Sunday in January, 1916, 'Mr Richards preached a strong anti-Conscription sermon: on Conscience which he had advertised. Many regulars absent but a large congregation of strangers.'[44] Matters had gone beyond the church's control, if indeed they had ever been within it. In the early spring of 1916 Richards was one of eight committee members of the No-Conscription Fellowship (from which he quickly resigned) to sign a leaflet against the Military Service Act: *Repeal the Act*. On 10 May they were summoned to appear at the Mansion House charged with prejudicing recruiting and military discipline. At the same time, and for the third time, Richards sent his resignation to The Downs, firm in his fidelity to the Gospel of Peace but in no doubt as to the divisive consequences of such firmness. The church considered his letter on 3 May, and this time his resignation was accepted.[45]

It was here that the nature of The Downs was revealed. One-third of the membership called a second meeting for the 24 May, 'there being a hope, which had hardly existed before, of inducing Mr Richards to reconsider his decision'. They urged him to remain, taking if necessary a break of six months, should he desire it. There was only one dissentient at a meeting at which eighteen members spoke, including 'several ladies'.[46]

The Mansion House trial, which was a tasteless affair, was held between these meetings, one of a series of notable actions of which Bertrand Russell's prosecution later in June has become the best known. Archibald Bodkin led for the Crown with the disconcerting indictment that 'war would become impossible if all men held the view that war is wrong'.[47]

Bodkin foolishly fought Richards with texts snatched from context, but it made little difference to the result: £100 fine with £10 in costs, or sixty-one days in prison.

On 15 June, between the Mansion House hearing and the appeal at Guildhall, Richards renewed his decision to leave The Downs. He preached his farewell sermon on 30 July and afterwards he was presented with a cheque for over £200 and the *Encyclopaedia Britannica*. His people were in no doubt as to their duties as Free Churchmen: they met his fine.

Indeed, on 31 May Alfred Haworth, Arthur's brother, had proposed that the church

> though holding diverse views as to the righteousness and necessity of the present war, strongly protest against the harsh treatment, amounting in many cases to persecution accorded to those who, guided by conscientious convictions, feel constrained to refuse all forms of military service. In passing this resolution they are mindful that nearly all the young men associated with the church and school, at the call of conscience, voluntarily joined His Majesty's Forces.[48]

Arthur Haworth himself contributed to Richards's farewell. On 31 July Richards, now that he had ceased to be in pastoral charge, received his call-up papers. It was an act of predictable administrative pettiness, but the implication that Free Church ordination was somehow inferior to State Church ordination (Anglican clergymen were not so pestered) enraged Haworth who agitated successfully for the removal of the anomaly. Richards was not sure as to the strict justice of this chivalrous impulse.[49]

Richards moved to London to become General Secretary of the Fellowship of Reconciliation. Then in April 1918 he went to Pembroke Chapel, the Liverpool Baptist Church once famous under Charles Birrell and now notorious for its socialist politics and its spiritual eccentricities. Edith Richards described its people as a band 'fighting their way to a Jerusalem . . . by way of agitation and demonstration'.[50] It was an uneasy interlude for both parties. Richards's theology, though broad enough, was not to Pembroke's taste, and his militant pacifism was outdistanced by their militant politics. Pembroke's attempt to harness its religious energies to the politics of the new Europe was exciting and sometimes appalling: it demonstrated, not least under Leyton Richards, that such a thing could not be done within orthodox Free Churchmanship.[51]

The Downs still hoped for Richards's return. As the church *Manual* put it: 'the great majority of members of the congregation, though not agreeing with Mr Richards views on military matters, probably only a few did that, were content, if not even wishful, to hear them stated; especially so for the sake of his preaching in general and other splendid qualities.'[52]

For the rest of the war the pulpit was filled by temporary pastors, of whom Dr Dunning of Boston, an old friend of Mackennal and the Faulkner Armitages, was the most soothing. Dunning was an elderly, distinguished American Congregationalist whose sermon on Mayoral Sunday in 1916 was heartwarming: 'from him we got the assurance that the heart of the real America was with the Allies.'[53] As he wrote to his wife: 'I gave out the National Hymn last Sunday morning. The people hadn't sung it for two years. They seem so grateful to me for telling them that their cause is right, and their sacrifices are going to be worth to the world all that they cost.'[54]

There was to be no abatement of sacrifice before November 1918. William Armitage's eldest son was killed in May 1917 and his second son in April 1918. Mayoral Sunday continued to be observed at The Downs. In October 1917 the church decided to search for a permanent minister: 'one speaker advocated unanimity in inviting Mr Richards back at once, while another made a very strong appeal to those who wanted Mr Richards, to give way for the sake of unity, and help to see if there were not some other Minister who would prove acceptable to all.'[55] The preachings 'with a view' endured by all Congregational churches with vacant pulpits, began again. None satisfied them, until, a month after the Armistice on 15 December 1918, they heard Henry Child Carter, the minister of Emmanuel Church, Cambridge and immediate past-chairman of the London Missionary Society. He preached without a 'view' but The Downs invited him unanimously to their pastorate. Carter refused. His first duty was at Cambridge 'to which so many students are returning after the mighty exodus to the war'.[56]

The remarkable thing about the invitation was that Carter, like Richards, had unswervingly opposed the war: but Carter, like Richards, was a man of indefinable power of personality, proof of the strong relationship between minister and people which characterized Congregationalism at its best. Carter's refusal paved the way for Richards's return. He began his second, unclouded, pastorate at The Downs in June 1919.

The divisions which Richards had provoked should not be underestimated. In 1913 the roll of communicants had stood at 296; in 1919 it was 257.[57] The impact of the war could not be undone: at its peak 160 men of the church and institute were serving in the forces, and Faulkner Armitage's war memorial porch commemorated eighteen men of the church who had been killed in action.[58] Post-war ministers were faced with an ageing congregation, and from the 1920s the upending of the cotton trade ensured that it was a declining congregation as well. The implications of this were still unclear in the 1920s and Richards attracted the admiration of many, not least among those who had fought, who had most criticized his war-time stand. The churchmanship of The Downs had been deepened, and thereby that of the Free Churches in general. This was a contribution which had no bearing on numbers. Leyton Richards's immediate successor, has thus expressed it:

> Bowdon Downs educated my understanding of the meaning of Christian fellowship. Here were *good* people. They were not conventionally pious, but they were civilized and tolerant because they were Christian. The pacifism of Leyton and Edith Richards in the war years educated (and divided) the church without disrupting its essential and enduring unity. . . . Much that all Christendom now takes for granted as it struggles with the irresolvably complex problem of relating Religion to Life, was the rare and lonely witness of the few in 1914. . . . Bowdon Downs was one of the churches which tried to face the inescapable implications of truly Christian fellowship: it engendered a little group — an *ecclesiola in ecclesia* — which made and maintained that witness. It was a witness to sensitivity and awareness.[59]

In 1923 Leyton Richards went reluctantly to Carrs Lane, Birmingham, before resting in Quakerism. The Downs families had a further link with national peace movements: William Armitage's niece, Alison Carver, had married H. R. L. Sheppard, of St Martin's-in-the-Fields, in June 1915, a country wedding almost pre-war in its expansiveness.[60]

It is arguable as to whether the pacifism of Richards, 'Dick' Sheppard and the Peace Pledge Union had developed in sophistication since the days of Henry Richard. There is a fundamental incompatibility between the Gospel and even the most Christian politics. Mackennal voiced it in 1900 when he yearned to see England as a sacrificial nation: 'I am sure that, so long as the vision of a martyred nation appears absurd and impossible, there will never be a Christian nation.'[61] Christians content with levels of faith below that of prophecy must sacrifice themselves to the compromises of politics. Perhaps this duty is seen more clearly than it was, and perhaps this is the chief lesson of the Great War.

It is strange that the Great War caught Free Churchmen with such surprise.[62] It was a logical conclusion to the decades of rearmament whose progress they had deplored. Baldwin Brown alerted them to it in 1878. Dr Mackennal warned them again twenty years later: 'If it were not so sad a spectacle, we might find boundless humour in the fact that Europe has been, for fifty years, massing armies which today it trembles to behold, perfecting weapons of precision until it is afraid to use them. . . .' He added: 'Commercial necessities give us no pledge of peace; enlightened self-interest is not to be trusted, the self is sure to dim the light; the fear of war will not prevent war.'[63]

This failure of Free Churchmen to draw conclusions might seem the more strange in 1914 in the light of their internationalism born of the missionary impulse and formed by their increasing sense of belonging to a global Christianity. This nascent ecumenism received its grandest infusion at the Edinburgh Missionary Conference of 1910.

Perhaps this internationalism was unduly compromised by the imperialism which grew with it. Certainly it was compounded by naivety. The Free Churchmen who made their way in the new atmosphere were heirs to the 'sentimentalists in drab'[64] of earlier days, the heirs of countless shopkeepers, partially excluded at the critical points of society from participation in affairs. This was the legacy of being Dissenters within the system, and their intense Victorian apprenticeship was no recompense. Matthew Arnold was right about them after all.

At the outbreak of war leading European Churchmen were at Constance to discuss peace. To the physical discomfort of sudden isolation in the heart of a mobilizing continent was added the spiritual strain of utter futility. Yet enough of their internationalism survived the war, disciplined and more detached now, to contribute to that ecumenical movement which has transformed Christian expression in the second half of the twentieth century. The level of prophecy remained, but for those whose calling lay in compromise, the consequences were seen more clearly.

Something of this can be seen with the outbreak of the Second World War. There was no sense of surprise about it, and in Britain at least the pacifist stand was recognized. Henry Carter of Cambridge, however, was mystified that conscription had ceased to be an issue, even for Nonconformists.[65] What was unthinkable in 1913 was not thought about in 1939. Such a change marked the end even of lip-service to voluntaryism. It was the natural result of the vast perspectives forced on Free Churchmen by the First World War, compounded in subsequent years. It owed much to the stand of those like Leyton Richards: conscription was less objectionable once an exception had been made for pacifists. It owed more to the experiences of those who had fought in the First War, the first in their families ever to do such a thing. For some of them there was the example of their padres, muddling through with them, no less admirable than the Richardses or Carters. Basil Willey has best described one, a minister from a seaside resort, tall and broad chested, loud voiced and direct, an apostle of liberty whose sole influence lay in what he was: 'To me the presence and influence of this excellent man were the greatest possible comfort and support. He was the living embodiment, and because of his cloth and his character the respected and beloved embodiment, of every value I clung to.'[66] Such natural rooted manliness was as effective in securing the painless transformation in attitudes as any amount of prophecy. It was the spirit of C. S. Horne. It was also the spirit of Leyton Richards, applied to a different end.

For the rest, the change was the result of language. The language of conquest is the language of compulsion, which is one of its fascinations for men of peace filled with a sense of mission. Mackennal wrote that 'the fancied necessities of militarism efface that moral courage, that chivalry and tenderness of honour, which the Gospel has called into being'.[67] As English Christians separated empire from imperialism, so they liked to separate chivalry from militarism: even Leyton Richards was enlisted for that cause, for when he died his original denomination felt that 'a great warrior joined the hosts in heaven'.[68]

Epilogue

Let our church be 'a gathering up of all that men can do. It has fifty roofs, it has a gigantic signal tower, it has blank walls like precipices, and round arch after round arch, and architrave after architrave. It is like a good and settled epic, or better still it is like the life of a healthy and adventurous man who, having accomplished all his journeys and taken the fleece of gold, comes home to tell his stories at evening and to pass among his own people the years that are left to him of his age. It has the experience, growth, and intensity of knowledge, all caught up with one unity. It conquers the site upon which it stands. . . .'

(Lutyens's intention for the parish church of St Jude,
Hampstead Garden Suburb, 20 December 1910, quoted in C. Hussey,
The Life of Sir Edwin Lutyens, 1950, p. 190.)

Bibliography

(London is the place of publication unless otherwise stated)

A complete list of sources for this book would be neither helpful nor practicable. Material used in its immediate preparation has been cited in the notes for each chapter, and the extent to which denominational handbooks, chapel records, biographies and private diaries, have formed an indispensable foundation for the study will have been apparent.

This note is to suggest the range of sound secondary reading now available for amateurs of English Nonconformity. There remain considerable gaps, but many have been filled in the past decade and more are about to be filled as a steady stream of dissertations appear, some of them swanlike enough to turn into books.

This is just as well, since the nature of the Nonconformity which flourished from the 1780s to the 1920s will very soon be as alien to Free Churchmen as to anybody else, and it would be shockingly wasteful to lose all sense of that vibrant, brief experience.

The best introduction to Victorian Nonconformity is W. Haslam Mills, *Grey Pastures*, 1924, a collection of essays, originally written for the *Manchester Guardian* and crying out for re-publication. This sympathetic re-creation of Congregationalism in Ashton-under-Lyne in the 1880s might be compared with the harder, fictionalized, recollection of an earlier Congregationalism in London and 'Cowfold' in 'Mark Rutherford's' *The Revolution in Tanner's Lane*, 1893 edn. The whole treatment of Dissent in the Victorian novel has been ably covered in V. Cunningham, *Everywhere Spoken Against: Dissent in the Victorian Novel*, Oxford, 1975.

Atmosphere thus provided, there remains foundation: H. Perkin, *The Origins of Modern English Society 1780-1880*, 1969. This will lead to A. D. Gilbert, *Religion and Society in Industrial England: Church, Chapel and Social Change 1740-1914*, 1976, and then to the equally important, but difficult, W. R. Ward, *Religion and Society in England 1790-1850*, 1972 (chiefly but justifiably about Methodism in north-western England), and the stimulating A. Everitt, *The Pattern of Rural Dissent: the Nineteenth Century*, Leicester, 1972 (a study with particular reference to Kent, Northamptonshire, Leicestershire and Lindsey).

Collections of documents and commentary are fashionable. Nonconformity has been well served by two such books, D. M. Thompson (ed.), *Nonconformity in the Nineteenth Century*, 1972 (its commentary forms a plain, elegant, excellent introduction to the subject), and J. H. Y. Briggs and I. Sellers (eds), *Victorian Nonconformity*, 1973 (notable for the variety and interest of its extracts).

249

The liturgical and theological expressions of Nonconformity might be followed profitably in H. Davies, *Worship and Theology in England*, Vol. III, *From Watts and Wesley to Maurice 1690-1850* and Vol. IV, *From Newman to Martineau 1830-1900*, Oxford, 1961-2; W. B. Glover, *Evangelical Nonconformists and Higher Criticism in the Nineteenth Century*, 1954, and J. W. Grant, *Free Churchmanship in England 1870-1940*, n.d. (*c.* 1950).

There is no good recent study of the architecture of Nonconformity. For a general introduction by a workmanlike architect there is still M. S. Briggs, *Puritan Architecture and its Future*, 1946; meanwhile Christopher Stell's magisterial work for the Royal Commission on Historic Monuments is eagerly awaited.

Denominational histories are in a state of flux. The Baptists are soundly covered by A. C. Underwood, *A History of the English Baptists*, 1947 and E. A. Payne *The Baptist Union: A Short History*, 1958. The forthcoming history by J. H. Y. Briggs, E. A. Payne and B. R. White is a promise of excellence. The Congregationalists produced A. Peel, *These Hundred Years*, 1931 and R. Tudur Jones, *Congregationalism in England 1662-1962*, 1962 (perhaps the last and among the best of the older type of denominational history). Methodist scholarship is prolific. Nonetheless W. S. Townsend, H. B. Workman and G. Eayrs, *A New History of Methodism*, 1909, 2 vols, has yet to be replaced, since so far only Volume 1 of R. Davies and G. Rupp (eds), *A History of the Methodist Church in Great Britain*, has appeared, and that was in 1965. Of the varieties of Methodism attention ought to be drawn to O. A. Beckerlegge, *The United Methodist Free Churches*, 1957; H. B. Kendall, *The Origin and History of the Primitive Methodist Church*, n.d. (a quarry if nothing else), 2 vols; T. Shaw, *The Bible Christians 1815-1907*, 1965. Attention must also be drawn to these important books about Methodism: B. Semmel, *The Methodist Revolution*, 1974; E. R. Taylor, *Methodism and Politics 1791-1851*, Cambridge, 1935 (reissued 1975); J. Kent, *The Age of Disunity*, 1966; B. Currie, *Methodism Divided: A Study in the Sociology of Ecumenicalism*, 1968. R. Moore, *Pit-Men, Preachers and Politics: The Effects of Methodism in a Durham Mining Community*, Cambridge, 1974 is a suggestive and often moving study of wider relevance than Durham — once the fearsome barrier of the first ninety-five pages is overcome.

For the smaller denominations, Elizabeth Isichei, *Victorian Quakers*, Oxford, 1970, is peerless. The Presbyterian Church of England is without a full recently written history and the student must turn to A. H. Drysdale, *History of the Presbyterians in England*, 1889. The Churches of Christ are about to be served by D. M. Thompson. For the Salvation Army there is material to be quarried from R. Sandall and A. R. Wiggins, *History of the Salvation Army 1865-1914*, 1947-68, 5 vols. For the Brethren's early years there is H. H. Rowdon, *The Origins of the Brethren*, 1967. The student of Unitarianism will need to turn to C. G. Bolam *et al.*, *The English Presbyterians from Elizabethan Puritanism to Modern Unitarianism*, 1968, and R. V. Holt, *The Unitarian Contribution to Social Progress in England*, 1938 (2nd edn 1952).

As a reminder that Protestant Dissent has strange bedfellows it is not entirely inappropriate to commend the urbane E. Royle, *Victorian Infidels*, Manchester, 1974, and the stimulating J. Bossy, *The English Catholic Community 1570-1850*, 1975.

There remain issues. For politics B. Manning and O. Greenwood, *The Protestant Dissenting Deputies*, Cambridge, 1952 is still the best starting place. G. I. T. Machin, *Politics and the Churches in Great Britain 1832-1868*, Oxford, 1977, went to press while the present book was in preparation. A key issue is usefully but nonetheless disappointingly covered in W. H. Mackintosh, *Disestablishment and Liberation*,

1972, but attention may be drawn to the essays by D. Fraser and D. M. Thompson on 'Edward Baines', and 'The Liberation Society 1844-1868' in Patricia Hollis (ed.), *Pressure From Without in Early Victorian England*, 1974. For a swiftly useful survey beginning in late Victorian times and petering out with Lloyd George there is S. Koss, *Nonconformity in Modern British Politics*, 1975.

The widening field between politics and social concern is excellently treated in P. D'A. Jones, *The Christian Socialist Revival*, Princeton, 1968 and S. Mayor, *The Churches and the Labour Movement*, 1967. It may be continued in K. S. Inglis, *Churches and the Working Classes in Victorian England*, 1963 and H. McLeod, *Class and Religion in the Late Victorian City*, 1974 (a sensitive study of London, but of more general application).

The reader who looks for Nonconformity and Temperance must delve into B. Harrison, *Drink and the Victorians: The Temperance Question in England 1815-1872*, 1971. Nonconformists galore may also be followed in an unlikely book, C. Binfield, *George Williams and the Y.M.C.A: A Study in Victorian Social Attitudes*, 1973. The Nonconformist contribution to municipal affairs may be gleaned from E. P. Hennock's studies of Leeds and Birmingham, *Fit and Proper Persons: Ideal and Reality in Nineteenth Century Urban Government*, 1973. Addicts of emotive educational controversies should start with J. Murphy, *Church, State and Schools in Britain 1800-1970*, 1971.

Suburban Nonconformity has yet to find a scholarly devotee prepared to become its apologist, but amateurs might turn to J. M. Richards, *The Castles on the Ground, The Anatomy of Suburbia*, 2nd edn 1973, even though religious Nonconformity is nowhere mentioned in it.

And for epilogue? C. Driver, *A Future for the Free Churches*, 1962; D. Jenkins, *The British, Their Identity and Their Religion*, 1975; and by implication, J. S. Whale, *Christian Reunion: Historic Divisions Reconsidered*, 1971.

And historians who wish to follow where this sort of life led their sort of mind are recommended to read R. M. Crawford, *'A Bit of a Rebel': The Life and Work of George Arnold Wood*, Sydney, 1975. It moves from Bowdon to Sydney, via Balliol and Mansfield.

Notes

PREFACE
1 *Jubilee of the Congregational Union. Manchester October 1881*, p. 13.
2 Tacket Street Congregational Church Ipswich, *Minute Book*, 1856-85 (East Suffolk Record Office, FK 2:2957).
3 A charming account of Dissent among the Taylors at Ongar and Lavenham at the turn of the century may be seen in J. Gilbert (ed.), *Autobiography and Other Memorials of Mrs Gilbert*, 1870-4, 2 vols, esp. vol. 1.
4 Thus the Quakers, most recently and notably in Elizabeth Isichei, *Victorian Quakers*, Oxford, 1970.
5 See too 'The Song against Grocers' in G. K. Chesterton, *Greybeards at Play and Other Comic Verse*, J. Sullivan (ed.), 1974, pp. 72-4.

CHAPTER 1
1 D. Jenkins, *The British: Their Identity and Their Religion*, 1975, p. 96.
2 The best, and best-flavoured, account of the slow removal of Dissenting disabilities remains, B. Manning and O. Greenwood, *The Protestant Dissenting Deputies*, Cambridge, 1952.
3 Elizabeth Isichei, *Victorian Quakers*, Oxford, 1970, pp. 44-53.
4 G. Packer (ed.), *The Centenary of the Methodist New Connexion 1797-1897*, n.d. (c. 1897); J. T. Hughes, 'The Story of the Leeds "Non-Cons" ', *Proceedings Wesley Historical Society*, Vol. xxxv, December 1965, pp. 81-7; March 1966, pp. 122-4; Vol. xxxvii, June 1970, pp. 133-9; Vol. xxxix, October 1973, pp. 73-6; O. A. Beckerlegge, *The United Methodist Free Churches*, 1957.
5 E. A. Payne, *The Baptist Union: A Short History*, 1958, pp. 125-43.
6 For 'Rivulet', 'Leicester' and the Congregational Union see A. Peel, *These Hundred Years*, 1931, pp. 221 ff., and 266 ff. and for 'Leicester' see also below ch. 9. Samuel Davidson is properly treated for the first time in a forthcoming article in the *Durham University Journal* by J. H. Lea. For the pattern of disruption in the eastern counties see J. C. G. Binfield, *Nonconformity in the Eastern Counties 1840-1885*, University of Cambridge Ph.D. dissertation, 1965, pp. 139-41, 248-69; 'The Thread of Disruption: Some Nineteenth-Century Churches in Eastern England', *Transactions Congregational Historical Society*, Vol. XX, No. 5, May 1967, pp. 156-65; 'Chapels in Crisis: Men and Issues in Victorian Eastern England', ibid., Vol. XX, No. 8, October 1968, pp. 237-54.

7 It is generally assumed that the Unitarians are their heirs, yet it is possible that more nineteenth-century Congregational Churches than Unitarian ones were originally Presbyterian: thus, in the five eastern counties in 1884, six of fifteen Unitarian Churches might claim to be older than 1750 — but three of these were originally Independent. At the same time over eighty Congregational Churches could claim to be older than 1750. The point is not entirely academic: which today more truly reflects historic Congregationalism — the United Reformed Church or the Congregational Federation?

8 A. D. Gilbert, *The Growth and Decline of Nonconformity in England and Wales, with Special Reference to the Period before 1850; An Historical Interpretation of Statistics of Religious Practice*, University of Oxford D.Phil dissertation, 1973. This chapter relies heavily on Dr Gilbert's work, now incorporated in his *Religion and Society in Industrial England 1740-1914*, 1976.

9 Gilbert thesis op. cit., pp. 119 ff. He gives the peak years of growth as 1805-6, 1820-1, 1827-8, 1832-3, 1849-50, 1859-60, 1875-6, 1881-2, 1904-5: he concludes this from Methodist statistics which he believes would have been echoed by Baptists and Congregationalists had they kept comparable records.

10 Ibid., pp. 419 ff.

11 Quoted in F. W. Wheldon, *A Norvic Centenary and the Men who Made it: 1846-1946*, Norwich, 1946, p. 45.

12 *General Baptist Year Book* 1880, pp. 3 ff. This was the least exuberant part of an address to the General Baptist New Connexion Assembly which incorporated within a single paragraph references to the exiled harpists of Babylon, Ulysses, Britannia, Queen Victoria, a popular ballad, and the audience themselves, Gladstone's 'warmest friends, and his best disciplined troops . . . the descendants of Cromwell's Ironsides — the Nonconformists of England'.

13 Gilbert thesis op. cit., pp. 133 ff.

14 Ibid., pp. 167 ff.

15 See below, chs 3 pp. 34-7, 4 pp. 72-7, 9 pp. 201-2.

16 See below, ch. 8 pp. 171-2.

17 W. R. Ward, *Religion and Society in England 1790-1850*, 1972, p. 1. This chapter owes much to Professor Ward's book.

18 J. Stoughton, *Reminiscences of Congregationalism Fifty Years Ago*, 1881, pp. 24, 67.

19 See below ch. 4 passim esp. pp. 72-7, 95-7.

20 *Congregational Year Book*, 1848, p. 8; see also C. Binfield, 'Thomas Binney and Congregationalism's "Special Mission" ', *Transactions Congregational Historical Society*, Vol. xxi, No. 1, June 1971, pp. 1-10.

21 See below ch. 9 pp. 170-2.

22 See below ch. 7 pp. 149 ff.

23 See below ch. 4 esp. pp. 72-7, 98-9.

24 Ward, op. cit., pp. 2-4.

25 Wesleyan *Minutes of Conference*, 1840, p. 115.

26 *Baptist Handbook*, 1871, p. 33.

27 H. Mann, *Census of Great Britain 1851: Religious Worship in England and Wales*, rev. edn 1854, p. 57. The following section is based on this.

28 It has since exercised all serious historians. The present concern is with their impact on the preacher in the pulpit and the man in the pew. The precise significance of the Census, and the idiosyncracies of Mann's analysis, are not at issue here, but may be followed in: K. S. Inglis, *Churches and the Working Classes in Victorian England*, 1963; D. M. Thompson, 'The 1851 Religious

Census: Problems and Possibilities', *Victorian Studies*, Vol. XI, No. 1, 1967, pp. 87-97; W. S. F. Pickering, 'The 1851 religious census – a useless experiment?', *British Journal of Sociology*, Vol. II, 1967-8, pp. 382-407.

29 Mann, ibid., pp. 86-7. He reached the aggregate attendances for morning, afternoon and evening services by assuming that half the afternoon attenders and a third of the evening attenders had not worshipped at earlier services.

30 See *Congregational Year Book*, 1855, pp. 69-73: the theme of a session on British Missions.

31 *Congregational Year Book*, 1862, pp. 60-72, on which the following paragraphs are based.

32 *Congregational Year Book*, 1863, pp. 29-30.

33 *Congregational Year Book*, 1861, p. 48.

34 *Congregational Year Book*, 1851, pp. 83 ff., esp. p. 89.

35 So he told the Free Churchmen of St Ives, and Halstead: *Eastern Counties Gazette*, 17 October 1863; *Halstead Times*, 2 September 1865.

36 *Congregational Year Book*, 1874, p. 51.

37 Ibid., pp. 116, 117.

38 Arthur Reed Ropes ('Adrian Ross') (1859-1933); his entry into the theatre resulted from a cold caught during the Boat Race, which he improved by writing a libretto for a comic opera, which led to the professional production of 'Joan of Arc' at the Opéra Comique in 1891; J. A. Venn, *Alumni Cantabrigienses*, Part 11, 5, p. 335; E. Hampden-Cook, *The Register of Mill Hill School 1807-1926*, priv. edn 1926, pp. 150-1. He was a member of Kensington Chapel from 1909 to 1933, and previously of Congregational Churches in Cambridge and Crouch End.

39 *Congregational Year Book*, 1871, pp. 89 ff.

40 [S. D. Spicer] *Albert Spicer 1847-1934: A Man of His Time by One of His Family*, 1938, p. 16.

41 Gilbert thesis, op. cit., pp. 398 ff; 375 ff.

42 *Congregational Year Book*, 1847, p. 47.

43 *Congregational Year Book*, 1870, p. 65.

44 *Congregational Year Book*, 1885, p. 93.

45 *Congregational Year Book*, 1868, pp. 73-81.

46 Ward, op. cit., p. 291.

47 Witham Congregational Church, *Minute Book*, 1822-49, 29 September 1848.

48 Primitive Methodist *Minutes of Conference*, 1875, p. 92.

49 Ward, op. cit., esp. p. 4.

50 *Congregational Year Book*, 1877, p. 88.

51 See below ch. 5 esp. pp. 102-3.

52 *Congregational Year Book*, 1866, p. 34.

53 E. Luscombe Hull, *Sermons preached at Union Chapel, Kings Lynn*, 1869, 2nd series, p. 193.

54 Compiled from J. Vincent and M. Stenton (eds), *McCalmont's Parliamentary Poll Book: British Election Results 1832-1918*, 1971. See also Binfield thesis, op. cit., p. 403.

55 For the Brotherhood Movement, see below pp. 211-2. Campbell's controversial *The New Theology*, appeared in 1907.

CHAPTER 2

1 *Minutes of the Primitive Methodist Conference*, 1819, p. 5; 1847, p. 22.

2 *Minutes of the Wesleyan Conference*, 1848, pp. 171-2.

3 *Congregational Year Book*, 1876, p. 115.

4 Wesleyan Methodist Association, *Minutes of the Annual Assembly of Delegates*, 1850, p. 38.

5 The implications of this are fascinatingly worked out in the context of a Durham mining valley between 1880s and 1960s in R. Moore, *Pit-Men, Preachers and Politics: The Effects of Methodism in a Durham Mining Community*, Cambridge, 1974, pp. 95 ff.

6 W. R. Ward, 'The Baptists and the Transformation of the Church, 1780-1830', *Baptist Quarterly*, Vol. XXV, No. 4, October 1973, pp. 167-84. This section owes much to Professor Ward's article.

7 St Andrews Street Baptist Church, Cambridge, *Robinson's Church Book of 1774 with additions to 1832*, October 1790.

8 H. Rogers, S. E. Dwight and E. Hickman (eds), *The Works of Jonathan Edwards*, 1837, Vol. 1. p. 426, quoted in Ward art. cit. p. 175.

9 M. M. Wilkin, *Joseph Kinghorn of Norwich*, 1855, p. 163.

10 These issues have been tentatively expressed with particular reference to three large, urban, Baptist Churches, in J. C. G. Binfield, 'Congregationalism's Two Sides of the Baptistery — A Paedobaptist View', *Baptist Quarterly*, Vol. XXVI, No. 3, July 1975, pp. 119-33.

11 *Jubilee of the Congregational Union, Manchester, October 1881*, pp. 38-9.

12 These issues are stimulatingly considered in D. Jenkins, *The British, Their Identity and Their Religion*, 1975, pp. 96 ff.

13 See below ch. 5 *passim*.

14 *Jubilee*, op. cit., p. 88.

15 Ella Sophia Bulley, *A Visit to Tunbridge Wells*, June 1856; MS. in possession of Revd H. A. Wilson. This entry, for 8 July, was written in cipher, and I am grateful to Dr and Mrs G. Newton for breaking the cipher.

16 Such questions are considered in J. S. Whale, *Christian Reunion: Historic Divisions Reconsidered*, 1971, esp. pp. 97 ff.

17 S. Spender, *World Within World*, 1951 (new edn 1964), pp. 1-2.

CHAPTER 3

1 *Pattisson's Interleaved Morant's Town and Hundred of Witham*, facing p. 110. Essex Record Office: T/P 142/1. The following paragraph is based chiefly on this.

2 For John Castle (1819-88), see *A Short Sketch of the Life of a Working Man, Showing in Several Instances the overruling and wonderful working of the Providence of God*, MS. 1871, Essex Record Office D/DU/490, esp. pp. 18-22. This has been largely reprinted, with notes and commentary, in A. F. J. Brown, *Essex People 1750-1900*, Essex Record Office Publications, No. 59, Chelmsford, 1972, pp. 116-32, esp. p. 119.

3 This paragraph is largely based on Witham Congregational Church, *Minute Books*, 1822-49 and 1849-83, E.R.O. D/NC 3/2 and 3; *Baptismal Register*, 1754-1849.

4 For Daniel Whittle Harvey (1786-1863), M.P. Colchester 1818-20, 1826-34, and Southwark 1835-40, see *Dictionary of National Biography*. There are frequent references to the Shaens in H. Solly, *These Eighty Years or the Story of an Unfinished Life*, 1893, 2 vols; the best known of the family was William Shaen (1820-87), solicitor of Bedford Row, and friend of all radical and libertarian causes from the Social Purity League and Bedford College, to artisans dwellings and women's suffrage, taking in George Holyoake, Josephine Butler, Bishop Colenso, Mazzini and Octavia Hill.

5 F. M. Thomas (ed.), *Fifty Years of Fleet Street. Being The Life and Recollections of Sir John R. Robinson*, 1904, p. 4.

6 This paragraph is chiefly based on Witham *Minute Books*, op. cit., records of the Witham British Schools, 1833-94, Essex Record Office DNC 3/20-29. B. Brown, *Reminiscences of Bateman Brown J.P.*, Peterborough 1905, *passim*. E. Hampden Cook *Register of Mill Hill School, London 1807-1926*, priv. edn 1926, *passim*.

7 R. W. Dixon, 'Reminiscences of the Old Dissent at Witham', *Transactions Congregational Historical Society*, Vol. V, October 1912, pp. 327-44, on which the following section is based.

8 Ibid., p. 332.

9 Ibid., p. 335.

10 Ibid., p. 335.

11 Ibid., p. 333.

12 Ibid., p. 339.

13 Ibid., p. 342.

14 Ibid., p. 339.

15 Thomas, op. cit., p. 7.

16 White's, *Essex*, 1848, pp. 41-2, 164, 185, 187, 188, Burke, *Landed Gentry*, 1937, under Blood of Ballykilty and Cranagher for a colourful descent from Neptune Blood, Dean of Kilfenora.

17 *Pattisson's Interleaved Morant. . . .*, op. cit. p. 111.

18 Ibid. This is a quotation from White's *Essex*, 1848, added by J. H. Pattisson.

19 'Which three societies conjointly raised a monument to him in that city': from an inscription in Witham Parish Church. I am grateful to Professor A. W. Bradley of Edinburgh for confirmation of this.

20 For Henry Crabb Robinson (1775-1867) see Edith J. Morley, *The Life and Times of Henry Crabb Robinson*, 1935; and D. Hudson (ed.), *The Diary of Henry Crabb Robinson: An Abridgement*, Oxford, 1967, esp. pp. vii-xv.

21 He had *Hebrew Melodies* in mind. Dixon, art. cit., p. 333.

22 W. H. E. Pattisson to H. C. Robinson, 20 February 1800, Dr Williams's Library H.C.R. 1800-3: 3.

23 Note of 13 May 1858 added to the letter of Elizabeth Pattisson to H.C.R., 13 February 1816, Dr Williams's Library H.C.R. 1806: 36.

24 Ibid.

25 Elizabeth Pattisson to Jacob Pattisson 15 July 1789, Essex Record Office D/DCM C1/2.

26 Elizabeth Pattisson to Hannah Pattisson 13 January 1801, E.R.O. D/DCM C1/2.

27 Elizabeth Pattisson to H. Crabb Robinson, 21 November 1794, D.W.L., H.C.R. 1725-99: 47.

28 Elizabeth Pattisson to H. C. Robinson 18 December 1794, D.W.L., H.C.R. 1725-99: 48.

29 Elizabeth Pattisson to H. C. Robinson, 29 March 1810, D.W.L., H.C.R. 1809-17: 21.

30 September 22 1815, T. Sadler (ed.), *Diary, Reminiscences and Correspondence of Henry Crabb Robinson*, 1869, 3 vols, Vol. 1, p. 501. Elizabeth Pattisson to H. C. Robinson, 13 February 1816, D.W.L., H.C.R. 1806: 36.

31 W. Francis to Jacob Pattisson, 29 June 1792, E.R.O., D/DCM C1/2.

32 Sadler, op. cit., Vol. 1, p. 24; for the Barbaulds see Betsy Rodgers, *Georgian Chronicle: Mrs Barbauld and her Family*, 1958, esp. pp. 64-84.

33 C. B. Jewson, *The Jacobin City: A Portrait of Norwich in its Reaction to the French Revolution 1788-1802*, 1975, esp. p. IX.

34 Ibid., pp. 58-61; Edith J. Morley, *The Life and Times of Henry Crabb Robinson*, 1935, p. 2. While Pattisson urged Robinson to publish an essay on 'Spies and Informers' there is no direct evidence that Amyot or Pattisson themselves wrote for *The Cabinet*: a key survives naming thirteen of the contributors, but they are not among them. I am grateful to J. Horth of the Norfolk and Norwich Library for this information.

35 H. C. Robinson to W. H. E. Pattisson, 26 May 1795, Edith J. Morley, *Henry Crabb Robinson on Books and their Writers*, 1938, Vol. III, p. 842.

36 H. C. Robinson to W. H. E. Pattisson, 9 May 1795, E.R.O. D/DCM C1/2. *Political Justice* appeared in February 1793: Godwin, son of a Dissenting minister in Norfolk and Suffolk, was a pupil in the late 1760s of Samuel Newton of Norwich.

37 H. C. Robinson to W. H. E. Pattisson, 25 April 1795, E.R.O. D/DCM C1/2.

38 Robinson to Pattisson, 9 May 1795, op. cit.

39 T. Amyot to W. H. E. Pattisson, 19 October 1796, E.R.O. D/DCM C1/2. For Thomas Amyot (1775-1850), Tory and antiquarian, see *D.N.B.*

40 W. H. E. Pattisson to H. C. Robinson, 5 December 1798, D.W.L., H.C.R. 1725-99: 119.

41 W. H. E. Pattisson to H. C. Robinson, 16 July 1803, D.W.L., H.C.R. 1800-3: 94.

42 W. H. E. Pattisson to H. C. Robinson, 2 December 1830 and 9 May 1831, D.W.L., H.C.R. 1830-1: 80, 124.

43 Pattisson to Robinson, 16 July 1803, op. cit.

44 Amyot to Pattisson, 19 October 1796, op. cit.

45 Pattisson to Robinson, 5 December 1798, op. cit.

46 W. H. E. Pattisson to Hannah Thornthwaite, 9 October 1799, E.R.O. D/DCM C1/2.

47 W. H. E. Pattisson to H. C. Robinson, 27 October 1799, D.W.L., H.C.R. 1725-99: 139.

48 Harriet Stock (later Mrs Lancelot Haslope) to Hannah Pattisson, 18 August 1800, E.R.O. D/DCM C1/2. William Pattisson married Hannah Thornthwaite on 13 March 1800.

49 H. C. Robinson to Hannah Pattisson, 5 April 1809, Edith J. Morley, op. cit., Vol. III, p. 845.

50 H. C. Robinson to William and Hannah Pattisson, 26 December 1810, ibid., pp. 846-7.

51 Entry for 28 December 1814, op. cit., Vol. 1, p. 157.

52 9 September 1815, quoted ibid., p. 172.

53 18 September 1815, ibid., p. 174.

54 17 and 19 October 1812, ibid., p. 111.

55 31 and 29 December 1814, ibid., p. 157.

56 3 January 1815, ibid., pp. 158-9.

57 H. C. Robinson to William and Hannah Pattisson, 6 February 1815, op. cit., Vol. III, pp. 849-50.

58 19 May 1812, op. cit., Vol. 1, p. 84.

59 12 June 1815, ibid., p. 169.

60 H. C. Robinson to Hannah Pattisson, 1 February 1819, op. cit., Vol. III, pp. 851-2.

61 Postscript dated 17 August 1803 to W. H. E. Pattisson to H. C. Robinson, 16 July 1803, op. cit.

62 Hannah Pattisson to H. C. Robinson, 22 November 1808, D.W.L., H.C.R. 1808: 155.

63 Habakkuk Crabb (1750-94) was at Royston from 1790; *D.N.B.*

64 E. Hodder, *The Life of Samuel Morley*, 1887, p. 13. Morley and his two brothers were at the school after 1816. Other pupils included S. W. Savill of Bocking, son of an Essex textile manufacturer, and W. A. Kent, related to Robinson's and the Pattissons' mutual cousins, the Isaacs. The United Reformed Church at Melbourn contains a tablet to Carver erected by his former pupils.

65 Hannah Pattisson to J. H. Pattisson, 14 March 1816, E.R.O., D/DCM C1/2.

66 Hannah Pattisson to H. C. Robinson, 30 January 1822, D.W.L., H.C.R. 1822: 74.

67 T. Sadler, op. cit., Vol. 1, p. 336.

68 For Lawrence see D. E. Williams, *The Life and Correspondence of Sir Thomas Lawrence Kt.*, 1831, 2 vols.

69 *D.N.B.*, 'Sir Thomas Lawrence 1769-1830'.

70 Sarah Goodin Barrett (1783-95) was the sister of Edward Moulton-Barrett, a man of chapel loyalties, chiefly Congregational, at Hope End, Sidmouth, and (of course) Wimpole Street. Lawrence painted her in 1795; the previous year he had sketched Godwin and Holcroft during the London treason trials.

71 From Kenneth Garlick's catalogue *raisonné: A Catalogue of the Paintings, Drawings and Pastels of Sir Thomas Lawrence*, Walpole Society 1962-4, Vol. XXXIX, Glasgow, 1964.

72 Edith J. Morley, op. cit., Vol. 1, pp. 13-14.

73 Ibid., p. 131 (Diary entry for 6 September 1813).

74 M. L. Smith, *Witham Congregational Church* 1965, p. 16 (E.R.O. WG).

75 Revd J. N. Goulty to Mr and Mrs W. H. E. Pattisson, 17 November 1814, forwarded by them to Robinson, 20 November. D.W.L., H.C.R. 1809-17: 114a. The boy was found to be an impostor. Goulty was a Norfolk man and a kinsman of Nelson.

76 Smith, op. cit., p. 16.

77 W. H. E. Pattisson to Revd J. Blackburn, 9 June 1822, New College London MSS. L 52/4/47.

78 Witham Congregational Church, *Minute Book*, 1822-49, E.R.O. D/NC 3/2, on which the following paragraphs are based.

79 The *Minute Book*, naturally, is imprecise. It seems unlikely that the charge involved sexual morals, or even financial ones. It is possible that there was political animus: the Pattissons had supported the Whig candidate at the recent election, driving with Robinson to vote at Maldon — where Robinson was shouted down when he spoke in favour of Catholic Emancipation, the chief issue of the contest. Sadler, op. cit., II, p. 330.

80 Ibid., p. 394 and records of the Witham British School, 1833-94, op. cit.

81 Witham Congregational Church, Sunday School Teachers' *Minute Book* 1849-77, 22 August 1849, E.R.O. D/NC 3/19.

82 W. H. E. Pattisson to H. C. Robinson, 5 September 1837, D.W.L., H.C.R. 1836: 50.

83 All Saints Church, Guithavon Street, was built 1841-2, for £5,000, of which William gave £100, and Jacob gave £150 as well as land for the vicarage. The schools were built in 1842. J. H. Pattisson's annotation in *Morant*, op. cit. This benevolence coincided with the first years of Vicar Bramston's long ministry in Witham.

84 In 1832 it was hoped that he would stand for Maldon, W. H. E. Pattisson to H. C. Robinson 24 September 1832, D.W.L., H.C.R. 1832: 53. He was abroad when the proposal was made and in fact had been dead for four days when his father

wrote to Robinson.
85 H. C. Robinson to J. H. Pattisson, 26 March 1860, D.W.L., H.C.R. 10.1.8. A painting of Venice fetched 2,400 guineas: 'the announcement produced a burst of applause', 26 March 1860, E. J. Morley, op. cit., Vol. II, p. 796.
86 H. C. Robinson to J. H. Pattisson, 5 January 1860, D.W.L., H.C.R. 10.1.6.
87 S. Spender, *World Within World*, 1951 (new edn 1964), p. 3.

CHAPTER 4

I

1 *Leeds Mercury*, 31 July 1830, quoted in R. W. Ram, *The Political Activities of Dissenters in the East and West Ridings of Yorkshire 1815-1850*, University of Hull M.A. dissertation, 1964, p. 119.
2 The phrase was probably coined by the Tory *Leeds Intelligencer* in 1829.
3 William Cobbett's phrase, quoted in J. C. Gill, *Parson Bull of Byerley*, 1963, p. 80.
4 *A Father's Dying Addresses*, 1848, printed by Unwin Brothers of London and Woking. There is a copy in Dr Williams's Library. The account which follows is taken from this.
5 So felt G. S. Phillips in the 1840s, quoted in J. F. C. Harrison, *Learning and Living 1790-1960*, 1961, p. 140.
6 Samuel Smiles's classic of 1859 originated in lectures delivered to a young men's mutual improvement society formed in Leeds in 1844.
7 For an account of this see R. G. Wilson, *Gentlemen Merchants: The Merchant Community in Leeds 1700-1830*, Manchester, 1971.
8 This is the problem to which E. P. Hennock addressed himself in his important and stimulating study of Leeds and Birmingham: *Fit and Proper Persons: Ideal and Reality in Nineteenth-Century Urban Government*, 1973.
9 This is the thesis of J. R. Lowerson, *The Political Career of Sir Edward Baines (1800-1890)*, University of Leeds M.A. dissertation, 1965, esp. pp. 2-10, on which this and the following paragraphs are based.
10 This paragraph owes much to J. F. C. Harrison, op. cit., pp. 8-21.
11 Leeds suffered severe depression in 1831, 1837, 1841-2, 1847-8; between 1856 and 1870 the only good years were held to be 1860, 1864 and 1866. Ibid., p. 15.
12 E. Baines, *Two Letters to Sir Robert Peel on the Social, Educational and Religious State of the Manufacturing Districts with Statistical Returns of the Means of Education and Religious Instruction*, 1843, quoted in Ram, op. cit., p. 3.
13 Quoted in Harrison, op. cit., p. 162.
14 In 1888 the Church of England provided seventy-nine churches, the Wesleyans forty-two, the Primitives twenty-five, and the Free Methodists and Congregationalists twenty-two each. The Church of England provided 50,755 sittings, the Wesleyans 28,225 and the Congregationalists lagged third with 12,061. K. W. Wadsworth, *A Century of Service: The Yorkshire Congregational Union and Home Missionary Society 1872-1972*, Leeds 1972, p. 19. In 1892 six councillors were Free Methodists, six were Primitive Methodists, and three were New Connexion Methodists. Hennock, op. cit., p. 221.
15 In 1851 there were thirteen Baptist Chapels in Leeds, housing 5.6 per cent of the town's churchgoers; the eleven Independent Chapels housed 8.7 per cent of churchgoers. R. J. Owen, *The Baptists in the Borough of Leeds During the Nineteenth Century: A Study of Local Church History*, University of Leeds M.Phil. dissertation, 1970, p. XI.

16 Charles Reed, son-in-law of the elder Edward Baines, was M.P. for Hackney 1868-74 and St Ives 1880. Edward Crossley, son-in-law of the younger Edward Baines, was M.P. for Sowerby, 1885-92.

17 For H. S. Baines, unsuccessful at Leeds North in 1895, see below, p. 99; Sir Max Muspratt, grandson of Thomas Baines of the *Liverpool Times*, was M.P. for Liverpool Exchange, 1910-18.

18 This paragraph owes much to Ram, op. cit., esp. pp. 40-8.

19 This section owes much to Hennock, op. cit., *passim* esp. pp. 10-13, 183-232, 361.

20 Ibid., p. 192.

21 M. Brock, *The Great Reform Act*, 1973, p. 17.

22 E. Baines, *The Life of Edward Baines*, 1851, pp. 38 ff; D. Read, *Press and People, 1790-1850. Opinion in Three English Cities*, 1961, pp. 60-1.

23 E. Baines, op. cit., pp. 45-8.

24 Ibid., p. 50.

25 Ibid., pp. 50, 146; Read op. cit., pp. 63, 64, 67, 77, 78-9.

26 Read, op. cit., p. 78.

27 E. Baines, op. cit., p. 59.

28 Ibid., pp. 92 ff; D. Read, op. cit., p. 113.

29 J. C. Gill, op. cit., pp. 63-4 and *passim*.

30 Thus in 1833-4 it generated a pamphlet war on the state of the University of Cambridge between R. M. Beverley, a Trinity contemporary of Matthew Talbot Baines, and Adam Sedgwick, a Fellow of Trinity: J. P. T. Bury (ed.), *Romilly's Cambridge Diary 1832-42*, Cambridge, 1967, pp. 46-7, 57, 59.

31 C. Newman Hall, *Autobiography*, 1898, pp. 172, 176.

32 T. Lloyd, *The General Election of 1880*, Oxford, 1968, p. 33, n. 1.

33 S. J. Reid (ed.), *Memoirs of Sir Wemyss Reid 1842-1885*, 1905, p. 160. Reid transferred from Kensington Chapel to East Parade, Leeds, in November 1870 and moved on to Headingley Hill in May 1873. East Parade *Members List*, 1841; Headingley Hill Congregational Church, *Church Roll*, 1866-1907.

34 A. W. Roberts, 'Leeds Liberalism and Late Victorian Politics', *Northern History*, 1970, V, pp. 141-3. R. R. James, *Lord Randolph Churchill*, 1959, p. 219.

35 A. W. Roberts, art. cit., p. 156; *The Times*, 28 July 1972 (obituary to Arthur Mann, 1876-1972); The Baines's *Mercury* did not publish betting news but it did publish the results of lotteries, and by 1901 a leading Leeds Baptist minister, P. T. Thompson of Blenheim Baptist Church, protested at its mercenary coverage of gambling news; a far cry from 'the great high-minded organ of the past', R. J. Owen, op. cit., pp. 246-7; S. J. Reid, op. cit., pp. 99-100.

II

1 He joined one year to the week before the official opening of East Parade Chapel, to which the Salem congregation moved. Salem Chapel, *Register Book*, 1833; East Parade, *Members List*, 1841.

2 E. Baines, *The Life of Edward Baines*, 1851, pp. 34, 35.

3 19 June 1835, ibid., p. 219.

4 Ibid., pp. 119-20.

5 Ibid., pp. 35, 359-64.

6 Ibid., pp. 122-3, 248.

7 Ibid., p. 279.

8 Ibid., pp. 11-15.

9 Ibid., pp. 15-32.

10 Ibid., pp. 63 ff., 208.
11 Ibid., pp. 84, 301.
12 Ibid., p. 68. That son died at his house in Leeds called St Anne's Hill, the name of Fox's beloved villa in Chertsey.
13 Ibid., p. 85; D. Read, *Press and People 1790-1850: Opinion in Three English Cities*, 1961, p. 108.
14 Baines, op. cit., pp. 77, 88-90, 106; Read op. cit., pp. 109 ff.
15 Quoted in R. W. Ram, *The Political Activities of Dissenters in the East and West Ridings of Yorkshire 1815-1850*, University of Hull M.A. dissertation, 1964, p. 26.
16 Of the 124,000 people in Leeds not more than 6,683 would be enfranchised; probably under 5,000. In May 1832 a survey showed that 5,547 might be enfranchised, of whom 212 might come from the working classes. Baines, op. cit., pp. 151-9.
17 Ibid., p. 181.
18 According to R. W. Ram, op. cit., pp. 185-6, five were Unitarians, two were Methodists, with one Congregationalist, one Baptist and a Catholic. In 1841-2 perhaps twenty-two councillors were Nonconformists, of whom perhaps twelve were Unitarians and six were Congregationalists: an interesting comparison with the Methodist preponderance fifty years later: see above ch. 4 Part I note 14.
19 J. Hamburger, *Intellectuals in Politics: John Stuart Mill and the Philosophic Radicals*, 1965, pp. 206, 223-4, 278.
20 Baines, op. cit., p. 194.
21 Ibid., p. 135.
22 J. C. Gill, *Parson Bull of Byerley*, 1963, p. 80.
23 Quoted in Read, op. cit., p. 123.
24 To use his own description of those who supported the Corn Laws, men 'insensible to all the calls of humanity and justice'. Baines, op. cit., p. 260.
25 Ibid., p. 254.
26 Ibid., pp. 312, 313.
27 B. Harrison, *Drink and the Victorians. The Temperance Question in England 1815-1872*, 1971, pp. 104-5, 110-12.
28 Baines, op. cit., p. 318.
29 Supposedly after a worldly minded woman applauded Baines's impartiality between Unitarians and Congregationalists as being 'all things to all men, that is the way to succeed in business'. Ibid., p. 5.
30 Ibid., pp. 285 ff., esp. p. 297.
31 H. R. Martin, *The Politics of the Congregationalists 1830-1856*, University of Durham Ph.D. dissertation, 1971, esp. pp. 110-18, 172, 180-1.

III

1 This information has been taken from Salem, *Register Book*, 1833- ; East Parade, *Members List*, 1841- ; East Parade and Trinity, *Register of Members*, 1894-1908.
2 Ibid., East Parade, *Church Books, passim*.
3 East Parade, *Church Book*, 1891, pp. 12-15. The architect was William Lambie Moffatt.
4 Trinity Church, Leeds, *Church Book*, 1902, p. 10; East Parade, *Building Committee Minute Book*, 1839- .
5 The East Parade Sunday School's membership was 572 but 'the excitement that was produced by the Queen's visit to the town [to open the Town Hall]

261

considerably augmented the applicants for admission, and on the 5 September [1858] the unprecedented number of 588 children were present'. East Parade, *Church Book*, 1859, *passim*, esp. p. 39.

6 Note appended to East Parade, *Members List*, 1841-   . There were 1,865 sittings: 882 on the ground floor and 983 in the galleries.

7 This section is based on the *Church Books* for 1859, 1862-8, 1870-5. Each book is a summary of the church's activities for the preceding year.

8 A. Peel (ed.), *Letters to a Victorian Editor*, 1929, p. 25.

9 J. R. Lowerson, *The Political Career of Sir Edward Baines (1800-1890)*, University of Leeds M.A. dissertation, 1965, p. 10.

10 D. Fraser, 'Edward Baines', in *Pressure from Without in Early Victorian England*, Patricia Hollis (ed.), 1974, pp. 185-6.

11 M. Arnold, *Culture and Anarchy*, 1869 (1889 popular edn), pp. XIII-XIV.

12 E. Baines to E. Baines junior, 15 October 1825. E. Baines *Life of Edward Baines*, 1851, p. 302.

13 *The Times*, 10 June 1890.

14 C. E. Mudie to H. Allon, 23 July 1864. A. Peel, op. cit., p. 19.

15 A. Peel, op. cit., p. 27.

16 D. Read, *Press and People 1790-1850: Opinion in Three English Cities*, 1961, p. 132.

17 Lowerson, op. cit., p. 36.

18 Read, op. cit., p. 186.

19 H. R. Martin considers that Baines was probably the most active Congregationalist in the Anti-Corn Law League, *The Politics of the Congregationalists 1830-1856*, University of Durham Ph.D. dissertation, 1971, pp. 213-14.

20 R. W. Ram, *The Political Activities of Dissenters in the East and West Ridings of Yorkshire 1815-1850*, University of Hull M.A. dissertation, 1964, pp. 107-30.

21 G. Kitson Clark, 'The Leeds Elite', *University of Leeds Review*, Vol. 17, No. 2, pp. 251-2.

22 F. Boase, *Modern English Biography*, 1908 (1965 edn), Vol. IV, p. 233.

23 B. Harrison, *Drink and the Victorians*, 1971, pp. 241, 259, 268, 277.

IV

1 J. Murphy, *Church, State and Schools in Britain 1800-1970*, 1971, p. 16.

2 The British and Foreign Schools Society, originating in 1808, was interdenominational, and attracted much Nonconformist support; the National Society of 1811 was Anglican.

3 In Ireland there was a board of seven commissioners, drawn from all denominations. In the schools under their supervision children received a secular education, with religious instruction given on at least one weekday. On every other weekday it was provided either before or after lessons. This avoided the Authorized Version, which would not have been acceptable to Catholics. Liverpool's Whig Council introduced the scheme in 1836 but the imposition of the Authorized Version by their Tory successors in 1841 led to the withdrawal of Catholic support. The system lasted in Ireland until 1870: Forster's Act boosted denominational schools and thus ensured its collapse. Murphy, op. cit., pp. 15-16, 18, 25, 64.

4 J. R. Lowerson, *The Political Career of Sir Edward Baines (1800-1890)*, University of Leeds M.A. dissertation, 1965, pp. 60 ff. The Leeds Institute began late in 1824.

5 F. G. Walcott, *The Origins of Culture and Anarchy: Matthew Arnold and Popular Education in England*, 1970, p. xv.

6 *Leeds Mercury*, 18 October 1834, quoted in Lowerson, op. cit., p. 137.

7 N. Gash, *Reaction and Reconstruction in English Politics 1832-1852*, Oxford, 1965, p. 77, n. 2.

8 J. F. C. Harrison, *Learning and Living, 1790-1960*, 1961, pp. 18 ff.

9 Quoted in J. T. Ward, *Sir James Graham*, 1967, pp. xvii, 196.

10 A. and C. Reed, *Memoirs of Andrew Reed D.D.*, 1863, p. 207.

11 Ibid., p. 212.

12 A. Peel, *These Hundred Years*, 1931, pp. 177-83, esp. p. 182.

13 J. Murphy, op. cit., p. 27.

14 A. Peel, op. cit., p. 177 (my italics).

15 E. Baines, *The Life of Edward Baines*, pp. 331-2.

16 Lowerson, op. cit., pp. 145-6.

17 This was a perverse if plausible argument since the 1839 proposals, which Nonconformists (Wesleyans excepted) generally approved, had been introduced in the same way, and the Anglican opposition had then voiced the constitutional objections which the Nonconformists in their turn raised in 1847. Given the fraught sectarianism of the 1840s, this was the surest way of getting any educational proposals through.

18 To Lansdowne's famous statement that 'it is universally admitted that governments are the worst of cultivators, the worst of manufacturers, and the worst of traders', the elder Baines added 'the worst of instructors'. Baines, op. cit., pp. 332-4, esp. p. 333.

19 *Leeds Mercury*, 2 March 1850, quoted in Lowerson, op. cit., p. 160.

20 *Nonconformist*, 25 April 1849, quoted in G. A. Weston, *The Baptists of North West England 1750-1850*, University of Sheffield Ph.D. dissertation, 1969, p. 517.

21 Walcott, op. cit., pp. 23-7.

22 Ibid., pp. 3-15. The following paragraphs owe much to this.

23 A. W. W. Dale, *The Life of R. W. Dale of Birmingham*, 1898, p. 163.

24 For the accepted, Arnoldian, view see Walcott, op. cit., pp. 63 ff. For an alternative assessment, see N. Morris 'State paternalism and *laissez-faire* in the 1860s' in *Studies in the Government and Control of Education since 1860*, 1970, pp. 13-20.

25 Lowerson, op. cit., p. 21.

26 The others were the Newcastle Commission, into elementary education, which reported in 1861, and the Clarendon Commission, dealing with the major public schools, which reported in 1864.

27 Lowerson, op. cit., pp. 228-30.

28 J. Murphy, op. cit., pp. 46-7; J. L. Paton, *John Brown Paton: a Biography*, 1914, p. 145.

29 *Congregational Year Book*, 1868, p. 405; Peel, op. cit., pp. 183-4.

30 Lowerson, op. cit., p. 243, quoting *Leeds Mercury*, 8 October 1870.

31 Paton, op. cit., p. 152.

32 P. T. Marsh, *The Victorian Church in Decline*, 1969, pp. 80-1.

33 E. R. B(aines) 'Memoir' in T. Baines, *The Industrial North in the last Decade of the Nineteenth Century*, Leeds, 1928, p. 4. For Talbot Baines (1852-1927) see below ch. 4 Part V pp. 99-100.

V

1 J. R. Lowerson, *The Political Career of Sir Edward Baines (1800-1890)*, University of Leeds M.A. dissertation, 1965, pp. 154, 158-9.

2 *Leeds Mercury*, 10 September 1859, quoted in Lowerson, op. cit., p. 191.

3 Lowerson, op. cit., pp. 195-7.

4 J. Vincent, *The Formation of the Liberal Party 1857-1868*, 1966, p. 225.

5 Ibid., p. 252; Lowerson, op. cit., pp. 212-4; F. B. Smith, *The Making of the Second Reform Bill*, Cambridge, 1966, p. 47. P. Guedalla (ed.), *Gladstone and Palmerston*, 1928, pp. 279 ff.

6 Smith, op. cit., p. 49.

7 B. and Pamela Russell (eds), *The Amberley Papers*, 1937, 2 vols., Vol. 1, p. 451; and *passim*, esp. pp. 367-400, 446-55.

8 Lowerson, op. cit., pp. 225-7.

9 *Leeds Poll Book*, Leeds, 1868.

10 Lowerson, op. cit., pp. 244 ff.

11 Vincent, op. cit., pp. 124-6.

12 For Sir John Barran Bt (1821-1905) see E. P. Hennock, *Fit and Proper Persons: Ideal and Reality in Nineteenth-Century Urban Government*, 1973, p. 212, and R. J. Owen, *The Baptists in the Borough of Leeds during the Nineteenth Century: A Study of Local Church History*, University of Leeds M.Phil. dissertation, 1970, *passim*.

13 R. Cobden to J. Bright, 21 December 1848, quoted in N. McCord, 'Cobden and Bright in Politics 1846-1857' in *Ideas and Institutions of Victorian England*, R. Robson (ed.), 1967, p. 98.

14 The following three paragraphs are based on A. W. Roberts, 'Leeds Liberalism and Late Victorian Politics', *Northern History*, V, 1970, pp. 133-55.

15 *Memorial to Edward Baines on the Completion of his 80th Year: Public Presentation in the Albert Hall, Leeds, December 3rd, 1880*, 1881.

16 F. Boase, *Modern English Biography*, 1908 (1965 edn), Vol. IV, p. 233; East Parade, *Church Book*, 1891, p. 25.

17 Hennock, op. cit., p. 225.

18 East Parade, *Church Book*, 1876, p. 19; 1886, pp. 6, 21; 1888, p. 7; 1891, pp 22-3, 72.

19 *Church Book*, 1876, 1891.

20 *Church Book*, 1876, p. 40; 1889, p. 47; 1891, pp. 73, 79.

21 *Church Book*, 1878, p. 8; 1879, p. 6. For the Leicester Conference see below ch. 9 pp. 197-9.

22 F. Wrigley, *The History of the Yorkshire Congregational Union*, 1923, p. 118.

23 East Parade, *Church Book*, 1877, pp. 6-7.

24 *Church Book*, 1877, p. 7; 1888, p. 9; 1891, pp. 35, 38, 43, 44, 46; 1892, p. 24.

25 *Church Book*, 1876, pp. 4, 19; 1884, pp. 5-6, 22.

26 *Church Book*, 1888, pp. 8-9; 1889, pp. 6-8; 1891, pp. 45-6;

27 *Church Book*, 1891, p. 6.

28 *Church Book*, 1881, p. 6.

29 Headingley Hill Congregational Church, *Year Books*, 1868-1929, *passim*; *Baptismal Register*, 1870- ; *Church Roll*, 1866-1907.

30 East Parade, *Church Book*, 1892, pp. 20, 21-2, 28-9.

31 *Church Book*, 1893, p. 17; 1895, p. 36; 1896, p. 8; 1897, p. 11; 1899, pp. 7, 8.

32 *Church Book*, 1900, p. 7; *Deacons Minutes*, June 1899 to March 1903.

33 *Church Book*, 1899, pp. 8, 10-12.

34 *Church Book*, 1900, pp. 11-14, 18-19; 1901, pp. 6-7; 1903, p. 17.

35 *Church Book*, 1903, p. 20; 1904, p. 21; 1905, p. 23.

36 *Church Book*, 1881, p. 23; 1887, p. 26.

37 Headingley Hill, *Church Roll*, 1866-1907.

38 East Parade, *Church Book*, 1891, p. 26.

39 For Herbert Stanhope Baines (1868-96) see Headingley Hill, *Church Roll*, 1866-1907; *Baptismal Register*, 1870- ; J. A. Venn, *Alumni Cantabrigienses*, Part II, Vol. I, p. 123.

40 T. Baines, *The Industrial North in the last Decade of the Nineteenth Century*, with Preface by Sir H. Bell and Memoir by E. R. B(aines), Leeds 1928, *passim*; J. A. Venn, op. cit., p. 123; A. T. Michell, *Rugby School Register*, Vol. II, 1842-74, Rugby 1902, p. 279.

41 J. Vincent, op. cit., pp. xvii-xviii.

CHAPTER 5

1 A. Miall, *The Life of Edward Miall*, 1884, pp. 160-2.

2 Ibid., p. 359.

3 For an impression of Samuel Augustus Tipple (1826-1916) see A. Porritt, *The Best I Remember*, 1922, pp. 4-6; and *More and More of Memories*, 1947, pp. 187-9.

4 J. Ewing Ritchie, *The London Pulpit*, 2nd edn 1858, pp. 212, 214.

5 E. H. Higginson reviewing Miall's, *The British Churches in Relation to the British People*, 1849, quoted in W. R. Ward, *Religion and Society in England 1790-1850*, 1972, p. 277.

6 J. Travis, *Seventy-Five Years*, 1914, pp. 179-80.

7 Ritchie, op. cit., pp. 212-18.

8 A. Miall, op. cit., p. 360.

9 A. W. W. Dale, *The Life of R. W. Dale of Birmingham*, 1898, p. 63.

10 J. Guinness Rogers, *An Autobiography*, 1903, p. 93.

11 F. A. Freer, *Edward White: His Life and Work*, 1902, pp. 178-9.

12 A. Miall, op. cit., p. 149.

13 This is the theme of J. S. Newton, *The Political Career of Edward Miall. Editor of the Nonconformist and Founder of the Liberation Society*, University of Durham Ph.D. dissertation, 1975.

14 A. Miall, op. cit., p. 159.

15 R. F. Horton, *An Autobiography*, 1917, p. 93.

16 W. R. Ward, op. cit., pp. 196-7.

17 G. Howell to G. Potter, 28 October 1871, quoted in Newton, op. cit., pp. 499-500.

18 W. H. Mills (ed.), *The Manchester Reform Club 1871-1921*, priv. edn Manchester, 1922, pp. 30-4. Mills (1874-1930) was brought up in the remarkable atmosphere of Albion Congregational Church, Ashton under Lyne. His uncle, William Mills (1813-64), was a former President of the Methodist New Connexion Conference. He himself was chief reporter for the *Manchester Guardian* from 1914 to 1919. Victorian Nonconformity, northern style, has not had a more gracefully accurate apologist.

19 Ibid., p. 34.

20 Ritchie, op. cit., p. 218.

21 Matthew Arnold, *Culture and Anarchy*, 1869 (1889 popular edn), p. 19.

22 A. Miall, op. cit., pp. 6-7.

23 Ibid., pp. 8-9.

24 Ibid., pp. 9-11.

25 Ibid., p. 20.
26 This account is taken from A. Miall, op. cit., pp. 18-40. For David Lloyd (1811-84) see *Congregational Year Book*, 1885, pp. 207-8.
27 M. Arnold, *Culture and Anarchy*, 1869 (1889 popular edn), p. 17.
28 A. Miall, op. cit., p. 54; H. R. Martin, *The Politics of the Congregationalists 1830-1856*, University of Durham Ph.D. dissertation, 1971, p. 16.
29 Newton, op. cit., *passim*, esp. p. 346.
30 Rogers, op. cit., p. 142.
31 A. Miall, op. cit., pp. 26-7, 46, 49, 50. The Baines affair is also discussed by Dr G. I. T. Machin in his forthcoming book on *Politics and the Churches in Great Britain, 1832-1868*, Oxford, 1977. I am grateful to Dr Machin for letting me see portions of his typescript.
32 A. Miall, op. cit., p. 53.
33 Ibid., pp. 59-60, 61.
34 Ibid., p. 70.
35 Quoted in Martin, op. cit., p. 232.
36 Ibid., pp. 285-6; 387.
37 *Nonconformist*, 28 April 1847.
38 See above ch. 4 Part IV p. 89.
39 A. Miall, op. cit., pp. 230 ff.
40 Ibid., p. 273.
41 Ibid., p. 304.
42 C. S. Miall, *Henry Richard, M.P.*, 1889, p. 261.
43 Martin, op. cit., p. 299. The Society is described blow by blow in W. H. Mackintosh, *Disestablishment and Liberation*, 1972.
44 D. M. Thompson, 'The Liberation Society, 1844-1868' in *Pressure from Without in Victorian England*, Patricia Hollis (ed.), 1974, p. 214.
45 J. S. Newton, op. cit., p. 441.
46 A. Miall, op. cit., pp. 93 ff; Thompson, art. cit., p. 216.
47 Martin, op. cit., p. 274.
48 F. A. Freer, op. cit., p. 47.
49 A. Miall, op. cit., pp. 92-3.
50 This paragraph is largely based on Martin, op. cit., pp. 307-21. Carvell Williams's career is analysed in A. H. Welch, *John Carvell Williams: The Nonconformist Watchdog*, University of Kansas Ph.D. dissertation, 1968.
51 A. Miall, op. cit., p. 96.
52 Ibid., pp. 92, 96-7; Martin, op. cit., 293 ff, 315-17.
53 Martin, op. cit. p. 321.
54 G. A. Weston, *The Baptists of North-western England, 1750-1850*, University of Sheffield Ph.D. dissertation, 1969, pp. 680, 685-6; Martin, op. cit., pp. 305, 321. Thompson, art. cit., pp. 227-9.
55 Weston, op. cit., pp. 685-6.
56 College St had 766 members in 1885. See T. H. S. Elwyn, *The Northamptonshire Baptist Association: A Short History 1764-1964*, 1964, pp. 44-5, 57, 58, 72-3. For J. Turland Brown, (1819-99) see *The Rev. John Turland Brown and College Street Church, Northampton: Memorial Volume*, Northampton, 1899, *passim*, esp. p. 6.
57 Martin, op. cit., p. 488; A. Miall, op. cit., p. 229. In 1844-5 its income had been £1,000. Miall, op. cit., p. 100. In 1850-1, its income had been £1,791, Martin, op. cit., p. 100.
58 *Camberwell Green Congregational Church Centenary Manual, 1880*, 1881, p. 55.

59 *Eclectic Review,* new series, Vol. IX, 1855, p. 105, quoted in Newton, op. cit., p. 467.

60 Miall, op. cit., pp. 108-10. From 1837 to 1841 Molesworth had been Baines's fellow member for Leeds.

61 Ibid., p. 126.

62 Ibid., pp. 124-8; Martin, op. cit., p. 376.

63 C. S. Miall, *Henry Richard M.P.,* 1889, p. 91.

64 A. Miall, op. cit., p. 186.

65 Ibid., pp. 182-7.

66 [F. G. Byles] *William Byles by his Youngest Son,* priv. edn, Weymouth, 1932, pp. 82 ff. For James Miall see below ch. 5 p. 124.

67 A. Miall, op. cit., pp. 320, 362.

68 P. Marsh, *The Victorian Church in Decline,* 1969, pp. 137-40, 144-7.

69 A. Miall, op. cit., p. 202; W. R. Ward, *Religion and Society in England 1790-1850,* 1972, p. 217; Martin, op. cit., p. 519; Newton, op. cit., pp. 295 ff., esp. 304-8.

70 A. Miall, pp. 260-4; C. S. Miall, *Henry Richard M.P.,* pp. 119-21; 147-50.

71 Ibid., pp. 151-2.

72 S. Mayor, *The Churches and the Labour Movement,* 1967, p. 212.

73 Martin, op. cit., p. 234.

74 A. Miall, op. cit., p. 60.

75 Ibid., p. 82.

76 Ibid., p. 83.

77 Martin, op. cit., pp. 234 ff; Newton, op. cit., pp. 479, 520-2.

78 A. Miall, op. cit., pp. 87, 109; Newton, op. cit., p. 441; Martin, op. cit., pp. 263-4.

79 F. B. Smith, *The Making of the Second Reform Bill,* Cambridge 1966, p. 22.

80 J. L. S. Sturgis, *John Bright and the Empire,* 1969, *passim,* esp. pp. 28, 36, 37.

81 A. Miall, op. cit., p. 190.

82 Ibid., op. cit., pp. 136-7, 140; A. W. W. Dale, op. cit., p. 63.

83 A. Miall, op. cit., pp. 259-60, 334-5.

84 Newton, op. cit., p. 479; Freer, op. cit., pp. 56-9; A. Miall, op. cit., pp. 292-5.

85 Quoted in Newton, op. cit., p. 514.

86 Ibid., p. 517.

87 A. Miall, op. cit., pp. 177-8.

88 Ibid., p. 301.

89 *Nonconformist,* 11 September 1867 and 11 November 1874, quoted in Newton, op. cit., pp. 477, 513.

90 For H. S. P. Winterbotham (1837-73) see *D.N.B.*

91 Charles Miall, editor of the *Nonconformist* from 1878-90, is pleasantly described in A. Porritt, *The Best I Remember,* 1922, pp. 39-40; for J. G. Miall (1805-96) see *Congregational Year Book,* 1897, pp. 209-11; there is a pleasant pen portrait in A. Mackennal, *Life of John Allison Macfadyen M.A., D.D.,* 1891, pp. 161-4; for J. D. Morell (1816-91) see F. Boase, *Modern English Biography,* 1897 (reprint 1965), Vol. II, p. 962.

92 Adding 'which means that before long no one will be so entitled, as is, indeed, obvious to see'. G. Keynes (ed.), J. M. Keynes, *Essays in Biography,* 1961 edn, p. 326.

CHAPTER 6

1 For an account of the implications of this, and the extent to which it affected

even the Liberal landslide of 1906, fought of course on the 1884 franchise, see A. K. Russell, *Liberal Landslide: The General Election of 1906*, Newton Abbot, 1973, pp. 15 ff.

2 Dorothea Price Hughes, *The Life of Hugh Price Hughes*, 1904, p. 357.

3 The five acts were: the Corrupt and Illegal Practices Prevention Act, 1883; the Representation of the People Act, 1884; the Redistribution of Seats Act, 1885; the Local Government Act, 1888, which provided for County Councils; the Local Government Act, 1894, which provided for Parish, Rural and Urban District Councils. All save the 1888 Act were Liberal measures.

4 There were exceptions, notably Ipswich, Norwich and Plymouth, until 1948.

5 A. Jones, *The Politics of Reform 1884*, Cambridge, 1972.

6 *A Diary of the Gladstone Government*, Edinburgh and London, 1885, p. 3.

7 Ibid., 1 April 1880; Jones op. cit., p. 17.

8 And *Iolanthe's* little Liberals and Conservatives had first delighted lovers of clean theatre and safe music in 1882.

9 *The Times* quoted in *A Diary*, op. cit., 30 March 1882.

10 Ibid., 10 July 1883.

11 The *Financial Reform Almanack*, 1885, quoted in *A Diary*, op. cit., for 25 April 1880.

12 Ibid., 17 February 1882.

13 Ibid., 1 December 1883.

14 Ibid., 28 February 1884; also 26 June, 8 July, 12 July, 20 October.

15 Jones, op. cit., p. 12.

16 H. Pelling, *Social Geography of British Elections 1885-1910*, 1967, p. 98.

17 Helen Caroline Colman, *Sydney Cozens-Hardy — A Memoir*, priv. edn Norwich, 1944, p. 35.

18 Admittedly Norfolk's other urban constituencies were beyond the normal run of things: King's Lynn's electorate remained suspiciously small, and Norwich was one of the surviving two member seats.

19 Pelling, op. cit., p. 98.

20 Of course none of the Methodist circuits fitted the division precisely. In 1885 the Primitives' Holt Circuit had 360 members and Briston had 410; to this should be added a proportion of the membership of the overlapping Fakenham and North Walsham circuits; in 1886 the Wesleyans' Holt circuit had 107 members, to which should be added a proportion from the overlapping Walsingham and Walsham circuits; in 1885 the U.M.F.C. Holt circuit had 436 members. In the preceding twenty years the Primitives had kept a reasonably steady membership, the Wesleyans had fluctuated (at Holt between 80 and 150) and the U.M.F.C. had steadily declined. These figures have been taken from Primitive Methodist *Minutes of Conference*, Wesleyan Methodist *Minutes of Conference*, United Methodist Free Churches *Minutes of the Annual Assembly*.

21 2,929 acres, with a gross annual value of £3,764: all of it in Norfolk, most of it near Letheringsett. J. Bateman *The Great Landowners of Great Britain and Ireland*, 4th edn 1883, reprinted, with introduction by D. Spring, Leicester 1971, p. 207.

22 He consulted with the architect, Jeckyll, at useful meeting places, as, for example, when they rode to hounds together. I owe this information to the late Mr B. Cozens-Hardy.

23 W. H. Cozens-Hardy's uncles, Jonathan Davey and John Cozens (1769-1841), were members of St Paul's Baptist Chapel, Norwich; in 1792 Cozens was

Secretary of the Norwich Revolution Society, and in 1796 Thelwall addressed an election crowd from Cozens's grocery shop. C. B. Jewson, *The Jacobin City*, 1975, *passim*, esp. pp. 29, 72.

24 E. Hodder, *The Life of Samuel Morley*, 1887, p. 103.

25 See below, esp. ch. 8, *passim*.

26 For the Willans family see below, ch. 7, esp. pp. 157-8.

27 H. Cozens-Hardy to J. J. Colman, 27 May 1879; I owe this reference to the late Mr B. Cozens-Hardy.

28 On 26 July 1866 Herbert Cozens-Hardy married, at Grafton Square Congregational Church, Maria, daughter of Thomas Hepburn J.P., of Clapham Common. Hepburn and W. H. Cozens-Hardy each settled £4,000 at 5 per cent p.a. on the couple, and W. H. Cozens-Hardy furnished their home, 48 Clarendon Road, Notting Hill, leased for £75 p.a. In 1875 they moved to a larger, detached, freehold villa, 50 Ladbroke Grove, which remained Herbert's town house until his death in 1920. This information comes from autobiographical jottings kept by Herbert Cozens-Hardy between 1870 and 1917, hereafter referred to as H. H. Cozens-Hardy, *Autobiography*. I am indebted to the executors of the 4th Lord Cozens-Hardy for permission to use this and other material in their possession.

29 H. H. Cozens-Hardy to J. J. Colman, 27 May 1879.

30 At the very least he would lose fees from his pupils – some 300 gns. annually. H. H. Cozens-Hardy, *Autobiography*, p. 7.

31 After 1892 his income usually exceeded 10,000 guineas, ibid., p. 8.

32 It is unclear whether this referred to the colour of her hair, her temper or a contemporary eruption of the Italian volcano. I owe this information to Mr R. C-H. Horne.

33 Maria Cozens-Hardy wrote an account of the 1885 election in diary form. Unless otherwise stated the following description of the contest is based on this account.

34 Hoare was a clever choice: a London banker, Hampstead to Cozens-Hardy's Notting Hill, an Anglican, but connected with the great Quaker banking families, popular in the county and younger than his opponent. His son was a better known Samuel Hoare, later Lord Templewood.

35 Mrs Louis Buxton of Bolwick was a Lee Warner.

36 R. W. Ketton Cremer, *Felbrigg. The Story of a House*, 1962, pp. 273-7.

37 To the concern of Mrs W. H. Cozens-Hardy Bastard had chaired a meeting at Salthouse when no Liberal *gentleman* had been available. He did it rather well.

38 Bullard was later unseated on petition. The figures were:

Bullard, (Sir) H.	Cons.	7,279
Colman, J. J.	Lib.	6,666
Wright, (Sir) R. S.	Lib.	6,251.

The Yarmouth and Lynn results were equally depressing.

39

Taylor, F.	Lib.	4,530
Buxton, Sir R. J. Bt	Cons.	3,588.

Taylor belonged to the Diss family, of whom Meadows Taylor, William Pattisson's master, was one. Buxton was not related to the Fowell Buxtons.

40

Cozens-Hardy, H. H.	Lib.	5,028
Hoare, S.	Cons.	3,342

41 H. H. Cozens-Hardy, *An Autobiography*, op. cit., on which the subsequent account is based.

42 See below, ch. 9, esp. pp. 201 ff.

CHAPTER 7

1 *Congregational Year Book*, 1847, pp. 164-73.

2 'Remarks on Ecclesiastical Architecture as Applied to Nonconformist Chapels', ibid., pp. 150-63, on which the following paragraphs are based.

3 He then quoted an exception to the rule: St Pancras, London, 'where the architect was obliged, in order to supply vestries, to attach to the main building, the form of a small temple, in the portico of which, he placed female figures as columns, which are technically denominated Caryatides — strange ornaments for a house of prayer!', ibid., p. 161.

4 The earliest *complete* copies would seem to be Unitarian, of which Gee Cross, Hyde, near Manchester (1847) is one of the best. 'Properly' Gothic Congregational Churches attributed to the 1840s, would seem to have been completed later: thus William Butterfield's charming Highbury Chapel, Bristol, opened in 1843, had its apse, tower and transept added by Edward Godwin in 1863; the apse was again enlarged in 1893 by (Sir) Frank Wills. The large and expensive Cavendish Chapel, Manchester, of 1848, had tower, spire, nave, aisles and transepts — but the apse held the organ gallery. For most Nonconformists the problem was how *not* to copy: as at Ryecroft Congregational Church, Ashton-under-Lyne, which sought to preserve the 'spirit of Gothic . . . in all its integrity and beauty, without having recourse to the old stereotyped plan of dividing the space into nave and aisles, after the manner of the Church of England', *Congregational Year Book*, 1854, p. 276.

5 Bowdon Downs Congregational Church, *British School Minute Book, 1848-1867*, £1,987.11s.6d. was raised and it was opened in January 1861: Dr J. D. Morell, the Inspector, and the school's examiners 'expressed their pleasure at its noble proportions'.

6 *Congregational Year Book*, 1847 pp. 11, 41. Thus, in 1855, 5,000 copies of the *Year Book* were published, and most were sold: an unprecedented number (*Congregational Year Book*, 1856, p. 19). But the 1847 *Year Book* sold disappointingly.

7 Ibid., p. 157; see also *Congregational Calendar*, 1845, p. 121: Sir John Summerson has compiled a scratch list of London architects most frequently illustrated in the architectural press of the 1860s: out of 160, seventeen were illustrated more than three times: Tarring came seventh in popularity, J. Summerson, *The London Building World of the Eighteen-Sixties*, 1973, p. 23.

8 Charles P. Pritchett transferred from the Congregational Church in York in August 1843. His wife Mary, joined in November 1852: she died in July 1859 and in December 1862 Charles was struck from the roll, as having 'joined Church of England'. He had, however, already left Huddersfield. James P. Pritchett joined Ramsden Street in September 1852 but transferred to Darlington Congregational Church in the same year. These were two of the six sons of J. P. Pritchett of York. Ramsden Street Congregational Church, Huddersfield, *Members List, 1826-1918*, in keeping of Huddersfield Central Library.

9 J. P. Pritchett of York (1789-1868) was a very distant connexion of Thomas and Joshua Wilson of Highbury, and a much closer connexion of a group of prominent London Anglican evangelicals. The son of a Welsh parson, he was articled in Southwark to one of the Medland family, Congregationalists who produced several architects in subsequent generations. He began his practice in York in 1813 and was active in York Congregationalism. He was the architect of the Lendal and Salem Congregational Chapels in York and of Queen Street Congregational Chapel in Leeds. I am indebted for this information to Mr G. A. H.

Bousfield. See also *D.N.B.*

10 A. W. Sykes, *Ramsden Street Independent Chapel, Huddersfield. Notes and Records of a Hundred Years 1825-1925*, Huddersfield, 1925, p. 11.

11 R. Bruce, 'Congregationalism in Huddersfield', *Congregational Year Book*, 1875, pp. 120, 121.

12 Sykes, op. cit., pp. 10, 14, 34.

13 Ibid., pp. 20-1, 24-5.

14 Richard Knill (1787-1857) is a key figure in much early nineteenth-century Nonconformist history. After his return from service in India and Russia, he held together and enthused congregations in many parts of the country, sometimes as in Huddersfield, Chester and Wotton under Edge, with his stated pastorates, more often by his visits on deputation for the London Missionary Society.

15 Sykes, op. cit., p. 34.

16 Ibid., pp. 36-7.

17 Hillhouse Congregational Church, *Minute Book of Origins and First Committee Meetings of Proposed Chapel at Hillhouse or Bradford Road*, 1863-7. The following account of the building of Hillhouse is based on this.

18 *Congregational Year Book*, 1863, p. 309.

19 See below, ch. 9, esp. p. 197.

20 As C. H. Jones pointed out, in the past twenty years these two congregations had jointly spent £1,000 a year on church provision in Huddersfield.

21 This information has come from Hillhouse Congregational Church, *Sunday School Subscription List*, January 1872 (when a debt of £525 remained); *Year Book*, 1874, p. 31: and *Year Books*, *passim*.

22 *Congregational Year Book*, 1865, p. 301.

23 Ibid., 1871, p. 414; 1866, p. 309; 1865, p. 300; 1872, p. 406.

24 The development of the profession is discussed in J. Summerson, op. cit., pp. 18-21.

25 *Huddersfield Examiner*, 12 September 1863, for William Willans (1800-63).

26 For Charles Henry Jones (1800-84), see ibid., 30 August 1884.
   For Sir T. F. Firth Bt (1825-1909), see E. G. Burnley and J. W. Walker, *Upper Independent Church, Heckmondwike, 1674-1924*, Heckmondwike, *c.* 1924, *passim*.
   For William Shaw (1821-97) see *Rochdale Observer*, 27 January 1897.
   For J. W. Willans (1831-1910) see *The Times*, 3 May 1910.
   For W. H. Willans (1833-1904) see *Who Was Who*, 1897-1916.
   For T. B. Willans (1836-97) see *Rochdale Times*, 26 May 1900.
   For J. E. Willans (1842-1926) see *Huddersfield Examiner*, 15 May 1926 and 21 September 1918.

27 H. H. Asquith, *Memories and Reflections*, 1928, Vol. I, p. 6.

28 Sykes, op. cit., p. 51.

29 See below, ch. 9, pp. 197-9.

30 This section is chiefly based on Milton Congregational Church, Huddersfield, *Minute Book*, 1881-9.

31 Stannard officiated in 1888 at the funeral of Asquith's mother.

32 Milton Congregational Church, *Year Book*, 1881, p. 10; 1883-4, pp. 12-13; 1882-3, p. 11.

33 Ibid., 1882-3, pp. 14-17.

34 *Jubilee Souvenir 1881-1931*, p. 31.

35 Ibid., p. 33.

36 Ibid., p. 19.

37 See below, ch. 9, pp. 200 ff.
38 Quoted in M. Bence-Jones, *Palaces of the Raj*, 1973, p. 187.

CHAPTER 8
1 A. Peel and J. A. R. Marriott, *Robert Forman Horton*, 1937, p. 362.
2 J. M. Richards, *The Castles on the Ground. The Anatomy of Suburbia*, 2nd edn 1973, p. 78.
3 Ibid., p. 28.
4 Ibid., pp. 2, 3.
5 Ibid., pp. 3, 19, 35.
6 T. Raffles Davison, *Modern Homes*, 1909, pp. 12, 79, 85, 132; his principles were charmingly demonstrated in one of his own rare buildings, The Quinta Congregational Schools, Shropshire — remarkably advanced for the late 1870s.
7 E. Armitage, *Diary*, March-May 1874: MS. in possession of Revd H. A. Wilson.
8 Ibid., May 1874.
9 Alexander Raleigh (1817-80) had been minister at Hare Court, Canonbury, since 1858. (Sir) Walter Raleigh, his son, became Professor of English Literature at Oxford in 1904. Lady Reed (1817-91) was the sister of (Sir) Edward Baines, recently defeated at Leeds, and the wife of Sir Charles Reed who had been M.P. for Hackney since 1868 but had recently been unseated on petition. She was the mother of Talbot Baines Reed, the writer. Annie Armitage, Amy, Caroline and Ella Sophia Bulley, were at Newnham in 1873, 1873-4, 1873, 1871-2, respectively.
10 *Congregational Year Book*, 1874, p. 414.
11 *Diary*, op. cit., October 1889.
12 From the estimates submitted by G. F. Armitage, 15 July 1889, in *Mansfield College Committee Minute Book 1885-1889*, in the possession of Mansfield College, Oxford.
13 *Mansfield College Subscription List*, in the possession of Mansfield College, Oxford. A 'league table' thus emerges:
The Manchester connexion £6,265.
The Spicer-Unwin connexion (chiefly London) £4,725.
The Pilkington-Rylands connexion £2,500.
The Wills connexion (chiefly in the south-west) £2,180.
The Samuel Morley connexion £1,600.
The Yorkshire Wool connexion (Willans, Crossley, Salt, Baines) £895.
The London professional connexion (Pye-Smith, Reed, Curwen) £874.
The Colman, Cozens-Hardy connexion £727.
14 *Mansfield College Committee Minute Book, 1885-1889*, 16 November 1885.
15 H. Guppy, *The John Rylands Library, Manchester: 1899-1924*, Manchester, 1924, pp. 13, 15, 17.
16 W. Haslam Mills (ed.), *The Manchester Reform Club 1871-1921*, Manchester, priv. edn 1922, *passim*, esp. p. 24.
17 *Manchester Guardian*, 19 January 1911.
18 *Diary*, op. cit., Wednesday, 2 September 1879. Elkanah Armitage was one of the officiating ministers.
19 Mills, op. cit., pp. 6-7.
20 H. Shaw, *Manchester Pioneers of the Cross*, n.d. (c. 1906), pp. 10-11; *The Times*, 27 November and 6 December 1972; see below ch. 10, pp. 217-18.
21 B. I'Anson, *The History of the Armytage or Armitage Family*, n.d. (c. 1915), pp. 113-15.

22 Mills, op. cit., pp. 7-8.

23 *Men of the Period: Lancashire*, 1895, Part 1, p. 49. The first half of the firm's history is excellently told in G. W. Armitage, *A History of Armitage and Rigby*, 1939, from a bound typescript in the possession of Major W. B. Armitage.

24 The phrase 'cottontot' was coined by the family of Lord Stanley of Alderley in the 1840s. Nancy Mitford (ed.), *The Ladies of Alderley*, re-issue 1967, p. xvii. The names of all these houses, save Dunham House, appear between the 1850s and 1914 in the *Manuals* of the Bowdon Downs Congregational Church: they were the houses of Armitage connexions. Dunham House was built by G. F. Armitage for a (Low) Anglican client.

25 *Warrington Examiner*, 11 May 1878, from which quotations in the following paragraphs are taken. Redmayne, the architect of the Manchester College of Art in 1880-1, did the Bowdon Downs Lecture Hall in 1882, details of which may be found in the Church *Manuals* of 1882 and 1883.

26 D. Macfadyen,

27 G. W. Armitage, op. cit., pp. 71 et seq. Mrs George Faulkner and William Armitage's first partner and brother-in-law, William Ward, were cousins.

28 *Altrincham Guardian*, 12 and 19 November 1937.

29 Dr J. S. Whale to author, 19 November 1973.

30 G. F. Armitage, *An Account of the Families of Armitage and Rigby and their connections from 1575 to 1934*, bound typescript 1936, *passim*, esp. p. 23. Several copies of this exist, and I am grateful to their owners, Major W. B. Armitage, Miss B. Preston and Revd H. A. Wilson, for further personal recollections.

31 *British Architect*, Vol. 35, 2 January 1891, pp. 5-6. This is apropos Armitage's redecorations for the Fine Art Society, New Bond Street. Part of the fireplace survives, in the William Morris Art Gallery at Walthamstow, attributed (1975) to the firm of William Morris and Co.

32 There is a suggestion that he was responsible for restoration work at Bramall Hall itself between 1883 and 1887, *British Architect*, op. cit., p. 5.

33 Rosamund Allwood, *George Faulkner Armitage and his work at Spenfield, Leeds*, Undergraduate Dissertation for the Department of Fine Art, University of Leeds, 1974, p. 44.

34 From a surviving Book of Plans and Sketches covering the years 1892-7, in the possession of Wolff and Alexander Ltd, 16 John Dalton Street, Manchester.

35 In 1873. This provides a good example of the patronage on which he built his business. Armitage and Rigby had their chief mills in Warrington; Faulkner's uncle, Samuel Rigby, was the chapel's leading personality and his eldest brother, Ziba Armitage, was a deacon. Four families, Rigbys, Armitages, Lees and Haworths, contributed half the cost of the Italianate building; William Armitage gave the communion table and pulpit panels, which cost £163. T. Hawthorn, *Centenary of Wycliffe Congregational Church, Bewsey Street, Warrington*; Warrington, 1951, *passim*, esp. p. 10.

36 G. W. O. Addleshaw, 'Architects, sculptors, designers and craftsmen 1770-1970 whose work is to be seen in Chester Cathedral', *Architectural History*, 1971, xiv, pp. 76, 97. I am indebted to Dean Addleshaw for much information about Armitage, some of whose early furniture is in his possession.

37 Seven of his commissions before 1891 were illustrated by T. Raffles Davison in *Sketches of Some Interiors Reprinted from the 'British Architect' Designed and Executed by G. Faulkner Armitage: Stamford: Altrincham*, n.d. The Devonshire Club commission again illustrates the connexion of patronage. Formerly

Crockford's, the gaming club, since 1874 it had housed Liberals who wanted an aggressive alternative to the Reform Club. Samuel Morley was a founder member and it offered dining- and committee-room space for the metropolitan launching of several Nonconformist causes, the early promotion of Mansfield College among them. Armitage's extensive renovations were completed by the end of 1889.

38 *British Architect*, 20 February 1891, p. 137.
39 *Sheffield Independent*, quoted in *British Architect*, 11 April 1890, p. 259.
40 I am indebted for this information to Mr Michael Darby of the Print Room, Victoria and Albert Museum.
41 'Silks and Satins', *The Art Journal*, 1891, pp. 19-20.
42 I'Anson, op. cit., p. 107.
43 It has been called 'screaming Gothic'; but the view of it across Clowes Park has also been likened to that of Salisbury Cathedral from the river: both were Anglican reactions to it.
44 Arthur H. Lee and Sons Ltd Brochure, *Seventieth Anniversary*, 1958; S. P. B. Mais, *Fifty Years of Fabrics*, priv. edn, A. H. Lee and Sons Ltd, Birkenhead, 1938; I am grateful for much information about the firm and family to Mr A. D. Lee.
45 I am indebted for information about this to Mr M. Darby. The best of the firm's designs are now in the Print Room of the Victoria and Albert Museum.
46 C. A. Lee, 'Hand Blocked and Embroidered Tapestries', *Journal of Royal Society of Arts*, No. 5126, January 1967, Vol. cxv, p. 92: this is the best source for Lee's work.
47 Lee Fabrics, *The One-Eyed Weaver: Being an Information Concerning the Versatility of the Needle*, n.d., p. 4.
48 C. A. Lee, art. cit., p. 101.
49 Ibid., pp. 92-4.
50 'The Foliage Society', *Times Literary Supplement*, 28 February 1975, p. 222. The tapestry is in the Whitworth Art Gallery, Manchester.
51 Undated letter (*c.* 1916), in possession of Major W. B. Armitage.
52 T. Ellison, *The Cotton Trade of Great Britain*, 1886, pp. 253-5.
53 I am grateful to Miss F. R. Mclaren, Miss A. L. Bulley and Mrs H. Marshall for details of West Down.
54 Quoted in [J. K. Hulme], *Botanic Gardens, Ness*, University of Liverpool, official guide: n.d., unpaginated. I am grateful to Mr Hulme and Miss A. L. Bulley for this information.
55 P. F. Clarke, *Lancashire and the New Liberalism*, Cambridge, 1971, p. 120.
56 The phrase is Edward Hubbard's — N. Pevsner and E. H. Hubbard, *The Buildings of England: Cheshire*, 1971, p. 250.
57 G. F. Armitage, op. cit., p. 29.
58 Pevsner, op. cit., p. 253.
59 The fullest account of the houses is in Julia Beck, *A Survey of the Work of Richard H. Watt in Knutsford*, Manchester Municipal School of Art, Dissertation, 1951.
60 Ibid., p. 46.
61 Pevsner, op. cit., p. 43.
62 Aileen and W. Tatton Brown, 'An Unprofessional Genius', *The Architectural Review*, Vol. LXXXVIII, October 1940, No. 527, p. 109.
63 Ibid., p. 111. It is now (1977) a chic French restaurant.
64 *Diary*, op. cit., 29 March 1906, Watt was sixty-three, not fifty-three.

65 It was opened 18 June 1908, *Congregational Year Book*, 1909, pp. 151-2. It has been replaced by a nasty Catholic basilica.
66 *Diary*, March 1913.
67 I am grateful to Miss B. Preston for this information.
68 *Manchester Guardian*, 20 July 1960.
69 'his Kensington abode — Pembroke Lodge . . . a rather suburban looking detached villa . . . with a small garden, and furnished and decorated itself after the familiar fashion of Glasgow, or Bradford or Altrincham', R. Jenkins, *Asquith*, 1964, p. 323. Law was an elder of St Columba's, Pont St.
70 J. D. Kornwolf, *M. H. Baillie Scott and the Arts and Crafts Movement*, 1972, pp. 35, 148-9, G. F. Armitage, op. cit., pp. 33-4.
71 Bernard Manning dismissed the father's hymnal, *Worship Song*, as spiritual Keating's Powder; Clough Williams-Ellis nicknamed the son, 'Holy Murder'.
72 *The Times*, 10 September 1975. I am grateful to C. B. Jewson for further information about Norman Jewson and Ernest Weaving.
73 P. Green, 'The Provenance of Pooh', *The Times Literary Supplement*, April 4, 1975, p. 375.

CHAPTER 9

1 Elizabeth Baldwin Brown, *In Memoriam: James Baldwin Brown, B.A.*, 1884, pp. 89-90.
2 W. B. Selbie, *The Life of Charles Silvester Horne*, 1920, p. 152.
3 Elizabeth Baldwin Brown, op. cit., pp. 48, 59.
4 Ibid., p. 129.
5 Selbie, op. cit., p. 184.
6 Ibid., pp. 45, 47, 48.
7 Ibid., p. 116.
8 Ella Sophia Bulley, *A Visit to Tunbridge Wells*, June 1856, manuscript journal in the possession of Revd H. A. Wilson.
9 Elizabeth Baldwin Brown, op. cit., p. 72.
10 Ibid., pp. 62, 71.
11 T. S. Raffles, *Memoirs of the Life and Ministry of the Rev. Thomas Raffles, D.D., LL.D.*, 2nd edn 1865, pp. 360-1.
12 Henry Stormonth Leifchild (1823-84) sculptor of 'The Mother of Moses leaving him on the Banks of the Nile' (1846), 'Rizpah' (1851), 'Lot's Wife', 'Bacchus and Ariadne', 'Minerva repressing the Wrath of Achilles'. In thirty-two years he exhibited thirty-eight sculptures at the Royal Academy.
13 Elizabeth Baldwin Brown, op. cit., p. 2.
14 Quoted in H. R. Martin, *The Politics of the Congregationalists, 1830-1856*, Durham Ph.D., 1971, p. 377. Brown *père* is mentioned *passim*.
15 It cost £5,000, which was raised by 1844. A church of seven members had been formed in February, 1843, two months before the official opening. R. Mansfield, *The History of Congregationalism in Derbyshire from the Methodist Revival to 1850*, Manchester, Ph.D., 1958, pp. 257-8.
16 Elizabeth Baldwin Brown, op. cit., pp. 7-8. Nonetheless the spiritual fruits of Brown's years in Derby included R. F. Horton's mother, and his father, T. G. Horton, was invited to the pastorate in the early 1850s, but went to Tonbridge Chapel, St Pancras, instead. A. Peel and J. A. R. Marriott, *Robert Forman Horton*, 1937, pp. 23-5.
17 Elizabeth Baldwin Brown, op. cit., p. 174.
18 J. Baldwin Brown, *Thomas Raffles D.D., LL.D. A Sketch*, n.d. (c. 1863), pp. 5-6.

19 *Watchman*, 9 July 1884, quoted Elizabeth Baldwin Brown, op. cit., p. 177.
20 Ibid., pp. 40-1.
21 Ibid., p. 17.
22 Ibid., pp. 115-16.
23 Ibid., John Hunter's memorial address, p. 114.
24 Ibid., pp. 134, 139, 140.
25 He hoped that the opening of the Palace on Sundays would produce a balanced relationship between Church and society, so that 'by all the harmonizing influences which are brought to bear on [the working classes] we may regain a hold on them, and lead them'. J. Wigley, *Nineteenth Century Sabbatarianism: A study of a Religious, Political and Social Phenomenon*, Sheffield Ph.D., 1972, pp. 90-3, 216-7.
26 F. A. Freer, *Edward White*, 1902, p. 57.
27 *Congregational Year Book*, 1879, pp. 98-9.
28 Elizabeth Baldwin Brown, op. cit., p. 141.
29 *Congregational Year Book*, 1879, p. 99.
30 C. Newman Hall, *An Autobiography*, 1898, pp. 271-4.
31 J. A. Spender and C. Asquith, *Life of Herbert Henry Asquith, Lord Oxford and Asquith*, 1932, Vol. I, p. 28.
32 W. L. Bradley, *P. T. Forsyth: The Man and His Work*, 1952, pp. 27-8. For Hillhouse and Milton Churches, Huddersfield see also above ch. 7, pp. 151-6, 158 ff.
33 Milton Congregational Church, *Year Book*, 1882, pp. 69-70.
34 Quoted in A. Peel, *These Hundred Years*, 1931, p. 266.
35 Bradley, op. cit., p. 31.
36 Elizabeth Baldwin Brown, op. cit., pp. 24-5.
37 *Congregational Year Book*, 1879, pp. 94-5.
38 Elkanah Armitage, *Diary*, 14 October 1878: MSS. in possession of Revd H. A. Wilson.
39 Elizabeth Baldwin Brown, op. cit., p. 55.
40 E. E. Cleal, *The Story of Congregationalism in Surrey*, 1908, p. 319, Elizabeth Baldwin Brown, op. cit., pp. 58, 69, 88; 104-6; 121; 132, 143.
41 Ibid., p. 171.
42 W. B. Selbie, op. cit., p. 303; R. F. Horton, 'A Tribute of Love' in *C. Silvester Horne: In Memoriam: April 15, 1865-May 2, 1914*, 1914, p. 14; T. Yates, 'The Pilgrim Knight', ibid., p. 27; H. Jeffs, ibid., p. 53; A. Porritt, *The Best I Remember*, 1922, p. 55; Selbie, op. cit., p. 263.
43 Selbie, op. cit., p. 34.
44 H. Cozens-Hardy, *The Glorious Years*, 1953, p. 192.
45 Selbie, op. cit., p. 265.
46 Ibid., p. 84.
47 H. Jeffs, *Press, Preachers & Politicians: Reminiscences, 1874 to 1932*, 1933, p. 127. Selbie, op. cit., p. 181.
48 Selbie, op. cit., p. 116: see above p. 191.
49 A. Mursell, *Memories of My Life*, 1913, p. 136.
50 ' "Whitefield's" and "Claremont": The Story of Two Congregational Central Missions.' Article extracted from untraced journal of 1905, in possession of Mr R. C-H. Horne.
51 Ibid.
52 Ibid.
53 Selbie, op. cit., p. 179.

54 This, and most of the following paragraph comes from ' "Whitefield's" and "Claremont" . . .', art. cit.

55 Ibid.

56 Charles Leach (1847-1919), originally a New Connexion Methodist, had held important pastorates between 1879 and 1908 in Birmingham, Queen's Park, Manchester (Cavendish Chapel), and Canonbury (Harecourt). In January 1910 he beat the sitting M.P., the Socialist Victor Grayson, into third place.

57 The only acceptable lines from a much longer poem on Cromwell, Selbie, op. cit., pp. 266-7.

58 Ibid., p. 109.

59 Ibid., p. 82.

60 Ibid., pp. 207, 218.

61 Horne's delightful phrase, ibid., p. 131.

62 The figures, inevitably open to discussion, are from S. Koss, *Nonconformity in Modern British Politics*, 1975, p. 228.

63 J. C. G. Binfield, 'Congregationalism's Two Sides of the Baptistery — A Paedo-baptist View', *The Baptist Quarterly*, vol. XXVI, July 1975, No. 3, pp. 121, 129.

64 Selbie, op. cit., pp. 195-7; 207-13; 215-16.

65 Letter of 20 January 1909 (*sic*: it should be 1910) in possession of Mr R. C-H. Horne.

66 Selbie, op. cit., pp. 127-9.

67 A. Porritt, *The Best I Remember*, 1922, p. 51. For a helpful modern account from the educationalists' view, see J. Murphy, *Church, State, and Schools in Britain 1800-1970*, 1971, esp. pp. 76-103.
   For a vivid Free Church account, see W. Evans and W. Claridge, *James Hirst Hollowell and the Movement for Civic Control in Education*, Manchester, 1911, esp. pp. 50 ff.

68 Selbie, op. cit., p. 241.

69 R. F. Horton, op. cit., p. 16.

70 Porritt, op. cit., pp. 53-4.

71 A. Porritt, 'A Biography in Brief' in *C. Silvester Horne: in Memoriam*, 1914, p. 12.

72 Elizabeth Baldwin Brown, op. cit., p. 133: see above pp. 195-6.

73 P. D'A. Jones, *The Christian Socialist Revival*, Princeton, 1968, p. 346.

74 H. J. S. Guntrip, *Smith and Wrigley of Leeds*, 1944, pp. 96-7.

75 S. Mayor, *The Churches and the Labour Movement*, 1967, pp. 71-2.

76 H. McLeod, *Class & Religion in the Late Victorian City*, 1974, pp. 65-6, 119.

77 Selbie, op. cit., p. 301.

78 *The Globe* (Toronto), Monday, 4 May 1914. I am indebted to Mr R. C-H. Horne for this reference.

79 P. T. Forsyth, *A Radiant Life: in Memory of Charles Silvester Horne*, Church Stretton, 15 May 1914.

80 R. J. Campbell, 'That High-Souled Man of God' in *C. Silvester Horne: in Memoriam*, 1914, p. 23.

81 'Anarchy and Brotherhood', Horne's spring address to the Congregational Union, 10 May 1910: *Congregational Year Book*, 1911, pp. 40-1. 'The Church as by Grace Established' was the title of his autumnal address, 11 October 1910.

CHAPTER 10

1 *Congregational Year Book*, 1879, p. 98, see also above, p. 196.

2 C. S. Horne to Dorothy Horne, 29 October 1912, quoted in W. B. Selbie, *The Life of Charles Silvester Horne*, 1920, p. 296.

3 For George Williams (1821-1905) see C. Binfield, *A Man In His Setting: The Relevance of George Williams*, National Council of Y.M.C.As, 1975, *passim*; C. Binfield, *George Williams and the Y.M.C.A: A Study in Victorian Social Attitudes*, 1972, *passim*.

4 *Manual for the Church and Congregation Worshipping in Paddington Chapel*, 1900, p. 33 and *passim*.

5 Paddington Chapel *Church Minute Book, 1813-64*, letter of 9 May 1815.

6 *Methodist Times*, 7 December 1899, quoted S. Koss, 'Wesleyanism and Empire', *The Historical Journal*, XVIII, 1, 1975, p. 114.

7 E. Armitage, *Diary*, 1 October 1890, in possession of Revd H. A. Wilson.

8 Ibid., 12-19 July; 6 October 1890.

9 H. Shaw, *Manchester Pioneers of the Cross*, n.d. (*c.* 1906), pp. 10-12.

10 *The Times*, 27 November 1972.

11 Quoted in G. W. Armitage, *A History of Armitage and Rigby*, 1939, pp. 17-18, bound typescript in possession of Major W. B. Armitage.

12 See above p. 170. 'It was a standing joke with the Rigbys that they entertained the Missionaries just as they were returning to the field so were fresh in their memories and received consequently, skins and other trophies, while Townfield's entertainment, coming just as they arrived on furlough, was blotted from their memories.' G. F. Armitage, *An Account of the Families of Armitage and Rigby and their Connections from 1575 to 1934*, 1936, p. 6, bound typescript in possession of Major W. B. Armitage.

13 W. Armitage, *Trip to South Africa Commencing March 4 1905*, MS. Diary in possession of Major W. B. Armitage, entries for 10 April; 14 March; 18 April; 1 May.

14 Edward Stallybrass (1794-1884) worked in Siberia, in the Baikal region, from 1817 to 1841; his work is assessed in E. A. Payne, *Out of Great Tribulation: Baptists in the U.S.S.R.*, 1974, pp. 11-12 and *Congregational Year Book*, 1885, pp. 229-30. He was a sensible fellow and when, from time to time, he and his colleague Swan got on each other's nerves, the two men would shut themselves up together and let fly, until the air was cleared and peace restored, and they could come out and get on with the job. [Irene M. Fletcher to author, 7 April 1973.]

15 J. D. Jones, *Three Score Years and Ten*, 1940, pp. 45-6.

16 E. Armitage, *Diary*, 12-16 October 1891.

17 S. Lavington Hart (1858-1951); Fellow of St Johns 1883; in China 1892-1929; Principal of Anglo-Chinese College, Tientsin, 1901-29.
   J. Walford Hart (1860-94); member of Lyndhurst Road Church, 1890-2; in China 1892-4; the Anglo-Chinese College was in part a memorial to him.
   They were the sons of T. Baron Hart (1818-91), minister from 1864-84 of the English Congregational Church in the Rue Royale Paris.

18 E. Armitage, *Diary*, 18 October 1891.

19 Ibid., 31 January; 23 October 1892. In January Armitage stayed with the Richard Pilkingtons of Rainford, and in October with the Windle Pilkingtons ('delightful people'); the news of Ward's decision came on 8 March. See also W. Lazenby, *Thrice Happy Place*, St Helens, 1975, pp. 93-4.

20 Ibid., 8-11 November; 25 November 1892: his St Helens flock presented him with £321 and a gold watch.

21 Waterhead Congregational Church, *Minute Book*, 1864-96, entries for 3 March,

1 June, 3 August, 24 August and 15 September 1892.

22 E. Armitage, *Diary*, 10-15 October 1892.

23 Ibid., 22 September 1895.

24 Ibid., 12-22 July 1891.

25 Ibid., 26 February 1892.

26 Ibid., 16, 19, 20 November 1890.

27 A. Peel, *These Hundred Years*, 1931, p. 328: Harriet Spicer, daughter of James Spicer of Woodford, was, it seems, the pioneer.

28 *Diary*, op. cit., 26 April 1891. She had regularly spoken at Waterhead's Sunday School Anniversary, and her Services of Song had long been performed in Congregational Churches. She had also, at least once, written a sermon for her husband: in 1874.

29 *Diary*, 20 October 1891.

30 Ibid., 3 May 1891. 'The students of the College give me anxiety. They resist the supernatural claims of Christianity. Smith and Wrigley are very nice fellows, but they head this resistance, I fancy.' Smith and Wrigley later shared a unique pastorate at Salem, Leeds.

31 Ibid., 23 October 1892.

32 Daniel Tomkins J.P. (1826-1902). I am indebted for this information to cuttings and correspondence in the possession of the Rt Revd O. S. Tomkins. The twin chapels, King Street and Middlegate, formed a joint Church; with 443 members, and a Sunday School of 657 scholars, in 1901. Prince's Street, Norwich had 699 members.

33 Tomkins's sister, Elsie, married into the Copeman family, who were connexions of the Colmans, and fellow supporters of Prince's Street.

34 See above p. 220. Mrs Barrett's family, the Bowers, were neighbours of Mrs Armitage's family, the Bulleys, at Montpellier Crescent, New Brighton: they too attended Rake Lane Church.

35 O. F. Tomkins to L. C. F. Tomkins, n.d. (*c*. October 1889); L. C. F. Tomkins to O. F. Tomkins, 13 October 1889. In possession of Rt Revd O. S. Tomkins, as are all the Tomkins letters subsequently quoted.

36 Undated cutting from the Norwich Y.M.C.A. magazine, *Progress*, in possession of Rt Revd O. S. Tomkins.

37 O. F. Tomkins to L. C. F. Tomkins, 11 February 1901; 17 December 1899; 13 July 1900.

38 O. F. Tomkins to L. C. F. Tomkins, 31 August 1895. He did not go to Harley College until 1896.

39 Orders of Service for 6 December and 24 October 1899: it seems that Tomkins was twice ordained, for, as he wrote to his sister Dora (n.d.), apropos F. B. Meyer, of Christ Church, Westminster Bridge Road: 'I never told you, did I, that he ordained me at his church in London, so that I have actually been ordained twice. I was afraid to tell Dr Barrett that however. I went to Hicks's service and Dr Guinness [Principal of Harley College] saw me in the audience, called me on to the platform and that was how it happened. But after all the form does not count for much, what we all need is the ordination and filling of the Holy Spirit, to do God's work aright. And that we can all have, if we "trust and obey".'

40 'Tamate' was the nearest native version of 'Chalmers'. For James Chalmers (1841-1901) see R. Lovett, *James Chalmers: His Autobiography and Letters*, 1902, *passim*, esp. p. 488; and also A. Porritt, *The Best I Remember*, 1922, pp. 149-50.

41 It seems that Chalmers appealed for an assistant when in England for the L.M.S.

Centenary in 1895. This appeal led Tomkins to apply to the L.M.S., which at the time did not have funds for such an appointment. The editor of the *Home Magazine* also learned of the appeal, and offered the necessary money. Undated cutting, December 1899, from *The Home Magazine*, in possession of Rt Revd O. S. Tomkins. I am also grateful to Mr C. B. Jewson for confirmation of the 'cannibal' joke; his mother was present at Tomkins's Ordination and Valedictory meetings in Norwich where the joke gained currency. Tomkins did become 'somewhat wasted away': he noted in a letter home that he weighed 11 stone 9 lb in June 1899 and 11 stone 2 lb in January 1901. O. F. Tomkins to Mr and Mrs D. Tomkins, 24 January 1901.

42 *Home Magazine*, art. cit.

43 O. F. Tomkins to Mr and Mrs D. Tomkins, from the Red Sea, 25 December 1899. This Ward must not be confused with R. J. Ward of St Helens.

44 O. F. Tomkins to Mr and Mrs D. Tomkins, 19 December 1899; 22 December 1899.

45 O. F. Tomkins to Mr and Mrs D. Tomkins, 19 December 1899; 21-23 January 1900.

46 O. F. Tomkins to Mr and Mrs D. Tomkins, 6 May 1900; 10 January 1901; 11 September 1900; Murray was a Liberal 'Swell' since his brother, the Master of Elibank, was a leading Liberal M.P.

47 O. F. Tomkins to Mr and Mrs D. Tomkins, 28 January 1901, pendent to letter of 24 January.

48 O. F. Tomkins to Mr and Mrs D. Tomkins, 10 October 1900.

49 O. F. Tomkins to Mr and Mrs D. Tomkins, 24 August-2 September 1900.

50 O. F. Tomkins to Mr and Mrs D. Tomkins, 10 October 1900.

51 Among them was Dr Ruth Massey of Wuchang, a connexion of Dr Mackennal's, who had also been one of the new missionaries at the Kensington Chapel valedictory services in October 1899; the Boxer Rebellion forced her to return to England for a period. Joseph Stonehouse of Peking, an L.M.S. missionary since 1882, was murdered on 23 March 1901.

52 As in a delightful letter of 24 December 1900, when Tomkins makes Tip, the collie dog which had belonged to Mrs Chalmers (Tamate Vaine) write to Tip, the young collie dog belonging to the Daniel Tomkinses, to describe a narrow escape from a crocodile: perfect ammunition for a children's Sunday sermonette.

53 O. F. Tomkins to Mr and Mrs D. Tomkins, 13 August 1900; 11-12 September 1900, 24 November 1900.

54 O. F. Tomkins to Mr and Mrs D. Tomkins, 27 March 1901.

55 O. F. Tomkins's Diary 1901, entry for 7 April. I have corrected the hasty entry to make for easier reading. It is tempting to think that Tomkins had a sense of impending danger. Indeed, on 5 March he had compiled a list of six missionaries under the age of thirty-three, who had died on service: but it is more likely that he was noting down material for a letter home. And in January he had come to an 'understanding' with the girl in Norfolk whom he hoped to marry and bring out to Daru.

56 Cutting in scrapbook compiled by Mrs Daniel Tomkins, concerning her son's death; in possession of Rt Revd O. S. Tomkins.

57 Extract from letter from Revd H. M. Dauncey, 3 February 1902, copied by L. C. F. Tomkins, in possession of Rt Revd O. S. Tomkins.

58 He sailed on 20 October 1903 and worked for the L.M.S. in China until 1913. After a wartime pastorate at Fowlmere, Cambridgeshire, followed by war work in France, he entered the Church of England.

59 Notes in possession of the author. Chalmers's life made Horton reflect how many great Englishmen were in fact Scotsmen, and he wrote: 'when the present Education Bill has wrecked the national education of England, a still larger proportion will be.'

60 E. Armitage, *Diary*, Inset for Spring 1890.

61 Ibid., 'Indian Journey', 10 December 1902 to Easter 1903.

62 F. Wrigley, *The History of the Yorkshire Congregational Union*, 1923, pp. 118-19.

63 As a descendant of one of James Chalmers's first companions has suggested: see C. Price, 'Tahiti wants Tiamoraa', *New Statesman*, 17 January 1975, p. 67.

64 *Minutes of the First Conference of the United Methodist Church*, 1907, pp. 11-13.

65 H. Smith, J. E. Swallow, W. Treffry (eds), *The Story of The United Methodist Church*, 1932, p. 11. I am grateful to Mr A. N. Cass for both these references.

CHAPTER 11

1 *Congregational Year Book*, 1879, p. 98.

2 *Methodist Times*, 27 April 1899, quoted in S. Koss, 'Wesleyanism and Empire', *The Historical Journal*, XVIII, 1, 1975, p. 112.

3 Cutting in scrapbook compiled by Mrs Daniel Tomkins, in possession of Rt Revd O. S. Tomkins.

4 Lynn Harold Hough, 'When Jimmy Ellerton Enlisted', *The Wellspring*, Vol. LXXII, No. 44: cutting in possession of Mr R. C-H. Horne.

5 See above ch. 7, pp. 157-8.

6 I am indebted to Mr K. Moore for confirmation of this. In 1867 Asquith joined St Leonard's Congregational Church, Sussex. Its minister, Andrew Reed, formerly of Norwich, was doubly connected to the Baines family, through his wife and his sister-in-law.

7 H. H. Cozens-Hardy, *Autobiography*, pp. 57-8, 61-3; in possession of the executors of 4th Lord Cozens-Hardy.

8 E. Armitage, *Diary*, 24 June 1914; in possession of Revd H. A. Wilson.

9 Ibid., 6 July.

10 W. Armitage, *Diary*, 12 July 1914; in possession of Major W. B. Armitage.

11 Ibid., 15, 28, 30 July.

12 W. Armitage, *Diary*, 27 March: it contains cuttings about the Ulster Crisis, 27 April 1914. E. Armitage, *Diary*, 27 November, 4 December 1913; 21 March 1914.

13 Ibid., 8 August 1914.

14 One of his nephews, Basil Carver, was already a Sandhurst cadet: a significant shift in family attitudes. Carver died in France in August 1916, from gas poisoning.

15 E. Armitage, *Diary*, 24 March 1913.

16 Ibid., 8 August 1914.

17 Ibid., 20 October 1914.

18 Ibid., 10 September 1914.

19 Ibid., 16 November, 20 October 1914.

20 Ibid., 30 August 1915; 10 December 1916.

21 Ibid., 2 April 1917.

22 Ibid., 5 February, 1919.

23 Ibid., 26 August 1914.

24 See above, ch. 8, esp. pp. 170-2.

25 E. Armitage, *Diary*, Christmas 1899; New Year 1901.

26 A. Mackennal to A. W. Whitley, 19 October 1901 quoted in D. Macfadyen, *Alexander Mackennal, B.A., D.D., His Life and Letters*, 1905, p. 259: see also pp. 243 et seq.

27 Ibid., pp. 252-3.

28 This and subsequent information is taken from the Church *Manuals* for 1913, 1914, 1915. The membership at The Downs itself, excluding branch churches, was 260 in January 1915. The church address list, of members *and* attenders, however, gives 512 names, with a further thirty-one at a distance.

29 To place this in a wider Free Church perspective: the *Baptist Times* reported by November 1914 that 13,255 Baptists had recruited, and regularly reported figures sent in by individual churches. K. W. Clements 'Baptists and the Outbreak of the First World War', *Baptist Quarterly*, Vol. XXVI, No. 2, April 1975, p. 76.

30 *Congregational Year Book*, 1916, pp. 48-57.

31 Ibid., pp. 58-71.

32 Armitage finally heard Micklem on 24 May: 'I liked him very much, and so did most. He is a really earnest and able young fellow and I should prefer him greatly.' W. Armitage, *Diary*, 24 May 1914; also 22 March and 15 May. Micklem became co-pastor with Arnold Thomas at Highbury, Bristol, a prelude to a uniquely distinguished career. His father had helped Herbert Cozens-Hardy in the 1885 election: see above ch. 6, p. 138.

33 His minister, Ambrose Shepherd of Elgin Place, announced the news of Peace from his pulpit with the phrase 'We are all pro-Boers now'. *Congregational Year Book*, 1916, p. 188. For Richards (1879-1948) see Edith R. Richards, *Private View of a Public Man: The Life of Leyton Richards*, 1950.

34 Edith Richards, op. cit., p. 35.

35 Ibid., p. 47.

36 Ibid., pp. 48, 51-3.

37 W. Armitage, *Diary*, 11 November 1914.

38 Ibid., 5 December; 8 December.

39 Edith Richards, op. cit., esp. pp. 59-62.

40 Johnson frequently lectured at The Downs Literary Society: thus 'Literary Society. Rev. Johnson's address on "Waste". Socialist. Co-operationist. I was in the chair', W. Armitage, *Diary*, 15 March 1915.

41 Ibid., 28 March 1915, 18 April 1915.

42 Ibid., 28 July 1915, 25 August 1915.

43 Ibid., Saturday, 30 October 1915.

44 Ibid., 23 November 1915; 12 December 1915; 9 January 1916.

45 Unless otherwise stated, this account is taken from the Church *Manual*, 1917, pp. 10-11.

46 Cutting in W. Armitage, *Diary*, May-June 1916.

47 Edith Richards, op. cit., p. 64.

48 W. Armitage, *Diary*: cutting.

49 Edith Richards, op. cit., pp. 68-9.

50 Ibid., p. 72.

51 The Pembroke story is excellently told in a typescript by I. Sellers, *Salute to Pembroke*, 1960, of which a copy is in Dr Williams's Library.

52 *Manual*, 1917, p. 11.

53 So recalled Faulkner Armitage: Harriet Westbrook Dunning (ed.), *Albert Elijah Dunning: A Book of Remembrance*, priv. edn, Norwood, Massachusetts, 1927, p. 117. Dunning (1844-1923) had been editor of the American *Congregationalist* between 1889 and 1911. William Armitage noted of the Mayoral service

(Faulkner's 4th) 'A large Congregation and good choir, and a very good sermon', W. Armitage, *Diary*, 29 October 1916.

54 Harriet Dunning, op. cit., p. 128.

55 *Manual*, 1918, p. 10.

56 *Manual*, 1919, p. 10.

57 It is almost impossible to get consistent figures, which tally with each other. These are taken from the church's *Communion Attendance Register*, 1913-19: they apply to The Downs itself, and do not include the branch churches.

58 *Centenary of the Church of Christ Bowdon Downs of the Congregational Order meeting at Bowdon, Cheshire 1839-1939* 1939, pp. 19, 21-2.

59 Dr J. S. Whale to author, 19 November 1973.

60 The Carvers were active Congregationalists at Marple: Alison Sheppard's sister-in-law Mrs Oswald Carver, whose husband was killed in the Dardanelles on the day of the wedding, later married the future Lord Montgomery of Alamein.

61 D. Macfadyen, op. cit., p. 258.

62 This section owes much to K. W. Clements art. cit., especially pp. 83 ff: he aptly describes the increasingly good pre-war relations between British and German churchmen, whom he sees as resembling 'two parties of passengers standing on the decks of their respective ships, waving cheerily across the water to each other, sincerely proffering hands of friendship — but unaware that the vessels on which they stood were on collision course' (p. 84).

63 D. Macfadyen, op. cit., pp. 247, 249.

64 The phrase is found in C. S. Miall, *Henry Richard M.P.*, 1889, p. 80.

65 I am indebted to Professor John Ferguson for this information.

66 B. Willey, *Spots of Time*, 1965, pp. 194 et seq., esp. p. 202.

67 D. Macfadyen, op. cit., p. 247.

68 *Congregational Year Book*, 1949, p. 503.

Index